ELIZABETH I

ELIZABETH I

RENAISSANCE PRINCE

A Biography

LISA HILTON

Weidenfeld & Nicolson
LONDON

First published in Great Britain in 2014
by Weidenfeld & Nicolson

1 3 5 7 9 10 8 6 4 2

A CIP catalogue record for this book
is available from the British Library.

HB ISBN: 978 0 2978 6522 3
TPB ISBN: 978 0 2978 6523 0

Typeset by Input Data Services Ltd, Bridgwater, Somerset

Printed and bound by CPI Group (UK) Ltd,
Croydon, CR0 4YY

Weidenfeld & Nicolson

The Orion Publishing Group Ltd
Orion House
5 Upper Saint Martin's Lane
London, WC2H 9EA
www.orionbooks.co.uk

The Orion Publishing Group's policy is to use papers that
are natural, renewable and recyclable products and made
from wood grown in sustainable forests. The logging and
manufacturing processes are expected to conform to the
environmental regulations of the country of origin.

To my daughter, Ottavia

ILLUSTRATIONS

Anne Boleyn, c. 1533–6 (black and coloured chalks on paper), by Hans Holbein the Younger (1497/8–1543). Royal Collection Trust © Her Majesty Queen Elizabeth II, 2014/Bridgeman Images

Thomas Wyatt, c. 1535–7 (coloured chalks with pen and ink on paper), by Hans Holbein the Younger. Royal Collection Trust © Her Majesty Queen Elizabeth II, 2014/Bridgeman Images

The Family of Henry VIII, c. 1545 (oil on canvas), English School (16th century). Royal Collection Trust © Her Majesty Queen Elizabeth II, 2014/Bridgeman Images

Elizabeth I when a Princess, c. 1546 (oil on panel), attributed to William Scrots (fl. 1537–53). Royal Collection Trust © Her Majesty Queen Elizabeth II, 2014/Bridgeman Images

Mary I, 1554 (oil on oak), by Hans Eworth (fl. 1520–74). Society of Antiquaries of London/Bridgeman Images

Edward VI when Prince of Wales, 1546 (oil on panel), attributed to William Scrots. Royal Collection Trust © Her Majesty Queen Elizabeth II, 2014/Pictorial Press Ltd/Alamy

Richard II, 1390 (oil on panel), by an unknown artist. Westminster Abbey, London/akg-images/De Agostini Picture Library/De Agostini Pictures

Elizabeth I, c. 1600 (oil on panel), English School (16th century). National Portrait Gallery, London/Bridgeman Images

The Clopton Portrait of Elizabeth I, c. 1560–65 (panel), English School (16th century). Private Collection. Photo © Philip Mould Ltd, London/Bridgeman Images

Elizabeth I and the Three Goddesses, 1569 (oil on panel), attributed to Hans Eworth or Joris Hoefnagel (1542–1601). Royal Collection Trust © Her Majesty Queen Elizabeth II, 2014/Bridgeman Images

William Cecil, 1558 (oil on canvas), English School (16th century). IAM/akg-images

Phillip II of Spain, c. 1553 (oil on canvas), by Titian (c. 1488/90–1576). Galleria Palatina, Palazzo Pitti, Florence © akg-images/Nimatallah

Robert Dudley, Earl of Leicester, *c.* 1557–1609 (drawing on paper), by Federico Zuccaro (1542–1609). © The Trustees of the British Museum

Niccolò Machiavelli, second half of 16th century (oil on canvas), by Santi di Tito (1536–1603). Palazzo Vecchio, Florence © GL Archive/Alamy

The Pelican portrait of Elizabeth I, *c.* 1574 (oil on panel), by Nicholas Hilliard (1547–1619). © Walker Art Gallery, National Museums Liverpool/Bridgeman Images

Ivan IV the Terrible (colour woodcut), by Hans Weigel (fl. 1577). Bibliothèque des Arts Décoratifs, Paris/Archives Charmet/Bridgeman Images

Murad III, 1808, by John Young. © Heritage Image Partnership Ltd/Alamy

Mehmet III (oil painting on panel), after Cristofano Dell' Altissimo (*c.* 1525–1605). © National Trust

The tomb of Battista Castiglione in St Mary's Church, Speen. Photograph © Peter Orr

Henry Lee, 1568 (panel), by Anthonis Mor (1517/20–76/7). National Portrait Gallery, London/Bridgeman Images

Francis Walsingham, *c.* 1585 (oil on panel), attributed to John de Critz the Elder (*c.* 1552–1642). © World History Archive/Alamy

Francis, Duke of Anjou, late 1560s, French School (16th century). © Heritage Image Partnership Ltd/Alamy

Mary Stuart, *c.* 1560 (oil on panel), follower of François Clouet (*c.* 1510–72). Victoria & Albert Museum, London/Bridgeman Images

The Armada portrait of Elizabeth I, *c.* 1588 (oil on panel), attributed to George Gower (1540–96). Woburn Abbey, Bedfordshire/Bridgeman Images

Elizabeth I in Old Age, *c.* 1610 (oil on panel), English School (17th century). Corsham Court, Wiltshire/Bridgeman Images

The signature of Elizabeth I on a letter to Lady Southwell, 15 October 1598. © Rex/Nigel R. Barklie

'Princes have mysterious spirits and properties, unknown to all others.'

Thomas Cromwell

PREFACE

etween 1569 and 1603, a painting by the Dutch artist Joris Hoefnagel was seen by the thousands of visitors who streamed
through the court of Elizabeth I at Whitehall. They came to
admire, to solicit, to petition, to intrigue. Some, it was said, came for
love, and others, it was also said, came to murder. All were conscious
of the presiding presence of the mysterious and magnificent ruler of
England, the nation's second Queen Regnant, 'Great Harry's' daughter, Elizabeth herself. But when they stood beneath *Queen Elizabeth
and the Three Goddesses*, what did they see?

This first known allegorical portrait of Elizabeth is a product of
the Protestant diaspora of the mid-sixteenth century. Ten years into
the Queen's reign, her contentious (and, by Elizabeth herself at least,
somewhat resented) position as the figurehead of religious reform
across Europe had already transcended her role as monarch of what
was then 'the isolated, impoverished island kingdom of England'. The
artist was a refugee from the Netherlands, where reformist rebels
were locked in conflict with the Catholic power of Spain. In choosing
to display Hoefnagel's picture so prominently, Elizabeth was making
a powerful statement about her conception of herself as a ruler, a
statement which relied on its viewers' ability to interpret the classical
visual language of the picture. To contemporaries then, 'seeing' the
picture properly required both an understanding of Elizabeth's place
in the confessional politics of Europe and the capacity to filter that
understanding through the 'new learning' which had revolutionised
European thought over the preceding centuries. Put simply, it is a
Renaissance picture, and it depicts a Renaissance prince.

The painting is a rendition of the Judgement of Paris, in which
Elizabeth, holding her orb and sceptre, faces the three goddesses

Juno, Minerva and Venus. Juno, the Queen of Heaven, holds her hand to the skies, expressing the endorsement of Elizabeth's judgement by God. The attributes of the three deities, a sceptre, a sheaf of roses and a quiver of arrows, lie on the ground, uniting the rival goddesses in their 'defeat' by Elizabeth, who has reconciled their respective qualities of power, intellect and beauty. Given the timing of the composition, when Elizabeth had not yet officially transformed herself into the Virgin Queen, it may be read as a cautious encouragement of a still-marriageable woman, but the audience at Whitehall might also have seen something else. Elizabeth is cast in the male role, as Paris, whose award of the prize in the ancient world's most lethal beauty contest to Venus brought about the Trojan War. One myth surrounding the foundation of the kingdom of Britain attributes it to Aeneas, one of the few inhabitants of Troy who escaped Greek devastation. So when the picture was seen by a German visitor, Baron Waldstein, at the palace in 1600, history might suggest that Elizabeth/Paris, who never did give an apple for Venus, in the end, had not only reconciled the qualities of the three goddesses, but in doing so had followed Aeneas in refounding her nation, battered yet triumphant after a great conflict.

In the twenty-first century, we might perceive something else. Hoefnagel's canvas is divided into two distinct parts. On the left stands Elizabeth, erect and crowned, stiff in her brocaded gown, her canopy of state just visible behind, enclosed by the forbidding wall of a palace. To the right, the goddesses are posed in a bright, gentle landscape, delicately ethereal, the trees in full leaf, the grass lush. Above them, in the distance, is another palace, not a gloomy defensive fortress, but a turreted fantasy, a tower of delight. To my eyes, the distinction in the picture is between the past and the future. Elizabeth I reigned from 1558 to 1603. In those forty-five years something occurred in England, something which recalibrated ideas about Englishness and nationhood and which left the country a very different place at the end of the period than at the beginning. In 1500, when Elizabeth's grandfather, the first Tudor monarch Henry VII, was on the throne, no conception of England as a unified state existed. Subjects' loyalties were divided between the *regnum* and the *sacerdotium*, that is, the worldly power of the king and the sacred power of the Pope. It was Elizabeth's father, Henry VIII, who first overturned this ancient division, yet it is not until the second half of Elizabeth's reign that the 'realm' of England was identified as a 'state', a usage in place by 1590. Elizabeth herself is absolutely central to the manner in which this shift is brought about, yet somehow the ever-burgeoning interest in the Queen and her Tudor ancestors – the mini-series, the films, the abundant literature, the documentaries – has had the effect of diminishing her, reducing her to little more than a bewigged farthingale with a mysterious sex life. The young woman confronting the classical goddesses of Hoefnagel's portrait is a very different creature from the perennially frozen mask of magnificence which conventionally characterises her reign. In the picture, Elizabeth is in motion, moving from the darkened constrictions of medievalism towards a recognisable world, one informed by the new learning the goddesses embody. She is stepping forward into the light, into the Renaissance, into a princely modernity.

CHAPTER ONE

Elizabeth I may have been the second of England's Queens Regnant, but she was descended from a tradition of ruling women in both England and Europe. The patrilineal claim of the Tudors was flimsy to say the least: a very little drop of royal blood had to be made to go a very long way, and much has been made of the propaganda employed by Elizabeth's grandfather and father, Henry VII and Henry VIII, to aggrandise the Tudor line at the expense of the royal claim which came through Henry VII's marriage to the Plantagenet heiress Elizabeth of York. If Elizabeth I consciously invoked the influence of five hundred years of powerful English queens, as well as ruling women among her contemporaries, this recasts her conception of herself within that structure of Tudor propaganda, which she not only inherited, but so successfully reconstructed. Nearly every biography of the Queen begins from the premise that her rule was in some way anomalous, by virtue of her gender. Often, the fact of Elizabeth's biological femininity has then been used as a basis from which to interpret nearly every aspect of her governance. In my view, this is simply wrong.

Elizabeth herself was happy to play on the conventions of gender when it suited her 'weak and feeble' woman's body to do so, but convention is not fact any more than rhetoric is reality. Arguably, contemporary conceptions of sexual difference were considerably more supple and sophisticated, and far less constricting, than those of the twenty-first century. Practically, Elizabeth's gender was significant in certain areas – the organisation of her household, for example, or her inability to lead her troops in battle – but Elizabeth's intellectual upbringing, and particularly the influence of the 'new learning', gave her a princely self-image not in the least circumscribed by femininity. Elizabeth saw herself primarily as a prince, in the sense that royalty, in the perceptual model of her times, negated gender. Furthermore, it was as a modern monarch, a 'Renaissance prince', that Elizabeth attempted to govern and refashion her realm. Elizabeth was not, primarily, an exceptional woman, she was an exceptional ruler, and one way in which she became so was to envision herself, as she once told the Venetian ambassador, as a 'prince from a line of princes', even where those princes were not necessarily male.

What, then, were the qualities of a 'Renaissance prince'? How can we recognise one, and how can it be claimed that Elizabeth was one? Definitions of the Renaissance itself are notoriously slippery. Everyone has an idea of what the Renaissance was, but in what exactly it consisted is more fluid, if not downright confusing. As a concept, it exists without the world of scholarship, and thus defies scholarly attempts to argue it out of existence; however, it is not quite possible, Dr Johnson-style, to aim a kick at Brunelleschi's dome in Florence and refute its absence thus. The Renaissance is a nineteenth-century definition of a movement in learning and the arts that may have begun in the tenth century, or the twelfth, or, according to some theories, never have begun at all. Nevertheless, two salient features are broadly accepted. Chronologically, the most acceptable definition of the Renaissance is the period between 1300 and 1600, to which might be added, psychologically, a sense that something was changing, something was happening, and that this 'something' was man's sense of his own place in the universe:

> The new man, the modern man, was a man who made himself, who constructed himself, and who was conscious of this creation. This was, precisely, the 'Renaissance man'.[1]

'Renaissance', of course, means 'rebirth', and what was reborn during the period in question was not only the classical learning of ancient Greece and Rome, which was being rediscovered across that period, but 'a renewed affirmation of the human',[2] which affected not just works of art (the most popular association of the Renaissance), but politics, medicine, civic life, education, war, architecture and ultimately religion. Perhaps it is useful to imagine the medieval social structure as a cycle, a wheel upon which, generation after generation, the same modes of living and the same systems of belief were enacted, and then, by contrast, to see the Renaissance as an arrow shot through this cycle, a linear trajectory of self-conscious progress and change. The impetus behind the arrow was the 'new learning', or 'humanism'.

Until the sixteenth century, serious education in England was the province of the shabby 'poor scholars' familiar from Chaucer. As one anxious father had it:

> I swear by God's body I would rather that my son should hang than study letters . . . it becomes the sons of gentlemen to blow the horn nicely, and to hunt skillfully and elegantly carry and train a hawk. But the study of letters should be left to the sons of rustics.[3]

By the end of Elizabeth's reign, it was such views that appeared embarrassingly backward. Humanist learning exploded medieval certainties as thoroughly, and sometimes as destructively, as a bomb. In the fallout, everything looked different. Again, it is difficult to speak precisely of a humanist 'project', but it is possible to speak, during the period of the Renaissance, of a humanist reality. That reality is characterised, above all, by curiosity, by an urge to 'illuminate in its totality and its richness the figure of man'. Humanism was not one set of thoughts or ideas which all practising humanists supported, but, rather, a collective conviction that the study of classical texts provided the opportunity to envisage the world anew. The word 'humanist' was in use in the universities of Italy by the fifteenth century, denoting one who practised *studia humanitatis*, that is, grammar, rhetoric, poetry, history and moral philosophy, based on the study of classical authors. This discipline represented the coalescence of three currents of intellectual activity which had been present, respectively, in Italy during the medieval period, but which, over the three hundred years in question, burgeoned into a tsunami of learning. The combination of rhetorical training of the bureaucrats of the Italian city-states, which had its roots in Roman custom, Latin grammar from the thirteenth century, and classical Greek literature brought to Europe after the fall of the Byzantine Empire to the Ottomans in 1453, revolutionised European thought between 1300 and 1600. The discovery of Greek and Latin manuscripts, their study and diffusion, and the translation of Greek into more accessible Latin produced a wealth of knowledge which Europe had never seen before. Scholars worked on history and mythology in order to better understand the texts, and produced works not just of literature and history, but mathematics, astronomy, medicine and biology. Humanism 'represented a body of scholarship and literature that was secular, without being scientific, and that occupied a place of its own, independent of, though not opposed to, both theology and the sciences.'[4] With the advent of the printing press in 1450, the total change in the intellectual climate effected by humanism was disseminated, again as never before, by the new possibility of mass production. What united humanists above all was that self-conscious belief that they lived in an age of dramatic progress, of reinvention, of wonder.

The 'new learning' was more than an intellectual and artistic movement: it transformed not only the way people thought, but the way they lived. Technological advances in warfare meant that towns looked physically different, and the way in which they were governed changed, too. The period saw feudalism give way to capitalism, and with this a fundamental shift in the methods and practice of authority from which emerged the nation-state. The very nature of power was being altered. Rulers were becoming liberated from the constraints of medieval social structure, they were able to consolidate their power through the deployment of standing armies, more effective taxation and a professionalised 'civil servant' class. As the influence of both nobility and Church diminished, rulers centralised power through their courts and began, notably, to engage with 'mercantilist' politics, designed to stimulate economic growth while depriving potential enemies of resources. Of course such changes were tremendously varied, taking place at different rates and by different means across time and place, but by the end of the period the emergent idea of the 'state' can be seen as reflecting this dramatic shift.

To arrive at a definition of a 'Renaissance prince' would thus require a blending of these two elements. The term could encompass, but not be limited to, patronage of the arts, of the 'new learning', within the period, but also an appreciation of this fresh concept of the state. The morphology of this state was first articulated by Machiavelli,[5] whose works *The Prince* and the *Discourses* were in circulation in manuscript from 1513, though they were not published until 1532. In 1559, the Vatican placed Machiavelli's work on its list of prohibited books, where they remained until the twentieth century. Even now, the name Machiavelli is suggestive of duplicity and cynicism, of ruthless self-interest, and the notorious moral catch-all of the 'ends justifying the means' (as though anything other than the ends might be proposed to justify them). Five centuries' worth of prejudice has its roots among Machiavelli's sixteenth-century readers – by 1590 Machiavelli had become a stock stage villain, a byword for manipulation and general trickiness. Christopher Marlowe's *The Jew of Malta* claims the Florentine writer as the reincarnation of the Duc de Guise, whom Elizabeth I once described as her 'greatest enemy', while the next year Shakespeare refers to that 'notorious Machiavel' in *Henry VI Part I*. Machiavelli's ideas represent the collision of two conflicting ideologies, two very distinct ways of looking at the world, an opposition which has its source in the developments of the new learning. Yet why did Machiavelli's first readers find these ideas as shocking and disturbing as they found them compelling? And why should they be so essential to a definition of a 'Renaissance prince'?

In many ways, Machiavelli is a very un-Renaissance writer. Given that he was a product of fifteenth-century Florence, still referred to in Italy today as 'the cradle of the Renaissance', his lack of interest in its intellectual and artistic achievements is almost startling. Machiavelli's unique concern is statecraft, the getting and maintaining of power. His attitude to the discoveries of humanism is strictly utilitarian. The classical history so revered by his contemporaries is employed not as any kind of moral example, but as a form of what now might be referred to as 'best practice' – what can be learned from the ancients on the acquisition and endurance of authority. *The Prince* is often understood as a 'mirror book' for rulers (the term refers to the instruction manuals which proliferated during the Renaissance, giving advice on everything from religious observation to table manners), a 'how to' manual for the contemporary ruler. Recent scholarship posits it as something more, a constitutional tract produced as a consequence of 'the change from feudalism to the princely state'.[6] Contrary to the stereotype, Machiavelli's works are more than an ABC for the forward-thinking tyrant; they are a philosophical reaction to the radical changes in the form and practice of governance which his age witnessed. Throughout the 1490s, Machiavelli had seen his own beloved city of Florence descend from a notionally free republic to a theocracy to a city under alien occupation by the French, to a ducal state governed by Lorenzo de Medici, the dedicatee of *The Prince*. The overarching preoccupation of the latter work and the *Discourses* is if and how a state which has been corrupted can regain and maintain its liberty. For Machiavelli, the ruler's primary duty was the preservation of the state at any cost. This was also one of the principal concerns of Elizabeth I and her ministers throughout her reign, indeed, arguably, it was the creation and secure maintenance of England as a state which was that reign's object.

In many ways, Elizabeth was much less a 'Renaissance' figure than her father. Though she was flatteringly (and inaccurately) compared to Lorenzo de Medici, the 'Magnificent', the archetypal Renaissance ruler whose death precipitated the collapse of the Florentine republic which Machiavelli sought to restore, she was, unlike Henry VIII, no artistic innovator. She built no palaces, patronised few significant painters, kept an appropriate though not by the standards of the time an astonishing court. Her artistic legacy is not startling, though by no means so impoverished as might first appear. Yet she did accomplish that primary objective, the securing of her state, in the wake of her father's revolutionary break from Rome and the brief, bloody restoration of Catholicism during the reign of her older sister Mary. Whether or not Elizabeth was a strong or a weak ruler; whether she guided the nation successfully through the upheavals of religious and legal reform, or created a cruel religious antagonism which obtained for centuries; whether she left England as a strong nation with a new sense of a united identity, or an exhausted and bankrupt country desperate for change, it is in this that Elizabeth remains unique, not only because she survived to govern at all, but because she did so *sui generis*, in a way which had never been seen before.

Henry VIII's long courtship of Elizabeth's mother, Anne Boleyn, his divorce from his first wife, Katherine of Aragon, and the subsequent, desperately dramatic fall of Queen Anne are the stuff of Tudor legend. Elizabeth's birth in 1533 produces such a crowd of spectres around her cradle, both the vindictive ghosts of the Plantagenet past and the insistent phantoms of hindsight, that it is sometimes difficult to remember that, then, no one knew how it would turn out. Writing a decade after the end of Elizabeth's queenship, Shakespeare, in *Henry VIII*, describes her birth, giving Archbishop Cranmer an encomium on the baby's future, an anticipatory eulogy of the 'maiden phoenix's' greatness:

> Her ashes new create another heir
> As great in admiration as herself
> So shall she leave her blessedness to one –
> When heaven shall call her out from this cloud of darkness
> Who from the sacred ashes of her honour
> Shall star-like rise, as great in fame as she was,
> And so stand fix'd.

And Henry joyfully replies:

> O Lord Archbishop,
> Thou hast made me now a man; never before
> This happy child did I get anything.
> This oracle of comfort has so pleas'd me
> That when I am in heaven I shall desire
> To see what this child does and praise my Maker.

We know, and Shakespeare's audience knew, that it didn't really happen like that. But this need to distort fact, to gloss, to reshape, tells us a great deal about Elizabeth's capacities as a ruler, contentious though her legacy may be. The idea of Elizabethan England as a 'Golden Age' was as much a myth when Shakespeare was writing as it is now, yet however much the reign is disassembled and criticised, the myth persisted. The play of *Henry VIII*, which reflects on Elizabeth's legacy, is a useful means to contextualise the two contrasting dynamics which defined Elizabeth's rule and to some extent created that myth. What Elizabeth did was to negotiate her way between two differing and incompatible ideologies, which we might call 'chivalric kingship' and 'statecraft', which left England a markedly different place on her death in 1603 from her accession in 1558. It is the conflict between these two ways of thinking which is the connective current of Shakespeare's history plays, and which is resolved, in *Henry VIII*, by Elizabeth herself.

The history plays, which begin in the thirteenth century with *King John* and end in the sixteenth with *Henry VIII*, represent a chronicle of the passing of the medieval world, and its replacement by a new order. Shakespeare's 'notably nostalgic'[7] portrayal of Henry's reign is haunted by another prince, the most famous of them all – Machiavelli. As the culmination of the history cycle, the play contrasts two political systems, the medieval and the modern, or the Christian and the Machiavellian. It was the incompatibility of the latter which Machiavelli's contemporaries found so shocking.

What Machiavelli did was to 'call the bluff on the belief . . . that all genuine value systems are compatible'.[8] The medieval model, that of 'chivalric kingship', posited that a Christian ruler could govern honourably, according to the tenets of the Church, and that there was no essential conflict between justice and expediency. This is not to say that the medieval monarch did not lie, cheat and murder (Elizabeth's own ancestors are ample proof), but that when they did so their actions were seen as deviations from a code, and judged accordingly. Machiavelli did not advocate immorality in the pursuit of gain, but what he did argue was that apparently immoral actions could, according to circumstance, be ethical. This was not a novel conundrum – it was discussed by many of the classical authors that humanist scholarship was rediscovering. Cicero and Quintilian – writers with whom Elizabeth I was familiar – discussed the idea that 'political success demands morally obnoxious acts from anyone seriously engaged in politics',[9] while the Stoics claimed that there could be no conflict between *honestum* and *utile*, the impulse towards truth and necessity, a view which many humanists maintained. This was the stance taken, for example, by Roger Ascham, Elizabeth's own tutor, whose disapproval of Machiavelli was expressed in his call for a return to the 'days of yore',[10] an idealised past where the true and the good were less problematically aligned. What Shakespeare recognised, and what Henry contends with in the play, is that the Renaissance had brought about challenges for rulers for which this traditional model proved inadequate.

Machiavelli's critics maintained that Christianity and Machiavellian statecraft were intrinsically opposed. *Henry VIII* demonstrates that the need for the latter is invoked by the limitations of the former, that is, while:

> Too much can be made of Machiavellian influence in Tudor political theory . . . it cannot be ignored . . . the forces that were activating English thought came into play because of political and social exigencies for which traditional patterns no longer sufficed. And among these forces Machiavelli was one.[11]

Europe was changing. The superstructure of the Church, which had imposed its hierarchy over the remnants of feudal government, was diminished in authority, indeed in England that authority was desuete. The princely state was emerging as the foundation of a very different political order, which required a different set of imperatives for government, which seemed inimical to the older idea of honourable or chivalric kingship. What the Christian ethic could not allow was the 'doubleness' of Machiavellian thinking, that a ruler might say one thing and do another. As Calvin had it, 'If the tongue speak otherwise than the heart thinketh, both be abominable before God'.[12]

Both Protestant and Catholic writers associated Machiavelli with mendacity, even with the 'father of lies', Satan himself. A sermon preached at St Paul's Cross in 1578 expressed horror at the idea of:

> the most wicked assertion of the unpure Atheist Machiavel, who shameth not in most ungodly manner to teach that princes need make no account of godliness and true religion.[13]

Yet as James I, Elizabeth's 'heir' as referenced in *Henry VIII*, had it, 'a king can never without secrecy do great things'. The Renaissance prince needed *The Prince*. Much of the action of the characters in Henry VIII echoes the book, and Machiavellian maxims – beware of the hatred of commoners, or of appropriating worldly goods – are present there. The challenge of the play is aligning the two variant thought systems required to achieve what Machiavelli described as 'the highest form of virtue', which is 'the ability to do whatever is necessary to preserve the state'. In the play, it is implied that such a reconciliation can only be effected by the divine right, yet this right, which Henry has arrogated to himself in his separation from Rome and the founding of the Church of England, is compromised by the 'un-Christian' political strategy employed to obtain it. The paradox is that a Christian king has succeeded by un-Christian methods. Cranmer's closing speech suggests that it is Elizabeth who will finish what her father began, allying the two systems morally, to secure a free and independent England.

While there is no direct evidence that Elizabeth herself owned a copy or read *The Prince*, it is impossible that she could have been ignorant of its ideas, which had been current in England for some time when she succeeded to the throne. Richard Morison, secretary to her father's minister Thomas Cromwell, who was in Italy until 1536, has been credited with using Machiavellian doctrines.[14] Mary Stuart's Lord Chancellor, Bishop Gardiner, in letters of advice to Philip of Spain between 1553 and 1555 lifts 3,000 words from Machiavelli's work. Elizabeth's ministers Francis Walsingham, William Cecil and Nicholas Bacon all read Machiavelli, Sir Christopher Hatton owned a copy, and in 1560 a translation of Machiavelli's *The Art of War* was dedicated to Elizabeth, a dedication repeatedly included in later editions. 'Given [Elizabeth's] extensive humanist education, her fluency in Italian and her life-long interest in philosophy, it is highly probable that she was, like most of her councillors, familiar with Machiavelli's ideas.'[15]

Elizabeth was very much a Renaissance ruler in that, like her father before her, she invested a good deal in her self-presentation as a scholar-king. She wrote and translated throughout her life, not only her own speeches, on which she worked closely with a secretary before handing them to her minister William Cecil for checking, but also letters in French, Italian, Greek and Latin as well as poems and prayers. One couplet references Machiavelli directly:

Never think you Fortune can bear the sway,
Where virtue's force can cause her to obey.

The central premise of *The Prince* is the perennial conflict between *virtu* and Fortune. A ruler, Machiavelli suggests, can control fate through the exercise of virtu. Virtu is not the same thing as virtue, that is, adhering to high moral standards. Virtu, derived from the Latin *virtus*, in turn from the root *vir*, 'man', can be understood as a combination of qualities – courage, fortitude and ingenuity among them – but it differs from virtue, goodness, by the 'goals achieved and the results of achieving them'. Virtu is counterposed with Fortune, conventionally depicted throughout the medieval period as a woman who turns and overturns the destinies of humankind on a wheel – mercurial, fickle, ever-changing, or as Machiavelli put it in a poem, 'apt to change her whirling in the middle of the spin'. 'Fortune is a woman', he writes, 'and if you want to master her you must beat her and compel her to struggle.' The ultimate goal for the prince is to 'govern Fortune' which can only be achieved by applying moral flexibility to political expediency. 'Only if men could properly discern the demands of the times and adjust their behaviour accordingly' is this possible. Different behaviour, in different contexts, can achieve the same result.

Elizabeth I has been described as 'one of the most perfect incarnations of the Machiavellian prince'.[16] The need to adapt to circumstance, to bow to necessity in order to better control it, was a lesson Elizabeth learned early, and upon which her literal, as well as political, survival may well have depended. The contrast between her reputation and that of her disastrously dogmatic sister Mary is a case in point, while her execution of Mary Stuart, which cost her a good deal of personal struggle, represents perhaps the best example of Machiavellian statecraft over 'chivalric kingship'. Knightly ideals, which had, in principle at least, underpinned an older form of politics, had no place in a new ideological age where political assassination was construed as an instrument of divine will.

Elizabeth presented herself as a Machiavelli-style politician in a 1585 letter to James of Scotland:

'if you suppose that princes' causes be veiled so covertly that no intelligence may bewray them, deceive not yourself, we old foxes can find shift to save ourselves by others' malice and come by knowledge of greatest secret specially if it touch our freehold'.

The reference the Queen catches here is to Machiavelli's example that 'The lion cannot protect himself from traps, and the fox cannot defend himself from wolves. One must therefore be a fox to recognise traps and a lion to frighten wolves.' That is, what will achieve a desired result in one context will fail in another. Mary Stuart's ambassador Maitland warned about Elizabeth's capacity for dissembling, claiming that she was 'all plain craft without true dealing'. That Elizabeth was influenced by Machiavelli is not exactly news, but in the conflict between Fortune and virtu referenced in the couplet, she does something else.

The poem was written to Walter Ralegh, in response to the latter's own complaint that, in the best language of courtly discourse, 'Fortune hath taken away my love'. The poem is dated to around 1589, at the cusp of Ralegh's influence before it began to decline in the face of Elizabeth's promotion of Robert Devereux, Earl of Essex. Four years later, Elizabeth was to translate one of the most important works of medieval thought, Boethius's *The Consolation of Philosophy*, and her response to Ralegh's verse reads like a rehearsal of the dialogue in Boethius, between Philosophy and Fortune, but also as a recasting of the gendered categories of Machiavelli's virtu and Fortune.

In *The Consolation*, Boethius suggests that only God can overcome fortune, whose power is limited to the sublunary, or material world. Elizabeth's verse advice to Ralegh plays with the conventions of courtly love, but also positions the Queen as God's representative. Ralegh's plea is couched in the conventional courtly terms – he is the swooning knight, she the inconstant mistress. Elizabeth's answer switches the roles. She portrays herself as Philosophy, or virtu, appropriating the 'male' role to herself, while Ralegh is encouraged to recover his 'courtly masculinity' (which by implication is compromised). In directing Ralegh towards virtu, she also implies that she has power over Fortune, enhancing her own divine status as God's representative on earth. Where Elizabeth is truly a Renaissance prince, then, a creature of her times, is in this refashioning of her own right to govern within a new political order which is *nevertheless justified by her arrogation of divine power to herself.* As *Henry VIII* suggests, this was something that Henry VIII himself never quite managed.

Henry was in many ways very much a prince of the Renaissance. The new learning may have come late to England – a fact of which the king was very much aware – but on his accession in 1509 he was determined to embrace it both intellectually and practically. There is a case to be made for elements of Renaissance sophistication having been introduced in England as early as the reign of Richard II, which closed the fifteenth century, but by that century's end a realm which had been ravaged by the Wars of the Roses for forty years still retained memories of a much more barbaric age. Henry VII showed his respect for developments in European culture by conferring the Order of the Garter on the Duke of Urbino, whose court in the Italian Marches epitomised the artistic and social ideal of Renaissance princedom, as captured in Baldassare Castiglione's The *Book of the Courtier*, perhaps the most influential 'mirror book' of the period. He commissioned Polydore Vergil to produce the first major study of

English history, and rebuilt Richmond Palace in the new style. Almost from the moment he ascended the throne, Henry VIII's ambition was to build upon these first, somewhat faltering gestures, to create a court which would ultimately equal that of his great rival, François I of France. English intellectuals such as Linacre and Colet transmitted the advances being made in Padua, Florence and Rome to the first Tudor court, while one of the greatest Renaissance scholars, Erasmus, spent the five years between 1510 and 1515 at Queens' College, Cambridge (he loathed it). Henry commissioned Pietro Torrigiano to create the tomb-monuments of his grandmother, Margaret Beaufort, his father, and his mother, Elizabeth of York, the latter of which remain at Westminster Abbey today. Henry's patronage of Holbein, or the court culture which produced writers such as Sir Thomas Wyatt, or the building of Nonsuch Palace, to take some of the most obvious examples, would qualify Henry as a 'Renaissance' ruler, yet while in his secession from Rome he brought about the conditions which foregrounded Elizabeth's rule, he did not succeed in aligning Church and state in the manner which renders his daughter unique. Had he lived longer perhaps he might have done so – certainly there is much speculation as to the extent of his reformist tendencies at the end of his life, and in his directions for the governance of his boy-heir Edward VI he attempted to establish a parliamentary paradigm which would permit this, yet the brevity of Edward's reign arrested this dynamic. (England under Edward remained an intellectually dynamic place, perhaps most notably in the atmosphere of St John's College, Cambridge, which was to have tremendous influence on the Elizabethan administration, but even considered in the most positive light, Edward himself remains a figure of promise, rather than achievement.) The particular challenges facing Elizabeth on her succession were brought about both by this legacy from her father and the attempts of her sister Mary to overturn it. Mary was very much a creature of the world Elizabeth is leaving behind her in the *Three Goddesses* portrait. Her persecution of the reformed faith was based on precisely the absolute distinctions which Machiavelli proposed a ruler might disavow. Mary consistently – and rather heroically – refused to abandon her own inner Catholic convictions, and was quite unable to make a distinction, in her own case or that of others, between what she believed and what she chose to make apparent. Herself highly educated, Mary was much less interested in advancing learning than she was in dragging England back to conformity. The realm inherited by Elizabeth in 1559 was thus poised between confessions, between ideologies, between conservatism and reform. But how did her own story begin?

Perhaps the starting point of the trajectory which was to carry the young woman of the *Three Goddesses* portrait into the Renaissance was her signature. When Elizabeth Tudor learned to write, she did so as a princess. Her first letters, formed under the tutelage of William Grindal, who taught her between 1544 and 1546, are notable for the clarity of their neat italic hand. Italic script spoke of classical education, associating its user with the erudite tradition of 'new learning' so prized by European elites. Yet, 'though prestigious in some contexts . . . [it] seems to have been viewed by some in the later part of the Tudor period as a childish, womanish, second hand skill'.[17] When Elizabeth came into her crown in 1558, one of the first things she did to signify her new status as Queen was to adopt what she called her 'skrating'hand, the runaway script which sprawls across her correspondence like a dancing spider. Like Hamlet, Elizabeth held it 'a baseness to write fair and laboured much/ How to forget that learning'.[18] No longer a polite young lady, eager to please with her accomplishments, the young Queen bestowed more attention than any of her Tudor predecessors on her signature, creating a swooping, intricate flourish derived from the huge ampersand displayed in the bottom right corner of her childhood writing manual, Palatino's *Il Libro Nuovo*. Notably, neither of the sample 'R's' the Queen melded in her signature were influenced by Palatino's model of the word 'Regina'; significantly, they are modelled on the letters which begin 'reverendissimo' and 'rarissimo', that is in the masculine rather than the feminine form. Elizabeth's signature is a tiny, poignant window into the mind of a young woman whose path to the throne had been so perilous as to make its completion almost incredible, it is also a measure of her apparently serene certainty of her own destiny. Teenage girls practise signatures, signing themselves into imagined futures with the crush of the week: Elizabeth wrote her future as a monarch. And she chose to do so not as a princess, but as a prince.

Elizabeth's decision to reinvent her signature shows us two things. First, that she was comfortable enough within the rarefied atmosphere of humanist learning to play with it, to appropriate it to her own ends, and second, in a gesture which foregrounds her much later manipulation of the Machiavellian concept of virtu in her exchange with Ralegh, that those ends involved a dissolution of gender categories. Something similar occurs in the *Three Goddesses* portrait. The Judgement of Paris perhaps had particular associations for Elizabeth, since it formed part of the six pageants performed at the coronation of her mother, Anne Boleyn. In Anne's procession to Westminster Abbey for her crowning, she paused at the Great Conduit, where the Judgement was acted out. Conventionally, the prize of the golden apple in the myth was given to Venus; in Anne's pageant the actor playing Paris paused at the last moment and gave the prize to Anne herself, announcing:

yet, to be plain,
Here is the fourth lady now in our presence,
Most worthy to have it of due congruence.

Anne's acceptance of the apple casts her in a conventional feminine role, as a woman to be judged and rewarded by a man, but in the *Three Goddesses* picture, it is, as we have noted, Elizabeth herself who is Paris, who has taken the authority of choice upon herself.

Throughout her reign, Elizabeth was to exploit the fluidity of gender categories which, in the perceptual paradigm of her age, surrounded those few exceptional individuals who enjoyed the status of sovereign rulers. This fluidity was represented in language. Elizabeth I referred to herself as a 'prince', as did her kinswoman and fellow Queen Regnant Mary Stuart. Sovereign monarchs were 'male', even when they were female. Perhaps the best analogy is with languages

where nouns are gendered: a thing, a table or a book, say, is catego-
rised by a preposition as male or female. Perhaps the use of the word
which most sums up Elizabeth's character is her glorious riposte to
Robert Cecil, 'The word *must* is not used to princes'. Also significant
to sovereign status was the distinction between the 'body natural'
and the 'body politic' of a prince. In Elizabeth's case, these potential
biological dualities were central to her authority, which she sought
to enforce through a mystic virginity, which confirmed her not only
as a head of state but as the quasi-divine figurehead of a new religion.

Elizabeth's realisation of this role is demonstrated visually in one
of the best-known images of her as Queen, the *Armada Portrait* of
1588. It is curious that the cultural legacy of Elizabeth I's personal rule
has been described as being 'of the word, not the eye'. No monarch
before or since has so effectively stamped an age with their image.
Elizabeth constructed her appearance with a precision which might
in contemporary terms be called 'branding' – the consistent details of
red hair, ivory skin, ornate ruff and elaborately jewelled costume rendering her instantly recognisable. The *Armada Portrait*, the zenith of
Elizabeth's age, at least so far as propaganda was concerned, fulfils all
the iconographic elements which so effectively annealed her image
to her reign. The most intact of three versions, in addition to as many
as six derivatives, the portrait is nevertheless novel in that it takes a
horizontal rather than a vertical perspective 'as though some new
and spectacular format had to be invented to match the magnitude
of the event'.[19] Elizabeth's hand rests upon a globe, after the manner
of a Roman emperor, above it is set the Crown Imperial, equating the
status of the Tudors with that of the Holy Roman Empire. Between
the columns behind the Queen we see the English fireships advancing into the Spanish fleet on the left, and on the right the enemy's
battered, ignominious retreat to the cruel Scottish coast – images of
shipwreck, it should be noted, were at the time used to imply heresy
– there is no doubt that the Spanish are being punished by the same
God who delivered victory to the Queen. All we see of Elizabeth is
her face, poised and smooth beneath her pearl-dressed wig, and the
long pale hands of which she was proud all her life. Her gown, with its
huge puffed sleeves, bows, embroidery and jewels, is less a garment

than a treasure trove, an insistent display of wealth and wonder. This is in no way a representation of a human being, rather the portrait captures a point of apotheosis, of the translation from monarch to immortal. The atypical perspective of the painting, whereby the chairs and tables which surround the Queen are observed simultaneously from differing viewpoints, reinforces the gesture of her hand set upon the globe; this is a ruler who commands not just guns and ships, merchants and soldiers, even, it is implied, storms and sun, but time and space themselves. The picture's background performs the same trick as Shakespeare's conclusion to *Henry VIII*, refashioning Elizabeth's life in smooth and triumphant continuity.

Here, then, are three moments where we might engage imaginatively with Elizabeth – the assiduous student of the new learning, swirling out her future with her quill; the young Queen, stepping forward into the sunlight of a dawning age; and the triumphant sovereign, her humanity excised beneath a gorgeous canvas of authority. It is in the gaps between these moments that Elizabeth created herself. In seeing her as a Renaissance prince, this book is just one way of looking at how she did so.

CHAPTER TWO

When the infant Princess Elizabeth awoke in her nursery on 20 May 1536, the landscape of her childhood was imperceptibly but irrevocably changed. Her mother, Queen Anne, had died the previous morning in the Tower precincts, her head struck from her body by the dancing blade of a French swordsman imported from Calais for the task. So many corpses, so many ghosts. Elizabeth's path to the throne was littered with a hundred and fifty years' worth of bodies. Since 1400, when the two strands of the great Plantagenet dynasty which had ruled England since 1154 divided and turned against one another, the preoccupation of the English crown had been heirs. The childless Richard II (with whom Elizabeth was later to identify herself) lost his throne to Henry Bolingbroke, subsequently Henry IV. The death of his son Henry V, the second Lancastrian king, in 1522, left the nation under the nominal leadership of a tiny baby, inaugurating the second phase of the Wars of the Roses, the dynastic conflict which dominated English politics until Henry Tudor seized the throne from Richard III in 1485. Richard's predecessor, Edward IV, had been a strong ruler, but he, too, left an heir in his minority, the romantic and mysterious king-who-never-was Edward V. Richard's own son, Edward of Middleham, the short-lived Prince of Wales, died like his cousin in childhood. With Henry's accession and celebrated reunion of the two strands of the dynasty in his marriage to Elizabeth of York, the succession seemed assured, though it passed to another Duke of York, Henry VIII, rather than his elder brother, Arthur Prince of Wales. It was hardly surprising, given this legacy of treachery, death and devastating insecurity, that when Henry married his brother's widow, Katherine of Aragon, he should have been even more concerned than his ancestors with the getting of a male heir, yet this was the one thing which, in his view, God denied him. Henry's struggles to release himself from his first marriage and wed Elizabeth's mother Anne precipitated the greatest confessional schism Europe had yet seen and set England on the course to Protestant isolation which became such a self-declared part of the emerging nationalist identity of his daughter's state.

Elizabeth was the product of that schism, and for two years, officially at least, she was his petted darling, the first child of that godly marriage which would people the courts of Europe with Tudor blood. Yet on 20 May 1536 all the small certainties of her world were severed. Historians have been arguing ever since about the effect this had on Elizabeth, but we cannot know how and when the two-year-old girl was informed of her mother's death or what her reaction was. This has not prevented generations of writers from imaginatively constructing the consequences of Elizabeth's loss, but statements such as 'Unresolved grief continued through Elizabeth's childhood . . . for Anne Boleyn's name could not be mentioned without provoking a fearful reaction from Henry VIII. Such a situation often leads to excessive mourning reactions on occasions of loss and later melancholia',[1] are merely speculative and without authority, though not uninteresting. That Elizabeth was nurturing a secret guilt at having fulfilled the desire of her Electra complex (the killing of her mother), that she was traumatised into evading marriage in later life, that she promoted a cult of her virginity in order to compensate for her inadequacy as a woman, that she needed to dominate and control those around her, has all been confidently and speciously attributed to the scars left by her mother's execution. That Anne's death had some effect on her daughter is reasonable; we simply do not know what that effect was, even if Elizabeth herself did.

This is not to say that Anne was not influential in her daughter's life. Her trial, her execution and the dissolution of her marriage invested her absence with a form of negative capability – an absence which has been understood as haunting her daughter's life ever after. Two weeks before her death, the queen had written to Henry, begging him not to punish their daughter in his resentment against her, a plea which, given the declared illegality of their marriage, Henry had no choice but to ignore: the most significant aspect of Anne's legacy to Elizabeth was the ambiguous status of her birth, the stain of illegitimacy which was to dog her well beyond her eventual accession to the throne. The comment of Elizabeth's governess, Lady Bryan, on the sudden alteration in Elizabeth's status, 'As my lady Elizabeth is put from the degree she was in, and what degree she is at now I know not but by hearsay, I know not how to order her or myself', summed up a confusion which spread from the royal nursery across the courts of Europe. There was not one moment of Elizabeth's entire life during which her status was unequivocally accepted. So while we can only surmise Elizabeth's feelings towards Anne from a (very) limited record of her actions, Elizabeth's refusal to accept her bastard status *did* at times invoke her mother, though in a symbolic or legalistic, rather than an emotional fashion.

The very circumstances of Elizabeth's birth have proved cause for debate. Was she, as one of her father's biographers asserted, 'the most unwelcome royal daughter in English history',[2] or the confirmation of God's blessing on a controversial marriage which both parents nevertheless confidently believed, in 1533, would go on to produce sons? On 26 August that year, Anne had formally 'taken to her chamber' at Greenwich to await the birth of her child, in a ceremony which closely followed that set out in the *Ryalle Book* for the delivery of Henry's mother, Elizabeth of York. Elizabeth's room had been decorated in blue arras cloth and gold fleur-de-lis, as any more complex decorative scheme was considered, according to the protocol, as 'not convenient about Women in such case'.[3] Anne selected tapestries featuring the story of St Ursula and the eleven thousand virgins, a prescient choice, while her bed, fitted with feather pillows and a crimson cover finished with ermine and gold edging, followed the model of her late mother-in-law. The bed was ceremonial as much as practical, functioning as a semi-throne, surmounted with a canopy of state embroidered with the crowns and arms of the royal couple. The canopy was 'a potent symbol of the queen's position, in which her claim to the authority of the crown derived from the fact that she shared a marriage bed with the king'. A pallet at the foot of the bed served for daytime use, and for the labour itself when the time came. Again following the precedent of fifteenth-century queens, the birthing chamber was furnished with two cradles, one upholstered and gilded to match the state bed, the second more simply carved in wood. The chamber also contained an altar and closet for Anne's devotions. After hearing Mass, Anne entertained the court (though not the king) in her Great Chamber, where she was served with wine and spices as she had been at her coronation. Then she retired with her women to remain enclosed until the birth. The birthing chamber was a powerful feminine space, a reliquary of sacred mystery. This still, entirely feminine world, where all the roles of the queen's household were taken by women, became the tense, beating heart of the court. As Anne waited out the long weeks in those dim, stifling rooms, she at least seemed serene as to the ritual's end. Anne had every intention of bringing forth a prince. The court doctors and astrologers had assured the royal couple that their child would be male, and letters (later hastily amended) had been prepared to announce the birth of Henry's true heir.

How the queen passed her time during her seclusion is not known – herbal baths were popular for women in late pregnancy, and quiet diversions such as embroidery or reading aloud were recommended; one imagines that, like all heavily pregnant women, Anne simply longed for it to be over. Nor is it known whether Anne made use of the sacred girdle of Our Lady which had been brought from Westminster Abbey in 1502 to lend succour to Elizabeth of York. Prayer was more or less the only painkiller on offer in this age of terrifyingly high maternal mortality, and birthing girdles, associated with various saints, had been used to encourage women in childbirth for centuries. Katherine of Aragon had used the Westminster girdle and had also lent it to her sister-in-law, Margaret Tudor. The use of such a relic by Anne would certainly have been controversial, given the attitude of the government at this stage of the Henrician Reformation to relics, pilgrimages and miracles, preaching on which was officially banned for a year in 1534, but there is an interesting possibility that Anne made use of a 'Protestantised' holy symbol, an amulet roll. These were scrolls containing prayers or holy stories which acted as textual interpretations of physical relics such as the Westminster girdle, invoking the same mystic connections. While disdain for relics was a principle of the reformed religion, a certain latent power still attached to them. One example of such a roll exists, related to five fifteenth-century versions. The extant roll was produced in 1533 as a response to the royal pregnancy, and features the legend of the mother and child martyrs Sts Quiricus and Julitta. These saints were not unknown in England (a half-dozen rural churches dedicated to them exist), but the invocation of St Quiricus as an intercessor is more firmly rooted in the French tradition, where he appears as the popular St Cyr, who visited Charlemagne in a dream. Given Anne's French education, and the publication of such rolls in London at the time of her pregnancy, she may have found Quiricus, in a textual, rather than a confessionally dubious relic form, an appealing form of spiritual aid.

After a reportedly difficult labour, Anne's confinement ended shortly after three o'clock on 7 September. (The nineteenth-century biographer Agnes Strickland has the queen announcing in a remarkably complete sentence for a woman who has just given birth that 'Henceforth they may with reason call this the Chamber of Virgins, for a virgin is now born in it on the vigil of that auspicious day when the church commemorates the nativity of our beloved lady the Blessed Virgin Mary'. If Miss Strickland had known of the existence of the amulet roll, she might have been less sanguine, as St Julitta met her martyrdom without her head at the hand of the tyrant king of Tarsus.)

Eustace Chapuys, ambassador to the Holy Roman Emperor Charles V, lost no time in pronouncing on the royal couple's despair and fury at the birth of a princess, but then Chapuys, whose master was the nephew of Katherine of Aragon, loathed Anne Boleyn and everything associated with Henry's second marriage. Despite his gloating, there is little contemporary evidence that Henry was more than conventionally disappointed by Elizabeth's sex, indeed he reassured Anne of his joy in the child and his love for them both. A celebratory *Te Deum* was sung at St Paul's, and, two months after Elizabeth's birth, Chapuys noted sourly that the king had been overheard by one of Anne's ladies saying that he should sooner beg for his bread on doorsteps than lose his wife. Unarguably, though, Anne had failed in what had always been the primary task of queens, and the succession remained perilously uncertain.

The recall of Henry's illegitimate son Henry Fitzroy to court shortly after Elizabeth's birth has been interpreted as an exhibition of the king's anxiety, of his need to prove that he could father sons, but the fourteen-year-old Fitzroy's marriage on 28 November to Mary Howard, daughter of the third duke of Norfolk, might equally be read as cementing a Boleyn triumph, as bringing the king's offspring safely into the Boleyn/Howard power nexus now that he had a legal heir. The idea that Elizabeth's birth was the beginning of the end for Anne is in no way borne out by contemporary reports – between October 1533 and June 1534 five witnesses reported king and queen to be 'merry' and in fine health.

Elizabeth's christening, on 10 September that year, also produced disparate accounts. Chapuys, gloating that the king's mistress had borne him a bastard girl, claimed that the ceremony was 'very cold and disagreeable, both to the court and the city',[4] while Edward Hall, the author of the 1542 *Hall's Chronicle*, which describes the history of the union of the royal houses of Lancaster and York, dwelt on the magnificence of the ceremony in the friars' church near Greenwich Palace, enumerating the dignitaries who attended and their roles, conjuring the image of the five hundred torches which accompanied the newly baptised princess back to her mother's arms. The fact that neither of Elizabeth's parents attended the ceremony was customary, and though Henry had cancelled the tournament planned for the birth of a prince, there was nothing lacking in the observances paid to a princess, from the Archbishop of Canterbury as godfather to the purple velvet stole in which the baby was wrapped.

Some writers have claimed that Queen Anne insisted on breast-feeding her daughter, others that 'we know virtually nothing of how the new princess was cared for in the first weeks of her life'.[5] In December 1533, again according to royal convention, Elizabeth was removed to her own household at Hatfield in Hertfordshire, travelling through London in great and deliberately circuitous style so that the people could catch a glimpse of the new Princess of Wales. (Chapuys reported with predictable distaste on the 'pompous solemnity' of this journey, but then he also believed that Elizabeth had been sent to Norfolk.) That Anne was 'heartbroken' at the severing of the 'extremely close bond' she had forged with her daughter is, again, a matter of supposition.[6] The 'merriment' between Anne and Henry reported at court suggests that whatever Anne's private feelings may have been she was not allowing them to show in public; moreover her place was at the king's side and, more importantly, in his bed, that she might conceive again as soon as possible. There is no reason to believe that Anne did not think it more suitable for her daughter to be raised in a quiet and orderly routine in the country, away from the pestilence of London, as had been the thinking and practice of generations of royal mothers before her.

And if Anne was unable to see her daughter often in person, Elizabeth's household was a stronghold of Boleyn affinity. In charge were the queen's aunt, Lady Anne Shelton, and her husband, Sir John, who served as steward, and Lady Margaret Bryan, who was half-sister to Anne Boleyn's mother, Elizabeth Howard. After acting as a lady-in-waiting to Katherine of Aragon, Lady Bryan was given charge of Mary Tudor, with whom she remained five years, before Henry began planning to marry Anne. By now in her sixties, Lady Bryan was called out of retirement to care for Elizabeth, which suggests that Anne and Henry trusted her competence and experience, but her role also called for considerable diplomacy. To the horror of Chapuys, in October 1533 the king decided that Mary, now officially styled 'the Lady Mary' in acknowledgement of her bastard status, should join her half-sister's household. 'The King, not satisfied with having taken away the name and title of Princess, has just given out that, in order to subdue the spirit of the Princess, he will deprive her of all her people,' choked the ambassador, adding that Mary had been reduced to the status of a 'lady's maid'. Mary's arrival created a background of tension, status-mongering and outright danger which pertained throughout her sister's life. Even as a tiny baby, Elizabeth was not safe from politics.

Of course, Elizabeth could have known nothing of the schemes and disputes into which her household was plunged with the appearance of her furious, confused and resentful teenage sibling. What is known of Lady Bryan's parenting appears to have followed a sensible, thoughtful model, in keeping with the practices of her age, which nonetheless were being influenced by the exciting developments of the Renaissance 'new learning'. The fifteenth and sixteenth centuries saw a regeneration of interest in medicine and pediatrics, promoted by printing and the increased use of the vernacular, which allowed physicians to combine practical experience and classical learning in a new way. Numerous texts on child-rearing and the treatment of childhood diseases were published, particularly in Germany, one of which, Eucharius Rösslin's *Der Rosegarten*, was the first 'scientific' pediatric manual to be translated into English, in 1533 and 1540. Swaddling, wrapping babies in tight linen bands to encourage their limbs to grow straight, was widely practised, but Rösslin took a daringly modern view: 'Imagine what goes on in him [the baby] as he feels the touch of rough hands on his tender skin and is chafed with coarse woolen cloth or scratchy swaddling bands. What do you think it feels like to lie on a hard board covered with prickly straw?'[7] Princess Elizabeth did not have to itch in scratchy bands or lie on straw, as Anne Boleyn provided suitably sumptuous clothes for her baby princess, including a gown of Russian velvet and embroidered purple satin sleeves, but Lady Bryan did follow some of the guidelines observed by Rösslin, such as weaning – late by modern standards – at two years on to pureed, sweetened food. She was concerned that Elizabeth, as a toddler, should not be allowed to sit up to table as it made her overexcited, and preferred her to stick to a plain, wholesome diet (which had little effect, as Elizabeth adored sweets all her life, and ruined her teeth with them). We don't know whether Elizabeth possessed the latest fashionable baby accessory, a tricycle-like contraption which aided children in learning to walk, but she was taken for airings in the park and was apparently a physically lively, as well as an exceptionally mentally alert, child, 'as goodly a child as hath been seen'.[8] Lady Bryan wrote regularly to court with details of Elizabeth's progress, and the child was visited quite frequently by her parents. Though her principal residence was Hatfield, Elizabeth was moved, again according to custom, between other royal residences to allow them to be cleaned, a necessity given the size of her household. In addition to the Sheltons, Lady Bryan and her first cofferer, William Cholmley, Elizabeth's retinue was the equivalent of that of a great magnate, with about twenty 'above stairs' offices, dispensed by her father, and a further one hundred servants' posts. Her progress between Hatfield, Eltham, Hunsdon, Richmond, Greenwich and Langley during her early childhood reflects the need for frequent changes of location for the purposes of hygiene and provisioning.

It was a move to Eltham in March 1534 which provoked one of the emblematic moments of the conflict between Elizabeth's sister and her mother. From the start, Mary had proved absolutely intractable on the subject of Elizabeth's status; on hearing the news that she was to remove to the princess's household she had remarked with considered disingenuousness that she wondered where, since the daughter of Anne Boleyn had no such title. When Mary refused point-blank to enter the litter which was to carry her to Eltham unless she was given her own proper title, an infuriated Lady Shelton had her pushed into it by force and confiscated her jewels as punishment. Mary compounded her disobedience by complaining vociferously that she lived in daily fear of being poisoned by the 'king's mistress'. Never much of a politician, Mary could only take a martyred satisfaction in the humiliations her stubbornness provoked. Her treatment by 'the concubine' was a much-vaunted scandal, but Anne Boleyn's attitude to Mary was based as much upon fear as spite, and Mary knew it.

If Elizabeth was to be promoted, Mary must be reduced, and Anne understandably saw any leniency towards Katherine of Aragon's daughter as undermining her own position. Anne's bullying of Mary requires consideration, though, as much of the impetus to abase the princess came from Henry, with Anne being blamed (again following a model which had affected previous 'foreign' queens whereby they were criticised for their husbands' actions rather than condemn the king himself), for a policy which Henry believed to be necessary to reinforce the validity of his annulment of the Aragon marriage. Nevertheless, Chapuys reported in January 1534 that Anne was complaining to the king that Mary ought to be supervised more closely, fearing that Henry's 'easiness' would allow Mary to continue to use her title, which could not be permitted as it would disparage Elizabeth. Anne sent messengers, including Cromwell, to discourage Henry from seeing his daughter, though the French ambassador claimed that the king's eyes filled with tears as he spoke of his obstinate daughter. Anne instructed Lady Alice Clere, Mary's custodian, to insist that Mary ate her breakfast at the common table, and that, if Mary tried to use her title, to box her ears. The hapless Alice was also scolded by Anne's brother, Lord Rochford, for treating Mary with 'too much honesty and humanity'.[9] At the time of the litter incident, Anne tried another tack, offering to intercede with the king if Mary could bring herself to some accommodation. Anne was invoking her queenly position here – intercession was an important traditional role in which queens could be the conduit for royal mercy – and Mary clearly grasped this, as she responded calmly that she knew of no queen in England but her mother, but if Madame de Boleyn would be so gracious as to speak to Henry she would be suitably grateful. Anne was predictably infuriated by this superb insolence. According to Chapuys, she began plotting to eliminate Mary. Anne received some satisfaction during the Eltham visit when, in April, Elizabeth was exposed quite naked to the visiting party of the French ambassador. This might seem peculiar, but the physical examination of dynastic brides was nothing unusual – Edward I's queen, Philippa of Hainault, had undergone such an examination, and at a far more embarrassing age – but in Elizabeth's case it was especially important, as deformity in children was attributed at the time to the sinful union of their parents. That Elizabeth should be proved flawless was encouraging, but Anne was troubled when it appeared that Elizabeth's entry into the international marriage market was being overshadowed by her sister.

Europe in the first half of the sixteenth century was dominated politically by the two great powers of France and the Holy Roman Empire. In 1516, Charles V had succeeded to the Spanish crown, followed in

1519 by his election as Holy Roman Emperor, thus giving him control over a vast territory which stretched from Gibraltar to the north of Holland, effectively encircling the French dominions ruled since 1515 by François I. Though François never took Charles up on his offer to settle their differences in single combat, the two monarchs were almost incessantly in conflict, particularly, though by no means exclusively, over control of their respective territories on the Italian peninsula. While England could in no way compare in land, wealth or military might with the two main players, her allegiance was useful to, and cultivated by, both, a counterweight in their endless tug of war. In the previous generation, Henry VII had sought to shore up his nascent dynasty by forming an alliance with Spain in the form of Katherine of Aragon, and subsequent English policy, while subject to the endless complexities and feints of sixteenth-century diplomacy, had remained broadly pro-Hapsburg.

France was England's traditional enemy, and Henry's enthusiasm for military glory had seen him manipulated by Charles's predecessors, Ferdinand of Aragon and the Emperor Maximilian, in 1514, into a war which was far more to their advantage than his. The marriage of Henry's sister Mary to Louis XII of France that year cemented an alliance with the French, which endured (despite Mary's swift widowhood and the accession of François in 1515) for some seven years, yet, despite the Treaty of London, brokered by Henry's minister Wolsey in 1518 and the meeting between François and Henry known as the Field of Cloth of Gold in 1520, war was again declared in 1522. Another peace treaty was signed in 1525, but Henry's pursuit of the Boleyn marriage necessitated a change in his foreign policy. Imperial troops sacked Rome in 1527, and the Pope, Clement VII, whose consent to an annulment of the Aragon marriage Henry urgently needed, found himself the prisoner of Charles V, Katherine's nephew. The Treaty of Cambrai in 1529, between François, the Emperor and the Pope, secured an imperial–papal alliance, halted French campaigns in Italy and left England isolated. Henry now deemed it politic to cultivate François's support for his marriage to Anne, which François was initially prepared to offer, in order to stave off a threatening alliance with Charles. Thus the early 1530s saw some tentative collusion with

England's break from Rome – the French king had strong-armed the theology faculty of the Sorbonne into declaring his marriage with Katherine invalid in 1530 and in 1532 a defensive alliance had been agreed at meetings at Boulogne and Calais. However, the appearance of Elizabeth herself disrupted this cooperation. When Henry discovered Anne was pregnant in early 1533, he had little choice but to marry her immediately, lest his longed-for heir be tainted with illegitimacy, but François was furious when Henry pressed on so precipitately with the wedding. For his part, François had been dancing round the question of the English royal divorce, since he needed papal support for his own project of marrying his son to the Pope's niece, Catherine de Medici, with the object of recovering French power on the Italian peninsula. Henry VIII professed himself disgusted with François's approaches to the Pope (though in fact they worked to his advantage, as they delayed the sentence of excommunication from Rome which was a consequence of his denial of papal authority), and by the time the Valois–Medici marriage took place, the two kings had resumed their usual quarrelsome relationship. François wanted an English alliance, but was chary of losing papal support to join England in isolation if he gave his full sanction to the Boleyn marriage.

In October 1534, the French had received a proposition that they should formally acknowledge the validity of Henry and Anne's union and recognise Elizabeth. In November, the Admiral of France, Brion, arrived with a proposal from François that Mary be betrothed to the dauphin. François thus sought to keep all his potential allies happy – joining the houses of Tudor and Valois while implying to Charles and the Pope that Mary, not Elizabeth, was still the 'right' heir. Henry initially treated the offer as a feint, but eventually conceded that Mary might marry Francois' third son, the duke of Angoulême, with the proviso that the couple renounce any claim to the English crown. Better still, Henry suggested, if François would persuade the Pope to revoke the sentence of excommunication against him, Angoulême could marry Elizabeth, in return for Henry's renunciation of his own ancient title to France and a significant parcel of land grants on the French coast. Brion showed no interest in a proposed visit to Elizabeth, instead asking Henry to proceed with the negotiations for

Mary's betrothal. Anne's anger was hysterical. Usually a model of the controlled court lady, she embarrassed herself by bursting into screeching laughter at an entertainment held for Brion, which clearly offended the Admiral.

Royal marriage brokering could be as graceful, precisely choreographed and meaningless as a stately pavane, and the game being played here had little to do with the eventual marital disposal of either Elizabeth or Mary, and everything with the contentious status of Henry's queen. If the French were promoting Mary, that status was by no means assured, particularly as Henry had implicitly acknowledged this in his insistence that Mary should formally renounce her claim (which theoretically was already legally void) on making a French marriage. Any hopes Anne may have had for the settlement of her daughter's future dissipated when the marriage negotiations collapsed at an inconclusive summit in Calais, which Cromwell, who favoured an alliance with the Emperor, cried off.

In January 1536, two crucial events took place. First, Katherine of Aragon died at Kimbolton. Recognising that she was ill with what modern assessments concur was cancer, she had written to Henry the previous month, commending 'our daughter' Mary to him and 'beseeching thou to be a good father unto her'. Henry's reaction to the news was repulsive. He accompanied Elizabeth to Mass dressed in yellow, their progress marked 'by trumpets and other great triumphs'.[10] Anne was reportedly overjoyed, but her triumph did not last. On the day of Katherine's funeral, she suffered a miscarriage. Reportedly, the foetus was male, and conventionally, the queen 'miscarried of her saviour'. Perhaps, though, it was not the child in her womb which had been protecting Anne, but a dying woman in Cambridgeshire. As long as Katherine of Aragon lived, Henry could not repudiate his wife. When she died, 'Anne's shield had been removed'.[11]

The idea that Anne's miscarriage heralded her downfall has been widely canvassed, but there is little evidence that this was the case. As late as April 1536, Henry continued publicly to endorse his marriage. That Anne had indeed miscarried a male child is confirmed by Chapuys, the chronicler Charles Wriothesley, who described her as being 'delivered of a male child before her time', and the poet

Lancelot de Carles, who confirmed that 'she gave birth prematurely to a son'. None of these writers mention that the foetus was in any way deformed, and yet this supposition has gained considerable currency, based on a comment made fifty years later by an exiled Catholic writer, Nicholas Sander, who claimed that the queen had been delivered of a formless lump of flesh. Even these words are too imprecise to support the claim of some disability or deformity, and it would certainly be strange that Chapuys did not remark upon it at the time had this been the case. That a deformed child was evidence of Anne's adultery in the king's mind, or that she was believed to be a witch, have been inferred from the suggestion, but since there was no deformed child the argument is circular. Had Anne's pregnancy run to term, and had the boy lived, then of course the story of the queen, and the English succession, would be very different, but this does not mean that the miscarriage in itself precipitated Anne's downfall.

In April 1536 Chapuys received orders from his master, Charles V, to finally recognise Anne at court, a gesture which was contrary to imperial policy since 1529. The Emperor believed it was now more advantageous that Anne remain queen, since if the papal sentence against him was enforced, and Henry put aside his wife as a consequence, there was a risk that the king would remarry. Any subsequent offspring would take precedence over Mary, the imperialists' preferred heir. Accordingly, the ambassador attended Mass, accompanied by Anne's brother Lord Rochford, with whom he had exchanged pleasantries before an interview with the king. 'As the king came during the offertory,' Chapuys reported, 'there was a large gathering of people and part of them to see what expressions *the concubine and I would make*: she did so courteously enough, for I was just behind the door through which she entered, she turned round to do me the reverence *comparable to that which I did her*'.[12] Here was the subtlety of Renaissance statecraft, an exchange of bows which could pass as the merest civil gesture and yet which nevertheless signified an important change of policy. The encounter was obviously staged, as the crowd waiting in anticipation to see it shows, and it reflects the desire of the king to see his wife acknowledged and a reciprocal willingness on the part of the imperial ambassador to gratify him. If Anne was teetering on the edge of the abyss, it would have been too serious a diplomatic concession for Henry to have demanded, even as a bluff to conceal his intentions; thus, officially, Anne was clearly in favour and so long as relations with the empire were concerned, would remain that way. Yet just over one month later, the queen was dead.

If the miscarriage is discounted, the sources of Anne Boleyn's demise have been ascribed to the machinations of two, sometimes overlapping, forces – the 'Aragonese' conservatives and Thomas Cromwell, a one-man faction all of his own. Henry himself hovers on the sidelines, a bloated tiger, ready to be soothed by pert little Jane Seymour's purrings. Or, again, Henry wanted Anne dead and set his most capable minister to conspire it. That Cromwell orchestrated the charges against Anne, and their inevitable conclusion, is undoubted; *why* he did so remains a matter of dispute among eminent historians. Highly convincing reasonings have been produced on both sides to demonstrate that, in his own words, Cromwell was 'a fantasiser et conspirer le dit affair' ('imagined and contrived'); his centrality in Anne's trial and execution remains, whether she is considered guilty or as the innocent victim of his machinations. It is the method of Cromwell's elaboration of the charges of incest, adultery and treason, though, which brings Anne's influence on her daughter into focus.

It has been argued that, as queen, Elizabeth's power was to some extent maintained by what has become known as the 'cult of Elizabeth', a practice of adoring and venerating the queen which blended the language of courtly love with that of religion, to present her as a semi-divine figure. 'Courtly love' long predated the Renaissance, but was very much a part of elite culture in the sixteenth century, revitalised by the influence and inclusion of the new humanist learning. In England, the tradition of courtly love is particularly associated with one earlier queen, Eleanor of Aquitaine, but by the sixteenth century the form promoted by Eleanor's father, Guillaume IX of Aquitaine, had become a culture universal among the European ruling classes. Courtly love and its correlative, chivalry, provided a code of conduct which pertained from the battlefield to the 'pastime' of the royal

chamber. It was a highly complex, witty, stylised, exclusive and sometimes subversive intellectual game in which both courtiers and kings
aspired to produce the most subtle and ingenious forms of homage to
their (often fictitious) lady loves.

This is the crucial element of courtly love – that it was a *game*,
albeit a highly sophisticated one. The form of a swooning knight
paying court to his impossible beloved was endlessly supple, a super-
language in which anything might be said, or, more deliciously,
unsaid. Sexual favours were not the object (though they were often
the consequence) of the game of love; well played, it could lead to preferment, patronage, an augmentation of status in the ruthless milieu
of court politics, the production and distribution of such poetry mirroring the dynamic of the courtier's life of endless waiting. It was also
a means of free expression under a tyrannical system where to speak
one's mind could be to lose one's head.

Anne's court, like Elizabeth's, was one of poetry, while the 'cult
of Elizabeth', if such there was, is based on a manipulation of the
tropes of courtly love, of that culture of romantic literary chivalry
which had played such a significant part in her parents' courtship.
And Anne Boleyn, until Cromwell decided to be literal rather than
literary-minded, was a mistress of the art. In one reading of Cromwell's actions in 1536, it was courtly love which he used to bring Anne
down, and it was Elizabeth's appropriation of her mother's practices,
if not her errors, which enabled her so triumphantly to manipulate
the mechanics of her mother's disgrace into her own unique form of
political glory.

In 1582, Elizabeth I wrote a poem on the departure of her last serious suitor, the Duke of Anjou:

> I grieve and dare not show my discontent
> I love and yet am forced to seem to hate:
> . . . I am, and not, I freeze and yet am burned
> Since from myself another self I turned.

Elizabeth is here demonstrating her own mastery of the conventions
of courtly love. The piece is very much a performance in the accepted

style. Paradoxes, 'I freeze and yet am burned', were characteristic of Renaissance poetry, known as 'Petrarchan contraries' after the Italian humanist whose sonnets had brought perfection to the earlier troubadour form of courtly love, and which were influential all over Europe. Thus Thomas Wyatt, 'of heat and cold when I complain/And say that heat doth cause my pain/When cold doth shake my every vein'. Elizabeth may have been describing her own feelings in her poem, but her feelings are not really the point. Participating in the convention displayed the Queen's skill at literary composition, the fact that Elizabeth's performance is highly derivative shows her ability to play the game of saying one thing – a tortured farewell to her last lover – while thinking another – a rather wistful good riddance, in Anjou's case.

It was just such a contrary that had originally opened the relationship between Elizabeth's parents. We know that Anne had been at court in the spring of 1522 when she appeared at a Shrovetide pageant given at York Place, the palace of Cardinal Wolsey. *Hall's Chronicle* described the castle which was constructed in the great chamber, with three towers decorated with banners showing three torn hearts, a lady's hand holding a man's heart and another turning a heart upside down. Anne was one of the eight ladies in white gowns displayed in the towers, representing Beauty, Honour, Constance, Bounty, Mercy and Pity, with Anne as Perseverance and her sister Mary as Kindness. Anne's role as Perseverance was especially apt, though it was Mary's, as Kindness, that was also to play a role in Elizabeth's life. Henry and seven other male 'virtues' attacked the castle, which surrendered under a siege of dates and oranges, after which the ladies were led out to dance. At the time, it was Mary, rather than Anne, who caught the royal eye, but four years later, by the time of the Shrovetide celebrations of 1526, there was no doubt of the king's attraction to her sister. Henry's motto was another heart, this time in a press, with the words 'declare I dare not' inscribed below. It is uncertain whether his feelings were already known at the time, since the love letters the king wrote to Anne are undated, but for the next decade Anne was to hold his attention as no other woman ever had or would.

Anne's ability to hold the king off for seven years is part of her legend. The brilliance of her strategy was to cast herself in the role of courtly lady, requiring Henry to play the perfect knight. Henry was nothing if not dogged in the pursuit of all the roles in which he cast himself – philosopher king, warrior, even husband – and 'this persona of courtly lover . . . was fully formed in Henry and had been signalling . . . for an answering adept to come and lift its latch. In Anne, he had her. She was the mistress of Petrarchan contraries: her blowing hot and cold made the perfect environment for the king's tender interest.'[13]

Once Henry had an idea in his mind, it was fixed. His minister Wolsey, who expertly managed the king for so long until he fell foul of that very certainty in the matter of the divorce, assessed his personality thus:

> I have often kneeled before him . . . an hour or two to persuade him from his will and appetite, but I could never bring to pass to dissuade him therefrom. Therefore . . . I warn you be advised and assured what matter you put in his head, for ye shall never pull it out again.

What Anne did was put the idea of marriage, and only marriage, into that stubborn crowned head. Her virginity was not the obstacle to his passion, it was the incentive. Anne's hymen became an instrument in Henry's divorce. When Henry instructed Wolsey to convey his wishes to the English envoys in Rome he was anxious to explain that he intended to divorce Katherine not out of lust for Anne but because his marriage was a sin in the sight of God. Anne's 'constant virginity' was an article in the case, both legally and within the terms which Anne and Henry constructed for their relationship – effectively, Anne was protected by the conventions of courtly love. Henry was not only anxious to prove his facility at the game of love to Anne, as his letters to her rather desperately show, but to the courts of Europe. By interpreting the role of courtly lady 'to its utmost potential [Anne] became more powerful than any man'.[14]

How did Anne Boleyn acquire such skill? Certainly, she came

from a family of courtiers. Elizabeth I's great-great-grandfather may have been in trade (something she shared with Catherine de Medici), but by the mid-fifteenth century Sir Geoffrey Boleyn, Lord Mayor of London, was well on his way to establishing a dynasty. Geoffrey's son, Sir William, married the daughter of the Earl of Ormond, while in the next generation his son, Anne's father Thomas, married Elizabeth Howard, daughter of the Earl of Surrey, whose brother became third Duke of Norfolk in 1524. By 1514, the Boleyns had consolidated their position at court, as Thomas was sent as ambassador to the Archduchess Margaret, regent of the Netherlands, that year. In 1513, his daughter Anne became one of eighteen ladies serving Margaret at Malines, in a household which included three future queens and the future Emperor Charles V. The magnificence and sophistication of the Burgundian court had greatly influenced those of two English monarchs, Edward IV and Henry VII, and would continue to be a model well into the sixteenth century, but Anne's time there was relatively brief, as she was present at the marriage of Henry's sister, Mary Tudor, to Louis XII of France in October 1514, and after Louis's death Anne joined the entourage of the new queen of France, François I's bride Queen Claude, where she remained for seven years. When she returned to England, the combination of her own wit and attractiveness and the rare polish she had acquired abroad made her exceptional. Anne was an elegant dancer, beautifully dressed, an accomplished musician and a fluent French speaker, but above all that she was clever, indeed brilliant, expert at the flashing flirtatious wordplay which relieved the claustrophobic tension of court life. Next to her, the English ladies, and their Spanish queen, looked like bumpkins.

As *maîtresse-en-titre* (if not in fact) and then as queen, Anne's court was not quite the sober and earnest hive of virtue that Latymer and Foxe portrayed. Henry and Anne were reported on many occasions to be 'very merry', 'pastime in the queen's chamber was never more', remarked her vice chamberlain.[15] 'Pastime' was the informal entertainment of the queen's rooms – music, cards, perhaps dancing, storytelling, word games, poetry reading. The 'pastime' was where gossip was whispered, where courtships were conducted in the candlelight, where the shafts of courtly wit darted and shone. Castiglione describes the custom of 'pastime' thus:

> among the other pleasant pastimes and music and dancing that continually were practised, sometimes neat questions were proposed, sometimes ingenious games were devised . . . in which under various disguises the company disclosed their thoughts figuratively to whom they liked best.[16]

Sex was very much present, as a reality or a delectable mirage, depending on the accounts of Anne's conduct one chooses to believe, but it was from this flirtatious atmosphere that Cromwell drew his weapons.

From this intense, intellectual and sensual environment, Cromwell conjured the names of seven men who were to be accused of adultery with Anne. Mark Smeaton, her Flemish musician, the only low-born man among them, was also the only one who pleaded guilty. Smeaton, Henry Norris, Sir Francis Weston, William Brereton and Anne's brother, Elizabeth's uncle Viscount Rochford, were executed. Sir Richard Page was exonerated of all charges. And Sir Thomas Wyatt went to the Tower, but not the block. It was Wyatt who witnessed, as his biographer beautifully puts it, 'a cataclysmic event, one of those gashes in history that tears, as Rilke said, the "till then from the ever since"'.[17]

Wyatt was an intimate member of Anne's circle, and the most accomplished of its poets. His exquisite lyric to Anne, 'Whoso List to Hunt', leaves a perfect representation of the language of love and longing which surrounded that circle and which Cromwell spun so chaotically out of control. With hindsight, 'Whoso List' reads as a fatal warning:

> Whoso list to hunt, I know where is an hind,
> But as for me, helas, I may no more.
> The vain travail hath wearied me so sore,
> I am of them that farthest cometh behind.
> Yet may I by no means my wearied mind

Draw from the deer, but as she fleeth afore
Fainting I follow. I leave off therefore
Sithens in a net I seek to hold the wind.
Who list her hunt, I put him out of doubt,
As well as I may spend his time in vain.
And graven with diamonds in letters plain,
There is written her fair neck round about:
Noli me tangere, for Caesar's I am
And wild for to hold, though I seem tame.

It is Wyatt's poetry which provides a fascinating key to the evidence which eventually indicted the queen.[18] Wyatt was imprisoned in the upper bell tower on 8 May 1536, and the following day, Cromwell began to assemble the jury for the trial. What did Wyatt reveal that allowed Cromwell to act? Or, rather, why was Wyatt's fate different from that of Norris, Brereton, Weston, Smeaton and Rochford? He expected to die, but instead found his sentence commuted to 'honorable detention'.

A poem contained in the Devonshire manuscript of 1536–7, which collates numerous works by Wyatt and his fellow court poets, contains the verses:

There never was file half so well filed,
To file a file for every smith's intent,
But I was made a filing instrument,
To frame other, while I was beguiled.

But reason hath at my folly smiled,
And pardoned me since that I me repent,
Of my lost years and time misspent,
For youth did me lead and falsehood guiled.

'File' is the key word, not 'frame'. In the sixteenth century it implied 'dishonour', or 'betray'. Wyatt's poem is, in a sense, a confession. He talked, and his reward was the pardon for conduct, the youthful folly, of which he repented. Wyatt's was not the only evidence, of course, which destroyed Anne, but the timing suggests that whatever he said 'enabled Cromwell to draw up his indictment [and] muster his juries'.[19] His words in the Tower were a good deal more precise that the elliptical subtleties which swirl through the poetry manuscripts. Yet poetry, curiously, occupied a significant place even at this moment of *extremis*. When Anne understood who her fellow prisoners were she made a bad, hysterical joke. She knew precisely why her 'lovers' had been selected, as players of the game of love at its highest, most ambiguously suggestive level. 'They may well make pallets now,' she giggled, punning on ballade/pallet, from sonnet to straw. And among the more extraordinary charges levelled against the queen was that she had laughed at Henry's verse-making, those earnest missives in which he sought to impress her with his own mastery of courtly love. In the account of Anne and her beaux sneering at the king's verse, 'which was made a great charge against them', we hear the sniggers of the 'pastime', of mockery of a man whose pen was as limp as his prick (as Rochford suicidally affirmed at his trial). Wyatt's biographer does not claim that Henry had Anne killed because she sniggered at his clumsiness with a couplet, but that Cromwell relied on 'a deliberate misinterpretation of a private language' to spring his trap, which was supported in law by Smeaton's confession and the Treason Act passed two years previously which made speaking against the king a treasonous offence.

It was this private language, though, which Elizabeth manipulated so superlatively to her own ends. It is also perhaps Anne's most significant legacy to her daughter. None of Thomas Wyatt's poems were published during Anne's lifetime, nor even in his own. But they were printed in Elizabeth's, in 1557, the year before her accession. *Tottel's Miscellany* contains ninety-six of Wyatt's poems, alongside forty by Henry Howard, Earl of Surrey, and the collection was the most widely disseminated and influential of the period. Here was the source of poetic inspiration for the courtiers who hymned Elizabeth, and for the other writers, including Shakespeare, who made the courtly sonnet the elastic, startling, finely wrought literary emblem of her age. The *Miscellany* is a direct linguistic link between Elizabeth's court and Anne's, an echoing connection between the two queens. At Elizabeth's court, though, and in the wider culture around the Queen, the language of courtly love was infused with religious veneration. Elizabeth became more than the 'mistress' in service to whom the courtier–lover achieves both identity and reward; she made herself, within the perceptual model of the Reformation, into a divine being.

CHAPTER THREE

How often in her childhood did Elizabeth hear the word 'bastard'? Kind Lady Bryan may have tried to shield her from the change in her status, but others, including her sister Mary, were not so gentle. Elizabeth's illegitimacy was tainted with something even worse – the ghost of incest. For Anne Boleyn might have been executed for high treason, but the grounds on which her marriage to Henry were dissolved were not her adultery, but Henry's previous relationship with her sister Mary, with whom he had had an affair in the 1520s. Under canon law, such a relationship rendered any subsequent union with a family member taboo, and though Mary herself was the product of just such a marriage (Henry's marriage to Katherine of Aragon, was, according to his own logic, illegitimate because she had previously been married to his brother Arthur, forbidden in the famous text from Leviticus 18:16 – 'Thou shalt not uncover the nakedness of thy brother's wife' – which sowed the theological seed for his first divorce), she positively relished taunting her sister with her bastard status. Elizabeth's sensitivity on the subject is signalled by her later discussions with the Venetian ambassador on the legality of Anne Boleyn's marriage, where she insisted on the legitimacy of her parents' union. In July 1536, Parliament repealed the Act which had made Elizabeth her father's rightful heir, and, though this was later overturned, the Queen remained technically a bastard all her life. Nor did the charge of incest ever die away. Writing in the 1580s, the Catholic rebel William Allen described Elizabeth as 'an incestuous bastard, begotten and born in sin, of an infamous courtesan Anne Bullen, afterwards executed for adultery, treason, heresy and incest . . . which Anne, her said supposed father kept by pretended marriage . . . as he did before both know and keep both the said

Anne's mother and sister.'[1] Mary Boleyn's 'Kindness' to Henry VIII at that long-ago feast would dog both Elizabeth's reputation and her mother's all her life.

Mary Tudor later referred to the allegation that Elizabeth was in fact Mark Smeaton's child, and cruelly referred to her as the 'Little Whore'. Nonetheless, she did show some tenderness towards her motherless little sister, and is credited with bringing Elizabeth to the Christmas court of 1536. By then, Henry's new wife, Jane Seymour, was just pregnant with the child who proved to be his only undisputed heir. Elizabeth's brother Edward was born at Hampton Court on 12 October 1537. The sisters were at court again for the christening three days later, with Mary standing as godmother and tiny Elizabeth, carried in the arms of Jane's brother Edward Seymour, holding the chrisom-cloth. Two weeks later, Queen Jane was dead, and Elizabeth's world changed again. Lady Bryan was to be governess of the new prince, replaced as Lady Mistress by Lady Troy, previously a member of Mary's household. At the same time, Katherine Champernowne, who had become one of the most significant women in Elizabeth's life, and who later married another member of Elizabeth's household, John Ashley, was appointed as governess. Along with Blanche Parry, the gentlewoman who had rocked Elizabeth's cradle and also taught her some of her native Welsh, Mistress Ashley remained close to Elizabeth all her life, and was responsible for her first education.

In 1539, Henry made a strategic dynastic marriage to Anne of Cleves, cementing an alliance with one of the small reformist corridor states that formed a buffer between Hapsburg territories in the Netherlands and Italy. Once again, Henry played the courtly lover, going 'incognito' to meet his bride at Rochester in a display of staged impatience, but it was a dismally unconvincing effort. Henry's reaction to Anne was one of outright repulsion, and, despite going forward dutifully with the marriage ceremony, he was so disgusted by the appearance and body odour of the 'Flanders Mare' that he was unable to consummate the union. Anne's reaction to Henry, who was no stranger to foul smells himself, thanks to the oozing sores on his ulcerous leg, is not recorded. Anne and Elizabeth are not mentioned as having met during the six months it took for her chaste marriage to be untangled, but she and Elizabeth did subsequently develop a relationship after the former queen had moved to her own property at Hever, where she apparently led rather a jolly existence.

Henry's next queen was a cousin of Anne Boleyn, Katherine, daughter of Thomas Howard, second Duke of Norfolk. As a young girl in the household of her step-grandmother, Katherine had had an affair with another relative, Francis Dereham, but the matter was hushed up and she obtained a place, aged about fifteen, as one of Anne of Cleves's maids of honour. Henry was soon besotted with the teenage beauty, marrying her within weeks of the annulment of his marriage to Anne. There is no real evidence of Katherine showing much interest in her youngest stepdaughter, though she did present Elizabeth with a few cheap trinkets, the kind of thing that pleases little girls, and had her to visit her at Chelsea and on a trip to see Edward at Waltham Cross. Elizabeth herself may have recalled these trips significantly, as she travelled in the royal barge at an age to remember it. But after four years of submitting to Henry's gouty attentions, Katherine took a lover, Thomas Culpeper. She was in the Tower by early 1542, and on 13 February suffered the same fate as Anne Boleyn.

Elizabeth was an extremely alert and intelligent child, but it is impossible to know what, if anything, she made of this sorry parade of stepmothers. It was a fact of sixteenth-century life that women died in childbed all the time – Elizabeth did not need the example of the death of a woman she had barely met, who died when she was four, to put her off maternity. As an adult, she was harsh in punishing sexual transgression when it in any way touched upon her authority – so if Katherine Howard is to be seen as an influence, it might be inferred that she was unsympathetic. But there is no reason at all to assume that Elizabeth was particularly interested by any of her three stepmothers before her father's last wife, Katherine Parr. Hers was a child's world, far from the court, with a child's preoccupations and concerns. Her illegitimate status certainly became an issue in later life, but, again, the external circumstances of her existence were happy and comfortable. She had teachers, activities, companions such as Lady Elizabeth Fitzgerald, who joined the royal sisters for a time at Hunsdon, and all the bustle of a large household, full of its own small events and dramas, to amuse and distract her. Much has been made of a letter from Lady Bryan soon after Anne Boleyn's disgrace in which she bemoans the state of Elizabeth's wardrobe, but the household accounts show that Elizabeth was well cared for in a relatively lavish manner appropriate to her station. Perhaps Mary called her names, but she was also a source of occasional treats and presents, and, anyway, siblings everywhere are perfectly foul to one another from time to time. Elizabeth did not spend her childhood cowed, poor and lonely, hoping desperately that the rays of her father's mercurial favour might once again beam upon her.

Henry was not even a particularly neglectful father by royal contemporary standards. He saw Elizabeth seldom, but he was kept aware of her progress, and in 1542, after dining with both his daughters at Pyrgo Park near Romford, he began to see more of them. In Elizabeth's case, this may have had as much to do with her age as anything else – she was, in her father's words, now exhibiting the qualities 'agreeable to her estate',[2] and small girls are not generally very interesting to busy middle-aged men. At nine or so, Elizabeth would have begun to be a civilised companion. For the last five years of the king's life, Elizabeth was given increasing signs that he loved and cherished her, and she reciprocated with a proud and powerful affection which endured in her as Queen.

Elizabeth's last stepmother, Katherine Parr, could not have been more different from poor, flighty Katherine Howard. Her own mother, Maud, had served as lady-in-waiting to Katherine of Aragon, and, after she was widowed for the second time aged thirty in 1542, Katherine became mistress of the robes in the household of Mary Tudor. Here she developed a romantic understanding with Thomas Seymour, Jane Seymour's brother, but this was brought to an abrupt end when Henry made clear that he, too, was interested in this attractive, rather serious woman. They married in a small ceremony on 12th July 1543 in the presence of both Elizabeth and Mary. Like many elite, educated ladies, Katherine had a deep interest in religious progressiveness, composing her own prayers and meditations and, as queen, holding a regular theological salon in her chamber. She was also considerably more interested than her predecessor in her step-children. Elizabeth's 'towardness' was remarked on by many who knew her; now Katherine saw to it that from 1544 she was able to share the lessons of her brother Edward, under the tutelage of John Cheke, the humanist – and reformist – professor of Greek at Cambridge, who had gathered about him an intellectual circle which was to include some of the key figures of Elizabeth's reign.

Elizabeth's tutors were both members of St John's, Cheke's college. William Grindal held the post until his death in 1548, after which he was replaced until 1550 by Roger Ascham, who left a detailed record of his studies with the future queen in a tract on education, *The Schoolmaster*, published in 1570. Ascham's book, which combines a perhaps surprisingly modern emphasis on a gentle and encouraging pedagogic method with an extraordinary depth and rigour, delineates the aims of a humanist education. For Ascham, Latin is the fulcrum of learning, and the purpose of its study, above all, is to achieve a command of expression which in turn will produce a polished clarity of reasoned thought. The student who began with Cicero's *De Oratore*:

> would not only take wholly away this butcherly fear in making of Latin but would also with ease and pleasure . . . work a true choice and placing of words, a right ordering of sentences, an easy understanding of the tongue, a readiness to speak, a facility to write, a true judgement both of his own and other's doings.

Ascham was building on a tradition of reformed education which had begun in Italy in the mid-fifteenth century. There, the *auctores octo*, medieval tracts on education, had been replaced by classical texts to introduce children to the works of ancient writers, to the extent that, in 1443, the University of Ferrara ordained that only those who could prove their credentials in *bonae litterae* – humanist studies – might be admitted to teach. Ascham believed that an ideal education consisted of three interdepending strands: the Latin of Tully, the Greek of Plato and Aristotle and the Holy Bible: 'I never knew yet scholar that gave himself to like and love and follow chiefly [these] authors, but he proved both learned, wise and also an honest man.'

Or *herself*, maybe, for Elizabeth also profited from an advancement in ideas about women's learning which in England had found its most celebrated exemplar in the 'school' established by Thomas More for his daughters and household, and which was known throughout Europe during the 1520s. More founded his system on the thorough method of double translation also adopted by Ascham, whereby the student would translate from Latin or Greek to English, and then retranslate their own rendering of the text. The curriculum followed in More's household was similar to that followed by Elizabeth, who, like More's daughters, read Latin, Greek, Spanish, French, Italian and German and studied mathematics, astronomy, natural philosophy, music and geography, while the study of grammar, rhetoric and logic was utilised in practice by debate and 'disputation'. Crucially, More's practice supported his view that women's intellectual capacity was in no way inferior to that of men:

> Nor do I think that the harvest is much affected whether it is a man or a woman who does the sowing. They *both* have the name of human being whose nature reason differentiates from that of beasts; *both*, I say, are *equally suited* for the knowledge of learning by which reason is cultivated . . .[3]

Another important precedent in terms of Elizabeth's education was that of her older sister Mary, whose studies were supervised by the Spanish humanist Juan Luís Vives. Mary studied the writings of contemporary humanists such as Erasmus and More himself, as well as Plato and Aristotle, and she too was an accomplished linguist. When Mary was seven, Vives produced a precursor to *The Schoolmaster*, *On a Plan of Study for Children*, directed towards the education of a future monarch. Mary's accomplishments are less well known than those of her sister (not least because she boasted of them less), but in her speeches as queen it is possible to discern many of the rhetorical elements derived from her education, which Elizabeth herself was to imitate.

An education equivalent to that received by the More girls or the Tudor princesses was obviously reserved for a very small number of women. But what made such an education extraordinary for those few was that, for the first time in England, women were possessed of an intellectual parity with men. Women's learning was not entirely unknown – indeed, during the early medieval period convents such as Wilton had been the focus of education for elite women – but Latin culture had generally been reserved for men. One positive consequence of this was the promotion by royal and aristocratic women of vernacular culture, but Latin had always been the language of power, of diplomacy and the law. Joined by Greek, considered essential by humanists for a true understanding of the Bible, Elizabeth's intellectual weapons were thus as finely honed as those of any of her male contemporaries. Like her brother Edward, with whom she shared her reading of Livy, Sophocles and Demosthenes, Elizabeth was educated as a prince.

As the children's household progressed from one nursery palace to another in between visits to court, Elizabeth and Edward apparently devoured the tasks set for them (and, since they were royal children, they were presumably never lazy or bored). One account captures the peaceful industry of this time: 'So pregnant ingenious were [Elizabeth and Edward] that they desired to look upon books as soon as the day began to break. Their morning hours were so welcome that they seemed to prevent the night's sleeping for the entertainment of the morrow's schooling.' Elizabeth was, however, excluded from the physical aspect of her brother's education. When Edward was called away to the 'knightly' training which formed part of his own, but not his sister's, education, Elizabeth 'in her private chamber betook herself to her Lute or Viol, and [wearied with that] to practice her needle'.⁴ Needlework was a far more conventional female accomplishment than making translations from Greek through Latin to English, but Elizabeth was proud enough of her embroidery to sleep on a pillow of her own decorating later in life, and to produce chair covers with her ladies. And while she might have been barred from the weapons drills thought suitable for Edward, Elizabeth acquired a lifelong taste for the brutal sport of cock-fighting from Ascham at this period, as well as the riding skills in which she delighted all her life.

Elizabeth was to live much of that life in little rooms. She was almost never alone, even at night, when one or more of her ladies would share her chamber, if not her bed. Like many 'cold bodies', Elizabeth loved fires and furs but hated stuffiness, and one senses a claustrophobia in her insistence, often to the inconvenience of her women, that windows be opened. No wonder she loved the open air, walking every morning in her garden or on a terrace, stalking lengths and lengths of galleries when the weather was poor, so that her puffing, court-bred maids struggled to keep up with her. Riding was a way to outrun herself, to be, for a few precious moments, free, and all her life Elizabeth adored hunting. She may not have been able to follow her brother in all the physical aspects of his education, but at riding she far outstripped him, galloping with a recklessness which later alarmed even her Master of the Horse, Robert Dudley, himself a brilliant equestrian. Of some 'good gallopers' sent from Ireland, he was to remark, 'she spareth not to try as fast as they can go. And I fear them much but she will prove them.'[5] When she could not ride, Elizabeth loved dancing, particularly, in her early years as Queen, the scandalous Volta, where the male partner lifted his lady between her skirts, often exposing her legs. Dancing and hunting were very much courtly accomplishments, but Elizabeth was a creature of her times in other respects, enjoying not only cockfights but bear-baiting. When required, Elizabeth could stand motionless in cere-monial majesty for hours – a skill which sorely tested the legs and back of many an ambassador – but active, even bloodthirsty, pur-suits seem to have provided a sense of excitement and release which she craved.

Confinement in palace etiquette and the physical endurance re-quired for ceremonial was her duty, but, while she accepted this, Elizabeth declared that 'I had rather be dead than put in custody'. To the later despair of her ministers, Elizabeth's need for movement and air translated into a refusal of any but the most minimal security measures: she was aware of the value of walking freely among her people in terms of maintaining her visibility and hence popularity, but it was also something that she required for its own sake. An interesting corollary of this has been proposed – that Elizabeth's insistence on preserving her independence to walk abroad necessitated the increasingly harsh measures taken against potential Catholic traitors later in the reign, that her freedom was paid for in their great suffering. Had the Queen been more willing to be guarded, the rack might have been less used.

For the present, though, thanks to Katherine, Elizabeth's spiritual and humanist education was progressing brilliantly. Katherine's influence has also been detected in the more tranquil relationship she enjoyed with her father. The dynastic portrait known as *The Family of Henry VIII* (1543/1547), depicting the interior and the garden of Whitehall Palace, includes Elizabeth on the right, separated from her father, Jane Seymour and the heir, Edward, by an ornate column, a distinction which is mirrored on the right by her sister Mary's pose. It has been proposed that the necklace Elizabeth wears in the picture is an 'A' medallion owned by her mother Anne Boleyn, and that Elizabeth had chosen to wear it as a gesture of solidarity to her mother. While this is not impossible, it seems extremely unlikely, but since the theory has been widely canvassed it is worth discussing. The most famous portrait of Anne Boleyn, the Hever portrait showing her wearing a 'B' pendant, was painted well after her death, and in fact there exists only one drawing, a Holbein showing the queen in a chemise and cap, which gives us any indication at all of what Anne looked like in her lifetime. For all that she was Henry's most famous queen, there is no painted record of her appearance during her brief reign. All the images which exist of her belong to the latter half of the sixteenth century, and in none of these is she wearing an 'A' necklace. We know that Anne possessed a 'B' and an 'AH', but there is no record in the royal accounts of her owning a single 'A'. It is quite possible that she did, and equally possible that Elizabeth inherited it; certainly the necklace she wears looks like an 'A', but it could equally be something else, or possibly have been painted in at a later date, as one expert suggests.[6] The principal scholar on portraits of Elizabeth makes no mention of the necklace in his discussion of the painting. Moreover, it is almost inconceivable that, had relations with her father been restored through the good offices of Katherine Parr, Elizabeth (at the age of eleven to thirteen) would have risked her father's wrath by such a gesture at this point. The idea that the necklace was a 'secret' between the girl and the unknown, probably Italian artist, seems equally unlikely, given the perceptiveness to allegorical detail in paintings of the time, which were meant to be 'read' symbolically by the cognoscenti. Elizabeth's position in the picture, beyond the column, is an instance of this; viewers of the portrait would have understood her illegitimate status from the stone barrier that separated her from the inner circle of her father's third wife and heir. The idea that Henry might have noticed and simply not minded seems equally extraordinary. And if Elizabeth was so determined to challenge her father by commemorating her mother in this fashion, why does the purported 'A' never reappear?

Elizabeth's presence in the picture correlates chronologically with the Act of Parliament of 1544 which restored her and Mary to the succession. Neither sister was re-legitimated, but both were formally designated, in order after Edward, as their father's heirs. At a reception on 26 June that year, at Whitehall, Henry dined with all three children and then presented them to the court informally over wine and sweets. Katherine Parr, who had no child and, given the state of Henry's health and girth, was never likely to have one by him, was pointedly not included in the party. So if there was 'triumph in [Elizabeth's] heart'[7] at her inclusion in the family picture at this moment, would this intelligent child have risked so much by doing something so crassly stupid?

Perhaps more interesting than this theory is the key the family portrait gives to the visual world Elizabeth knew as a child at her father's court. Pictures such as this were relatively rare in princely courts in comparison with tapestries, which were considered by contemporaries as being more prestigious objects. Tapestries usually travelled with their peripatetic owners (for his wedding a century earlier Philip of Burgundy transported fifteen carts' worth of them), and their function was to create 'instant splendour and magic'.[6] As a means of impressing onlookers, tapestries were intimately connected with their owners, appearing and vanishing as they came and went. They 'defined the spaces of political power, their dazzling visual richness and carefully selected iconography circumscribing the realm of the ruler'.[8] Tapestries were also an instance of the intricacy of the trans-European networks which connected merchants, artisans and consumers in the Renaissance. Gold and silver thread was sent from Venice, wool from England, silk from northern Italy and dyes from Turkey. Knowledgeable contemporaries were alert to the finish of the pieces – the greater the number of warp yarns, the finer the thread had to be, and the better quality the appearance of the tapestry. Pictorial detail and the presence of precious threads were noted and judged. It is hard, now, to appreciate the wonder that tapestries could create to sixteenth-century eyes, but in torch or candlelight, animated by the movement of bodies in crowded rooms, their 'full size figures would appear to move and mingle with similarly dressed inhabitants', in a shimmering, living dance. They were not flat, practical wall insulations, but 'interactive tableaux',[9] and the stories they portrayed were the familiar soap operas of their world. Henry VIII, like his father, collected numerous tapestries, including, in 1528, a set of the Raphael series *The Acts of the Apostles*. One of these, *The Healing of the Lame Man*, which divided the visual space into three sections in between the twisted vine columns of St Peter's, has been identified as the source for the compositional structure of the family group. The tracery on the column next to Elizabeth and the friezes on the walls above her connect the piece aptly with an innovation introduced during Jane Seymour's queenship, when Holbein produced a goblet for her, one of the first pieces of metalwork north of the Alps to employ a design of Moorish tracery. Holbein had encountered the styles, known as *grotesque* and *rinceaux*, of linear compositions in frieze and twining vegetable and floral garlands, at the French court at Fontainebleau, whence it had been imported from Lombardy. Though these styles derived from classical antiquity, the use of tracery was new, and originated in Islamic art, spread particularly through Persian book bindings coming from Venice.

The world of *The Family of Henry VIII* is a miniature of the Renaissance, a melding of assertive princely magnificence with exotic imagery, Italian art and Christianity in the language of the new learning, which Elizabeth's education had so precisely fitted her to understand.

CHAPTER FOUR

E lizabeth proudly displayed her learning in her first extant
letter, written in Italian to Katherine Parr in July 1544. The
two had not seen one another for a year, Elizabeth being occupied with her studies and Katherine at court, where she was serving
as regent while her ulcerous, lumbering husband was making his
last stab at playing the chivalric hero on a vainglorious campaign in
France. Elizabeth expresses both conventional and loving concern
for her father, 'humbly beseeching' the queen to 'recommend me to
him, praying always for his sweet blessing and similarly entreating
our Lord God to send him best success and obtaining of victory over
his enemies in order that your Highness and I may as soon as possible
rejoice with him on his happy return'. She soon had her wish, being
received by the king along with her sister Mary at Leeds Castle on
his return from France, after which she returned to the schoolroom
with Edward and began work on a project more ambitious than the
Italian letter, a translation from the French of *Le Miroir de l'âme pécheresse* (*The Mirror of the Sinful Soul*) by Marguerite of Navarre, planned
as a New Year's gift for Katherine. Twenty-seven pages of theological
translation is an extraordinary achievement for an eleven-year-old,
though the child Elizabeth is still visible in the obvious rush she
made to complete her present, the spelling errors increasing as she
hurried along. Elizabeth embroidered a beautiful cover (which still
exists) for her work, of silver thread on blue cloth, with KP in the
centre of four pansies. The charm of the presentation sits somewhat
uneasily with the text itself, not least as it contains observations
such as: 'Thou hast made separation of my bed and did put thy false
lovers in my place and committed fornication with them.' Elizabeth may have been a dab hand with a needle, but there was never

anything meek or ladylike about her mind. The pleasure and the terrors of the flesh were not then considered unsuitable material for princesses.

As Queen, Elizabeth's physical body was to become an object of obsessive interest. 'In the war of faith which divided Europe, Elizabeth's body . . . was the focal point of the conflict'.[1] To an extent, though, this had always been the case. Across Europe, the Queen's body was a mystic vessel, the point of translation of the king's line, a source both of succour and suspicion. The physical intimacy between royal couples often led to a deflection of criticism of a king on to the body of a queen, a means of positing 'unmanly' behaviour as the consequence of feminine power. King John's child-queen Isabelle of Angoulême, for example, in the thirteenth century, was accused by contemporary chroniclers of causing the king's disastrous losses on the Continent, of draining his virility so that he preferred to make love to her rather than fight with his magnates, while Eleanor of Provence, forty years later, was known as the 'nicatrix', the night bird, whispering poison into her husband's ear in the privacy of their bed. Stories of licentious and incestuous queens abounded from the Bible to the histories of the Crusades to the poetry of Boccaccio, 'a cultural stereotype from which to mount an assault on female rule'.[2] One response of queens was to disassociate themselves from images of potentially corrupt sexuality through identifying with the Virgin Mary, as Anne Boleyn had done in her Book of Hours. In choosing to translate Marguerite of Navarre's work, Elizabeth was associating herself with a similar tradition of queenship, as well as creating a literary connection with two women who had influenced her mother, and formed her own self-conception as an educated woman fit to rule.

During her time in France, Anne had undoubtedly been in the service of Queen Claude, rather than François I's sister Marguerite as has sometimes been supposed, but Anne was also acquainted with Marguerite's mother, Louise of Savoy. Louise herself had been trained at the court of Anne of Beaujeu, a daughter of Louis XII and a powerful regent during the minorities of both her brother and cousin, Charles VIII and Louis XII respectively. Anne of Beaujeu was known as a promoter of women's learning, a devotee of the scholar Christine de

Pisan, and the author of a manual, the *Enseignements*, dedicated to her daughter Suzanne. She had also been responsible for the educations of Margaret of Austria, in whose court Anne Boleyn initially served, and Diane de Poitiers, the mistress of Henri III. Louise gave Marguerite a princely education, so much so that as a patron, poetess and sponsor of the new humanist learning, Marguerite's own court became known as the 'New Parnassus'. The French historian Michelet termed her the 'Mother' of the French Renaissance. She thus represented a tradition of ruling women whose accomplishments embodied those of the Renaissance and from whose authority Elizabeth, in her translation, could draw.

Louise herself ruled for a time as regent, being assigned full royal powers by her son François in 1523 when he left on campaign to Italy. She, François and Marguerite created a series of verse epistles to one another, casting themselves as a trinity, in which Marguerite herself embodied youthful royal femininity while Louise represented a latter-day Virgin, a model of prudence and wisdom. The *Epitres* displace the physical body and sexuality of the regent on to her daughter, with Marguerite acting as a sort of 'body double' for Louise[3] while Louise carefully depicted herself with icons suggestive of chastity and learning. Thus the *Epitres* show Marguerite and her mother dividing the two aspects of queenly femininity, sacred and physical, between them, so negating the compromise to Louise's authority represented by her assailable corporeal self. This doubling is referenced in *Le Miroir de l'âme pécheresse* by Marguerite's references to the tensions of the soul imprisoned within the body: 'Ma pauvre âme, extase et prisonniere / Les pieds lies par concupiscence . . . Esperance de fin ne doit avoir'.[4]

Marguerite's feelings towards Anne Boleyn have been debated, but it is clear that Anne herself desired to cultivate a friendship. She had been Marguerite's guest when she visited Boulogne with Henry as his betrothed in 1532; afterwards she corresponded with Marguerite, and also passed on messages through her relatives. In 1533 the Duke of Norfolk was charged to tell her that Anne was 'as affectionate to your highness as if she were your own sister', while the following year Lord Rochford informed Marguerite of her regret at being unable to meet Marguerite and her brother in France due to her pregnancy. Poignantly, Anne expressed the following year that 'her greatest wish, next to having a son, was to see you again'.[5] Such effusive courtesies were customary, and it does not do to read too much into the relationship between Anne and Marguerite, but Anne's biographer proposes that she attempted to imitate the Queen of Navarre's learning by collecting books and illuminated manuscripts from authors and artists patronised by Marguerite, and even that the French original of *Le Miroir de l'âme pécheresse* from which Elizabeth made her translation could have been owned by Anne. If so, Elizabeth's translation was not only a highly appropriate gift to Katherine in religious, intellectual and queenly terms, but an indication of affection to her stepmother, as a rendering of one of the few mementoes of her birth mother that she possessed.

Anne Boleyn's possession of a Book of Hours, a devotional collection based on the Divine Office used in monasteries, has sometimes been cited as evidence of her reformist tendencies due to a reference in French to the Day of Judgement. This is disputable, since possession and use of such a book, well established in medieval tradition, was entirely concordant with orthodox religious practice. Anne's book does connect her with one aspect of the imagery surrounding her daughter, that of the Virgin Mary. Marian identification was a dominant motif in the representation of English queenship. Matilda of Scotland, Henry I's queen, had been close to Gundulph of Rochester, who had promoted the cult of the mother of Christ, celebrating the feast of the Immaculate Conception in the early twelfth century, before it was officially recognised by the Church. Ever since, the connection between the Queen of Heaven and the quasi-mystical power of the queen had been a significant dynamic. In Anne's book, she has written a note above an illustration of the Annunciation, the great moment when Mary receives the news that she bears God's Son:

By daily prove you shall me find
To be to you both loving and kind.

In Elizabeth's own manuscript book of devotions is a French prayer which also alludes to Mary: 'je te loveray en magnificat ton nom, o mon Pere' ('I will praise thee, O My Father, magnifying Thy name'). The line is a melding of Protestant and Catholic themes, combining the Magnificat, the first Marian hymn, with the resonance of the Psalms so important to reformers. Elizabeth made frequent reference to Mary, describing herself as 'God's handmaid' in a speech to Parliament of 1576 and in the 1569 text known as 'Queen Elizabeth's Prayer Book'. At a masque in July 1564 Elizabeth observed to the Spanish ambassador, indicating her black and white costume, 'These are my colours'. Black represented constancy and white virginity, so combined they signalled constant virginity. That an English queen should identify herself with the cult of Mary was nothing new, except that in Elizabeth's time there was no more cult of Mary. It is also crass to suggest that Elizabeth deliberately set herself up as a Virgin substitute in response to some mass psychological desire to replace Mary on the part of her subjects. Elizabeth did arrogate to herself some of the mystic power of the Virgin, though, and the way in which she did so is a product of the courtly love dynamic employed by her mother.

The impact of Anne Boleyn's religion on her daughter is another instance of a preference amongst some historians for facile emotive connections rather than thorough examination of the evolving and complex definitions of terms such as 'protestant' and 'evangelical' which often serve to obscure, rather than clarify, the theological revolution which began with Henry VIII's rejection of papal supremacy and continued well into Elizabeth's reign and beyond. Statements such as '. . . in time Anne would probably have turned Protestant . . . she and her father were described by the Spanish Ambassador as "more Lutheran than Luther himself". She was a great evangelical' are a case in point.[6] 'Protestant' as a term was first used in German in 1529 at the Diet of Speyer, and was current in English in 1533, but for much of the Edwardine period the term 'reformed' was more frequently used. 'Evangelical' did not necessarily mean Protestant, since it could be applied to Catholic reformers such as Erasmus as well as more radical thinkers such as Luther or Zwingli.

The question is rendered more difficult by the fact that 'Lutheranism' was often used as a shorthand by Romance language speakers to categorise generally those who rejected papal supremacy, while not necessarily accepting other 'Protestant' doctrines such as the Presence of Christ at the offering of the Host. In 1560, for example, the Guise Cardinal of Lorraine wrote to his beleaguered sister in Scotland that the French would punish 'those wicked Lutherans',[7] which was hardly an accurate summation of the beliefs of the Scots Congregational Lords. Aside from the fact that Chapuys was, as ever, a hostile witness, using the most provocatively negative terms to describe the 'concubine' to his orthodox master, the fact that he described Anne and her father in this manner is in no way indicative that Anne herself followed Luther's doctrines. Indeed, as we shall see, this linguistic confusion pertained in Elizabeth's subsequent dealings with the Ottoman Empire, where both she and her ambassador were referred to as 'Lutheran' at the Sultan's court well into the seventeenth century.

So how 'Protestant' was Anne Boleyn? Was she such a crucial influence in the English Reformation, both in her own practice and her direction of her husband's emerging Church? Much has been made of Anne's interest in the gospel, in particular her possession of a translation of the Bible into French by Jacques Lefèvre d'Etaples, as well as an English edition of his *Epistres et Evangiles*, which was dedicated to her. Yet an interest in the gospels in the vernacular had become common in educated circles in the 1520s and 1530s, among pious, progressive courtiers who read about, thought about and discussed their religion without taking issue with the essential tenets of the Catholic Church. According to William Latymer, one of Anne's chaplains, and later Dean of Peterborough under Elizabeth, who prepared a life of Anne for the queen early in her reign, Anne frequently discussed the gospel with Henry. Latymer is the only chronicler to make this claim, and, again, it is hardly proof that Anne was pushing her husband towards reform. If nothing else, Henry enjoyed debates which showed off his theological credentials – he had been extremely proud of the title *Fidei Defensor*, conferred upon him by Pope Leo X in 1521 in affirmation of his tract *The Defence of the Seven Sacraments* (in which the king supported the sacrament of marriage and the authority of Rome), which was revoked in 1530 and reconferred by Parliament eight years after Anne's death. As an intelligent and talented conversationalist, the topic might well have been one which Anne knew would interest and flatter her husband, but a conversation is hardly a religious revolution. Equally, Henry might well have had quite enough of doctrinal hairsplitting by the time he married Anne. Three copies of Thomas Cromwell's 1536 instructions to the clergy include the provision of the Bible in Latin and English for every church, that 'every man that will to look and read thereon',[8] a stipulation which, it has been claimed, was linked directly to Anne's promotion of the vernacular Bible, since the item was removed after Anne's execution and the majority of the injunctions do not include it. However, there is no evidence whatsoever of any direct connection with Anne, nor any dating of the drafts which do include the provision of the Bible, so 'it is the merest surmise to see her hand in this'.[9]

Moreover, interest in vernacular culture in general, and (since the fourteenth century) the Bible, had been a particular feature of English queenship for five hundred years. While many elite women had some knowledge of Latin in the medieval period, the area in which they were best able to participate in cultural patronage was the vernacular, in French from Anglo-Norman times and subsequently in English. Since Matilda of Flanders had collaborated with Archbishop Lanfranc on Church reform in the eleventh century, the association between royal women and vernacular pious literature had been powerful. Matilda's successor, Matilda of Scotland, commissioned two significant works, a *Life* of her mother, Saint Margaret, and the poem 'The Voyage of St Brendan', while the continued patronage of the convent at Wilton connected royal women with a tradition of women's intellectualism stretching back to the Confessor's queen, Edith. It was Richard II's first wife, Anne of Bohemia, who took the then controversial step of promoting the vernacular Bible, a precedent which has been overlooked in its endorsement of a movement that came to fruition in the time of the next Queen Anne. In the thirteenth century, a collection of laws was produced covering the 'Sachsenspiegel', an area of land spreading out from Magdeburg, the first capital of the Holy Roman Empire, and which included Bohemia. These laws made special provision for the inheritance of certain objects by women, including books, particularly those of a religious nature. Anne's father, Charles IV, endorsed vernacular religious texts, and when Anne arrived in England as a bride in 1381, she brought with her the New Testament in Latin, Czech and German. Translations of the gospels were also produced for the queen in English, and her commitment to pious reading therein was praised at her funeral by Archbishop Arundel. At the time, accessible translations of the Bible were considered heretical by many, but not by Anne. John Wycliffe, the Oxford theologian, promoted and translated the Bible in English, and his project can be connected (though not conflated) with Lollardism, the late fourteenth-century drive for reform which stressed the primacy of faith rather than adherence to the temporal authority of Rome. In 1383, Wycliffe submitted a petition in favour of his translation, observing that 'It is lawful for the noble Queen of England the sister of the Emperor to have the Gospel written in three languages . . . and it would savour of the pride of Lucifer to call her a heretic for such a reason as this! And since the Germans wish in this matter reasonably to defend their own tongue, so ought the English to defend theirs'.[10] After Anne of Bohemia's death, the Lollards made use of Arundel's funeral oration to promote the English gospel in a 1407 tract. In possessing and discussing the gospel in the vernacular, then, Anne Boleyn was arguably participating in a tradition of English queenship which long pre-dated the Lutheran controversy. Anne's time as queen was so short that it is difficult to assess her participation in many of the activities associated with English queens, but from Henry's insistence on the protocols of her coronation and anointing to her own desire to follow the prescribed rituals when she took her chamber for the birth of her daughter, we see that such associations were particularly important in cementing her (disputed) royal authority, and her interest in the gospels is entirely consistent with this.

The case for Anne as an active reformer is also compromised by the fact that her activities were most notable by their absence. That Anne was responsible for promoting sympathetic clerics to bishoprics has been accepted in several cases, but there is no direct evidence for her individual involvement, while Church preferments in the years anticipating and following the break with Rome were governed by service to the king, and, crucially, support for his decision to divorce Katherine of Aragon and abjure papal authority.

> What we have are some scraps of evidence of isolated instances of possible interest . . . not requiring any specific pious commitment . . . To read this as compelling evidence of Anne's supposed 'evangelical' religious sympathies or her desire to further 'reformed' religion is to infer too much.[11]

Imprisoned in the Tower, Anne was recorded as saying, 'I would to God I had my bishops for they would all go to the king for me',[12] but this implies less a conviction of support for her faith than a pathetic political naivety. Anne may have considered those bishops who had supported her marriage as being on her side, but they owed their places, and their loyalty, to Henry, not his disgraced queen, and not one of them attempted to save her.

Anne's personal beliefs also appear to have been entirely orthodox within the parameters of the Henrician Reformation. The question is not, perhaps, how 'Protestant' Anne was, but how Catholic she remained. Certainly she supported the reform which had made her a queen, but nothing she actually did is indicative of Lutheran leanings. At Easter 1533, when she was pregnant with Elizabeth, Anne mentioned to the Duke of Norfolk that she wished to make a pilgrimage to the shrine at Walsingham, sacred to Our Lady and hence particularly associated with birth. This sits uneasily with her supposed contempt for the external manifestations of the old faith. In early 1536, Tristram Revel, formerly of Christ's College, Cambridge, offered to present her with a translation of *Farrago rerum theologicarum*, a text by Francis Lambertus which disputed the Presence at Mass. Anne refused to accept it. As a prisoner, she asked her gaoler, Sir William Kingston, 'shall I be in heaven, for I have done many good deeds in my days?', a statement which it was simply impossible for a Lutheran who believed in justification by faith alone to utter.

Equally, Anne was hysterically desperate to receive the host while in the Tower and to be confessed and absolved after her trial. Finally, Lancelot de Carles, who lived at the residence of the French ambassador and wrote a poem on Anne's fall, notes an eyewitness account of her speech from the scaffold in which Anne invited prayers to Jesus for her sins, that they might not delay her progress to heaven, which suggests that she continued to believe in the doctrine of purgatory. Fundamentally and indisputably, Anne lived and died a Catholic.

Why, then, should so many inferences have been made which connect Anne's religion with the Protestantism of her daughter? The case rests mainly on William Latymer's account of Anne's life and the work of the martyrologist John Foxe. Latymer presents Anne as a model of a pious queen, dispensing alms to the poor and urging her chaplains to reprimand her if they observed her to 'yield to any manner of sensuality'.[13] Foxe concurs with this image, but goes further, claiming by 1559 that the nation is indebted to Anne 'for the restoration and piety of the church'. He claims that Anne promoted the gospel and maintained a scrupulously virtuous court. Both writers had an interest in emphasising Anne's piety to their new queen, and both, by implication, were stressing that it was impossible that such a godly woman might have been guilty of the repellent adulteries of which she had been convicted. The editor of Latymer's life confirms that it is, at best, an airbrushed account: '[he] deliberately suppressed all material relating to Anne which is not consistent with [his] portrait of a pious and solemn reformer'. Contemporary observers of Anne's inner circle present her court as a somewhat racier environment, but even given the obvious motivation of both Latymer and Foxe to present an idealised picture of Anne, neither of them say anything precise about the nature of her own religious belief. Both Latymer and Foxe were ardent reformers, and both were working with the aim not just of rehabilitating Elizabeth's disgraced mother, but of pushing forward a reformist agenda. The 1559 religious settlement was not a conclusion, they hoped, but a beginning, the first step on the path to more radical reform. We might read something unattractively manipulative in their accounts, an attempt to impress an emotional connection with reform on a daughter who had never known her mother, and who might be persuaded towards further reform by a belief that she was pursuing her mother's legacy. Elizabeth was robust enough to resist such beguilements, but this has not prevented some historians from doing so.

Anne's religious legacy was less literal, more literary. The courtly lover's relationship with his unkind lady corresponds, within the new Protestant dynamic of the Reformation, to man's relationship with God. Where the structure of the Catholic Church was displaced, the worshipper became his own conduit for holy favour, pursuing a state of grace endlessly, often desperately, with no guarantee of satisfaction. Only continued effort, continued communication, can guard against uncertainty. The pleading, the extravagant devotion Elizabeth evokes in her courtiers' verses, and which sounds so stagy and insincere to modern ears. is a mirroring of a new language which was desperately earnest in the context of the Elizabethan Church, that of the worshipper appealing to the deity.

It is to Katherine that one of Elizabeth's principal biographers ascribes her newly acquired zeal for reformed religion, a zeal which transformed her spiritually, but also produced one of the effective transformations of her image which were later to characterise her queenship.

Elizabeth's translation of Marguerite of Navarre's work can be used as evidence of her own conversion to the reformed faith which, for her, was always to be filtered through the pious prism of royal supremacy over the Church. During the Boulogne campaign in 1544, Elizabeth had been able to observe Katherine Parr in the role of regent, as a woman competently governing powerful men. It is also considered likely that she and Katherine were reading *Le Miroir de l'âme pécheresse* together. A letter from Katherine to Henry, in which she explains her increasing adherence to the doctrine of justification by faith alone – one of the principal tenets of reformed religion – is linguistically and thematically similar to Marguerite of Navarre's work. Katherine's letter equates royal grace with divine grace – 'I make like account with your Majesty as I do with God'.[14] She implies that Henry is God's chosen instrument, who will direct the realm towards the true faith. Like Katherine, Elizabeth would come to see the royal supremacy – the leadership of her father's Church – as a melding of sacred and worldly monarchy, but with one essential difference. Katherine was in the position in which Elizabeth's courtiers were to find themselves, seeking a relationship with their God which was parlayed through the figure of the monarch. Elizabeth became that monarch. And here we see, intellectually, a binding of both her paternal and maternal legacies. From Anne Boleyn, Elizabeth could absorb the language of courtly love, channelled through reform into the casting of courtier as suitor for both her own and divine grace, that combination of ruler and godhead which was embodied – literally – in Henry's Church. This blending of sacred and profane love is expressed in a lyric (possibly by Elizabeth's master of the tilt, Sir Henry Lee) and included in Robert Dowland's *A Musical Banquet*, published towards the end of Elizabeth's reign in 1597:

> But ah poor Knight, though thus in dream he ranged,
> Hoping to serve this Saint in sort most meet. . .
> Ah me, he cries, Goddess my limbs grow faint,
> Though I time's prisoner be, be you my Saint.[15]

Elizabeth's spiritual awakening was expressed externally by a transformation in her appearance. A portrait of 1546–7, possibly painted as a gift to Edward VI in an exchange of paintings by William Scrots between the siblings, shows Elizabeth in similar clothing to that of the slightly earlier *Family of Henry VIII*. Elizabeth wears a wide-sleeved, ornately worked red gown, an elegant headdress decorated with pearls, and holds a 'girdle book' below her waist attached by a jewelled belt. The positioning of the book, in the same place as her brother's codpiece, accentuated by his dagger in the companion picture, suggests Elizabeth's learning and her maidenly modesty. Four years later, though, she has adopted a far more demure costume, which attracted the nickname 'Sweet Sister Temperance' from her pious brother. The later *Clopton Portrait* gives an indication of how Elizabeth had changed her style to reflect her new, reformed, religious belief. Though still richly jewelled and furred, Elizabeth is depicted in a plain black gown, her hair caught under the severe black cap. The royal 'Saint's' attire would grow ever more extravagantly elaborate over the years, as her authority evolved with her image, but Elizabeth's self-presentation during Edward's reign is a clear indication of the commitment to reform realised during her period in her last stepmother's household.

Elizabeth's next venture in translation was also a tribute to Katherine, a collection of the queen's own *Prayers and Meditations* into French, Latin and Italian, this time as a gift to her father. Again, Elizabeth makes reference to English queenship traditions, including the eglantine device of her grandmother, Elizabeth of York, along with four yellow-centred Tudor roses in gold and silver on a crimson background. It was her first use of the emblem, a symbol of purity, of which she became particularly fond. The present was accompanied by Elizabeth's only known letter to Henry, dated from Hertford on 30 December. It is an earnest and affectionate production, Elizabeth clearly trying to impress her father with her accomplishments and diligence, but also figuring herself confidently and emphatically as Henry's loving heir. It begins: 'To the most glorious and mighty King Henry VIII', her 'matchless and most benevolent' father, whom 'philosophers regard as a god on earth'. She continues that 'it seemed fitting to me that this task should be undertaken by myself, your daughter and one who should be not only the imitator of your virtues but also heir to them'. Elizabeth seems certain of two points here, firstly that her father's royal supremacy over the Church is theologically legitimate, and secondly that she is in no way unsuitable to follow his kingly example, except, as she adds, 'if there be any error in it, it may yet merit pardon on account of my ignorance, my youth, my short time of study and my goodwill'. She concludes by drawing the strands of her gift warmly together: 'Wherefore I do not doubt . . . that you will feel that this holy work which is the more highly to be valued as having been compiled by the Queen your wife, may have its value ever so little enhanced by being translated by your daughter.'

Elizabeth was at court with her father on three occasions during the following year, and this was perhaps the period when she grew closest to him, a closeness rendered poignant by the fact that Henry, once considered the most beautiful prince in Christendom, was visibly sickening. Obese, irascible, plagued by weeping sores and the peevish selfishness of chronic pain, the king was dying.

CHAPTER FIVE

Henry VIII died on 28 January 1547. Edward's uncle, Edward Seymour, then Earl of Hertford, brought the nine-year-old boy to Enfield, where Elizabeth had retired after her father's last Christmas court, on the pretext that he was being taken to London to be created Prince of Wales. Once brother and sister were together, they were informed of Henry's death. Later chroniclers had it that the new king clung to his fourteen-year-old sister and that the children wept together for some hours, a likely if not necessarily factual reaction. Some weeks later, Edward wrote to Elizabeth that they ought to restrain their mourning for Henry, whose soul was surely in heaven, which frankly sounds much more like him. Elizabeth was well past Latin truisms, but, as she observed the reconfiguration of her life after her father's death, it seemed that the worldly glory of Henry, who 'had bestridden England like a colossus',[1] had been brief indeed. The royal schoolroom was broken up, Edward was naturally preoccupied with his new role, and Katherine Parr, Henry's devoted and dutiful wife, was finally free to pursue the longings of her heart. Within four months, she was married to handsome Thomas Seymour, and her sober, reforming head appeared to have been completely turned.

There is something very nasty about Katherine's collusion in what happened to Elizabeth while the girl was under her charge in her Queen Dowager's homes at Hanworth, Chelsea and Sudeley Castle in Gloucestershire. The arrangement was a practical and sensible provision, as Elizabeth, though she was now a rich young woman in her own right after inheriting £3,000 in her father's will, with a projected £10,000 dowry, was still too young to live unchaperoned, and she and Katherine clearly had a close relationship. Unfortunately, Elizabeth soon developed another close relationship with Katherine's new husband. The junior uncle of the king, Thomas Seymour had dared to suggest to his elder brother Edward, now ensconced as Lord Protector under his new title of Duke of Somerset, that he might marry Elizabeth, but such an audaciously ambitious proposal would never have been sanctioned by the council. Seymour's proposal to Katherine may have been the best alternative so far as he was concerned, but for Katherine, who had experienced two duty matches, latterly with an old and physically repulsive man, this was love. And clearly erotic love, heady and impassioned, powerful enough to make her forget both her own dignity and her duty to her royal charge.

Katherine Parr soon became pregnant, and Thomas Seymour began to visit Elizabeth in her bedroom. He flirted with her, and Elizabeth flirted back. He teased her by threatening to climb under the bedcovers, saw her barelegged in her shift. Giggling and whispering and the agonising excitement of 'accidental' touches – anyone who was ever a teenager can remember how that feels, and Elizabeth was a teenager who had been starved of easy physical affection. Seymour playfully spanked her buttocks, he kissed her, protesting to Elizabeth's governess Katherine Ashley that it was all in fun. Mistress Ashley reported her concerns to Katherine Parr, who not only dismissed them, but began to participate in what modern eyes would regard as very unwholesome sex games. The Seymours teased Elizabeth together, and Katherine even held Elizabeth's arms behind her back as she struggled while her husband tore her gown 'into a hundred pieces'.[2] Elizabeth felt encouraged; she became bold enough to allow Seymour to take her in his arms while the household was at Hanworth in spring 1548, which, when Katherine saw it, finally seemed to shake her out of her delirium. Elizabeth's cofferer Thomas Parry had already observed the Queen Dowager's jealousy of the pair; now Katherine stood on what was left of her dignity and ordered Elizabeth from her house. Elizabeth, bewildered, fell into self-righteous protest, but Katherine refused to acknowledge her own part in the whole squalid business and Elizabeth was packed off several days later to the home of Sir Anthony Denny at Cheshunt in Hertfordshire.

Elizabeth was not the first silly girl to develop a crush on an older married man, and Thomas Seymour was not the first unscrupulous man to exploit it, but he was the Lord High Admiral of England, and she was the King's sister. Elizabeth's sophisticated reading had not prepared her for the visceral pull of physical desire, but Seymour knew exactly what he was doing. His suave persuasiveness with women meant that even Mistress Ashley, who had once favoured the match between the Admiral and her charge, was brought to excuse his threatening and disgraceful behaviour. The scandal might have reached no further than the Seymour household had Katherine not died in childbed on 7 September 1548. Elizabeth received the news at Cheshunt, and the measure of her grief may be inferred from the fact that she shortly afterwards fell ill. Mistress Ashley, however, saw her mistress's loss as a chance to revive Seymour's scheme, and set about persuading Elizabeth that Seymour would be an excellent husband. Despite her earlier qualms, she was obviously attracted to Seymour herself, and something of his creepy sexiness comes out in his message to her, 'whether her great Buttocks were grown any less or no?'. Quite what Seymour did to these two intelligent women who were supposed to have Elizabeth's welfare at heart is impossible to know, but Katherine Ashley now proved herself as much of an idiot as the Dowager Queen had been.

Mistress Ashley wheedled and cajoled on both sides, persuading Seymour to renew his suit and Elizabeth to admit it. Should not Elizabeth write to Seymour? Even if she could not prevent herself from smiling and blushing at the mention of his name, Elizabeth wanted no more to do with him, telling her governess firmly that she would not write, lest it be perceived that she was encouraging him, and moreover that any marriage she made should be the business of her brother and his council. Via Parry, Mistress Ashley sent an extraordinary message to Seymour, claiming for her own part that 'she would her Grace were your wife of any man's living'. Seymour responded that this would be impossible, but Mistress Ashley, transformed into a kamikaze Emma, gossiped to Thomas Parry about the incidents at Hanworth, assuring him that Elizabeth would make a delightful wife for Seymour. Parry was appalled. He disliked Seymour for his treatment of Katherine Parr, describing him as 'an evil jealous man', 'covetous' and 'oppressive'. Perhaps it was Parry who talked. Certainly, by Christmas, Elizabeth's reputation was in the gutter. She had departed for Cheshunt because she was pregnant with Seymour's child; she had been meeting him in secret since his wife's death; they had enjoyed moonlight trysts on the Thames . . . juicy celebrity gossip about a rich, handsome politician and the country's most eligible heiress, were it not for the fact that in the claustrophobic world of the Tudor court, words were deadly weapons.

On 17 January 1549, Thomas Seymour was arrested for high treason. His flirtation with Elizabeth was not the principal cause, but it became the most talked about. The Lord Admiral had been using his charms on Elizabeth's brother, too, persuading the rather joyless little boy that life would be a lot more fun with him as Protector instead of stuffy old Uncle Somerset. What he was accused of compassing was the possession of two Tudors, the king as his charge and Elizabeth as his wife. His rapacious stupidity cost him his head, and nearly cost Elizabeth her position. If Elizabeth had any inkling of the complexities of her mother's arrest and trial, now, with chilling suddenness, she too was seeing how quickly flirtations, whispers, romantic promises could be turned on an axe edge. Katherine Ashley and Thomas Parry followed Seymour to the Tower. Conspiring to marry Elizabeth without the king's consent was a treasonable offence, and Elizabeth found herself facing criminal interrogation for the first time. At Hatfield, she was confronted by Sir Robert Tyrwhitt, a member of Katherine Parr's former household. His wife had served Katherine in her chamber, and had first-hand knowledge of the liaison between Seymour and Elizabeth. By the time Elizabeth was questioned, both Thomas Parry and Katherine Ashley had already signed depositions attesting to Seymour's dealings with the princess, Parry reporting that he had been drawn into discussions of Elizabeth's landholdings and finances, and Katherine confessing to the bedroom games in embarrassing detail.

Elizabeth did not blame her servants. She knew that they had resisted for some time, to the extent that, even though they had been questioned separately, Tyrwhitt complained 'They all sing one song, and so I think they would not do, unless they had set the knot before, for surely they would confess or else they could not so well agree.' But Katherine Ashley was moved to a particularly miserable cell, with only straw to stop the window from where she complained piteously that she could not sleep for the cold, nor see in daylight. Eventually, though, she and Parry, terrified by where their meddling had brought them, broke down. Elizabeth was moved to tears by their plight, but Tyrwhitt could not draw her. She admitted that she had had many conversations with Seymour, but had stated repeatedly that she could and would never marry, within the realm or without, without the permission of the king, Somerset and the council. Tyrwhitt wrote to Somerset that Elizabeth 'had a very good wit, and nothing is gotten of her but by great policy'.[3] Anyone would have been frightened and intimidated in such circumstance; that Elizabeth was able so adamantly to retain her composure evinces an impressive psychological toughness. She was shamefully aware of her imprudence with Seymour, but she would not let that error destroy her. Even under such duress, Ashley and Parry affirmed that she had never said or done anything of which the council could disapprove, and with this certainty of her innocence Elizabeth went on the attack. She insisted to Somerset that a proclamation be issued refuting the slanders against her, but refused to implicate any rumour-mongers, lest her reputation among the people be further damaged. Elizabeth was always conscious of her public. In March, she went further, writing to Somerset that Katherine Ashley, who remained in prison, 'hath been with me a long time and many years and hath taken great labour and pain in bringing me up in learning and honesty'. She added cleverly that if Katherine's incarceration continued, it would lead her to conclude that Somerset did not truly believe in her innocence. Katherine and Parry were freed, but Elizabeth was not permitted to retain her beloved governess, who was replaced at Hatfield by Lady Tyrwhitt. Elizabeth sobbed and sulked but the council had no sympathy. Reasonably enough, they considered that Mistress Ashley had been unpardonably careless of her mistress's reputation and would not countenance her return.

The Seymour affair might have brought Elizabeth's teenage neck

precariously close to the executioner's block. In fact, relations between Edward and Elizabeth continued untroubled by the scandal.
It is impossible to know what Edward felt when his uncle was executed on 20 March, but it is plausible that he felt some sympathy for
Elizabeth. They were both extremely young, neither was inured to
the brutal realities of Tudor political life and both had been moved,
in their different ways, by Seymour's charms. Elizabeth's internalisa-
tion of the lessons she had learned was reflected in a further change
in her appearance. When Mary of Guise, widow to the Scots king
James V, and mother to Mary Stuart, Queen of Scots, visited Edward
at Whitehall in October 1551, Elizabeth took care to present herself as
the modest model of a Protestant princess. In an environment where
magnificence was all, where display was a measure of power, Elizabeth conspicuously refused the trappings of court splendour. As John
Fox noted approvingly, the young woman had 'so little delight in the
glittering gazes of the world, in gay apparel, rich attire and precious
jewels', that she spared barely a glance to those left to her by her
father. While the ladies of Edward's court appeared in silk gowns,
with their 'double curled' hair falling to naked shoulders, Elizabeth
'altered nothing, but to the shame of them all kept her old maidenly
shamefastness'. It was a potent statement, and one which Elizabeth
had learned could be vital to her very survival. With Seymour, Elizabeth had seen how swiftly even those with every appearance of
security and power could be toppled, while in the loss of Kat she
had learned of the irrelevance of affective bonds when confronted
by political power. Moreover, she had also learned that presentation,
'image', could contribute to a defence of innocence. These lessons
were to be tried to their limits in her subsequent confrontations with
Mary.

For the events of 1548–9 further soured Elizabeth's relationship
with her sister. When their father died, Mary, who was more than old
enough to have her own household, had invited Elizabeth to join it.
She had been disgusted by Katherine's hasty marriage, writing to her
sister of the 'scarcely cold body of the King our father so shamefully
dishonoured by the Queen our stepmother'. Elizabeth had replied
tactfully that she thought it best to submit to Henry's wishes in the

matter, and recalling Mary to the kindness and affection Katherine Parr had shown her. Obviously she had no desire to be boxed up with Mary and her priests, but she diplomatically suggested that she ought not to show herself ungrateful. Now Mary had been proved right. Her sister, the daughter of the hated 'concubine', had shown that blood will out in the loose atmosphere of Katherine's household. Edward, for his part, seemed more concerned with Mary's religious recalcitrance than Elizabeth's sexual indiscretion. Mary continued blithely to hear Mass, provoking a severe reprimand from her devoutly Protestant brother: '. . . your exalted rank, the conditions of the times, all magnify your offence. It is a scandalous thing that so high a person should deny our sovereignty.' He threatened, a miniature version of his father, that he would have his laws obeyed, and any who dared to break them would be 'watched and denounced'.[4] Once again unwelcome at court, shunted from manor to manor, Mary could find no support in Elizabeth.

Mary had the conviction to deny her brother's authority and retain her commitment to her faith, a quality which Elizabeth singularly failed to manifest, at least outwardly, in her sister's reign. Did Mary later feel contempt for Elizabeth's confessional suppleness, even as she earnestly sought to return her sister to what she believed was the True Faith? Moreover, might Elizabeth's staunch Protestantism under Edward have been, in some measure, a similar act of hypocrisy to that she demonstrated when she subsequently consented to hear Mass? Elizabeth's personal faith has best been described as a 'discreet evangelicalism',[5] reformist, yes, but not so austerely so as the Edwardian Protestants might have wished. As Queen, Elizabeth insisted on retaining the religious settlement as it had been formulated for her brother in 1552, whereby an essentially Catholic structure was overlaid with Protestant theology, creating a contrary dynamic which perhaps reflected the 'unique ambiguity'[6] of Elizabeth's own views. She remained attached, for example, to some aspects of the stately ceremonial worship she had known in the last years of her father's reign and the first of her brother's – her Chapel Royal continued to use choral scores from 1549 in the first year of her reign, and she insisted that her own communion table be adorned with a silver cross and candlesticks. She was perhaps less personally sympathetic to Protestant zealots than Catholic die-hards, yet on occasion, such as when the Dean of St Paul's gave her a heavily decorated prayer book which resembled a Catholic missal, she could react with fury. However, she persisted, and largely succeeded, in resisting further Protestant reform throughout her reign, so that the Church in 1603 remained structurally identical to that of 1559. Elizabeth's essential piety, though, is not questionable. Her ardent adherence to her father's Church was both a confirmation of religious belief and an endorsement of her own 'royalness', which latter was once more to be challenged as Mary came to the throne.

CHAPTER SIX

The three most important men in Elizabeth's life were William Cecil, Robert Dudley and Philip of Spain. It is hard to assess which of them had the most significant effect on her queenship, but collectively with Elizabeth herself, they formed a curious quadrant of political power which, at times, determined the direction of European politics in the later sixteenth century.

Cecil was born in 1520 into a Lincolnshire family with an established tradition of royal service. His Welsh grandfather, David, had been a military man since the 1490s, and was a client of Elizabeth's paternal grandmother, Margaret Beaufort, who assisted his father, Richard, to a post as a page of the King's Chamber, which enabled him to be present at the Field of Cloth of Gold in 1520. Aged fifteen, William Cecil went up to St John's College, Cambridge, founded in Margaret Beaufort's memory, where he met John Cheke, the Greek scholar who was at the heart of the group of Cambridge divines who guided the Edwardian Church into being. Cecil's first wife, Mary (who died in 1543), was Cheke's sister. He also became close to Roger Ascham, Elizabeth's tutor – *The Schoolmaster*, dedicated to Cecil by Ascham's widow, opens with a scene in Cecil's chamber. In 1540, Cecil came to London, where he studied law at Gray's Inn, before entering the service of the Protector, the Duke of Somerset.

The family connection with reform continued into his second marriage in 1546, to Mildred, the daughter of Anthony Cooke. Another reformist, Cooke was close to Katherine Parr, whose views on women's education he shared. His daughters, like Elizabeth herself, had been thoroughly schooled in the new humanist curriculum. In terms of Elizabeth's future relationship with Cecil, this is interesting

– Cecil was not uncomfortable with brilliant, educated women, and he was perfectly accustomed to the idea that his own wife (with whom he enjoyed a long and happy marriage) might be his intellectual equal. It was in Katherine Parr's home, in an atmosphere of piety and feminine learning, that Cecil first met Elizabeth in 1549. When Somerset fell that same year, Cecil successfully attached himself to Robert Dudley's father, the Duke of Northumberland, who engaged him to administer a part of Elizabeth's lands, a connection which continued discreetly through Mary Tudor's reign. It was to Cecil that Elizabeth turned immediately on her accession, and he was to remain by her side until his death. There are almost as many historical Cecils as there are Elizabeths, but whether he is seen as the cynical manipulator of a weak and indecisive prince, or the tool of a far less scrupulous politician, or any of the variants in between, what is notable is that their relationship is always interpreted symbiotically. However their partnership is assessed, it remains a partnership – Elizabeth 'made' Cecil in the wordly sense, but Cecil was also responsible for the making of Elizabeth.

In contrast, Elizabeth's romance with Dudley, her 'sweet Robin', initially appears much more simple, as one of history's most captivating love affairs. Whether or not the relationship was an affair in the modern understanding of the word is perhaps the least interesting thing about it. 'Did they or didn't they?' is a question to which we will never know the answer, not that this has prevented generations of historians from speculating. The facts stop at the bedroom door. Regardless of who did, or didn't, put what where, Leicester is one of the most influential figures of the reign, not only because Elizabeth loved and trusted him, which she did, but because of his role in the emergent statecraft of her government. Leicester was the focus of Cecil's fear and Catholic calumny; he was a shield, a scandal, at times a plaything and one of the main instruments in Elizabeth's progress from pretender to legend. It is pleasing to conjure the two lovers, side by side, curling their signatures for ever into the works of one of their favourite authors, much more to consider the implications of their choice of book. Leicester was the most active non-royal patron of bookbinders of the sixteenth century, leaving 220 volumes at Leicester House alone on his death, and he was also connected via his father's patronage of John Cheke to the scholarly circle emanating from St John's which played such a part in Elizabeth's education. John Ashley later recalled the 'friendly fellowship' and 'free talk' of Elizabeth's household when she was aged about sixteen, under the tutelage of Ascham; he remembered many 'pleasant studies' of Aristotle and Cicero,[1] and it is tempting to imagine the young Robert Dudley participating in these rarefied discussions. This was the atmosphere which formed not only Elizabeth's mind, but her faith, and Leicester was to become, along with Cecil, one of the principal proponents of reform. The earl was much more than the sexy swaggerer who famously stole Elizabeth's heart during the springtime of her queenship; he was a respected scholar and scientist, a patron and much closer in temperament, if not in style, to the other great professional politician of Elizabeth's reign, Cecil. His efforts at a more traditional type of aristocratic leadership never amounted, embarrassingly, to much more than that; he embodied the tension between old and new styles of governance – chivalry and statecraft – which defined Elizabeth's rule. His importance to the Queen is indicated by her extraordinary request, when she lay ill with smallpox in 1562, that he should be appointed Protector of the kingdom. She also stated vehemently that 'as God was her witness nothing improper had ever passed between them'.[2] There is no compelling reason not to take her word for it.

Robert's presence is not recorded at Hatfield during Elizabeth's early years. In 1566, he noted to the French ambassador that he had known the Queen since she was eight years old (i.e. in 1541). We do not know how and when exactly they met; it is likely though by no means confirmed that Robert, who was three months older than Elizabeth, was educated for a time in the household of her brother Prince Edward. Elizabeth was not present at either her father's funeral, which was customary, or her brother's coronation, which was not, and again we do not know if Robert attended either ceremony. But the children had been within one another's orbit since birth. Leicester's detractors subsequently presented him as an arriviste, an opportunist who had risen to power clutching at the skirts of the Queen, but, like so much of what was written about their relationship, this was simply untrue. Through his grandmother, Elizabeth Grey, Robert was descended from the thirteenth Earl of Warwick, the father-in-law of Richard Neville, known as the 'Kingmaker', the puppet master of the Wars of the Roses: in his family tree twined the great magnate houses of the period – Neville, Talbot, Beauchamp, Lisle. His grandfather Edmund Dudley, a member of Henry VII's council, had his head swept off by that zealous new broom Henry VIII in 1510, but not before he managed to father four children with his wife, Elizabeth Grey (the niece of John Grey, the first husband of Queen Elizabeth Woodville). Elizabeth then married Arthur Plantagenet, an illegitimate son of Edward IV. Edmund and Elizabeth's son John, Robert's father, became the ward of Sir Edward Guildford, eventually marrying Guildford's daughter Jane and producing a prodigious offspring of thirteen, eight of whom survived into adulthood. John worked assiduously to dispel the shadow of his father's attainder, and in 1543 was created Viscount Lisle in right of his mother, being promoted again to the Earldom of Warwick (again through his matrilineal connections with the Beauchamp family) in 1547. By the end of Henry VIII's reign he was not only a close adviser to the king but one of the principal supporters of religious reform. It was clear at the beginning of Edward VI's reign that the government would be led by his uncle, Edward Seymour, the Duke of Somerset, along with his rival John Dudley, who was elevated to the Dukedom of Northumberland in 1551. The ceremony at Hampton Court included two Dudley connections, Henry Sidney and Henry Neville, who were knighted alongside one William Cecil, Secretary to the King since the previous autumn. Until 1550, Cecil had been Somerset's man, but in adroitly changing sides, he not only saved his own career after Somerset's Protectorship came to an end, but assisted John Dudley in assuming control of both the king and his council. Three months later, Seymour was executed for treason, and Dudley's power appeared undisputed: 'Nothing is done except at his command,' reported the imperial ambassador.[3] Far from being a parvenu, Robert Dudley gained his experience in government from his father at a time when he was the most powerful man in the realm. Elizabeth and Robert Dudley were both recorded as being at court at the same time on at least two occasions, in 1549 and 1550, but in the spring of 1553, as her brother lay dying, she was staying quietly in the country. It was Robert, not Elizabeth, who was witness to his father's attempt at a *coup d'état*.

When Edward VI died on 6 July, there was no heir male to the English crown, precisely the situation which his father had changed the world to avoid. Edward's sisters, Mary and Elizabeth, had of course both been declared illegitimate, though their places in the succession had been restored by the Act of Parliament in 1543 and confirmed by their father's will. The offspring of Henry's sisters, Margaret and Mary, offered competing claims. Mary Stuart, Queen of Scots, the granddaughter of Henry's elder sister Margaret, was officially excluded from the crown, but as the vagaries of Elizabeth and Mary's status over the years had proved, this was not necessarily binding. Margaret's daughter by her second marriage, Margaret Douglas, was also of dubious legitimacy since her parents had been divorced. Henry's younger sister Mary had produced Frances and Eleanor Brandon by her own second marriage to the Duke of Suffolk, and Frances herself had three girls, Jane, Katherine and Mary, by her husband Henry Grey, Marquess of Dorset. Eleanor died in 1547; her daughter, Margaret Clifford, was the last of the nine potential claimants. All of these women would play significant roles in Elizabeth Tudor's life. According to Henry VIII's Act of Succession, it was Frances Brandon who led the field after his own daughters – if Elizabeth were ultimately to inherit and die without heirs, then the throne would wholly remain and come to the heirs of the body of the Lady Frances. Interestingly, William Cecil was a cousin of the Grey girls, through his wife Mildred Cooke, but though he aided and supported John Dudley in what he was to attempt, the impetus behind the 1553 coup came very much from the young king himself.

Elizabeth's own proto-evangelism had been commended by her fanatically reformist brother. In the aftermath of the Seymour scandal she had been astute in presenting herself as the premiere Protestant princess. But Edward, as well as being considerably more independent minded than has often been assumed, was also something of a prig. Elizabeth was a bastard, and Mary was a Catholic bastard.

Surely the crown would be safer on the head of a woman whose religion, as well as her birth, was impeccable? Lady Jane Grey was, to him, the obvious choice. So in the last months of his life, Edward, assisted by Cecil and John Dudley, set about overturning his father's will. With absolute disregard for the law, and for the consciences of his councillors, who had sworn the oath prescribed by the Succession Act, he finalised his own 'Device for the Succession'. When precisely the 'Device' was drafted is uncertain, but Edward made one crucial amendment to the document before it was finalised. Originally, he stipulated that the crown should pass to any male heirs of Frances Grey, and then to any male offspring of her daughters in turn. But then the sentence 'to the Lady Jane's heirs male' was altered to 'to the Lady Jane *and* her male heirs' (italics mine). Mary and Elizabeth were set aside: it was the Greys who would become the next royal dynasty of England.

And if the Duke of Northumberland had anything to do with it, those heirs male would be Dudleys. On 25 May, Jane Grey was married to Robert's brother Guildford Dudley at the family's London home, Durham House. Already, the French and imperial ambassadors were speculating on how long the ailing Edward had to live. In John Dudley's eyes, his son had just married England's next queen. Just over two months later, Edward lay dead at Greenwich. On 9 July, Edward's council swore allegiance to Jane, and next day at 5 p.m. she was proclaimed in London by the sheriff and the royal heralds. She was residing at the Tower, not only the traditional residence for monarchs before their coronation, but London's most secure fortress. The choice was both ominous and appropriate, as from the first there seemed no chance that her claim would prevail. Mary, who had prudently refused Northumberland's invitation to visit her brother's deathbed, had retreated to Norfolk, from where she wrote to the council asserting her right. Cecil had made contingency plans for flight, as well as the extraordinary political backflip he would have to accomplish to preserve his head if Mary prevailed (it is an instance of Cecil's preternatural political prescience that he had recruited a priest, Henry Watkyns, to serve at his home in Wimbledon at Easter 1553 in anticipation of exactly this.) And Elizabeth? She practised the strategy which as queen she was to turn into such an exasperating art. She waited.

In the Tower, Northumberland grew increasingly frantic. None of the women he had assumed he could manipulate seemed to be behaving. Mary was aggressively mustering her affinity in the eastern counties, while Jane had taken so well to queenship that when the Marquess of Winchester visited her to display the crown jewels, explaining that a new crown would have to be made for her consort Guildford Dudley, Jane announced that she rather thought she might just make him Duke of Clarence, after all. On 14 July, Northumberland, confirmed in his commission as leader of Queen Jane's army, rode out with his other sons to confront Mary. At Framlingham in Suffolk, in a gesture more famously imitated by her sister, Mary reviewed her troops on horseback before dismounting when her horse was startled and walking among her men. Even as her popularity soared, half-hearted enthusiasm for Jane was leaching away. Robert Dudley proclaimed her at King's Lynn on 18 July, but by then most of his father's troops had deserted. The next day, Jane's last as queen, her council simply gave up. Orders (signed by Cecil among others) were dispatched to Northumberland to disarm while the Earl of Arundel and Lord Paget set off to grovel to Mary, who was proclaimed at nine o'clock that evening. By August, Northumberland, Robert and his four brothers were in the Tower. They were still there on 19 March 1554, when Elizabeth joined them.

O trustless State of miserable Men
That build your Bliss on hope of earthly Thing,
And vainly think yourselves half happy then,
When painted Faces with smooth flattering
Do fawn on you and your wide Praises sing . . .
All is but feigned.

The lines are Edmund Spenser's, from his commemorative poem to Leicester, *The Ruines of Time*, written after the earl's death, but

The only portrait taken from life of Elizabeth's mother, Anne Boleyn.

Did Thomas Wyatt's evidence help bring about Anne Boleyn's downfall?

The scandal of her mother's death behind her, Elizabeth (right) returns to the Tudor fold.

(above left) Princess Elizabeth: prim and scholarly, the model of a Protestant princess.

(above right) Many of the rhetorical tropes Elizabeth adopted were learned from her sister, Mary.

(right) Edward VI: Elizabeth's companion-in-learning.

The connection between these two pictures, of the childless Richard II and Elizabeth in her coronation robes, demonstrates Elizabeth's early commitment to sacred virginity.

A meek monarch? The conservative Elizabeth of the early reign.

Queen Elizabeth and the Three Goddesses. From medieval to modern, stepping into the future.

(left) William Cecil, (below left) Philip II of Spain and (below right) Robert Dudley: the three most important men in the Queen's life.

Machiavelli's work embodied the conflict between chivalric kingship and statecraft which dominated Elizabeth's governance.

the sentiments could not have been more appropriate to the circumstances of the Dudley men incarcerated in the Tower. The vagaries of Fortune were a constant reference for medieval and Renaissance poets, not least Elizabeth herself in her later translation of Boethius's *Consolations of Philosophy*; the vanity of trusting to the caprice of fate could not have been more cruelly illustrated to the two young people imprisoned by the Thames. Elizabeth and Robert did not meet in the Tower, though each was aware of the other's presence, yet this shared experience not only of imprisonment, but of the appalling tension of waiting helplessly as outside the axeman struck again and again was unique to their relationship. But what was Elizabeth doing there?

During the upheavals which had raised her sister to the throne, Elizabeth had remained deliberately aloof. The chronicler William Camden claims that in response to an envoy from John Dudley she emphasised that she would do nothing to impede Mary's claim.[4] Ten days after Mary was proclaimed, Elizabeth arrived in London to await her. The brief ascendancy of the Northumberland/Grey party had seen both Tudor women proclaimed as bastards yet again, notably in two sermons preached by the Bishop of London, Nicholas Ridley, at St Paul's Cross on the Sundays preceding Mary's proclamation. Elizabeth's arrival at her new London residence, Somerset House, was a carefully staged rebuff to such calumnies. It was the procession of a feudal prince, two thousand horsemen strong, the men liveried in the Tudor colours of white and green. It was also a slight – a very slight – hint that Elizabeth, too, had men to command. On 31 July, Elizabeth rode out to meet the new queen at Wanstead, and on 3 August was by her side when she made her formal entry into the City. When Mary was crowned in September, Elizabeth took precedence after the queen in the coronation procession and banquet. Whatever Mary's personal feelings for her sister at this stage, in public all was concord. After the fraught progress of her accession, Mary needed a display of loyalty from her sister, and Elizabeth provided it with every appearance of good faith.

Yet already there were hints that Mary had been unable to overcome her long-standing hatred of the girl who had displaced her.

The Venetian ambassador, Giovanni Michiel, described Elizabeth in a report of 1557 making three notable points. Elizabeth is 'a young woman believed to be no less beautiful in her soul than in her body, though her face is pretty rather than beautiful, her figure is, however, tall and well-shaped, with good colour, though olive skinned, and beautiful eyes and hands, as she is well aware'. He goes on to describe the superiority of Elizabeth's learning over Mary's: 'She surpasses the Queen in her knowledge of languages . . . speaks Italian better than the Queen (and prides herself on it, not speaking any other language with Italians).' Finally, he comments on Elizabeth being 'proud and haughty', despite 'being born of such a mother'. Elizabeth 'has no less self-esteem, nor does she believe herself less legitimate'. Michiel explains that Elizabeth defended her mother's marriage, claiming that Anne Boleyn had 'wanted nothing but marriage with the King, with the authority of the Church and of its Archbishop, therefore if she was deceived, she acted in good faith, which may not have compromised her marriage, nor her own [i.e. Elizabeth's] birth, for she was born in the same faith'.[5] Here is a picture of a very attractive young woman who is not afraid of displaying her accomplishments at her sister's expense. Moreover, Elizabeth *did* apparently speak of her mother, and stood up for her when challenged. Michiel is not quoting a specific incident here, or a conversation held directly with Elizabeth; he is citing what he has heard about the court. In the Italian, he claims Elizabeth 'allega a favor suo' (alleges in her favour); that is, 'she speaks of this', not 'she said this'. So it is possible that the ambassador is quoting statements made on more than one occasion – and plausibly, given that the sisters' legitimacy was the hot topic in 1553, not 1557, much earlier. Beautiful, clever, proud Elizabeth is speaking out in her mother's defence. The reference to 'faith' is particularly interesting. Elizabeth is not saying that she was born into the Protestant faith, but into the same faith as Anne, that is, the reformed Catholicism of the Henrician settlement. She is no heretic, but the faith she was born into, and which, she argues, justified her mother's marriage, was one which acknowledged the king, not the Pope, as head of the Church. It is a spectacularly subtle piece of defiance. No wonder Mary was infuriated. That Elizabeth was making such remarks early in the reign is also supported by the fact that Mary was soon provoked into making the very unqueenly remark that her sister had a look of Mark Smeaton about her, him being such a handsome man. To choose the lowest born of Anne Boleyn's alleged lovers was a particularly low blow.

So Elizabeth's very presence was an irritation, more so because (as ever) the succession was uncertain and she was the next heir. But it was faith which really catalysed Mary's loathing. Practically her first action as queen was to repeal the religious statutes of the previous reign, and to reinforce her own status by declaring the marriage of Henry VIII and Katherine of Aragon lawful (a step Elizabeth herself never took). Elizabeth initially refused to appear at Mass, but as Mary's promises of toleration rapidly evaporated, she shrewdly sought an interview with Mary and requested on her knees that she be given books and instruction to guide her towards conformity. When she eventually did attend Mass it was only after failing to plead illness, and she accomplished the performance with an adolescent display of pique, 'wearing a suffering air' and grumbling that she had a stomach ache. Mary was not deceived, complaining to the imperial ambassador Renard that 'she only went to Mass out of hypocrisy, she had not a single servant or maid of honour who was not a heretic, she talked every day with heretics and lent an ear to all their evil designs, and that it would be a disgrace to the kingdom to allow a bastard to succeed'.[6] Elizabeth wisely decided to return to the country, but not before requesting some ornaments for her chapel from her sister. Mary sent the accoutrements, as well as an elegant fur hood, but muttered to Renard that she feared great evil from her sister if she was not 'dealt with'.[7]

The best way to preclude Elizabeth's succession was to produce an heir, and in November Mary angrily rejected a request from the Commons that she should marry an English subject in favour of her own beloved project, a union with Philip of Spain. She would marry as God directed her, she declared, and in a scene of pious melodrama witnessed by Renard, she announced in private that she believed Heaven had selected Philip as her only possible bridegroom. By 14 January 1554 the terms of the marriage were being announced at

Whitehall, but in the city streets the same people who had greeted Mary so joyously 'with shouting and crying . . . and ringing of the bells'[8] just six months earlier now stood mute, lowering their heads in ominous silence as Philip's envoys passed by.

Silent dissent soon passed into open rebellion. When Mary acceded to the crown, she had released a significant prisoner from the Tower, Edward Courtenay, Earl of Devon. Courtenay was descended from Edward IV through his sixth daughter, Catherine of York, and therefore had a tenuous claim of his own. He was also a Catholic, whose father had been executed for treason by Henry VIII. Apparently, prison hadn't done much for Courtenay intellectually, but he was young and English. If Mary had paused to think, she might have done well to marry Courtenay herself, but he was not the royal bridegroom she had set her heart on. Mary's councillors then suggested that Courtenay marry Elizabeth, but while this might have neutralised her in religious terms, Mary could see that having a married heiress presumptive would be even worse than a defiant single one; moreover, Charles V counselled against the match. But several English magnates, incensed by Mary's determination on the Spanish marriage, thought differently. By early January a plot was in train. Four uprisings in Kent, Devon, Leicestershire and the Welsh March were planned, to converge on London with the aim of dethroning Mary and crowning Elizabeth queen with Courtenay as her consort. The scheme, originally timed for mid-March, failed even before it began, as Mary was aware of the ringleaders' activities by early January, while on the 21st Courtenay broke down under questioning and confessed. Three of the planned uprisings barely happened at all. Nonetheless, Sir Thomas Wyatt of Kent, the elder son of the Thomas Wyatt who had so loved Anne Boleyn, in poetry if not in fact, mustered his men on 25 January and marched on London. Shockingly for Mary, when the octogenarian Duke of Norfolk confronted him at Rochester, many of his troops gleefully defected, and those who stayed loyal sneaked back through the city with their coats turned inside out to hide Mary's arms on their liveries. Clearly London's loyalty was not to be taken for granted, and if the capital fell Mary was lost. But she had proved her bravery when she defied John Dudley, and she was the granddaughter of a true warrior queen, Isabella of Castile. Mary rode to the Guildhall on 1 February, and the speech she gave invoked many of the images her sister was later so effectively to employ. And interestingly, though she used the maternal trope which Elizabeth too made use of, she melded the image of a loving, protective mother with that of a prince:

> I cannot tell how naturally the mother loveth the child, for I was never mother of any. But certainly, if a prince and governor may as naturally and earnestly love her subjects, as the mother doth the child, then assure yourselves that I being your lady and mistress, do as earnestly and tenderly love and favour you.[9]

Here, in Mary's greatest speech, is the rhetoric which Elizabeth made her own. She is martial prince and authoritative governor, she is mother, but she is also, suggesting the language of chivalry, 'lady and mistress', an appeal for protection in the language of court-ly love. This was the language which was to coalesce in Elizabeth's reign into such a crucial apparatus for the function of the Queen Regnant's majesty. Nor did Mary neglect to brandish her coronation ring, which wedded her to the nation. And the nation kept its vows. After considerable alarm when Wyatt reached London, when some of the rebels came close to the palace of Whitehall itself, he found the ancient gates at Ludgate barred against him. One week after Mary's speech, he was in the Tower.

If indeed it was Thomas Wyatt senior whose confession had sealed Anne Boleyn's fate, then the interrogation of his son almost finished the life of her daughter. Questioned on 25 February and again at Westminster on 15 March, Wyatt confirmed that he had written to Elizabeth, but only to advise her to 'get away' for her own safety. Elizabeth had written nothing down, but had sent a verbal message by a servant, William St Loe, that she thanked Wyatt for his concern and would proceed as she thought best. This studied neutrality was supported by St Loe, who, despite the 'marvelous tossing' given by the interrogators, roundly denied any more damning communication. But there was more. While at court the previous autumn,

Elizabeth had been observed in a lengthy conversation with another conspirator, Sir William Pickering, and according to the French ambassador, Antoine de Noailles, was 'highly familiar' with yet another, Sir James Crofts. Elizabeth had written to Mary in late January, when the government knew of the rebellion, refusing a summons to court on the grounds of ill health, and somehow a copy of her letter had turned up in that same ambassador's papers. (The French, anxious to prevent Mary's marriage to Philip, were believed to support the rebels.) St Loe, defend his mistress as he might, had compromised himself by appearing alongside two more rebels at Tonbridge. And then there was the fact that Crofts, whose mission had been to declare the Welsh March for Elizabeth, had paused en route there at Ashridge and tried to persuade Elizabeth to remove to Donnington, which could be defended better. Elizabeth had refused, again claiming illness, but her initial reluctance to join her sister was seen as evidence of her involvement with the plot.

Was Elizabeth guilty of treacherous conspiracy in the Wyatt rebellion? Mary certainly believed so. Once the immediate threat from the rebels was quashed, she again ordered her sister to court. The illness of which Elizabeth had spoken does not appear to have been a feint – the pains in her arms and legs and the swollen appearance of her face suggests nephritis, an inflammation of the kidneys often caused by deficiency in the immune system. Given that Elizabeth later suffered from androgenic alopecia, or female-pattern baldness, which is associated with the production of the stress hormone androgen, it is possible that this illness was also brought on by extreme anxiety, as the immune system can also give way under psychological pressure, making the sufferer more vulnerable to infection. Androgen is one of the hormones associated with nephritis. Anne Boleyn also suffered from sudden illnesses at times of tension, and Elizabeth was periodically afflicted in the same manner. Certainly, she had every reason to be appallingly tense. Her reluctance to attend court may also have been simple fear. Now the gloves were off, it was quite possible that she would 'disappear', as the inconvenient York princes had done within (almost) living memory. In a Lenten sermon, Bishop Gardiner had just preached that the queen would be 'merciful to the body of the commonwealth', but that this could only be accomplished if 'the rotten and hurtful members of that were cut off and consumed'. Lady Jane had gone to the scaffold an hour after her husband Guildford Dudley on 12 February; her father's support for the rebels had exhausted Mary's clemency. Elizabeth had every reason to believe, when she finally entered London on the 23rd, that she would be next.

Nonetheless, ever aware of the importance of appearances, Elizabeth made a good, if rather pathetic show. Renard had disseminated a rumour that the swelling in her body was due to pregnancy, a slander for which Elizabeth showed her scorn by dressing in white and having the curtains of her litter drawn open, so that her suffering countenance might give the spiteful ambassador the lie. As the interrogations went on, Elizabeth was effectively imprisoned at Whitehall, where Mary refused to see her. After Wyatt had delivered his testimony at Westminster, she was finally visited on 16 March and charged with engagement in the conspiracy and informed that she would be sent to the Tower for questioning. Guards were stationed outside her chamber and many of her servants sent away. On Saturday 18 March, the Earl of Sussex and the Marquess of Winchester arrived to accompany Elizabeth to the Tower. She pleaded for time to write to her sister, so winningly that Sussex gave in to her request. One imagines that she had already rehearsed what she was going to say in those long hours behind a barred door, but she wrote extremely slowly, so slowly that the tide which was to take her downriver turned. (The last opportunity for her to have departed in daylight that day would have been about 1 p.m.; we can therefore surmise that the 'Tide Letter' was composed at about midday.) When she had finished, having bought another night of relative freedom, Elizabeth hatched in the remaining space on the paper, to prevent any other hand tampering with her words.

In terms of the evidence which has survived, Elizabeth had done virtually nothing to incriminate herself. She had remained aloof from the conspiracy, but what exactly she knew is uncertain. As queen, she consistently tended to avoid action until the last possible moment, refusing to intervene until she was required to do so. She prevaricated, but not passively. Had Wyatt's coup in 1554 succeeded, she could have ridden to her coronation with a clear conscience; when it failed, she was theoretically free of any taint. And yet not now, not quite. The papers of the French ambassador confirm that he was in contact, if not with Elizabeth herself, then with the rebels. On 26 January, he reported that Elizabeth was to remove to Donnington and that the castle was being fortified. Elizabeth had refused Sir James's request to leave for Donnington on the 22nd. Had she planned to go to Donnington and wait, well-defended, to see how events fell out, and been prevented by illness? Or had the rebels merely hoped that she would go there? Either way, Mary knew that men and munitions had been gathered. So how far what Elizabeth wrote to her sister now was true no longer mattered. What she wrote was a direct appeal to her sister's majesty, to the justice required of a prince. Her words had to give Mary pause, at least for long enough to allow Elizabeth to gain a purchase on her freedom.

'If any ever did try the old saying that a king's word was more than another man's oath I most humbly beseech your Majesty to verify it in me . . . that I be not condemned without answer and due proof which it seems that now I am for that without cause provided I am by your counsel from you commanded to go unto the tower, a place more wonted for a false traitor than a true subject.' She roundly denied the two principal charges, of communicating with Wyatt and the French ambassador: 'as for the traitor Wyatt he might peradventure write me a letter, but on my faith I never received any from him. And as for the copy of the letter sent to the French king, I pray God confound me eternally if I ever sent him word, message, token or letter. ' Elizabeth recalled Thomas Seymour's pleas to see his brother: 'In late days I heard my lord of Somerset say that if his brother had been suffered to speak with him he had never suffered', adding that it was the 'persuasions' of others which had persuaded the Duke of Somerset otherwise and that such persons 'are not to be compared to your majesty'. Such 'persuasions', she argued, should not set two sisters at odds. The 'Tide Letter' was a superb performance, but it did no good. Mary still refused to see Elizabeth and berated Sussex for permitting her to write. The next day, Palm Sunday, Elizabeth entered the Tower.

The hagiographic account of her arrival given in John Foxe's *Acts and Monuments* has Elizabeth playing to the crowd as only she knew how. Landing at 'Traitors' Gate', Elizabeth supposedly announced: 'Here landeth as true a subject, being prisoner, as ever landed at these stairs'. She then staged an impromptu sit-in and refused to get up from the flagstones, remarking that she was better off there 'than in a worse place'. When one of her attendants broke down at the sight of his mistress so demeaned, she informed the onlookers that there was no need, since 'she knew her truth to be such that no man would have cause to weep for her'.[10] In fact, Elizabeth landed at Tower Wharf and walked across the wooden bridge on the St Paul's side of the Tower. The only drama was the fright she got from the roaring of the lions in the royal menagerie. And while her prison was not the dank dungeon of romantic legend, her lodgings were a particularly spiteful choice on Mary's part, as the four rooms allotted to Elizabeth in the royal apartments of the Tower were those used by Anne Boleyn for her coronation and occupied once again before her death.

Elizabeth was just twenty-one years old. She had no access to counsel, much less a lawyer. She knew when she entered the Tower that it was only her own words, in response to the forthcoming interrogations, which would save her life. In the words of a text credited to Robert Dudley during his imprisonment on the other side of the fortress:

Where, when the wicked ruled,
And bore the sway by might,
No one would please to take my part,
Or once defend my right.

The sentiments are mawkish and the rhyme too pat for this to be a convincing production, though the sense of helpless isolation was something both Elizabeth and Robert shared.

Elizabeth's only weapon was her wits. She was examined on Good Friday, five days after her arrival. She recalled rather grandly that she did indeed possess a house at Donnington, but that she had never slept there. She admitted that Crofts had tried to persuade her to go, but pointed out that going to her own house could hardly be construed as a crime. The crucial issue was that since the house *had* been furnished with 'arms and provisions', did Elizabeth know of it, or agree to it? Mary's original letter to Elizabeth summoning her to court in early February hinted at the possibility of Elizabeth's going to Donnington, but Elizabeth had not taken the bait and confirmed it. The first encounter could be judged a draw. Renard was still pushing Mary to declaring Elizabeth guilty, but divisions had now emerged in her council. For Elizabeth's enemies, there was still the possibility that Wyatt might confess something more, but he went to his death on 11 April affirming that neither Elizabeth nor Courtenay 'was privy of my rising or commotion before I began'. Next day, the interrogators confronted Elizabeth again, and once more found no new evidence. As Wyatt's pickled entrails were nailed up at Newgate, two men were put in the pillory for claiming that it was he who had cleared her name. Elizabeth, though, remained fearful. When Sir Henry Bedingfield appeared at the Tower on 4 May at the head of a hundred guards, she asked, startled, if the scaffold erected for the beheading of Jane Grey had been dismantled. The only relief she could find from the unbearable uncertainty was to pace the privy garden and the chamber of her lodgings, circling again and again like the caged beasts in the menagerie close by. On the sixty-second day of her imprisonment, Elizabeth finally learned that she was to be released, but that Bedingfield would be, in effect, her new gaoler.

CHAPTER SEVEN

Elizabeth's new home was to be Woodstock, in Oxfordshire. Her journey there described the divisions of a divided country. Mary Tudor's early policy of religious toleration would collapse within two years of her accession, and from February 1555 the fires of Smithfield would be stoked with Protestants prepared to die for their faith. Three hundred men and women burned for their beliefs during Mary's reign, and, beyond London, the country in 1554 was already beginning to split into confessional enclaves. From Richmond, where she had remained for only a night after leaving the Tower, Elizabeth passed through Windsor, West Wycombe and Rycote, accompanied everywhere on her route by cheering crowds. Bedingfield reported nervously that 'Men betwixt London and these parts be not good and whole in matters of religion',[1] as resistance to Rome remained strong in villages which rang their bells as Elizabeth's litter travelled by. So many gifts of flowers and cakes were offered at High Wycombe that the princess had to beg the kind local ladies to stop, as the scent of sugar and spice was so overpowering. Sir Henry encountered a farmer named Christopher Cook outside Woburn, who had waited to catch a glimpse of the princess, and their conversation, he noted disapprovingly, proved Cook 'a very Protestant'. Oxfordshire, where the university remained a bastion of the Old Faith, was more reassuring. After four days, the party arrived at the dilapidated but serviceable manor house of Woodstock, most recently improved by Elizabeth's grandfather. The size of the property, with its two huge courtyards, presented an immediate problem to Bedingfield, who fretted that there were only three lockable doors.

It is hard not to feel sorry for Bedingfield. His account of his term of duty as Elizabeth's keeper reads like a chamber farce. An honest, dogged, but poorly educated man, his mind was no match for the quicksilver temperament of his charge, and his task, to watch Elizabeth closely while treating her 'in such good and honourable sort as may be agreeable to . . . her estate and degree',[2] was not lightened by the fact that most of the household were Elizabeth's adherents. Thomas Parry was no longer an official part of the princess's retinue, but he hovered at the Bull Inn at Woodstock, whence Bedingfield could not dislodge him, as it was Elizabeth herself who paid the bills for the household's maintenance, and she therefore required her cofferer nearby. One senses a euphoric insolence in Elizabeth's treatment of Bedingfield; perhaps it was having escaped with her life that made her tease him so mercilessly, yet she remained aware of her status as prisoner, and, as the weeks dragged on, she fell into a sullen depression.

Bedingfield found it almost impossible to keep track of the comings and goings of his prisoner's insurrectionary household. Parry was holding court at the Bull, receiving as many as forty visitors a day, suspicious gifts of books and potentially seditious pheasants arrived for Elizabeth, who complained vociferously about everything – her rooms, the air, the exile of one of the most Protestant of her women, Elizabeth Sandes, the lack of an English Bible, that her cloth of estate was not erected. Elizabeth knew that only by applying to her sister could she hope for some mitigation of her condition, but Mary refused to be 'molested by such her disguise and colourful letters'.[3] She petitioned Bedingfield constantly to be permitted to write to Mary, but another request, to be allowed to come to court in July, was merely ignored. In September, Bedingfield announced grudgingly that he had received permission from the council for her to write once more, a permission which, having sought it so long, Elizabeth now chose to ignore for a week before demanding the requisite materials. Then she complained of a headache. Then she washed her hair. Then she announced that she required a secretary to write to the council, and, since she was not permitted one, Bedingfield himself must do it. Bedingfield complied, but took back his writing desk. Elizabeth stole one of his pens. Bedingfield sneered at the airs of this 'grand lady', Elizabeth told him bluntly that he was a joke of a gaoler. This sort of petty sniping ground on for almost a year.

While Elizabeth's world had been reduced to the boundaries of Woodstock, with little diversion beyond baiting Parry, Mary had married her Spanish king on 26 July. In November, the queen's first parliament as a married woman immediately called for the return of Cardinal Reginald Pole, the exiled papal legate, and on the 30th of the month, after both Lords and Commons had passed a resolution to return the country to Catholicism, Pole formally absolved England from the taint of heresy and schism. Though considerable propaganda efforts were deployed to present the Marian Church as a 'national' one (precisely the strategy employed so much more successfully under Elizabeth), Mary's marriage and her fervent joy at the restoration of her faith left little doubt in most minds that, in religion, England once more belonged to Rome. The crowning triumph for Mary was her conviction that she had felt a child 'quicken' in her womb. The queen was pregnant, and whatever threat her sister had presented could now be seen as negligible.

At last, on 17 April, Elizabeth received the summons she had been hoping for. Bedingfield was even instructed that he need not trouble himself with reinforcing her guard for the journey. Elizabeth set off with a set of baby linen which she had embroidered in red as a gift for the next Tudor heir. She arrived at Hampton Court by the end of the month, though she was obliged to remain in her lodgings, which had been built for her brother Edward, for a further two weeks, until she received a visit from Bishop Gardiner. Elizabeth was required to submit 'to the Queen's grace'. Recognising this as a tacit admittance of guilt, Elizabeth refused. After a further week of waiting, Elizabeth was conducted to Mary's apartments by torchlight at ten in the evening. Elizabeth knelt before her sister, averring that she was a true subject, but when Mary scolded her for her refusal to confess, Elizabeth would only concede that she would not say she had been wrongfully punished before the queen. Mary was exasperated. Elizabeth had captured her sister's feelings in the couplet she had scratched with a diamond on to one of the window panes at Woodstock: 'Much suspected by me/Nothing proved can be.' It was infuriating. Mary was convinced of Elizabeth's guilt, yet she felt obliged to restore her to some measure of favour, perhaps because of the influence of the third party at this night-time interview, her husband, Philip of Spain. According to one source, Philip was lurking behind a tapestry during the encounter between the sisters, and it may have been at his desire that Mary eventually brought herself to exchange a few 'comfortable words' with Elizabeth.

The term of Mary's 'pregnancy' had already come and gone. On 30 April, the bells had been rung in the capital at the false report that the queen had been delivered of a son, and even if Mary was still convinced that she was with child, Philip was more realistic. Until an Anglo-Spanish succession was secured, he needed Elizabeth. By early August, even Mary could maintain the fiction no longer, and thanks to Philip's influence Elizabeth enjoyed a renewed measure of status as the court moved to Oatlands and on to Greenwich during the summer of 1555. She was even allowed to attend his official leave-taking on 25 August, when he sailed from Greenwich. Just over a month later, Elizabeth received permission to return to her own house at Hatfield. One wonders whether brother-in-law or sister was more relieved to be gone.

Speculating on feelings at nearly five centuries' distance is never a wise idea, particularly when it comes to an individual so intensely private as Elizabeth I. But as she departed for Hertfordshire, Elizabeth might well have felt that after the wretchedness of the past two years, her ordeal in the Tower and her imprisonment at Woodstock, something extraordinary was beginning. The signs were there. Her popularity was almost embarrassingly evident. Tactfully, she had requested her gentlemen to restrain the cheering crowds as she departed court, but there could be little doubt that where Mary had once been beloved, she was now loathed. The bonfires which had been lit to acclaim her accession had been transformed into horrific funeral pyres. Mary's holy fanaticism had prompted even Philip's own chaplain, Alfonso a Castro, to advocate restraint. In a sermon delivered when the burnings began, he observed, 'they learned it not in Scripture to burn a man for his conscience'. When Elizabeth had arrived at Hampton Court in the spring, disgraced, her birth still called into question (for though Mary had thus far resisted Gardiner's suggestion to have her once more declared a bastard, it remained a possibility) and, to her sister's smug eyes, painfully unmarried, she was very much the poor relation. Now, vindicated, free, and most importantly healthy and Protestant, it seemed that under the terms of her father's will she might indeed succeed. Short of a miracle, there would be no heir, and the sickness which would kill Mary in two years was already making itself known.

Elizabeth was quick to re-establish her household on its old footing. Thomas Parry returned, as did Katherine Ashley, and Roger Ascham arrived to resume her programme of studies. On the surface, Elizabeth's life had resumed its quiet, scholarly tenor, yet she had barely had time to recover from the upheavals of the recent past before her name was once again being associated with treason. Once again, the unfortunate Katherine Ashley was the source.

In 1550, Elizabeth had obtained Durham Place on the Thames in London, between Whitehall and the then Lord Protector's residence at Somerset House, as part of her father's bequests. It was a spacious property, with a large garden, but Elizabeth never lived there (in spite, or perhaps because, of the fact that it was once used by Anne Boleyn). After Seymour's fall, the Duke of Northumberland, Robert Dudley's father, arranged for Elizabeth to take Somerset House, the first truly Renaissance building in England. In the spring of 1556, Somerset House was searched, and a number of 'seditious' materials recovered, including books, pamphlets containing 'libels' on Mary and Philip, and a box of drawings and paintings which insulted the royal couple and the Catholic religion. The box, or cabinet, belonged to Katherine Ashley, who departed from Hatfield in May for her third spell in the Tower. But why were Elizabeth and her household yet again under scrutiny?

Mary's fourth parliament, which met three days after Elizabeth left court, was her most difficult to date. Martyrdom was one thing, but money was another. Two principal bills were proposed, one to return the crown properties originally confiscated by the Church, and the second to confiscate the properties of those reformists (eight hundred or so) who had voluntarily gone into exile to avoid Mary's persecution. Both bills were extremely unpopular, and though the crown managed to inch the first through – effectively by locking the Commons in the house and starving them into submission – the second was vehemently opposed by Sir Anthony Kingston, who also took the measure of locking the Commons in, though this time the door was bolted from the inside. In a passionate speech, he challenged the House not to pass a bill which was contrary to so many consciences, and the crown's proposal was defeated. Among those who voted against it was William Cecil. Kingston was connected with another disaffected gentleman, Sir Henry Dudley, and through him to his father-in-law, Christopher Ashton. Dudley was a distant relative of Robert Dudley (precisely, his father's second cousin once removed), and had been a Northumberland client during the days of the duke's ascendancy, travelling to France to promote the cause of Jane Grey. He was in Paris again at the end of 1555, where he discussed the implications of Mary's Spanish marriage with none other than the French king himself.

The Dudley plot might almost be seen as a prototype of the continentally based conspiracies of Elizabeth's reign, in which religious division in England was (prospectively) exploited to the advantage of either France or Spain. Christopher Ashton and Anthony Kingston agreed between them that Dudley would lead an invasion force from France, via Portsmouth, which would join with a rebel force raised by Kingston. Together they would march on London, dust off Edward Courtenay (presently kicking his heels in Venice), marry him to Elizabeth and 'dispose' of Mary – the original plan seems to have been exile with Philip, though wilder accounts suggest they intended to murder the queen. In February 1556, however, the French and Spanish kings signed a truce at Vaucelles, and the plot was put into abeyance. What was crucial, the French ambassador in London, Noailles, was informed, was that Elizabeth should not be involved: 'And above all, make sure that Madame Elizabeth does not begin ... to undertake what I have written to you. For that would spoil everything and lose the benefit which they can hope for from their schemes.'[4]

There are two ways of reading this. One, that Elizabeth was ignorant of the plan and that the French ambassador was being warned that she should not be involved in it. Or two, that the French ambassador thought that Elizabeth was already informed of the plan 'what I have written to you', and was poised ready to act; that is, she was fully aware of and had acquiesced to the coup. But had there been the least bit of evidence of this, why would Mary not have leaped upon the excuse to dispose of her troublesome sister once and for all? Perhaps she was allowing the plot to play itself out and then strike at Elizabeth when she had firm proof, for, incredibly, Dudley and Ashton now succeeded in robbing the Exchequer. They carried out the burglary to fund the scheme in lieu of monies from Henry II and got as far as actually touching the bullion stores. By the time this was revealed to Cardinal Pole, the Archbishop of Canterbury and principal councillor to Mary, the pair had sailed for France to organise the invasion. In March, the London group of plotters had been rounded up and Kingston was dead, possibly a suicide as he was taken into custody. Elizabeth expressed her shock and outrage in her highest style, writing to Mary that:

> Among earthly things I chiefly wish this one, that there were as good surgeons for making anatomies of hearts that might show my thoughts to Your Majesty as there are expert physicians of the bodies, able to express the inward griefs of their maladies to their patient. For then I doubt not but know well that whatsoever other should suggest by malice, yet your majesty should be sure by knowledge, so that the more such misty clouds obfuscates the clear light of my truth, the more my tried thoughts should glister to the dimming of their hidden malice.

Having unravelled all that, it is a tiny bit tempting to wonder whether Elizabeth's tongue was a little in her cheek.

Mary was not entirely blinded by obfuscating clouds, and though she later sent a diamond ring and a polite message to Elizabeth, still

Somerset House was searched and arrests were made at Hatfield in May. Along with Katherine Ashley and three more of Elizabeth's women, Elizabeth's Italian tutor, Battista Castiglione, and another servant, Francis Verney, were taken away. 'The number of persons imprisoned increases daily,' reported the Venetian ambassador excitedly, '. . . which has caused great general vexation . . . Among the domestics is a certain Battista . . . who has twice before been imprisoned on her [Elizabeth's] account, he being much suspected on the score of religion.'

Francis Verney was one of the members of Elizabeth's household who had provoked Bedingfield's suspicions during her confinement at Woodstock. A Protestant from a Buckinghamshire gentry family, he had hung around the Bull with Parry and had apparently managed to poke his nose into several letters from Mary's council. Both he and his brother Edmund had the government's eyes on them. 'If there be any practice of ill, within all England, this Verney is privy to it',[5] Bedingfield was warned. By June, Elizabeth was informed that four confessions of knowledge of the Dudley plot had been extracted, but Mary's envoys assured her that she herself was not suspected.

Mary did not believe her sister to be innocent. But Philip, in Brussels, insisted she be exonerated. If Elizabeth were eliminated, the next heir was Mary Queen of Scots, the future Queen of France, an intolerable outcome for what had been very much a dynastic Hapsburg marriage. So Mary, desperately loyal to her husband, excused her sister, who loftily refused an invitation to attend court. It can only have been a painful decision for Mary, to whom her negligible value as a woman, rather than as a conduit for Spanish ambition, had been made hatefully plain.

In a sense, though, the Dudley plot is something of a red herring. It was a crazy scheme, and one which only briefly had the backing of the serious military power of the French king. What deserves more scrutiny is the Italian connection – the arrest of Castiglione and the evidence which this provides that Elizabeth's household had been connected with anti-Mary propaganda for some years.

In the summer of 1556, Sir William Cecil and his wife Mildred received a pleasant invitation to the country house of Sir Philip Hoby at Bisham. Lady Cecil was pregnant, and Sir Philip considerately offered to send his carriage if the Cecils would consent to be of the party. It was very much a family gathering – among the guests were Cecil's brother-in-law, Sir Thomas Hoby, and his wife Elizabeth, Mildred's younger sister. The planned gathering on a July afternoon collects together some of the most influential characters of what might be termed the 'Marian resistance', which, through Battista Castiglione, leads back to Katherine Ashley and her 'libellous pamphlets' and, from there, to Elizabeth.

Another member of the group was Richard Morison, whom Elizabeth's tutor Roger Ascham had accompanied as secretary when Morison was ambassador to the imperial court in 1550. Morison had attracted unwelcome attention during his embassy for staging public readings of the works of Machiavelli. He was also a colleague of Bernardino Ochino, one of a small number of Italian religious reformists who had a significant influence on the progress of Protestantism in England. The Reformation in Italy itself was of brief duration. Between a programme of concentrated oppression from the Church and the Holy Roman Empire, which controlled much of the peninsula, the movement to reform was thoroughly quashed in about seventy years. Yet Italy briefly provided a significant locus of dissent for English exiles during Mary Tudor's reign and, moreover, continued to inject English reform with the energy of Renaissance humanism. Padua, governed by the republic of Venice and hence beyond the reach of imperial authority, was a particular centre for those seeking refuge from Catholic persecution. Its university was a magnet for humanists while (curiously) the superlative art of its public buildings, adorned with works by Giotto and Mantegna, provided dissident reformists with a background of some of the finest achievements of the Catholic Renaissance. The Hoby brothers were Italophiles, and, between 1548 and 1555, accompanied for a time by John Cheke, their travels on the peninsula brought them the acquaintance of many Italian reformists, among them Pietro Bizzani, whom Cheke made a fellow of St John's, Bernardino Ochino and later Jacopo Aconcio. The journeyings of the Hoby group were an unofficial exile. As Mary's persecutions intensified, they gave out that they were benefiting from a leisurely tour of Italy's cultural centres and healthful spas. It is possible that among the 'refugees of conscience' they may also have encountered Francis Walsingham, later Secretary to Elizabeth, who was present there between 1554 and 1556.

Thomas Hoby himself is best remembered for his travel writings and for his 1522 translation of that essential sixteenth-century text, Castiglione's *Il Cortigiano*. He also translated an anti-papal text, Francesco Negri's *Tragedy of Free Will*, which he dedicated to Katherine Parr's brother, the Marquess of Northampton, whose service he entered in 1551. Another Italian reformist associated with the circle, a close friend of Bizzani, was Elizabeth's tutor Battista Castiglione (a distant relation of the famous author), who had joined her household in 1544. Researchers concur that it is probable that Castiglione's first two spells in prison were associated with the Seymour and Wyatt incidents. Castiglione later became one of Elizabeth's gentlemen of the chamber and served her until his death at the age of eighty-two.

Not all members of the Hoby circle felt obliged to take their consciences on a Grand Tour. Some, like William Cecil, reached a compromise with the regime (Cecil voted against the Exile bill while simultaneously becoming High Steward of Cardinal Pole's manor near his own home at Wimbledon), while working discreetly against it. Elizabeth appointed Cecil surveyor of her lands in 1550; in 1553, for a fee of £20 per annum, he gave her advice on her property, some of which lay close to his own family home at Burghley. With one exception, they did not meet during Mary's reign, but they kept in contact through Thomas Parry, a relative of Cecil's whose name appears occasionally in the latter's accounts. Both Elizabeth and Cecil, in a strategy which prefigured the essential harmony of their future political relationship, were prepared to keep their heads down during the Marian ascendancy, to see which way the wind blew: 'We are used to the great old Protestant narrative of English history which has Mary's reign as a monstrous aberration . . . in 1555, there was no triumph of Tudor Protestantism.'[6]

But neither Elizabeth nor her future minister were entirely submissive. Cecil tolerated the presence on his land of a printing press owned by one John Day, which from the very day of Mary's coronation issued tracts against her. And Elizabeth, whatever the extent of her involvement in the Wyatt and Dudley rebellions, was harbouring a rebel in her own household, in the form of Castiglione.

John Cheke, the centre of this circle of covert dissidents, was less able to accommodate himself to the times. He had left England after one spell in the Tower, then, as he travelled between Brussels and Antwerp, he was taken on the orders of Philip of Spain and returned to captivity. Prison was too much for him. Although he had written to Cecil earlier that year to warn him of the spiritual consequences of conformity, the second spell in the Tower broke him. Just two weeks after Sir Philip Hoby's planned party, he made two formal recantations of his reformist faith and was received back into the Catholic fold by Cardinal Pole, with Mary's court as witnesses. He died soon afterwards, unable to forgive himself.

Elizabeth's reaction to Cheke's betrayal of his beliefs is not recorded, but, interestingly, she communicated briefly with Cecil at the time on an innocuous matter concerning her estates in Northamptonshire. By then, the Dudley conspiracy was dead and, thanks to King Philip, she was officially innocent. However, the Cheke–Cecil–Hoby circle gives some clue as to what exactly those 'pamphlets' were which had so incriminated the hapless Katherine Ashley. The influence of Italian reformists at large in London had been observed by the imperial ambassador, Renard: 'there are countless Italians here . . . who go about talking as evilly as they know how in merchant circles'.[7] Richard Morison was known to be involved in 'resistance' literature (as well as being a promoter of Machiavelli), and it is notable that many of the libels issued against Mary and Philip had a distinctly Italian slant, emanating from the cities – Venice, Ferrara, and that particular centre for the Marian diaspora, Padua. Due to its relative religious freedom, the city was an ideal centre for the production of inflammatory tracts. In May 1555, the Venetian ambassador reported that more than 1,000 copies of a *Dialogue* 'full of scandalous and seditious things against the religion and government'[8] had been distributed in London. He also reported on two books in translation, *The Mourning of Milan* and *The Lament of Naples*, which warned the English against the example of Spanish domination on the peninsula.

Elizabeth was an impressive Italian scholar. Her use of the language is widely reported and she continued to display her skills throughout her queenship, conversing in Italian with Francesco Gradenigo in 1596, and discussing her love for the language with the Venetian ambassador Giovanni Scaramelli in 1603. One scholar speaks of Elizabeth's 'determined turning of an intellectual accomplishment into a political tool',[9] which she certainly did as queen, but what if Italian also provides a further clue to her connections with the 'resistance' in the mid-1550s? Where else could Katherine Ashley have obtained such clandestine 'pamphlets' other than through Castiglione? The Venetian ambassador's report hints at his involvement:

> Certain knaves in this country endeavor daily to disturb the peace and quiet and present state of the kingdom, so as if possible to introduce some novelty and insurrection . . . and although all diligence has been used for the discovery of the authors, no light on the subject has yet been obtained, save that an Italian has been put in the Tower, he being a master for teaching the Italian tongue to Milady Elizabeth, some suspicion having been apparently obtained of him.

The tutor was very much part of the Hoby–Cecil network; he was a known reformist close to Elizabeth. If Castiglione was trafficking in forbidden literature, it suggests that Elizabeth's involvement in anti-Mary propaganda was more considerable than has previously been emphasised.

Somerset House was the site for the discovery of the seditious material. It was also the location of a meeting between Elizabeth and William Cecil in March 1558.[10] The details of this encounter are scant, so much so that they have long been overlooked, but it is possible that Somerset House was a sort of headquarters in the capital for

Elizabeth's government-in-waiting. In February that year, Elizabeth had installed herself in her London home with a large contingent of staff and servants. A month later, a servant recorded a boatman's tariff totalling five pence for the journey by water of William Cecil to Somerset House, where he met with the princess. Cecil's biographer concludes that 'it was a meeting that helped to shape the course of her reign and his life'.

It seems, though, that there is a strong possibility that Cecil's communications with Elizabeth, via this network, were more extensive than has been considered. The nature of the 'pamphlets' which indicted Katherine Ashley appears very similar to the tracts described by the Venetian ambassador. Thus it can be posited that Elizabeth herself, via Castiglione, was consistently implicated in the Marian resistance, beyond the very public alarms of the Wyatt and Dudley plots.

CHAPTER EIGHT

Elizabeth remained only a week in London in February 1558. As she returned to the country, Philip of Spain was attending to a report from Renard which advised him that there was little alternative other than to accept Elizabeth as Mary's successor. Philip's wife still had ten months to live, but a second phantom pregnancy had only confirmed her redundancy in her husband's eyes. Elizabeth's cautious optimism of the last four years was confirmed. She would rule. Throughout the year, as Mary's health declined, Elizabeth began mustering her forces for the accession. In October, Mary finally brought herself to concede what everyone in the political world already accepted, and added a codicil to her will, accepting the provision of Henry VIII's own, that Elizabeth would succeed. Since on her death her husband would obtain 'no further governance in England', Philip sent the Count of Feria as an envoy to safeguard Spanish interests under the new regime. One of Feria's first reports concerned William Cecil, who it was rumoured would have the post of Secretary, though Feria dispiritedly viewed this endorsement of a man suspected of being a heretic (most interesting, given Cecil's outwardly impeccable conformity) as an indication that the new queen would not be 'well-disposed in matters of religion'. Officially, Elizabeth was still hedging her bets. Confronted with Mary's wish that she would maintain Catholicism, Elizabeth replied to her sister's envoy Jane Dormer that 'She prayed God that the earth might open and swallow her up alive if she were not a true Roman Catholic.' Given that by November Feria had made a list of the men whom he believed Elizabeth would favour, which included the Earl of Bedford, Robert Dudley, Sir Nicholas Throckmorton, Sir Peter Carew, John Harington and Thomas Parry, as well as Cecil, and that all of these men had known reformist leanings, Elizabeth can hardly have expected her sister to believe her. But then, she no longer cared.

Mary died towards dawn on 17 November. The news reached Hatfield even before Elizabeth was proclaimed in London. Cecil was primed at his desk, and Elizabeth had plenty of time to prepare her reaction. She did not receive Mary's councillors under an oak tree, pausing for a few faint, feminine moments before quoting Psalm 118, 'This is the Lord's doing, it is marvellous in our eyes' (though it is quite the sort of thing one can imagine her doing); instead, having politely expressed her sorrow at Mary's loss and her own 'amazement', she explained how she intended to begin her government. In her first speech as Queen of England, Elizabeth announced, 'I am but one body naturally considered, though by His permission a body politic to govern'. In her last parliament, in 1601, Elizabeth was to say much the same thing:

> I know the title of a King is a glorious title. But assure yourself that the Shining Glory of Princely Authority hath not so Dazzled the Eyes of our Understanding but that we know and remember that we also are to yield and Account of our own Actions before the Great Judge . . . For myself I was never so enticed with the Glorious name of King, or Royal Authority of a Queen as delighted that God had made me His instrument to maintain his Truth and Glory.

The distinction between the 'two bodies' of the monarch to which Elizabeth chose to make reference in her first regal communication was primarily a legal one. It is best explained by a statement from the crown lawyers made in connection with landholdings in the royal Duchy of Lancaster in the fourth year of her reign:

> For the King has in him two bodies, viz. a Body natural and a Body politic. His Body natural (if it be considered in itself) is a Body mortal, subject to all Infirmities that come by Nature or Accident, to the Imbecility of Infancy or old Age, and to the like Defects that happen to the natural Bodies of other people. But his Body politic is a Body that cannot be seen or handled, consisting of Policy and

Government . . . and this Body is utterly void of Infancy, and old Age, and other natural Defects and Imbecilities, which the Body natural is subject to, and for this Cause, what the King does in His Body politic, cannot be invalidated or frustrated by any Disability in his natural Body.[1]

That is, the body politic is immortal, as distinct from the body natural, which is material. The distinction summarised in the Lancaster case draws upon ancient tradition concerning the 'angelic' quality of the royal body politic. The fifteenth-century lawyer Sir John Fortescue explains thus: 'the holy sprites and angels that may not sin, wax old, be sick or hurt himself, have more power than we, that may harm ourselves with all these defaults. So is the king's power more.' Kingship was therefore, within the division of the two bodies, possessed of both political and spiritual determinants in the belief in the sempiternity of the royal body politic. Association with 'holy angels' was a consistent factor in the understanding of sacramental kingship throughout Europe by the thirteenth century, but was of particular relevance to England in the sixteenth. The fusing of the stately and the spiritual in the royal supremacy was reinforced in the recitation of the Athanasian Creed, which affirms the parity of the three elements of the Holy Trinity. In contrast with Protestant churches on the Continent, the creed was repeatedly cited at English church services (the Book of Common Prayer provides nineteen occasions for its recitation, one of three approved in the 39 Articles). Fortescue's explanation of the 'angelic' power of kingship is translated through the thinking of Michael Psellus, an eleventh-century divine whose theories of 'angelology' provided Milton, in the next century, with the source for his discussions of the relationship between spirit and matter. Where the angelic quality of the royal body politic seems especially pertinent to Elizabeth is that angelic matter, the holy spirit of royalty, was sexless. In her very first statement to the royal councillors, then, Elizabeth is highlighting the *irrelevance* of her 'body natural's' femininity.

⁓

Baldassare Castiglione's *Il Cortigiano* was one of the most influential 'mirror books' of the sixteenth century. Just as the name implies, 'mirror books' offered a reflection of ideal conduct which the reader could imitate. Written at Urbino from 1508 and published in English in 1561, *Il Cortigiano* is half philosophical treatise, half conduct manual, delineating the ideal qualities of the courtier, and also of the 'perfect lady'. Dispute over women's capacities, their intellect, their fitness for government had been a standard topic for scholars and divines for centuries, the *querelle des femmes* which continues today. In a statement which reflects the views of Thomas More on women's intellectual capacities, Castiglione is in no doubt as to women's intelligence and receptiveness to education:

> I say that all the things that men can understand, the same women can understand too; and where the intellect of one penetrates, there also can that of the other penetrate

but he also makes an interesting distinction:

> Do you not believe that there are many to be found who would know how to govern cities and armies as well as men do? But I have not laid these duties on them because I am fashioning a court lady, and not a Queen.[2]

That is, while Castiglione is entirely clear about ladies' abilities (and in a text premised strongly on the importance of nobility this is an important qualification), he knows that queens are something else, something different.

As is the case today, 'femininity' invoked engagement with an intricate fascia of cultural expectations and social norms which were nonetheless fluid and intransient. European treatises from the fifteenth century emphasise that the woman born to rule be granted educational rights denied to others, that her conduct and judgement be those of a man. Mary Tudor may have been England's first Queen Regnant, but, alongside her sister's legacy, Elizabeth I could also draw on a five-hundred-year tradition of English queenship, a sacred office replete with ritualised and actual authority.

Practically, English queens had always been exceptional in terms of their legal status. Common law recognised three states of female existence, each of which was defined in relation to male authority, that is, maiden, wife and widow. It was only as widows that women could be officially released from male guardianship – or ownership – and conduct their own affairs. In reality, '*de facto*', women could and did command a considerable degree of power, but their '*de jure*', legal status, remained technically limited. Queens, however, were more independent before the law than any other woman, as they had the status of *femme sole* even while their husbands were living. They could sue and be sued, acquire property and land, and witness its granting or other legal transactions, they could hear oaths, appoint ecclesiastics, preside over court cases and make wills. In the Anglo-Norman realm, the spread of crown territories between England and France made shared rule between a king and his spouse a practical necessity, and one which accorded naturally with the legal status of queen. Hence, for example, we find Matilda of Flanders acting as regent for William I in Normandy, or Matilda of Scotland, the wife of Henry I, presiding over the first known assembly of the court of the Exchequer at Winchester in IIII.

If a queen functioned practically in a different fashion from other women, might this not reflect a slippage of categorisation in other respects? Early Scandinavian (as distinct from Christian European) culture attests a more flexible status for 'woman' which is, in part, connected as much with activity as with sex. Linguistically, activities, rather than individuals, were gendered in Old Norse; thus a woman who practised organised piracy (and a remarkable number did) was *viking*, what she did determining who she was. The gap between *de jure* and *de facto* status was contemplated by Scandinavian law as an area in which, in the case of necessity, the principle of sex could be overridden. In the *wergild* system, a compensation structure for men who had been murdered, an unmarried daughter could legally function as a son if there were no other direct male relatives. Female exception could be institutionalised, as it subsequently was in Tudor England.

Anglo-Saxon culture was equally typified by a much more fluid conception of gender roles. Sexual difference, it is argued, was less a consequence of biological distinction than of the way in which an individual accessed and interacted with power. Effectively, sex was dependent on status. As Anglo-Saxon culture was permeated by Christianity, such power could be acquired and used in spiritual terms, and here many of the traits which contributed to the mystical power of English queenship begin to emerge. Women had traditionally been seen as 'peaceweavers', able to negotiate truces or alliances verbally, in contrast to the violent forms of resolution demanded by a warrior society. This role evolves into the motif of intercession, whereby a queen might prevail upon a king to be merciful, persuading him to gentleness through her femininity without compromising his masculine status. Intercession became increasingly ritualised throughout the medieval period, as the idea of 'peaceweaving' melded with Christian humility and pity. To be a hero was no longer predicated on aggression, it also required a degree of spiritual militancy, which in turn meant that gender could be transcended. In Anglo-Saxon culture, a woman could be *geworht werlice* (made male) through faith. The early hagiographies of Christian England feature frequent examples of 'transvestite saints', that is, women who have overcome biological femininity by achieving spiritual masculinity. Aelfric, a tenth-century divine, explained this: 'If a woman is made manfully and strong in accordance with God's will, she will be counted among the men who sit at God's table.' As the soul became an arena of battle, so gender distinctions could meld into a form of heroic femininity, an anticipatory form of a new feminine power, as confirmed in the sixth-century *Life of the Holy Radegund*:

He [Christ] wins mighty victories through the female sex and despite their frail physique He confers glory and greatness on women through strength of mind. By faith, Christ makes them strong who were born weak so that . . . they garner praise for their creator who his heavenly treasure in earthen vessels.

The medieval construct of the *virago*, a 'third sex' category for women whose power exceeded the conventional confines of gender, evolves from the heroic femininity of the early Christian period. The term was applied to Henry I's queen, Matilda of Scotland, in recognition of her learning and piety, yet its potentially subversive ambiguity can be discerned in contemporary reactions to Matilda's daughter, known as the Empress, who represented the possibility of an English Queen Regnant for the first time. *The Anglo-Saxon Chronicle* reports that when Henry I's court was at Windsor for Christmas 1127, the king 'caused archbishops and bishops and abbots and earls and all the thegns that were there to swear to give England and Normandy after his death into the hand of his daughter'. Henry subsequently reviewed the accession and the resulting confusion plunged England into civil war, but it is crucial to note that Matilda's failure to achieve the crown was not simply a consequence of her sex. Initially, many magnates had found the idea of a woman ruler hard to swallow, but several, including the Empress's half-brother Robert of Gloucester, changed their minds, and therefore their side, under the influence of a passage from Scripture:

It seemed to some that by the weakness of their sex they should not be allowed to enter into the inheritance of their father. But the Lord, when asked, promulgated a law, that everything their father possessed should pass to the daughters.

The civil war of the twelfth century was *not* fought to prevent England being governed by a woman; indeed, the Empress's rival King Stephen owed his claim to his matrilineal descent as grandson of William I through his daughter Adela. Among the many factors which contributed to Empress Matilda's failure, that of her conduct is highly relevant. As we have seen, Scandinavian and Anglo-Saxon culture recognised gender as a fluid category which depended to a great extent upon action in relation to power. As many of the male protagonists on either side spent much of the civil war as hostages, the conflict was directed to a considerable extent by two women, Henry I's daughter the Empress Matilda and the wife of her rival, Matilda of Boulogne. What each did was quite similar; how they did it, and how this was perceived, affected the success of their respective causes.

As Queen, Elizabeth I consistently emphasised her status as the daughter of Henry VIII, in both words and images. This was a counter not only to the disputed legality of her parents' marriage, and to the allegations that she was not even the king's child (receiving visitors before a great swagger portrait of Henry, highlighting her notable resemblance to him, was one way of making the point), but a means of channelling female power through patrilineal authority. Previous English queens had demonstrated that power-wielding women could be 'lauded, rather than perceived as transgressive, provided that power was modified within a context of appropriately feminine piety and submissiveness'.[3] One pro-Empress writer tries to ground her attempt at the crown within such a context, emphasising that she acted on her father's wishes, 'meekly' 'submitting' to his will.[4] Matilda of Boulogne was careful always to present herself in a similar manner, as the defender of her son's rights, or the dutiful wife prosecuting her husband's wishes; she was conciliatory rather than confrontational. Empress Matilda might have styled herself 'Lady of the English' but to her critics her comportment was anything but ladylike. She was 'above feminine softness',[5] discourteous, stubborn and demanding, refusing petitioners and demanding money from the citizens of London, who briefly harboured her at Westminster. The same source which criticises the Empress, however, praises Matilda of Boulogne as *astute pectoris virilisque constantiae femina* – having the virile, courageous breast of a man, but the constancy or fortitude of a woman. That a queen might be possessed of the heart and stomach of a king was not entirely Elizabeth Tudor's idea. Where Matilda of Boulogne succeeded and the Empress so conspicuously failed was in manipulating the concept of the virago in displaying a 'manlike' courage tempered by conventional femininity. Or as Elizabeth herself was to put it, 'though I be a woman, I have as good a courage answerable to my place as ever my father had'. The nexus of gender and power was a net of intersecting tightropes, the strength of one affecting the purchase gained on the other. Militarily and tactically, Empress Matilda was never possessed of sufficient power to permit her to forget her femininity, an error her successor rarely committed.

Elizabeth I enjoyed the most seamless accession to the crown since that of Henry VI over a century earlier. Just six hours separated the announcement of Mary Tudor's death and Elizabeth's proclamation as Queen. Governing queens were no historical novelty, especially as Elizabeth was succeeding one, and so far as contemporaries were concerned there had never been so many women in charge at the same time in European history. Yet someone, apparently, still hadn't got the message. No study of Elizabeth is complete without a quote from the sixteenth-century shock Jock, John Knox, in his 1558 *First Blast of the Trumpet Against the Monstrous Regiment of Women*:

> To promote a woman to bear rule, superiority, dominion or empire above any realm, nation or city is repugnant to nature, contumely to God, a thing most contrarious to His revealed will and approved ordinance and finally it is the subversion of good order, and all equity and justice.

Knox's target (to his great subsequent embarrassment)was not Elizabeth herself, but the ruling Catholic women who in his view were thwarting the spread of Protestantism – the regents Catherine de Medici and Marie de Guise in France and Scotland, and Mary Tudor in England. Knox was a vociferous and powerful fanatic, but his views were by no means so representative of those of his period as it may seem. His invective is a tower of furious rhetoric, peculiarly personal. One might as well take the editorials of the *Daily Mail*, perennially outraged, permanently panicked that civilisation teeters on the cusp of destruction, as indicative of the progress of twenty-first-century history. Knox certainly had his adherents, but the idea that women were unfit to rule was outdated before he put pen to paper, both biologically and biblically.

In 1560, a Geneva translation of the Bible, dedicated to Elizabeth I, features a marginal note on the creation of Eve, arguing that man before the creation of woman was 'like to an unperfect building'. Eve's appearance signified that man was 'perfect'. This is not quite what one expects to find within the Judeo-Christian tradition of original sin ruining the party before it even got started, but it does signal an insight into the flexible definitions of gender present in Scandinavian and Anglo-Saxon linguistic structures, as well as the mutable femininity of the medieval virago. Before the eighteenth century, it can be argued, female biology was viewed very differently. Until it was possible to understand the structure and function of the female genitals, it was assumed that women's essential sex organs were the same as those of men, but simply inverted. No technical term existed in Latin, Greek or the European vernaculars for the vagina as a tube or sheath. When the eighteenth century discovered the make-up of the sexual organs, 'an anatomy and physiology of incommensurability replaced a metaphysics of hierarchy in the representation of woman in relation to man'.[6] In other words, the Renaissance privileged cultural understandings of gender (like the early Scandinavians) over distinctions based upon biological difference. This is not to suggest that society was anything other than 'intensely gendered',[7] as Knox's hysteria exemplifies, but that Enlightenment relegated a person's rank, economic role or social function to second place behind the incontrovertible absolute of biological sex. In the Renaissance, however, 'there was no true, deep, essential sex that differentiated cultural man from woman'. Where gender intersected with power, at the highest political and social levels, the distinction could be negated. It was perfectly possible for a woman to be considered, in the words of one of Elizabeth's defenders, the Marian exile John Bale, as an 'ideal prince'. Consequently, Knox's objections to female rule are much less significant than might first appear.

Bearing in mind the legal and theological distinction between the king's two bodies, John Aylmer suggested in *An Harborow for Faithful and True Subjects* that female rulers might simply be treated as honorary men, since their 'body natural' was not the salient issue: 'If it were unnatural for a woman to rule because she lacketh a man's strength, then old kings which be most meet to rule for wit and experience, because they lack strength, should be unmeet for the feebleness of the body.' Moreover, dissent towards God's anointed on the grounds of gender teetered precariously on the edge of heresy. In a 1554 letter to Knox, his correspondent observes that 'it is a hazardous thing for godly persons to set themselves in opposition to political regulations, especially as the gospel does not seem to unsettle or abrogate political rights'. Aylmer similarly justifies female rule as the acceptance of God's will: 'if nature hath given it to them by birth, how dare we pull it from them by violence? If God hath called them to it . . . why should we repine at that which is God's will and order . . . if He able women, should we unable them? If he meant not they should minister, He could have provided other.' God's will was unequivocal, and while Elizabeth was never averse to playing upon the conventions of her gender, obedience to the Providential instrument of her body politic was what she demanded.

Practically, hostility to the very idea of female rule was both ambivalent and short-lived. Equal power had already been conferred on England's first Queen Regnant, Mary, in an act passed two months after the Wyatt rebellion, which declared that 'the regal power of this realm is in the Queen's Majesty as fully and absolutely as ever it was in any of her most noble Progenitors Kings of this realm'. Despite the persistent demands that Elizabeth marry, her own sovereignty had to be kept discrete, as Mary's had been, lest an erosion of royal power degrade that of her subjects. It was very much Mary's marriage, rather than her gender *per se*, which began her descent into unpopularity. The arguments of figures such as Knox seem ultimately to have been based more on hostility to Catholicism than to female rule *per se*, and even Knox in the end conceded his point, recognising Elizabeth as another Deborah, the Old Testament heroine who brought peace to the tribes of Israel. But perhaps the best comment on the ambiguous interplay between the natural and political bodies of the monarch came from the old lady who, glimpsing Elizabeth on progress, remarked in astonishment: 'What? The Queen is a woman?'

CHAPTER NINE

To the Mantovan envoy Il Schifanoya, Elizabeth's arrival for her coronation at Westminster Abbey on 16 January 1559 sounded like the 'end of the world'. Bells, organs, fifes, trumpets and drums banged and blasted in a chorus of triumph that was impressive, if not refined. Political prince she may have been, but Elizabeth went to her coronation as a woman, 'in her hair', as her sister, mother, grandmother and great-grandmother had done. Loose hair was a symbol of virginity: the Queen came to the sacred ceremony of her anointing as a bride.

The first of Elizabeth's surviving state papers, for 17 November 1558, the day of Mary Tudor's death, included a memorandum to appoint 'Commissioners for the Coronation'. A further note of 18 December shows that five such commissioners had by then been selected. Sir Richard Sackville, privy councillor and under-secretary at the Exchequer, was made the event manager, with one of his first jobs being to arrange a fitting for Elizabeth's crown and ring. Both Elizabeth and Cecil were anxious about the form of the service, as the last time it had been employed was for Mary, and it might therefore have contained objectionably Catholic emphases. As Edward VI had done, Elizabeth used the *ordo* of the 1375 *Liber Regalis*, devised by the Abbot of Westminster, as well as referring to the *Little Device* drawn up for Richard III. Elizabeth was aware that the staging of her coronation was an essential opportunity to cement her legitimacy with her new subjects, but something more was required than a display of magnificence: namely, a means of accommodating a new, but as yet not fully realised, religious order within the ceremony itself. Effectively, from Henry VIII onwards (with the brief exception of Edward VI's minority), the Tudor monarchy had evolved as one sustained succession crisis, and as the third of her dynasty to be crowned in a space of twelve years it was essential that Elizabeth's coronation oath reflected the altered relationship between the crown and the Church imposed by her father's assertion of royal supremacy. The ceremony had to be carefully calibrated against those of Elizabeth's siblings, between continuity with Mary's reign, emphasising the legitimacy of a Queen Regnant, and the coronation of Edward VI, which had established the Protestant settlement which many in Elizabeth's council had already determined the reign should pursue.

'In pompous ceremonies a secret of government doth much consist, for that the people are naturally both taken and held with exterior shows,' observed Sir John Hayward,[1] and Elizabeth was determined on maximum pomp. In a rare instance of extravagance, the outlay on her coronation exceeded £20,000, more than 10 per cent of the projected revenue for the first year of the reign. The City of London also spent a fortune on the pageants the corporations chose to devise for the event, so much so that they rather gauchely reminded the Queen of their expenditure twice during the proceedings, once at Fleet Bridge and once at Cheapside. Coronations proceeded in four stages: the journey to take ceremonial possession of the Tower, thus securing London, the procession to Westminster, the coronation itself and the state banquet. Il Schifanoya describes Elizabeth's departure by water from Whitehall to the Tower on 12 January:

> The necessary ships, galleys, brigantines and co. were prepared as sumptuously as possible to accompany her Majesty and her Court thither by the Thames, which reminded me of Ascension Day at Venice, when the Signory go to espouse the Sea . . . her Majesty, accompanied by many knights, barons, ladies and by the whole Court, embarked in her barge, which was covered in its usual tapestries, both externally and internally and was towed by a long galley rowed by 40 men in their shirts, accompanied by a band of music, as usual when the Queen goes by water.[2]

The envoy was himself a member of Elizabeth's coronation procession, which he estimated at more than 1,000 people. Two mules drew the Queen's chariot, which was covered in cloth of gold and gold and silver tissue, while those of her ladies were draped in gold and crimson satin with crimson damask cushions (somehow Schifanoya learned that 24,000 gilt nails had been used in their construction). Elizabeth wore a gold crown covered with jewels, glowing like a jewel herself in her cloth of gold gown with a gold coif over her red-gold Tudor hair. She might have been the star of the show, but this was very much an interactive performance, a unique psychological opportunity to place herself not only in her people's eyes, but in their hearts. Thus the procession proceeded slowly, allowing maximum opportunity for ordinary folk to view the Queen (and indeed the coronation tableaux remained in place for three days afterwards, the better that people could study their meanings). At Fenchurch, Elizabeth was welcomed by a child on behalf of the city, and as the little boy concentrated fiercely on his lines, onlookers observed 'a perpetual attentiveness' in Elizabeth's face and 'a marvellous change in look as the child's words touched . . . her person'. Whatever her personal view of the poetry – and it was the City, not she, who had commissioned the pageants, Elizabeth was attentive to every nuance of its reception in her countenance. She was often to compare the role of prince with that of an actor on a stage, and in this, effectively her debut performance, she acquitted herself perfectly.

The next tableau had a deep personal significance for Elizabeth. At Gracechurch Street she encountered a triple-gated structure with three stages erected above the central gate, festooned in red and white Tudor roses, the lowest of which featured Henry VII and Elizabeth of York, the next Henry VIII and Anne Boleyn and at the top Elizabeth herself, standing alone. The Queen had, of course, made this journey before, a quarter of a century earlier, in her mother's belly, and here now was Anne, her disgrace formally obliterated at the moment of her daughter's triumph. Anne's own coronation in 1533 had featured a pageant at St Paul's, where three 'sibyls' held up three tablets proclaiming 'Come, my love, thou shall be crowned', 'Lord God direct my ways' and 'Trust in God', with, beneath their feet, a banner reading 'Queen Anne shall bear a new son of the king's blood and there shall be a golden world unto thy people'. Some of

those who witnessed Elizabeth's procession would have recalled the
'wafers', scraps of paper inscribed with the sibyls' message, which had
been scattered through the crowd as Anne rode by. Anne's placing
between the Yorkist heiress, her daughter's namesake, and Elizabeth herself not only legitimated her marriage and thus Elizabeth's
place in the Tudor line, but inevitably invoked comparisons with the
Virgin, whose mother was another Anne. The City could not have
sent a clearer message of their acceptance of the new order.

At Cheapside, Elizabeth was given a crimson satin purse containing a thousand marks in gold, and her simple, gracious acceptance
speech drove the crowds wild:

> I thank my Lord Mayor, his brethren and you all. And whereas your
> request is that I should continue your good Lady and Queen, be ye
> assured that I will be as good unto you as ever queen was unto her
> people. No will in me can lack, neither, do I trust, shall there lack
> any power. And persuade yourselves that for the safety and quiet-
> ness of you all, I will not spare if need be to spend my blood. God
> thank you all.

One old man was moved to tears, to which Elizabeth kindly responded: 'I warrant you it is for gladness.' In Little Conduit, Elizabeth
inquired as to the meaning of another display, and heard that it signified Time, leading his daughter Truth from a cave. 'And Time', she
responded 'hath brought me hither.' In St Paul's churchyard Elizabeth heard a Latin address from the schoolboys, then moved down
through Ludgate to Fleet Street where the last pageant stood. In
political terms, this was perhaps the most significant. Once again,
Anne Boleyn's coronation was invoked, this time by association with
that of Edward VI. In 1533 Anne's symbol, the falcon, had flown from
a 'cloud' of fine sarsenet into a nest of Tudor roses, accompanying
verses declaring that God had conferred imperial authority on her
as queen and on Henry's issue by her. The bird had appeared in the
same manner at Edward's 1547 ceremony, this time transformed into
Jane Seymour's falcon. (NB It is tempting for scholars to read much
significance into this mirroring, but it should be recalled that the

Tudors had a tendency to economising in public displays – in 1501, for the marriage of Katherine of Aragon and Prince Arthur, Henry VII had painted up four 'beasts', two lions, a hart and an elk, from previous pageants, which reappeared relentlessly throughout the festivities.) The scriptwriter for Anne's ceremony, Nicholas Udell, was the tutor of Richard Mulcaster, who wrote the scenario for Elizabeth's Fleet Street reception. Mulcaster, as John Knox was grudgingly to do, invoked the biblical queen Deborah, whose judgement enabled the Israelites to take the pagan land of Canaan, in a staged riposte to attacks on female rule.

In the pageant, Deborah was Anglicised into a conciliar ruler, dressed in parliamentary robes and standing above the figures of the three estates, nobility, commons and clergy. Mulcaster elaborated that the purpose of the pageant was to 'put [Elizabeth] in remembrance to consult the worthy government of her people ... that it behoveth both men and women so ruling to use advice of good council'. Royal imperialism and Godly Reformation were tied, by implication, to a polity created by Parliament under Edward VI. The meaning of that legacy was 'the conjunction and coupling together of our Sovereign Lady with the Gospel and verity of God's holy word, for the peaceable government of all her good subjects'. The powers of royal supremacy, for this imperial Deborah, would be subject to parliamentary limitation. According to one writer,[3] this argument 'infuriated' Elizabeth, but this is rather unsubtle speculation, given the quiet constitutional revolution about to be enacted at the Abbey.

On leaving the City, Elizabeth returned to Whitehall to await the coronation itself, which was to take place on Sunday 16 January. For the spectators this was the chance to see the full Elizabethan court and administration assembled together. At the head of the procession marched the messengers of her chamber, the serjeant porter and the gentleman harbinger (whose charge was the preparation of royal residences). Servants of the chamber, squires, ushers, chaplains and clerks of the Privy Seal followed, then the serjeant at law and the Queen's judges, then a crocodile of the Lord Chief Baron, Lord Chief Justice of Common Pleas, the Master of the Rolls and the Lord Chief Justice of England. After them the knights and peers, then the officers of state, led by the Earl of Arundel bearing the royal sword. The Duke of Norfolk, as Earl Marshal, and the Earl of Oxford, Lord Chamberlain, preceded four foreign ambassadors, followed by the Marquess of Winchester, the Lord Treasurer and Sir Nicholas Bacon, Lord Keeper of the Great Seal. The Archbishop of York had to walk alone, as the see of Canterbury remained vacant, then came the treasurer and comptroller of the royal household, after that the Secretary, William Cecil. Then Elizabeth, in her magnificent litter, surrounded by footmen, with Robert Dudley leading her own horse behind her. Six ladies on palfreys came after, then the three chariots containing the peeresses and her ladies. The royal guard brought up the rear.

On coronation day, the streets around the Abbey were prepared with fresh gravel and blue cloth. The cloth of gold carpet and blue velvet and cloth of gold cushions were laid out ready for the ceremony. From Whitehall, Elizabeth proceeded to Westminster Hall to be dressed in her robes of state and greet Bishop Oglethorpe of Carlisle, who was to crown her. (The Archbishop of York, Nicholas Heath, remained unconvinced – with reason – as to Elizabeth's commitment to Catholicism, and Cranmer had 'unfortunately been burned by Mary'.[4]) The reformist tone of the coronation was also set by the appointment of the Earl of Huntingdon to carry the royal spurs and the Earl of Bedford to carry the staff of St Edward, Protestants both. And for those who had an ear, it was notable that Elizabeth entered the Abbey not to the glorious – and very Catholic – *Laudes Regiae*, used since the coronation of Charlemagne, and for English monarchs from Queen Matilda of Flanders in 1068 to her father Henry VIII, but to *Salva Festa Dies*, 'Hail Thee, Festival Day'.

On 31 January 1547, in the first known proclamation to deal with the succession of the reign, Archbishop Cranmer altered the form for Edward VI's coronation in line with the 1534 Act of Supremacy. Conventionally, a king had been 'elect chosen and required . . . by all three of the estates of the realm to take upon him the Crown and royal dignity of England'. Cranmer's adaptation stated that 'the

laws of God and man' had already made Edward heir to 'the Royal Dignity and Crown Imperial', therefore announcing that Edward was King of England and Supreme Head of the Church by divine, rather than human, agency, an argument which was reinforced by the recasting of the ceremony itself, where it was stated that 'kings be God's anointed not in respect of the Oil the bishop useth, but in consideration of their power, which is Ordained, and . . . their Persons which are *elected by God*'.[5] Since the fourteenth century, the coronation oath had elaborated five requests to the monarch on behalf of their subjects – to confirm the laws and liberties that previous kings had granted to the English people, to do likewise in respect of the liberties of the clergy, to promise peace and concord to clergy, Church and people, to practise justice and mercy and to observe the laws 'as shall be chosen by your people'. Cranmer altered this so that the constitution of law, liberty, peace and concord was determined by the crown to the Church and the people, but not to the clergy, abandoned the second clause altogether and amended the fifth so that it was the people, not the king, who were to consent to new laws. At first consideration, this seemed an affirmation of the ruler's divine right, but in legal terms it meant something different.

The Edwardine reform of the Church was 'momentous'[6] in that it was accomplished not by royal prerogative, but by statute, thus changing the form of the law itself. Acts of Parliament became not only 'declaratory statements or definitions of the law as it was thought to exist', but new laws in their own right, and thus the potential of statute was no longer limited in its authority. That is, the legislation which created a new and Protestant order was not the will of the king, but generated by Parliament. So the casting of Deborah as a parliamentary ruler in the Fleet pageant was less a comment on the limitations of female authority than a recasting of royal authority in general. If the truncated reforms of Edward's reign were to pass smoothly into law under Elizabeth, it was legally essential that she be crowned in the same fashion as her nine-year-old brother had been, to reassert the royal supremacy in a manner which would constitutionally permit the continuation of that reformation by her advisers.

This legal nicety explains the confusion surrounding the

coronation oath sworn by the Queen. After processing in her crimson coronation robes from Westminster Hall to the Abbey on a blue carpet a third of a mile long, Elizabeth was conducted to a stage in the centre of the Abbey 'crossing' with the High altar to the east and the choir to the west. Bishop Oglethorpe asked if the people would have her as Queen from each of the four corners of this stage, and when the enthusiastic cries had died down Elizabeth offered at the altar, then seated herself in a chair of estate to hear the sermon, then knelt for the Lord's Prayer. There was then some rather awkward manoeuvring with books. The Queen gave a book to 'a lord' who handed it to the bishop, who gave it back and read from another book, after which Cecil popped up and handed a further 'booke' to the bishop, who then read from it. One historian suggests that Elizabeth swore the oath 'in the usual form' and suggests that the 'booke' was probably the Latin text of the coronation pardon.[7] Yet to know what Queen Elizabeth actually swore it is necessary to look forward in time, as there is no record of the words she spoke.

Given the constitutional redirection explained above, it is highly unlikely that Elizabeth swore the same oath as Mary, who had emphatically not used the 1547 form at her coronation. One clue as to the words comes from the 1644 trial for treason of the then Archbishop of Canterbury, William Laud. Laud claimed that he had *not* altered the coronation oath of Charles I in order to enhance royal prerogative at the expense of parliamentary statute. Whatever alterations had been made, he stated, had occurred under Edward VI and Elizabeth I. We know that Charles I used the same oath as Elizabeth's successor James I (with an amendment restoring the pre-Reformation formula that the king was to observe existing laws). Yet James's oath contained one formula found nowhere in any extant text, hence Laud's attribution to the 1547 or the 1559 ceremony. Yet since this was not used in 1547, it can only have been added in 1559, that is, expressly for Elizabeth. In Cecil's articles for the coronation before 18 December 1558 is a reminder to provide a copy of the oath for the Queen, and when her coronation began Owen Oglethorpe had no copy at all. The unique clause with which Cecil emerged at the vital moment was that in respect of the law the sovereign was to act 'according to the laws of God and the true profession of the Gospel established in the kingdom'. So there was nothing 'usual' about the vow Elizabeth made to her people in the Abbey that day; on the contrary, her oath was, like her, unique. And while such focus on the words she spoke might appear a nicety, her coronation 'forced the political culture of the Tudor monarchy into a new mould', one which would have a profound impact on Elizabeth's queenship and the future governance of the nation.

Elizabeth was already committed to the use of the reformist liturgy, as indicated by the appointment of the evangelical Edmund Allen as her chaplain. She had instructed that the host no longer be elevated during Mass and had famously stalked out of the service in the Chapel Royal on her first Christmas Day as Queen in 1558 when this was done in contravention of her wishes. On 27 December, she issued a proclamation ordering the Litany, Lord's Prayer and Creed to be recited in English, and announced that her first parliament would debate changes in 'matters and ceremonies of religion'. Her opinion of the idolatrous practices of the religion to which she had declared herself so devoted just months before is summed up in her verdict on the chrism with which she was anointed. Elizabeth was crowned with the oil used by Mary, who had procured it from the Bishop of Arras. The new Queen complained that it was greasy and smelly: 'Likewise for their holy oil, it is great superstition to give credit to it, or to any such feigned things invented by Satan to blind the simple people. Their oil is olive oil, which was brought out of Spain, very good for salads.'

Elizabeth herself rejected the doctrine of transubstantiation, yet the coronation Mass followed the Order of Communion of 1548, which remained technically in force. The Queen made three modifications – the Epistle and Gospel were read in English, the host was not elevated after the Latin consecration and, in plain contravention of the law as it then stood, Elizabeth received communion in both kinds (that is, she received both the sacred bread and the wine), discreetly administered by George Carew, new dean of the Chapel Royal, behind a traverse on the south side of the altar. At the moment of her crowning, the dukes, marquesses, earls and viscounts raised their coronets 'and then they put on the same and so to continue all day long until the Queen's Highness be withdrawn into her chamber at night'.

The first English Queen to undergo a coronation ceremony was Judith, the daughter of the French king Charles the Bald, who in 856 married Aethelwulf, King of the West Saxons. She was consecrated by the Bishop of Reims, who placed a diadem on her head and 'formally conferred on her the title of Queen, which was something not customary before then'. The latest crowning of an English monarch, that of Queen Elizabeth II in 1953, was not in essence so very different from the ninth-century rite celebrated in a field in northern France. Consecration and coronation were what set the monarch apart. We can glimpse something of the moment Elizabeth I experienced in its replication in the coronation of Elizabeth II, when the Abbey is filled with a heart-stopping radiance of lifted gems. As she looked down from the dais, Elizabeth saw a silvered sea of proud English loyalty, at this moment of her apotheosis. She was Queen. From now until her death, Elizabeth would be unique, sacred, magical.

CHAPTER TEN

For Elizabeth, as for all Renaissance rulers, the concept of 'magnificence' was central to her self-presentation. Discussed by Aristotle in the *Nicomachean Ethics*, it was defined as a virtue, 'an attribute of expenditures of the kind which we call honourable'. Magnificence could not be the province of the poor, since their limited means prevented them from dispensing large sums 'fittingly', but 'great expenditure is becoming to those who have suitable means . . . for all these things will bring them greatness and prestige'. In the *Rhetoric*, Aristotle lists magnificence and liberality among the constituents of virtue, while Cicero, in *De Inventione*, discusses the idea in relation to the four cardinal virtues – justice, courage, temperance and prudence, as applied to the sovereign dignity of rulers. These were writers whom Elizabeth spent her childhood discussing and translating with her tutors Ascham and Grindal, but even had her education been less rigorous, the visual and sensual world in which she grew up consistently reinforced the importance of dress, architecture, music, entertainment and precious objects as crucial components of status. Magnificent display communicated authority and power; it was a form of government, and, in the case of anointed monarchs, of the mystical connection with their divine right to rule. As her reign progressed, when Elizabeth walked or rode among her people, she did so as a goddess. The refined classical allusions with which her courtier-poets dazzled were not available to any but a small minority of her subjects, and while the seemingly endless conjurings of the Queen as Diana, Venus, Astraea, Belphoebe served varying symbolic requirements within the coterie of the elite throughout her reign, her status, her *magnificenza*, was signalled to the majority in a more immediately accessible sensual and visual fashion.

For a start, she was clean. The famously reported remark that Elizabeth I took a bath every three months 'whether she needed one or no' belies the fact that she was quite scrupulous about hygiene, bathing regularly in warm scented water and making use of the up-to-date bathrooms installed in several of her palaces. Perfumes created an important associative connection, and while the sixteenth century was in general an unbelievably filthy place by modern standards, Elizabeth's immediate environment was a fragrant one. There was a strong perceived link between not only odour and health, but morality, and washing was a key mark of gentility. Elizabeth and her courtiers used *aquamaniles*, specially shaped vessels for pouring water over the hands on formal occasions, scented with different perfumes according to the season – 'Saracen ointment' was used in autumn, for example, and in winter myrrh. Elizabeth used 'Spanish soap', which had been introduced by a much earlier queen, Eleanor of Castile, a fashionable mixture of salted wood ash and scent. Also available were scented mouth pastilles to sweeten the breath, oils and 'pommes' (balls made from powdered gum decorated with gold, which released their scent in the warmth of the hands). Her clothing , bedlinen and the cushions on which she would recline on the floor among her ladies were scented with lavender and spices, while perfume was burned in metal pans to scent her rooms. The queen's chamber made use of two pounds of orris root for this purpose in six months alone in 1564. Even Elizabeth's fires used heavily scented woods such as juniper and apple, as well as herbs. All this not only created a special, perhaps slightly intoxicating aura around the Queen, but, for many, recalled the scent of churches – the ruler and the altar smelled the same.

Even after the brutal depredations of the Edwardine reformation, church was the only place where many people had access to delicious scents, vivid colours and rich fabrics. Elizabeth's spiritual association with Marianism has been much discussed, but for those lucky enough to catch a glimpse of her this association was also visual. Many of the 'popish' trappings of Catholicism so despised by the reformers had begun, initially at least, as simple sensory messages to congregations which were largely illiterate and unable to understand the Latin in which services were conducted. Golden chalices, incense or the beautiful blue of the precious lapis lazuli paint used to depict the Virgin's cloak reinforced the sanctity of holy space. As they disappeared, the appearance of the governing class, most of all the Queen, acquired a concomitant importance. The right to govern had always been imposed through the eyes, now its spiritual dimension could be arrogated to the clothing and trappings of the powerful.

In the sixteenth century, you were what you wore. Clothes conveyed an immediate message of rank, and sumptuary laws, which governed the quality of materials to be worn by different classes of society, attempted – often with limited success – to enforce social order sartorially. Cloth was extremely precious, not just the tapestries which fluttered from the walls in elite homes, but clothes themselves – even the saddlecloths of horses had a measured value which could pinpoint status to the contemporary eye. Sumptuary legislation claimed to be protecting people from themselves; for example, Henry VIII's 1533 Act was promulgated against 'costly apparel' which contributed to the 'utter impoverishment and undoing of many light persons inclined to pride, the mother of all vices'.[1] Under Elizabeth, the aristocracy fought a rearguard action with clothing, determined to protect their privileges from the increasingly wealthy gentry and mercantile classes, thus Elizabeth made use of magistrates to enforce her Acts of Apparel, which imposed such proscriptions as forbidding velvet or satin to anyone under the degree of baron. Not just the quality of fabric, but the style of its cut was censured – certain fashions were seen as the exclusive prerogative of the higher ranks, hence the unfortunate man arrested in Blackfriars in 1565 for sporting 'a very monstrous and outrageous great pair of hose'.[2] In 1597, Elizabeth issued a precise proclamation on the subject of silk, gold and silver lace, but by then the craze for fashionable clothing was too deeply entrenched, and the Acts were repealed in 1604.

Elizabeth's tutor Roger Ascham had appealed in *The Schoolmaster* in 1570 against 'outrage in apparel', arguing that the court ought to set an example, but this was one injunction of her old master that Elizabeth was delighted to ignore. Not only did Elizabeth love clothes, but the logic of the sumptuary laws and the requirements of princely magnificence practically obliged her to be as extravagant as possible. Perhaps Elizabeth was aware of Alexandre Piccolomini's fashion guide, *Raffaella*, published in 1540, which gave tips to women on how to use dress to make the best of themselves. 'Raffaella' advised women to accentuate their best points – if they had fine hands, for example, they should show them off by putting on and drawing off elegant gloves, a technique Elizabeth was certainly noted as displaying. 'Raffaella' also warned of dressing in styles which were too young – God could more easily pardon youthful frivolity, but in old age 'loss and shame' could result from overly fashionable attire. This advice Elizabeth also gleefully ignored. Her first pair of high-heeled shoes was ordered when she was sixty-two, and she possessed more than 3,000 dresses, in the most refined and exotic fabrics – damask, silk and velvet from Italy, luxuriant furs, and, perhaps the greatest if simplest signifier of standing, the freshest, purest linen.

Linen was worn next to the skin, for comfort and hygiene, as clothes could rarely be washed, though a form of 'dry cleaning' using ingredients such as ash and pumice was employed. From 1561, Elizabeth worse silk stockings, along with her stiff whalebone stays and the farthingale, the support for her skirts which changed shape over the years from the conical Spanish style to the boxy French, which stuck out from the hips, then the wheel-shaped 'great farthingale'. Huge skirts were another signifier of status, as it took training to manage them gracefully, but they were also an easy target for the moralists. They denounced 'these bottle arsed bums', which they associated with continental, hence Catholic fashions for their 'papery and devilishness'. (Ironically, the devout Protestants who over the century became known as 'Puritans' adopted the most 'Catholic' style of all, the simple black and white costumes of the 'Spanish' style.) John Knox, never one to miss an opportunity for deriding womankind, complained that female rulers disturbed the order of nature with their 'gorgeous apparel', which was 'abominable and odious'. The complaint was as old as the hills – Eleanor of Aquitaine had been denounced in the twelfth century for wearing earrings, long linen headdresses and fur-trimmed trains – but as Elizabeth's reign progressed, women were also, interestingly, criticised for adopting masculine styles – men's beaver hats, doublet-like bodices with padded shoulders and ruffs, a disturbingly subversive trend which was 'stinking before the face of God and offensive to man'.

The ruff, perhaps the garment which most of all signifies 'Elizabethan', drove Puritans like Philip Stubbes, in his 1583 *Anatomy of Abuses*, into a lacy froth of fury. Ruffs were extremely high-maintenance, and practically functionless, having no purpose but decoration and requiring damp linen to be set in place with heated wands at 'starching houses', introduced in the 1560s (and which soon acquired a reputation as pick-up joints, rather like the milliners' shops of Victorian London). Three proclamations were issued against 'outrageous' ruffs, but the trend grew ever more elaborate; to Stubbes's horror ruffs were decorated with silk and laced with gold and silver, 'they goeth flip flap in the wind like rags that flew abroad, lying upon their shoulders like the dishclout of a slut'.[3]

Elizabeth's dresses and accessories were not only beautiful, precious and defiantly extravagant, they were also alive with meaning. The 3,000 dresses in her possession at her death formed 'a moving billboard of advertisement and signification'.[4] Emblems – roses, fleurs-de-lis, pomegranates, fountains, serpents – made her dresses a rustling, stirring tableau vivant. Sometimes this could be subversive, as in the masculine fashions of the 1570s, where Elizabeth set the trend for doublets and jerkins commissioned from her tailor, William Whittell. Queens who transgressed gendered dress codes had been severely censured in the past (Eleanor of Aquitaine was the scandal of Europe in the twelfth century for donning breeches and riding astride), and it is interesting that Elizabeth chose to adopt these fashions – admittedly very flattering – during the period when her diplomatic courtships were coming to an end. Masculine styling repositioned her from a marriageable woman to a martial prince. Official portraits, meanwhile, disseminated both obvious and subtle allegorical messages. The *Rainbow Portrait* of 1600–3 features a golden pearl-bordered cloak decorated with ears and eyes, a clear and slightly disturbing reference to Elizabeth's all-seeing authority (and, perhaps, to those in the know, to the 'spiery' which had kept the Queen safe so long). The motto makes it apparent:

Be serv'd with eyes, and listening ears of those
Who can from all parts give intelligence
To gall his foe, or timely to prevent,
At home his malice, and intendiment.

On her left sleeve coils a serpent, a symbol of wisdom, associated with prudence, but also, perhaps, an intriguing reference to Elizabeth's descent, via her great-grandmother Elizabeth Woodville, from the mythological serpent-goddess Melusina. Edward IV's queen was the daughter of Jacquetta St Pol, who in turn was descended from French counts of Lusignan, whose blood mingled with that of the house of York. The Lusignans claimed Melusina as an ancestress, a magical serpent woman whose story winds back into the legends of the Crusader kings of the French Holy Land, Outremer. Melusina was the protectress of the Lusignans, and the association in the fifteenth century led to both Elizabeth Woodville and her mother being accused of witchcraft. That Elizabeth should be invoking such an association can only be speculation, but it would fit intriguingly with the mysticism of the portrait, as an allusion to the dynastic power of Elizabeth's maternal ancestors.

In Shakespeare's late play *A Winter's Tale*, an ageing queen, Hermione, protects herself by becoming her own statue, transforming herself into her own image. In the 1998 film *Elizabeth*, much is made of the moment when the Queen, played by Cate Blanchett, paints on the official 'mask' so familiar from the portraits, as a symbol of her renunciation of love and her dedication to the realm. Elizabeth's make-up was an essential and very effective part of her image, and though its application was not quite the moment of operatic climax it appears in the film, it was nonetheless an authoritative, even a subversive statement. By using make-up so openly, Elizabeth was playing upon the cultural conventions of her era and redefining herself in terms of the perceived relationship between women, nature and art.

The debate over the relative superiority of nature and artifice was very much a Renaissance preoccupation, and again it was one with which Elizabeth was familiar. Essentially, the 'Aristotelian' view was that art could, at best, only imitate nature, as opposed to the 'Platonic' conception that art could produce superior creations to those found naturally. The debate was gendered in that the Aristotelian model privileged the masculine as superior to the 'natural' feminine and the Platonic posited a 'masculine' freedom of form (art) over 'feminine' matter (nature). A degree of synthesis between these two philosophical matrices was formulated by Thomas Aquinas, who saw nature as an intermediary between the creations of the human and the divine. The two most significant writers on the subject of Elizabeth's day, Philip Sidney and George Puttenham, thus allied art with both the masculine and the divine. For Sidney in the *Apology*, the poet is 'not enclosed within the narrow warrant of her [nature's] gifts, but freely ranging only within the zodiac of her own wit', while for Puttenham, in the 1585 *Art of English Poesie*, the poet improves 'the causes where she is impotent and defective'. Both writers propose that the artist is more 'virile' than nature herself, transcending the confines of biology to 'create' in a divine fashion.

A different view was taken by the thirteenth-century feminist writer Christine de Pisan. That Elizabeth had some awareness of Christine's work has been suggested by several scholars, as an inventory of Henry VIII shows her to have been in possession, aged fourteen, of a collection of tapestries (now lost) which illustrated Christine's most celebrated work, *The City of Ladies*. The book was translated in 1521 and the manuscript was recorded at Henry's court, but Elizabeth herself never mentioned Christine, though the potential influence of the text is intriguing, as it details the lives of significant queens and offers theories on how to resist misogyny. In another work, the *Vision*, Christine suggests a united model of nature and art, using the image of nature as a cook who feeds Chaos, forming and directing matter; rather than opposing art, nature can absorb both female biology and female intellectual endeavour. The Queen's use of make-up can be interpreted in the light of all three arguments, as a political necessity which also, literally, painted over the boundaries between her woman's body and her princely self.

Make-up was the province of women at two extreme ends of the social spectrum, aristocrats and prostitutes. Moralists disapproved of the vanity and wastefulness of cosmetics, their deplorable unchastity and perhaps most of all for their deceptiveness. If creativity was permitted to men, women, confined by their bodies, had better make do with what God gave them – 'What a contempt of God is this, to prefer the work of thine own finger to the work of God'.[5] In painting their faces, women were disguising that mortal body, transforming themselves, even challenging the social order by using 'artistry' not just to render themselves more attractive, but to redefine themselves as agents. A late Elizabethan text, Richard Haydock's 1598 *Tract Containing the Art of Curious Painting, Carving and Building*, makes the connection with artisanship clear by including a criticism of make-up, 'where a known natural shape is defaced, that an unknown Artificial hue may be painted on'.

Elizabeth's famous porcelain complexion was smoothed on like modern foundation from a foaming mixture of eggwhite, borax, alum and poppy seed, though mercury was also much used (sometimes to deadly effect on the wearer). Her face was then powdered with ground alabaster, and the cheeks and lips coloured with 'Venetian crayon', another alabaster compound, coloured with ingredients such as crushed rose petals and cochineal. Red lips were seen as a sign of good breeding, as well as youthfulness, while the luminescent glow of Elizabeth's skin evoked a jewel-like quality, a glow reminiscent of the haloes around holy figures in religious painting, the effect enhanced later in the reign by the fashion for stiff, filmy ruffs which framed the face. Elizabeth's make-up was not designed to enhance the natural prettiness which she certainly possessed as a young woman. It was defiantly unnatural, a mask of singularity, not seductiveness. The white-lead complexion (which some women attempted to naturalise by painting artificial blue veins across it), vermilion lips, darkened eyebrows and rouged cheeks advertised Elizabeth as her own creation. For Sidney, art was allied with both the divine and the masculine. Elizabeth's ostentatious painting staked a claim on these categories. Following Christine de Pisan's argument, the image she imposed on herself was not 'unnatural' in that what attracted censure in other women was appropriate for a queen. Perhaps Elizabeth, like Hermione in the play, became a prisoner of the protective image in which she encased herself, but Elizabeth also turned the moralists' criticisms back on themselves with her artistry, rendering reprehensible artifice the prerogative of a prince.

Jewellery is as much part of the Elizabethan 'brand' as her white complexion or elaborate ruffs. Jewels were, of course, a display of wealth, but they also engaged those who gave them and those who wore them in a symbolic language. Pearls, with their associations of sacred chastity and purity, were much favoured by the Queen, but sapphires and emeralds, which recalled the description of the heavenly Jerusalem, its walls built of gems, also had mystical properties. Jewel 'dictionaries', lapidaries, explain such properties. Sapphire was considered particularly appropriate for kings to wear on their fingers, believed to dissolve discord – hence, perhaps, the choice of Elizabeth's sapphire ring to be sent as the token of his accession to her patient heir James of Scotland. Diamond made its wearer indomitable, carnelian promoted concord, emerald was associated with eloquence. Thus the jewels which encrusted Elizabeth's gowns also spoke of her personal qualities. Elizabeth's jewels, many of which are listed in the inventories of the New Year gift-givings, often featured her symbols, the crescent moon, the phoenix, the pelican, the sieve. In 1571 the Spanish ambassador reported a gift from the Earl of Leicester of a jewel fashioned as Elizabeth on her throne with the countries of France and Spain submerged at her feet, and Mary Stuart grovelling in the waves. In 1587, Elizabeth received two hands in gold holding a trowel, a reference to the rebuilding of Jerusalem by the Israelites. Both these jewels have been read as encouragements to the Queen to pursue her 'godly programme' more assiduously.[6] Jewels could be celebratory, like the magnificent phoenix in gold and rubies presented by Lord Howard, or playful, like the curious Antony and Cleopatra on the prow of a ship. They swarmed with creatures – crabs, tortoises, butterflies, with flowers and leaves, with bows and arrows and swords, each conveying a narrative, a joke, a hope. Jewellery was also a means for Elizabeth to connect with people – cameo rings and bejewelled miniatures featuring her image were fashionable at court (though Elizabeth, ever stingy, tended to give away the miniature and expect the hapless recipient to provide a suitably costly setting), while medals with the Queen's portrait and a suitable emblem were a more accessible means of demonstrating loyalty. Worn on the clothing, such medals were an adaptation of the holy medals which had been used to commemorate particular saints or pilgrimages before the Reformation – so popular with the Duke of Norfolk that he rattled, it was said – another instance of the monarch's absorption of religious imagery. For jewellery, when worn by a king, had particular spiritual qualities. Precious objects were spiritually profitable:

> out of my delight in the beauty of the house of God – the loveliness
> of the many coloured gems has called me away from external cares
> . . . transferring that which is material to that which is immaterial.[7]

The light emitted by jewels, in a much darker age, indicated holiness. Elizabeth sparkled, she gleamed, she *shone* with the radiance of the anointed.

CHAPTER ELEVEN

William Cecil was perhaps Elizabeth's greatest friend, Robert Dudley her great love, but the longest, and most curious relationship she experienced with any man was possibly that with her former brother-in-law, Philip of Spain. Six years her senior, the leader of the greatest superpower in the known world was the contemporary of the lone monarch of Europe's pariah Protestant state, her relative, sometime, some said, admirer and ultimately most implacable enemy. For decades, the two were constantly in one another's thoughts, neither able to act without consideration of the other's movements, bound together by their most profound differences. Philip had been proposed as a bridegroom for Elizabeth when she was just nine, and, like a dysfunctional long-distance marriage, the tie between them was broken only by Philip's death in 1598. While their relations were governed by the impersonal demands of political strategy, they were also coloured by their mutual status as members of that very tiny elite of God's anointed. As with another relation and enemy, Mary Stuart, there was at the core of Elizabeth's feelings for Philip an acknowledgement of the mystical status of monarchy which only they could be expected to understand.

Though the prospect of a childhood betrothal had come to nothing, Philip was the first, and most powerful, suitor for Elizabeth's hand as Queen, after the humiliating failure of his first attempt at a Tudor matrimonial alliance with Mary. In the aftermath of the Dudley plot in 1555, the Venetian ambassador confirmed that it had been Philip's intervention with her sister Mary which saved Elizabeth from imprisonment, if not the scaffold: 'There is no doubt whatever but that had not her Majesty been restrained by the King . . . she for any trifling cause would gladly have inflicted every sort of punishment on her'. After the embarrassing fiasco of Mary's phantom pregnancy, the ambassador noted that Philip was much pleased with his charming, vivacious sister-in-law, whose intelligence and spirit could not have been in greater contrast to his dour, disappointed and lumpen wife, and it was not long before court gossips were giving out that Philip was in love with Elizabeth, to Mary's natural horror. That Philip's feelings towards Elizabeth were only ever conditioned by strategy is abundantly clear, but, as Queen, Elizabeth did not quite dispel the rumours. To flirt with Mary's husband while her sister lived would have been suicidal, but to have it believed that the world's most powerful man had been suffering from unrequited passion for his beleaguered sister-in-law after the fact was not displeasing. When Philip authorised his envoy Count Feria to propose for the Queen as his proxy in early 1559 he specified that he was acting contrary to his own inclinations, explaining that 'If it was not to serve God, believe me, I would not have gone into this.' Only the prize of retaining England within the Catholic fold could prompt him to the sacrifice.

Two weeks after Philip's authorisation, Elizabeth's first parliament met. Its primary goal, in the words of Sir Nicholas Bacon, Lord Keeper of the Great Seal, in his opening speech, was 'the well making of laws for the according and uniting of the people of this realm into an uniform order of religion, to the honour and glory of God, the establishment of his Church and tranquility of the realm'.[1] While Parliament debated the form of the bill for her supremacy over the Church, it was inconceivable that Elizabeth might seriously entertain Philip's proposition, since to do so would be to undermine the very principles of that supremacy. Since Philip had been married to her sister, he and Elizabeth were related within the prohibited 'degrees' specified by the Catholic Church, as set out in the Book of Leviticus. Marriage within the degrees had been a complex legal problem for European monarchs throughout the medieval period; indeed, Henry VIII had invoked it in relation to his divorce from his brother's widow, Katherine of Aragon, but solutions had commonly been achieved by dispensations from the Pope permitting related couples to marry. Such a dispensation, Feria was instructed to stress, could dissolve the objection to a marriage between the monarchs of England and Spain, but this would require Elizabeth to concede authority to the Pope in such matters. Not only would this contradict the conditions for governance over the Church which Cecil was presently so carefully calibrating in the Commons, it would effectively deny Elizabeth's own claim to the throne, since acceptance of a dispensation would be an admission that the papal ruling on Henry and Katherine's marriage was authoritative, and that Elizabeth herself was, indeed, therefore a bastard.

Moreover, in an objection which was to influence the diplomatic choreography of her marriage negotiations for the next twenty years, Elizabeth was acutely aware of the unpopularity of a foreign match. While Philip was a tremendous matrimonial prize, not only in terms of his power as a counterpoint to the threat of France, but also economically, through the crucial trade links with the Spanish-controlled Netherlands, the main centre for English trade with the Continent, Elizabeth had pointed out bluntly to Feria before she became Queen that Philip's marriage to Mary had lost her sister the affection of her people. When she received the king's formal proposal in February 1559, however, Elizabeth was obliged to play for time. If Cecil and his allies in Parliament could pass the supremacy bill in the form that they wished, it would definitively set England aside from the Catholic monarchies of Europe. In the meantime, negotiations were proceeding between France and Spain towards the Peace of Câteau Cambrésis, which would resolve the lifetime's conflict between the two countries over dominance in Italy and, Elizabeth and Cecil hoped, achieve the restoration of Calais in addition to peace between England and France.

(In 1557, the French had contravened the truce they held with Spain in Flanders. Despite the clause in her marriage treaty that 'This realm of England, by occasion of this matrimony, shall not directly or indirectly be entangled with the war', Mary Tudor gave in to pressure from Philip and reluctantly declared war on France on 7 June that year. In January, 27,000 French troops, commanded by the Duc de Guise, and not a little aided by the fatal Tudor stinginess – Mary had economised on the Calais garrison with disastrous consequences

– succeeded in taking the last pathetic scrap of the once mighty Angevin Empire in just eight days. The English had held Calais since 1347; the city was the last, crucial symbol of pretensions to continental power. Mary's reputation never recovered from its loss.)

It was therefore vital that Elizabeth at least pretend to entertain Philip's proposal in order to ensure Spanish support at the conference as the supremacy bill continued under debate. On 3 April, Câteau Cambrésis was concluded with the achievement of only the latter of the English objectives. Despite some nominal diplomatic flummery about a potential restoration of Calais after eight years, it was painfully apparent that the last remnant of England's French territories was gone for good, a humiliation Cecil felt very deeply. Two weeks previously, Elizabeth had been emboldened to inform Feria coolly that there was no possibility of her accepting his master, as she was, simply, a heretic. This was both an acknowledgement of the revolutionary gesture her government was poised to make and an acceptance on her own part of a decisively Protestant destiny. In refusing the greatest suitor she was ever to have, Elizabeth was thus making a profound political and theological gesture, one which would ultimately make of her prospective husband a potential nemesis.

The bill which Cecil prepared for his Queen's signature on 29 April 1559 was based on the 'uncompromisingly radical'[2] 'Device for the alteration of religion', which historians now concur was drafted by the Secretary himself. As the members took their seats earlier that year, Cecil had already begun a propaganda campaign in the City of London. Week after week Protestant divines, including many returned Marian exiles, preached at St Paul's Cross on the evils of the papacy and the need for true and reformed religion which would safeguard English freedoms. On 8 February, Elizabeth heard a sermon at Whitehall from Dr Richard Cox, her brother's former tutor, who had escaped persecution under Mary by fleeing to Frankfurt. It was a clear indication of the new order, which the bill presented to the Commons the following day was to establish. Under the guidance of Sir Anthony Cooke, Cecil's father-in-law, and Elizabeth's kinsman Sir Francis Knollys, the bill was guided towards presentation in the Lords on 28 February. Among conservatives it provoked outrage. Both sides invoked centuries of precedent, and the collated arguments of scholars, lawyers and theologians. Most pertinent for many objectors was the issue of Elizabeth herself – as the Archbishop of York dared to state, 'preach or minister the holy sacraments a woman may not, neither may she be Supreme Head of the Church of Christ'.[3] After Easter, on 10 April, a new amendment was presented. Elizabeth, the Commons were informed, was too humble to accept the title of 'supreme head', but would be known as 'supreme governor'. Since two of the most strident opponents of the bill, the bishops of Winchester and Lincoln, were now conveniently lodged in the Tower, charged with contempt of common authority on the warrant of the Privy Council, this rendition received a milder reception. Simultaneously, the Lords were voting on the Act of Uniformity, which required the restoration of the 1552 Edwardian Prayer Book, to be used by all ministers of the Church on pain of dismissal – a practical legal basis for the use of the Protestant religious service in English. Government and Church officials were obliged to accept both this and Elizabeth's declared governorship, and any who refused to accept supremacy or uniformity could now be lawfully punished, on an expanding scale from fines for a first offence to the ultimate crime of high treason. In the 'Device', Cecil had been calmly lucid about the threats to the realm these revolutionary measures would provoke. He predicted the excommunication of Elizabeth and the placing of England under papal interdict; he foresaw the fury of the Catholic powers and the possibility of a French invasion via Scotland. He predicted domestic dissent and even the dissatisfaction of reformers who felt that the government had not gone far enough. And what Cecil knew, Elizabeth knew.

Elizabeth was aware of her own confessional exceptionalism. A monarch who practised the reformed faith, she did so, uniquely, within a religious structure – the Church of England – of which she herself was the figurehead. In a prayer she composed herself, she was later to thank God for keeping her 'from my earliest days . . . back from the deep abysses of natural ignorance and damnable superstitions that I might enjoy the great sun of righteousness which brings with its rays life and salvation, while still leaving so many kings, princes and princesses in ignorance under the power of Satan'.[4] Elizabeth never wished to cast herself as a defender of the reformed Gospel; this became a position into which she evolved under the influence of pragmatic as much as spiritual conditions, but there can be no clearer indication of Elizabeth's private views on her religion than her active compliance within this first legal structuring of religious reformation. Her famous remark about not wishing to make windows into men's souls may well have been an acknowledgement of her reluctance to intrude on the ultimate compact between God and conscience, but from the outset of her reign she was prepared to enforce conformity, and to do so ruthlessly. The Protestant princess had come into her own, and whatever the inconsistencies of her personal practice she had stood by her Secretary in enshrining that inheritance in statute. Elizabeth could not possibly have known the personal anguish that would ensue, the challenges with which her own ethics would be confronted, or envisage the length and complexity of the process of establishing England as a secure Protestant polity, but she knew as she gave her signature to the bills that she was turning her face irrevocably from the Catholic haven offered by her brother-in-law's unwilling yet dutiful arms.

In so decisively rejecting papal authority, Elizabeth and her ministers threw down an implicit gauntlet to Spain. The conflict which came to dominate so many aspects of her reign, and which would result most famously (if not conclusively) in the Armada, had its roots in the alliance between the Spanish crown and Rome which had obtained since 1493. As part of a series of diplomatic favours advantageous to his own dynastic ambitions on the Italian peninsula, the Borgia Pope, Alexander VI, that year promulgated the bull *Inter Caetera*, dividing the recently discovered territories of the New World between Spain and Portugal along an axis drawn from the Azores islands. Territories to the east of the line were to be held as papal fiefdoms by Portugal, those to the west by Spain. In 1494, the Pope bestowed the title of 'Catholic Kings' upon Isabella of Castile and her husband Ferdinand of Aragon – the parents of Katherine of Aragon – in recognition of their conquest of Granada, the last remaining

Muslim state of the Iberian Caliphate. The title reflected an alliance between secular and sacred power crucial to Spanish dominance of the next century:

> . . . the assumption of this exemplary duty to preserve the True Faith was understood . . . as a quid pro quo for the near-miraculous acquisition of a vast and profitable empire. To challenge one was to deny the other, as Spain's future enemies well understood.[5]

Yet to view Elizabeth's Spanish policy as a defensive response to Philip's aggressive imperialism is to misunderstand the English (if not the Tudor) element of the conflict between the two nations. Philip shared with Elizabeth a self-perception of his role as the instrument of God's will, but, tyrannical evangelist of the Counter-Reformation as he undoubtedly was, English policy from the outset was aggressive as much as reactive. Cecil's 'Device' represented not only a clear statement to Elizabeth's subjects as to how the relationship between state and religion would henceforth function, but a belligerent isolationism motivated by the belief that attack was the best form of defence. The Act of Uniformity was by no means the end of the Elizabethan Reformation, whose form, in 1559, remained both incoherent and uncertain, but it was indisputable that no accommodation could be made with Roman Catholicism; the Old Faith did not permit of a relativism which could acquiesce in Elizabeth's authority to govern. Initially, though, both Spain and England sought to encourage peace. Despite the disappointment of Cateau Cambrésis, Philip had been diligent in promoting the English case and, with an eye to France, was keen to cement the amity of existing Anglo-imperial treaties with the distribution of 'pensions' to leading Protestants including the Earl of Leicester and Cecil himself.

Though there were to be many skirmishes on the way, it would take almost thirty years for Elizabeth and her brother-in-law to find themselves at war. Initially, Philip was prepared to support Elizabeth's 'heretical' state during its vulnerable early years, while Elizabeth herself never showed any inclination to diminish Catholic authority in Europe at large. She maintained for many years – sometimes with spectacular hypocrisy – that her primary commitment was to retaining peace with Spain:

> The King of Spain doth challenge me to be the quarreler, and the beginner of all these wars; in which he doth me the greatest wrong that can be; for my conscience doth not accuse my thoughts wherein I have done him the least injury.[6]

For his part, Philip moved only reluctantly towards an aggressive stance on England. Anglo-Spanish enmity was not an inevitable condition, but one which came about, slowly, through a mixture of 'spiritual ambitions and temporal grievances'[7] in which France, Scotland, the Netherlands, Rome and the New World all played a part. Nor were the policies of the papacy and Spain so closely aligned as many English people came to believe. When England confronted the 'tyrannous prosperity'[8] of Spain in 1588, few cared to recall that, had it not been for Elizabeth's rejected suitor, there might well have been no plucky Protestant England to set sail against the Armada.

CHAPTER TWELVE

Shortly after Elizabeth's accession, the Hapsburg ambassador Baron Pollweider summed up the conundrum which was to preoccupy not only the Queen's own ministers and the royal houses of Europe, but every generation of historians since – 'For that she would wish to remain a maid and never marry is inconceivable'. The bald facts are that she did, and she did. *Why* Elizabeth never married, despite her repeated public declarations of her willingness to do so, is the intriguing question.

At a wedding masque towards the end of her life, in 1600, Elizabeth was asked to join the dancing by one of her ladies, Mistress Fitton. What role should she take? asked the Queen. 'Affection,' replied Mistress Fitton. 'Affection is false,' answered Elizabeth. And yet she rose and danced. It is a very Elizabethan response, both playful and cynical. Did Elizabeth mean that all affection was not to be trusted, or that she, as Affection, was false? She performed her role, dancing at the wedding nonetheless.

Elizabeth proved that she did not believe that marriage for love was a possibility for her, no matter what sentimental gestures she occasionally indulged. Love was sport, marriage among the sixteenth-century ruling classes was business. In an age when all politics was dynastic politics, that is, family politics, no royal woman could expect that erotic attraction would have a role in her marriage. She was lucky if she was able to meet the bridegroom first. Betrothals, counter-proposals and the eventual bestowing of a woman's dowry, cognatic kinship network and person were among the tools of diplomacy, to be proffered or withdrawn according to political exigency. Like the majority of royal women, Elizabeth had been on the marriage market practically since birth, and she stubbornly remained there until her late forties, an age when many of her contemporaries were grandmothers. Courtships were a part of statecraft; they were also flattering and amusing, yet from an early age Elizabeth never intended them to be anything more.

Recalling his charge in the schoolroom, Elizabeth's teacher Ascham wrote that 'in her whole manner of life she more resembled Hippolyte than Phaedra. Which observation I then referred, not to the graces of her person, but wholly to the chastity of her mind.' In classical mythology, Hippolyte was killed after rejecting the sexual advances of his stepmother Phaedra. Since he had rejected her rival, Aphrodite, the goddess of virginity, Artemis (Diana), took pity on him and brought him back to life, which he then devoted chastely to hunting.

As soon as she was old enough to speak for herself, Elizabeth made her aversion to marriage perfectly apparent. Several suitors had been suggested during her brother's reign, including the Earl of Pembroke and Prince Frederick of Denmark, while the imperial ambassadors muttered darkly about the intentions of two Dudleys (Robert Dudley's father and his elder brother Ambrose) to put aside their wives and take the princess for themselves. And, of course, there had been the terrifying scandal of Seymour. However, serious gestures towards her betrothal were not made until it became apparent in the next reign that Mary Tudor would have no child. Philip of Spain proposed his nephew, the Archduke Ferdinand, or even his own eleven-year-old son Don Carlos by his first marriage to Maria Manuela of Portugal, but his favoured candidate was Emanuele Filiberto, Duke of Savoy. Despite considerable pressure for her during 1556 to accept the latter match, Elizabeth declared that she would rather die than have him, pointing out cruelly to Mary that 'the afflictions suffered by her' had vanquished any wish she might have had to take a husband, and that as for Don Carlos, she would not marry 'even were they to give her the King's son or find any greater prince'. This is fairly unequivocal, but the reasons for Elizabeth's objections to marriage were to evolve over time. That she had a personal dislike of marriage she made clear, though she was never precise as to exactly why. She knew of her mother's end, and of that of her stepmother

Katherine Howard, as well as the deaths after childbirth of Queen Jane and Katherine Parr and the horrible consequences of her attraction to Thomas Seymour. Perhaps, then, she was terrified of sex, but equally she had observed Mary throw away her people's goodwill on a loathed foreign marriage to a man who patently had no feelings for her beyond courtesy. Mary's obsession with bearing a son had resulted in appalling humiliation; moreover, since she was now unlikely to bear a child, Elizabeth knew that she stood to become Queen. It was irrational to marry at this juncture, particularly a Catholic candidate, and quite unnecessary when in a short time she might be able to choose for herself. Or perhaps, as she herself said, she had no desire to marry at all.

As Queen, having turned down her former brother-in-law, Elizabeth's hand was besought by Charles, Archduke of Austria, but the only person who was seriously interested in the marriage was the Spanish ambassador de Quadra. A prospective visit never came off, and religious differences were politely supplied as the reason why the match could not go forward, but no great enthusiasm was shown on either side. A more suitable, and determined contender, was Erik of Sweden, who spent practically his whole reign in pursuit of Elizabeth. In 1556, Erik had made a gaffe by sending an ambassador directly to Elizabeth, rather than to Queen Mary, who still had another six months to live. Another delegation appeared after the accession, but despite the fact that Erik himself was very much a prince of the Renaissance, a skilled singer and lutenist, a composer and a collector of fine manuscripts, his ambassadors' behaviour was less polished – 'those of most consequence at Court speak derisively of them, inasmuch as the envoy can only speak ridiculously and has no sense of decorum . . . they spend much money and are yet held as naught'.[1] Undeterred, Erik sent his younger brother, John Duke of Finland, to London in 1559, but Elizabeth was unimpressed by the Duke's scattering of silver coins in the streets and his claim that his brother would turn them to gold if he could marry the English Queen. 'The barbaric King of Sweden went to great expense for this marriage,' she admitted, 'but how could we have agreed with such a difference in manners?' She later sent Erik a rather heavy-handed gift, a copy of Castiglione's manual *Il Cortigiano*. Poor Erik was desperate to come to England to persuade Elizabeth, but was detained in 1560 by the business of being crowned, so he sent yet more ambassadors and more gifts, two ships' worth in 1560 (including eighteen horses), and twice set sail in 1561, only to be turned back by storms. His determination was such that royal souvenir sellers had already prepared woodcuts of the happy couple, and Elizabeth was obliged to write to the mayor of London in 1561 to have them suppressed. Erik continued to write elegant Latin letters to Elizabeth, and in September 1565 his sister, Princess Cecilia, Margravine of Baden-Rodemachern, arrived at court. The excitement of her visit was much increased when she gave birth to a son shortly after landing, and Elizabeth gave her a splendid welcome, but relations turned sour when the Swedish princess got herself into dreadful debt and had to retire to the Continent to evade her creditors.

In many ways, Erik would have been a highly suitable husband for Elizabeth. He was young and decent-looking, and, better still, Protestant. Swedish dominance of the Baltic trade routes secured by the marriage would have been of great advantage to both nations, and Swedish politics were to remain of much interest to Elizabeth later in the reign. Unfortunately, Erik's family, the Vasas, tended to run mad. By 1567 Erik had grown so paranoid about imagined plots against him that he personally murdered several high-ranking courtiers and was deposed and imprisoned by his brothers. He died in 1577, poisoned with arsenic in a dish of pea soup.

Erik's courtship left two legacies in England. The first was the musical manuscripts known as the Winchester part books, one of the most significant artefacts in the history of English music. They are very much Renaissance productions: French chansons set to Italian madrigals printed in Antwerp, a great centre for Italian music. Erik was trying to show Elizabeth that he was endowed with at least some of the courtier's qualities demanded by Castiglione; three of the villanelle tunes from the manuscript were used by Philip Sidney as settings of his *Certaine Sonnets* in 1570, a plaintive echo of the Swedish king's hopeless romance. The second was Helena Snakenborg, an exceptionally beautiful maid of honour to Princess Cecilia. During her visit, Katherine Parr's brother, William, the Marquess of North-ampton, fell in love with Helena, and Elizabeth gave her a place in her own household to permit their marriage to go ahead. Helena and Elizabeth grew close, so much so that when the Marchioness of Northampton was widowed after her sadly brief marriage of five months, she returned to Elizabeth's chamber and remained there for forty years.

Helena Snakenborg's marriage was that extraordinary thing, a love match, yet all that concerned Elizabeth's ministers was that she do her duty, settle on a candidate and produce a son as rapidly as possible. 'God send our mistress a husband,' wrote Cecil shortly after her accession, 'and by him a son, that we may hope our posterity shall have a masculine succession.' In 1564, at a point when Eliza-beth's court was beset by scandals and overshadowed by the question of the succession, he grumbled 'God give Her Majesty by this chance a disposition hereof that either by her marriage or some common order we subjects may know where to lean.'

In between these two complaints came Robert Dudley. That Eliza-beth loved him could hardly be doubted – certainly she was prepared to make a fool of herself over him and assuredly many people be-lieved that she would marry him – but did she ever have any real intention of doing so? The crown was barely on Elizabeth's head before her government was petitioning her to marry. During her first parliament she responded to a motion that she should take a husband quickly with a further iteration of her preference for the single state. She would have married, she explained, already, if she had desired to obey her sister, or from fear, or from ambition. Yet she had not. She had been 'constant' in her 'determination'. She concluded with one of her most famous statements: 'this shall be for me sufficient: that a marble stone shall declare that a queen, having reigned such a time, lived and died a virgin.' Of course no one believed her. What woman would not wish to marry? What woman could imagine governing alone? Yet this was never how Elizabeth saw herself. It was twenty years before she convinced her ministers into the grudging accept-ance that she had meant what she said. It is surprising that Elizabeth is so often characterised as a fickle, mercurial ruler. In this instance she set and maintained a course with perfect clarity; it took rather longer for the rest of the world to catch up.

If Elizabeth is taken at her own word, then her relationship with Robert Dudley might, rather, be characterised as a passionate and compromising flirtation than an affair which teetered on the brink of marriage. In 1559, Dudley was the perfect choice for a romantic friendship, given that he had been married to his wife Amy Robsart for nine years. Yes, he was young and dashing and handsome, a splendid dancer and a wonderful horseman; yes, Elizabeth knew and trusted him; and, yes, there was within them both the trauma of the Tower, but above all, Robert was *safe*. And Elizabeth, whose youth had been marred by so many constrictions, who had had to negotiate her way through such a maze of conflicting loyalties and temptations, did what any young single woman who suddenly found herself free and rich and happy would do. She enjoyed herself.

Robert had another function for Elizabeth. As they hunted and danced their way through the first summer of her reign, the possibility, already mooted by gossiping ambassadors, that he would find a way to divorce Amy and marry Elizabeth, kept her numerous other suitors conveniently at bay. The Duke of Norfolk and the Earls of Arundel and Westmorland were proposed as husbands, though only Arundel, who spent a good deal of time and money currying favour for the match, seemed to think he had a chance, and there was also talk of Sir William Pickering, whom Elizabeth was reputed to find attractive, though he himself confirmed that he was aware of her intention to remain unmarried. The Earl of Arran, the Protestant successor to the Scots crown after Mary Stuart, was also in the running, and Archduke Charles had also revived his lukewarm suit.

That Elizabeth would show favour to the Dudleys was not remarkable. On her accession, Robert's brother Ambrose Dudley followed his father into the post of Master of the Ordnance, while Robert's sisters Mary Sidney and Katherine, Countess of Huntingdon, became ladies of the bedchamber. As Master of the Horse, Robert was responsible not only for Elizabeth's stables but for the stage management of her public pageantry, while his physical proximity to the Queen when they rode out not only created a rare and delicious private intimacy, but gave him power, as one well placed to put suits or ask for favours. What troubled Elizabeth's ministers was the pattern of favouritism the Queen now began to show. She granted considerable lands to Dudley, and in April 1559 made him a knight of the Garter, along with the Duke of Norfolk, the Marquess of Northampton and the Earl of Rutland, all of whom were considerably higher-ranking than he. In November she granted him the Lord Lieutenantship of Windsor, which provoked a quarrel with the anxious Duke of Norfolk. No one was quite sure what it would mean if Elizabeth were to marry a commoner. English queens had done so before – as far back as the twelfth century Adeliza of Louvain had married William d'Aubigne and Isabelle d'Angoulême had married Hugh de Lusignan. Catherine de Valois had married one Owen ap Maredudd, which was the reason the grandson of a Welsh servant came to ascend the throne of England – however, these women were remarrying as royal widows. The only precedent for a Queen Regnant's marriage was Mary's to Philip of Spain. Philip had been granted the title of king, but was never crowned and anointed, as the marriage treaty stipulated that, though he was to aid his wife in governance, sovereignty remained vested in her. This had caused personal tension between the couple, and in the realm at large, when Mary submitted her sovereign will to her husband's in the disastrous affair of Calais.

Another example might be the marriage of Edward IV to a commoner, Elizabeth Woodville, whose huge family aroused enormous resentment, and arguably another round of civil war, by their incursions into the established aristocracy. Mary Tudor's marriage had been wildly unpopular, but might not the factionalism which would come about from the elevation of a dubious magnate dynasty prove equally divisive and damaging? The imperial ambassador Baron Bruener thought so: 'If she marry the said my Lord Robert, she will incur so much enmity that she may lay herself down one evening as Queen of England and rise the next morning as plain Mistress Elizabeth.'[2] The only other precedent for a queen co-ruling as anything other than a royal spouse or mother was the scandalous regime of Isabelle of France, the widow of Edward II, who, during the minority of her son, had made her lover, Roger Mortimer, *de facto* king. Sex and favourites, as Edward II had shown with Piers Gaveston and Hugh Despenser, could be a deadly combination, and while English kings had always taken mistresses as a matter of course, the idea of an unchaste female ruler was appalling. In September 1560, Cecil confided to the Spanish ambassador that he perceived 'the most manifest ruin impending over the Queen through her intimacy with Lord Robert. The Lord Robert had made himself master of the business of the State and the person of the Queen.'

From other sources, Feria reported, he had heard that Elizabeth even visited Dudley in his bedroom at night. Elizabeth's First Lady of the Bedchamber, Katherine Ashley, formerly her governess, dared to plead with Elizabeth herself, on her knees, about such scandalous rumours, warning of the 'evil speaking' around the pair and the consequent damage to Elizabeth's reputation. Elizabeth responded rather sadly that such talk was absurd, but that she wanted Robert close to her because 'in this world she had so much sorrow and tribulation and so little joy'. Elizabeth herself knew that the gossip was false – as she pointed out to Mistress Ashley, was she not always surrounded safely by her ladies – yet the poison had already spread far beyond the court. Writing from Brussels, Sir Thomas Challoner confided that 'these folks are broad mouthed of one too much in favour,' adding that he himself considered the 'scandal most false'. The Swedish ambassador felt obliged to defend the Queen from allegations that she was sleeping with Dudley, writing to his master that he saw 'no signs of an immodest life, but I did see many signs of chastity, virginity and true modesty.' The fact that he had to make such protestations at all showed that the damage Mistress Ashley feared had already been done. It grew worse with the sudden, mysterious death of Amy Dudley.

A quarter of a century after Amy Dudley was found dead at the foot of a staircase at Cumnor Place, near Oxford, on 8 September 1560, a Catholic propagandist tract, *Leicester's Commonwealth*, claimed that Robert Dudley had ordered the murder of his wife. Rumours that he had been planning to do so, and that Amy herself was fearful of being poisoned, had been current for some time. The writer of the most comprehensive history of Amy's end concludes that Dudley's dealings in the case are 'but conjecture',[3] and Dudley was exonerated from all blame, yet the disappearance of his wife provided an abrupt caesura in the relationship with Elizabeth. The Queen had carelessly ignored the gossips until now, but Amy's death could not be so easily dismissed. Dudley's reputation was severely compromised, and she felt it necessary to send him away from court while an inquest into Amy's accident was conducted. The verdict was finally pronounced at Cumnor Assizes in August the following year, long after Dudley had been reinstated, when the jury concluded that 'the aforesaid Lady Amy . . . accidentally fell precipitously down the aforesaid steps . . . and then broke her own neck, on account of which fracture of the neck the same Lady Amy there and then died instantly. . . and was found there . . . without any other mark or wound on her body'. In fact, Amy had also sustained two deep wounds on her head, which may well have been caused by the fall; the jury brought in a verdict of 'misfortune'. This did not hold back a wave of international outrage.

Writing from Paris, Sir Nicholas Throckmorton expressed his mortification:

> I am almost at my wits' end and know not what to say: one laugheth at us, another threateneth, another revileth her Majesty, and some let not to say what religion is this that a subject shall kill his wife and the Prince not only bear withal but marry with him . . . Alas that I ever lived to see this day. All the estimation that we had got clean is gone, and the infamy passeth the same so far, as my heart bleedeth to think upon the slanderous bruits I hear . . .[4]

Humiliatingly, Elizabeth was obliged to defend herself to another of her suitors, the Duke of Holstein, who had expressed his shock at the allegations that the lovers had conspired to get rid of Amy: 'she will consider it a favour if he will believe none of the rumours which he hears, if they are inconsistent with her true honour and royal dignity'.

If Elizabeth had ever had any intention of marrying Robert Dudley, Amy's death was the worst possible impediment to it. If she were to take him now, she would be considered little better than a murderess. This did not prevent continued talk of the likelihood of that marriage, particularly as they remained extremely close, and Elizabeth continued to heap favours on him to such an extent that, speaking later, she observed that she could not displace him even were she so minded, as he had clients and relatives in every import- ant post in the country; but even five years after the discovery of Amy's broken body, Cecil wrote in a memo of pros and cons he had drawn up against the marriage that Dudley was 'infamed by his wife's death'. Elizabeth was extremely sensitive about any slight to her royal dignity, so to have taken Dudley with this taint upon him, though she herself was entirely convinced of his innocence, was now impossible.

Elizabeth's care for her princely status was something she never again neglected. Over the pattern of her relationship with Dudley it is notable that their recorded quarrels generally exploded when she felt she had been in some way compromised or diminished by him. In 1562, he received a tart reminder of this when Mistress Ashley, meddlesome as ever, dispatched a servant named John Dymock to the Swedish court with letters to King Erik explaining that she, Katherine, knew that her mistress was 'well-minded' towards him. Mistress Ashley was clearly still listening to the persistent rumours of marriage between Elizabeth and Dudley, and the scheme was meant to encourage Erik, but she, and the rest of the court, had Elizabeth's answer when the Queen discovered not only the plan, but the fact that Dudley had sent two thugs to apprehend Dymock, who claimed they would watch all night for him, for fear of 'losing Lord Robert's favour forever'.[5] Elizabeth rounded on Dudley and gave him a public tongue-lashing, 'with great rage and great checks and taunts', adding that 'She would never marry him, nor none so mean as he'.[6] There was her answer, as cruelly plain as could be, though again it took some time for those around her, most of all Dudley himself, to accept it.

The contention that 'Amy's sudden and violent death . . . and the rumours and scandal that went with it, soon extinguished . . . hope. Elizabeth, unable to marry the only man she perhaps truly loved, was to remain single the rest of her life, it was the making of the Virgin Queen'[7] is in no way proveable. Clearly Amy's death, and the ignominy that came with it, horrified Elizabeth, but to attribute the complex national myth that grew up around her virginity to this one event seems overly reductive. Elizabeth had declared her commitment to virginity long before, both privately and in front of Parliament, while the 'cult of the virgin queen' (which some historians do not accept at all) was of lengthy and supple duration, responding flexibly to variant needs, and displaying different motifs, as the reign and the requirements of the nation progressed.

Writing in 1579, Petruccio Ubaldini, an Italian who had served both Elizabeth's father and brother, and who worked in an unofficial capacity as a writer of diplomatic letters to Italian rulers, produced a detailed pen portrait of Elizabeth, in which he compared her with her sister Mary in their differing views on marriage:

> . . . between her sister Mary and her [Elizabeth], there was no little emulation of virtue, but so very inclined her sister always was to marrying, also procuring marriage for the women in her royal service, as she is alien to getting married, which she does not only not seek for herself, as would be suitable, but neither does she for the other women.

Elizabeth's attempt to keep her maids of honour maids has often been remarked upon, and was often scandalously unsuccessful, and it has been suggested that she sought to retain her own mystique as a virgin by unkindly preventing her ladies from marrying. Equally, though, this may have been better served by surrounding herself with married women, who would be less likely to distract attention from the Queen's famous flirtatiousness with her male courtiers. Elizabeth's commitment to virginity, and her dislike of marriage among her women, accorded with the endorsement of celibacy supplied by St Paul, who, while he recognised the necessity of marriage (to avoid the sin of fornication), affirmed that virginity was a superior state, in emulation of Christ and His Mother. 'I say to the unmarried . . . it is good for them if they so continue.' Virginity was seen as a purer state, one which brought the individual closer to God and freed them from worldly concerns.

This view was reinforced by scholastic divines, such including Saints Augustine and Jerome: 'Death came through Eve, life has come through Mary. For this reason the gift of virginity has poured most abundantly on women, seeing that it was through a woman that it began', the latter wrote.[8] Confirmed by the New Testament, the mystical power of (particularly female) virginity had been endorsed over thousands of years, across pagan, medieval and humanist tradition, from the sexual purity of the knights of *Le Morte d'Arthur* to the endless iconography of the medieval Church, to the work of Ubaldini himself, who published a book on six celebrated women which included a description of Venda of Poland, a pre-Christian warrior queen whose virginity was read as key to her military success. At a primary level, beneath the complex propaganda of the imagery of the Virgin Queen, perhaps lay something more simple, a pious woman's commitment to what her faith upheld as a holy state, a state which she preferred to see replicated in those around her, and which also had implications for the 'chastity' of her court and thus her fitness to rule.

An alternate argument has been posited, which is that Elizabeth did not show any early commitment to virginity, and that her remaining single had more to do with conciliar wranglings – that there was, at no time, any single candidate of whom her ministers could wholeheartedly approve. The image of the Virgin Queen thus became as much a consequence of necessity – making the best of a bad unmarried job – as a conscious decision on the Queen's part. Her later deification as a virgin goddess was created in the absence of any plausible husband. But what if this had been Elizabeth's intention all along? In addition to what she herself consistently said on the subject of virginity, Elizabeth did make a powerful early statement in her choice of pose for her coronation portrait.

❦

Elizabeth's identification with Richard II in the aftermath of the Earl of Essex's rebellion at the end of her reign has become one of the commonplaces of the Elizabethan narrative, but Elizabeth's identification with Richard belongs equally to the beginning as the end of her reign. During a conversation with William Lambarde, the royal archivist, the Queen mentioned a portrait of Richard II, believed lost, but recovered by Lord Lumley. 'I am Richard II, know ye not that?' Elizabeth observed. The comment refers to a performance of Shakespeare's tragedy given before the Essex revolt, but also evokes Elizabeth's own coronation portrait, which is visible in a seventeenth-century copy, and is remarkably similar to the coronation portrait of Richard.

Known as the *Westminster Portrait*, the painting of Richard dates from the 1490s, and is an extremely rare example of individual portraiture in northern Europe for the period. The king is seated full frontal, crowned and wearing a collar and ermine cloak, the orb in his right hand, the sceptre in his left. In Elizabeth's portrait, this is reversed, as is the tear-drop effect created by the cloaks of both monarchs, which enclose their hands and torsos, emphasising the symbols of majesty they bear. It is likely that Richard's face was drawn from a pattern (a practice common in Italy in the fourteenth century and which was employed by Elizabeth's own court painters), thus, conceivably, the same model could have been used for both. The upright pose, the cast of the hands, the etiolated crowned head and impassive, smooth face, as well as the red-gold hair (for, despite later restoration, the face in the Richard portrait is considered to be original), are greatly alike. Both pictures are examples of the medieval *divina majestas*, the divinely ordained countenance of the ruler, locating them within a tradition of sacred royal images which dates back to the Romans. Both summon a holy presence in their relation to earlier religious icons, and both form part of what has been called the 'Renaissance ruler image cult'[9] which was widely disseminated across Europe.

In invoking this unique image – for there are no other medieval coronation portraits – in her own first representation as Queen, Elizabeth is physically modelling herself on the last English monarch with an unquestioned claim to the throne. The pictures create a link that overarches Elizabeth's bastardisation, the contested status of her mother's marriage, transcending her grandfather Henry VII's seizure of the throne by conquest, beyond the conflicting claims of York and Lancaster and the Wars of the Roses, beyond the usurpation of Richard by Henry IV: 'the painting, in short, iconographically abolishes a century and a half of both English history and royal iconography and returns us to the last moment when the legitimacy of the monarchy was not a problem'.[10] The mirroring is revealing in that it not only implies the extent of Elizabeth's determination on her unqualified right to rule, but several further parallels with Richard which serve to illuminate Elizabeth's conception of herself as a divinely appointed and, crucially, chaste monarch.

In Richard's relationship with his first wife, Anne of Bohemia, it is possible to detect a commitment to chastity which stretched back to the last Anglo-Saxon King of England, Edward the Confessor, and which adumbrates Elizabeth's status as Virgin Queen. Soon after the fifteen-year-old Anne's marriage to Richard in 1582, the young Queen had sought a papal dispensation for celebrating the feast day of her namesake St Anne, the mother of the Virgin. St Anne and her husband Joachim had waited twenty years for the blessing of a child. Might it be possible that Queen Anne's veneration of the saint was connected to her own fear that she would have to wait many years for a child? It is mere speculation to assume that Richard and Anne did not enjoy a perfectly normal sex life, but the fact remains that they had no children, and there are several hints that Richard had committed himself to a chaste life. In 1385, when his wife was nineteen, Richard II summoned the last feudal host ever called out in England to ride north against the Scots. About 14,000 men, the greatest army England had yet seen, the majority of the English nobility and the last contingent of fighting priests, participated in an expedition whose achievements were in inverse proportion to its magnificence. Richard's Scots expedition proved feeble and futile, but when he returned he issued a proclamation naming an eleven-year-old boy, Roger Mortimer, as his adoptive heir. Why should he have anticipated that his young and healthy wife would have no children at such an early stage? Richard's declaration may well have been a political tactic, aimed at neutralising factional competition, but his certainty that he would produce no heir is curious. Officially, the subject was taboo, as Parliament made clear a decade later in the pugnacious demand 'Who is it that dares say the King shall have no issue?', but even if it had become apparent by then that Queen Anne was unable to bear a child, this could not have been forecast in 1485. Two other pieces of evidence suggest that Richard was committed from the start to a chaste marriage, and that his marriage was indeed never consummated. In 1594, the king gave permission for his close friend Thomas Mowbray to use a badge traditionally reserved for the monarch's eldest son, displaying a crowned leopard. The use in the grant of the pluperfect tense 'si quem procreassemus' ('if we had begotten the same') has been read as indicating that Richard accepted his childless condition. The same year, Richard took delivery of the *Wilton Diptych*, the hauntingly exquisite double-panelled painting which represents one of the great artistic achievements of his reign, featuring himself being presented to the Virgin and Christ Child by a trio of Saints: Edward the Confessor, the Anglo-Saxon boy-king Edmund and John the Baptist. Richard's arms are impaled with those of the Confessor, suggesting that like his predecessor he, too, had rejected full marriage for a spiritual union with his country. Indeed, in 1395 Richard altered the royal arms, which he formally adopted on the Confessor's feast, quartering the fleur-de-lis and lions passant guardant with the Confessor's, emphasising his commitment as 'a prince of glorious peace',[11] an aspiration which Elizabeth I also shared. Richard's second marriage, in 1396, was an extraordinary affirmation of his commitment to chastity, given his by then urgent need for an heir. His bride, Isabelle of France, was nine years old, so there could be no hope of offspring for some years. It did, however, accord with his self-conception as a divine figure who ruled as God's Elect, which was deeply (and presciently, in the case of Elizabeth I) linked to celibacy. If theories as to Richard II's devotion to a chaste life are correct, then the connection with the coronation portrait signals something more than a shaking out of the wrinkles in the dynastic blanket; it foregrounds him, uniquely, as a prototype of the celibate adult monarch.

The sanctity of monarchy had been emphasised as never before in Elizabeth I's coronation, and we have seen how effectively Elizabeth absorbed and exploited the interplay between the formalised erotic desire of the courtly love tradition and religious devotion. Royal divinity was also a key component of Richard's understanding of his kingship. Chroniclers of the nine-year-old boy's coronation presented him as a Christ figure, the saviour of his troubled people, and several historians have noted in the *Wilton Diptych* unmistakeable tokens of his literal belief in his anointed divinity. Richard was alert to the iconographic power of the royal image, not only in his coronation portrait or the *Diptych*, but in the richly visual court culture which he encouraged, a more elaborate and ritualistic backdrop for monarchy than England had ever seen before. As Elizabeth's later reign was to celebrate her as a virgin goddess, so Richard's vaunted his divine right. It was Richard who introduced the titles 'Your Highness' and 'Your Majesty', which one nervous commentator ventured were not 'human but divine honours . . . hardly suitable for mere mortals'.[12]

The debacle of the 1385 Scots campaign might have suggested to Richard that war-making was not really his forte, so while he was not averse to arrogating the chivalric aura of his more successful predecessors to his own crown, he preferred to emphasise the more spiritual aspects of the knightly ideal. A fantastically mystical document commissioned from Philippe de Mézières by King Charles VI of France to encourage the match with his daughter conjures a vision of Richard as a second Arthur, the king who would finally lead England to the new Jerusalem. De Mézières connected Richard with the chaste heroes of Arthurian legend, where the Holy Grail may be glimpsed only by the pure, and also, implicitly with his Crusader ancestors, for whom the attainment of the Holy City was predicated, in theory at least, on sexual abstinence. There is no way of knowing whether Richard II was a virgin any more than Elizabeth I was, but implicitly or explicitly, the two rulers shared a need to transform that characteristic – which may have begun as a personal idiosyncrasy and developed into a political necessity – into a transcendental destiny.

Personally, Elizabeth seemed serenely assured of her own divine status. In response to the German humanist Paul Schede's *Ad Elisabetham*, where the poet casts himself in the conventional role of Petrarchan pleader – 'I place myself beneath your royal yoke/make me your bondsman, lady, and be mistress/To a free born slave' – Elizabeth (as ever enjoying the opportunity to show off in Latin) responds 'Quem regum pudeat tantum coulisse poetam/ Nos ex semideis qui facit esse deos?', 'What king would be shamed to cherish such a poet/ Who makes us from demigods to be gods?' The conscious connection with Richard II casts a different light on the romantic career of the Virgin Queen. Alongside her own statements, Elizabeth's use of her coronation portrait might be read as a commitment to holy virginity, that she will rule not as a woman but that the authority of her kingly body will be reinforced by a commitment to chastity which will elevate even her mortal body to the precincts of the angelic.

CHAPTER THIRTEEN

S table relations between Elizabeth and Philip were particularly necessary at this juncture given French ambitions both
in Scotland and England itself. Like Elizabeth, Philip viewed
the rise of the Guise faction and their protégée Mary Stuart at the
Valois court with deep suspicion. The alliance between Scotland
and France had been a matter of anxious interest for England and
Spain since the aftermath of the Battle of Pinkie Cleugh in September 1547 when English troops had defeated the Scots in the last
confrontation of the 'Rough Wooings', a series of attempts by the
English to amalgamate the two crowns of England and Scotland by
force, through the marriage of Henry VIII's heir Edward to
Mary Stuart, Queen of Scotland in her own right since 1542. The
new King of France, Henri II, had other ideas. The loss of Calais
had reversed the situation whereby the English had a bridgehead
in France; instead, Henri aimed to establish a French outpost in
England. He envisaged a Franco-British empire which would ultimately unite the realms of England, Scotland and France in one
immense power bloc. From the French perspective, the prospects
of the Tudor dynasty were bleak. Edward was a feeble teenager, his
sister Mary Tudor, whose claim to the throne had never been dis-
avowed by Catholic Europe, was thirty-four and unmarried, while
Elizabeth herself was dismissed as a bastard. The next heir in
French eyes was Mary Stuart, the child of Marie de Guise and James
V, whose mother had governed Scotland as regent since her husband's death. When Mary appealed to France for aid a month after
the battle, Henri saw an opportunity to mould his dream. By the
treaty of Haddington, on 7 July 1548, French military aid to Scotland
was formalised in the dynastic union of little Mary and the heir to

the French crown, Henri's son François. Writing to the Estates of Scotland after Mary's arrival in France, Henri declared that 'in consequence, her affairs and subjects are with ours the same thing, never separated'.[1] Henri's vision was far-sighted. When Edward died, as it increasingly appeared that he would, it might be possible that the combined forces of Scotland and France could enforce Mary Stuart's claim. In a bellicose letter to the Ottoman Sultan of 1550, Henri boasted:

> I have pacified the Kingdom of Scotland which I hold and possess with the same power and authority as I have in France, to which two kingdoms I have joined and united another, England, its kingship, its subjects and its rights, which . . . I can dispose of as my own in such a way that the said three kingdoms together can now be deemed a single monarchy.[2]

Among the French magnates who actively promoted Henri's project were Mary Stuart's uncles, the sons of Claude de Lorraine, Duc de Guise. The two eldest, the heir, François, and Charles, Cardinal of Lorraine, were given places on the Privy Council and in 1546 Diane de Poitiers, the king's powerful mistress, married her daughter to the third Guise brother, Claude II. In 1548, François married the granddaughter of Louis XII of France, Anne d'Este, acquiring a huge dowry and a significant Italian alliance for the Guise, as Anne's father, Ercole, Duke of Ferrara, was a major bankroller of French royal debt. With their sister Marie governing Scotland and the next Queen of France safely ensconced at the French court, the Guises commanded a huge and formidable power network. Yet their support for a Franco-British empire was compromised just ten years after its inception: as the biographer of the Guises observes, 'it was at the heart of this project that the Reformation rebellion would strike first'.[3] Though Henri II had initially continued his father's policy of persecuting Protestants, by the mid-1550s, when such persecution was beginning in Mary Tudor's England, executions had declined. In 1557, though, two Protestant brothers from Meaux attempted unsuccessfully to assassinate the French king. In January that year, the French had contravened the truce agreed with the Spanish in Flanders and Philip of Spain had pressured his wife to declare war, which the English reluctantly did on 7 June. On 10 August the French suffered a crushing defeat at Saint-Quentin, which many anxious Catholics interpreted as a sign of divine disapproval for the harbouring of heretics. For the Guises, confessional differences were not necessarily the central issue at this juncture, but they were quick to take advantage of the mood of national crisis and the confusion of their anxious king. Recalled from campaign in Italy, the Duc de Guise arrived in Paris on 6 October and prepared to attack Calais, the last pathetic scrap of the once-mighty Angevin Empire, which he accomplished successfully in just eight days in January 1558. Hailed as the saviour of the nation, it appeared that the Guise star was ascending even higher. When the marriage of sixteen-year-old Mary Stuart to François was celebrated that April at the cathedral of Notre-Dame in Paris, their stronghold on power in the next generation seemed complete.

Mary Stuart wore white to her wedding, always one of her preferred colours, though it was traditionally the shade of mourning for French queens. A sense of dramatic irony is inevitable; perhaps Mary sensed that the idyllic upbringing she had enjoyed in the gorgeous chateaux of the French monarchy was lost for ever. Certainly her childhood could not have been in greater contrast to that of her kinswoman Elizabeth, who had been raised in as near to the school of hard knocks as a princess could be. One of Mary's biographers asks perceptively whether indeed her charmed life at the French court was fit preparation for the tribulations she would have to face,[4] but as she followed her uncle François along the great nave, all was celebration and serenity, on the surface at least.

When the Treaty of Câteau Cambrésis was signed in April 1559, François de Guise became a figurehead for the disaffected French magnates and veteran soldiers who saw the settlement as dishonourable. Yet the family were too powerful, and too essential in Henri's project for the Franco-British empire, to be entirely marginalised. In February, Henri's daughter Claude had married their cousin, the Duc de Lorraine, in a series of festivities which horrified

Elizabeth's ambassador when he noticed that Mary Stuart and her husband had quartered their arms with those of both Scotland and England. The young couple had been calling themselves 'King and Queen Dauphins of Scotland, England and France' since January that year, but this display of the arms was a brazen and aggressive statement of intent. It was soon to be put to the proof. On 1 July, Henri's vizor was shattered by a lance as he ran in the celebratory tournament to mark the peace with Spain. Nine days later he was dead, and Mary Stuart was now in fact Queen of both Scotland and France.

The 'black legend' of the Guises derives from this moment, when they swooped down upon the physically and intellectually limited new king and his mother, Catherine de Medici, and carried them off to the Louvre. Like Richard III of England, they are portrayed as panto characters of history, the wicked uncles rubbing their hands in the background as they send their innocent young relatives to their doom. In terms of strategy, there is considerable continuity between the reigns of Henri and François II, while their position on Protestant heresy was in no measure so clear cut or decisive as either they or subsequently hostile chroniclers were prepared to concede. In Scotland, however, conflict between the old faith and the new had already provoked a crisis. Riots had broken out in May, prompting Henri, just before his death, to communicate his intention to send an army to crush the insurrectionary reformers to the Pope. When the Guises achieved their velvet revolution, the Protestant Lords of the Congregation were quick to fulminate against 'the fury and rage of the tyrants of this world . . . the insatiable covetousness of the Guises generation'.[5] In promoting their ambitions in Scotland, the Guises made two mistakes. Firstly, they assumed that asserting their niece's Catholic credentials in Scotland would be a strength, and second they underestimated the consequences of their imperialist attitude on Elizabeth's policy. While the French court was at Amboise in December 1559, the arms of Mary and François were again displayed, accompanied by a Latin inscription, the translation of which reads:

Gaul and warlike Britain were in perpetual hostility . . . Now the Gauls and the distant Britons are in a single territory – Mary's dowry gathers them together in one Empire.

With Marie de Guise writing frantically to her brothers for troops to aid her in quelling the chaos in Scotland, an English declaration of support for the Congregation could prove disastrous. But the arrogance of such statements was an intolerable provocation, and Elizabeth swiftly recognised that she could not afford to remain neutral.

In the 'Device' he had composed in 1558, the all-seeing Cecil had noted that the Reformation in England was to a considerable extent dependent on the balance of power across the northern border. It has been argued that English anxiety over Mary Stuart's display of English arms has been exaggerated – did not Elizabeth after all continue to use those of France? Yet the English claim in France had been desuete for a century, and now with Calais gone was meaningless, while French power in Scotland was a genuine menace. Initially, though, Elizabeth was reluctant to engage with Scotland, where the Lords of the Congregation were, in her view, rebelling against their sovereign, and until the death of Henri II had confined herself to sending carefully rehearsed envoys to Edinburgh, who gave a good many flowery speeches without committing either English money or English troops. As Sir Nicholas Throckmorton's furious reports of Mary and François's pretensions arrived (he had even been served at dinner from silver plate bearing the arms), Cecil prepared another radical memorandum, 'of certain points meet for restoring the realm of Scotland to the ancient weal'.

The terms of what became the Treaty of Edinburgh stipulated that Mary Stuart could nominate the twelve councillors who would govern the country, with the acceptance of the Scots parliament. No position was to be given to a French subject. If these terms were not kept, England had the right to intervene in Scotland in order to safeguard the Protestant faith. If Mary Stuart, influenced by the 'greedy and tyrannous affection of France', was unwilling to agree to this, then the crown should pass by consent of the Estates of Scotland to the next heir. It took another forty-four years for Cecil to get his way, but in the end this is precisely what happened. Cecil saw in 1559, as the Guises did not, that reformation was a splinter that, with sufficient strength and perseverance, could be levered into creating a permanent rift.

In December, the arguments for and against intervention in Scotland were debated at Whitehall, where most of Elizabeth's advisers took a conservative view. England was simply not strong enough to confront the French, therefore it was unwise, as well as unnecessary, to give overt support to the Congregation. When Cecil received intelligence on 26 December that the French navy was prepared to sail, with 15,000 German mercenaries ready to deploy, the council met again, and this time voted with only the exception of the Earl of Arundel to go to war. Elizabeth listened to the arguments the following day, but still refused to sanction the initiative. Cecil was so frustrated that he even prepared a letter of resignation, but he continued to insist to the Queen that she had to take action against her mortal enemies, Mary and the Guises. Only when Elizabeth heard that François II had issued letters patent confirming the Marquis d'Elbeuf (Mary Stuart's youngest Guise uncle) as his official Lieutenant in not just Scotland but England, too, did she allow herself to be swayed.

Why was Elizabeth so obdurate? She knew that she was poor, and weak. Confronting the French was a huge risk, one that could potentially bring her government and her Church down. How could she not be acutely sensitive to Mary's claim, given that her own remained so contentious in European eyes? Moreover, she was a new queen, still in her twenties, and she had occupied her throne for less than two years. She had to establish her authority with her own councillors, experienced though they were, to remind them that it was her will and hers alone which would ultimately determine policy. Finally, it was her own belief in the sanctity of monarchy, in the justice of her birthright, which had sustained her throughout the tumultuous years of her siblings' rule, and however powerful the political arguments in favour of the Lords of the Congregation, they remained in rebellion against their anointed queen. For Elizabeth this was the most significant, even mystical factor, one with which it is perhaps hard to empathise from the distance of our own age, when *realpolitik* is the only politics, yet the conflict between chivalry and statecraft at which Elizabeth was subsequently to become so adept was still emerging in the mid-sixteenth century. Ideology may have been the future, but the divine right was by no means a thing of the past, and Elizabeth would not be prepared to challenge it for a long time to come.

Adherents of the Scots Nationalist cause rarely mention that it was the despised English who saved them from French occupation in 1560. By the Treaty of Berwick in March, Elizabeth finally agreed to send military aid to the Protestant Lords. Six thousand troops were mustered and the port of Leith was blockaded. The French went so far as to appeal to Philip of Spain, but Philip was more concerned at that time with the threat of a Guisard empire than with reformist heretics, maintaining that the Scots should govern their own affairs. The Lords demanded the withdrawal of all French troops, who had no stomach to linger: by June the Frenchmen besieged at Leith were eating *fricassée de rat*. Marie de Guise succumbed to illness and died on 10 June, and by early July Cecil had completed (though not ratified) the Treaty of Edinburgh, which was to become 'the touchstone of his career; he would measure everything by it, and judge everything against it, for nearly thirty years'.[6] Triumphantly, the Scots Lords proclaimed in August that they no longer accepted papal jurisdiction and that the Mass was now outlawed.

The Guises remained the dominant political faction in France, but the country was now descending into the civil wars which would engulf it over the next three decades. As they had risen on the sudden death of one Valois king, they began to fall on that of another, for at the end of the year Mary Stuart's young husband, as feeble in body as he was stunted in mind, died of an infected abscess in his ear. Another woman ruler, Catherine de Medici, now assumed the Regency of the kingdom, but for Elizabeth, who had prided herself on being, famously, 'the best match in her parish', it meant that she now had a rival in the dance of diplomatic courtship for which she had already developed an agile taste. Beautiful, impeccably regal, Mary Stuart was now back on the marriage market, and, worse still, it appeared that she would soon be back in Scotland.

CHAPTER FOURTEEN

Mary's attitude on her return to her kingdom in 1561 was cautiously conciliatory. She confirmed that she would make no attempt to dispute Scotland's religious settlement, so long as she might practise her own faith in private, but she refused, very sweetly, to ratify the Treaty of Edinburgh on the grounds that she ought first to establish and consult her new Council in Scotland. Cecil had no truck with such evasiveness, writing to Thomas Randolph, the English ambassador to Scotland, of his fears that Mary intended to overturn the Congregation's accords, while Elizabeth was simply infuriated. In a rare moment of impetuous temper, she refused her permission for Mary to pass through England, which allowed Mary to portray herself as the victim of the piece. She mortified Throckmorton by claiming ingenuously that since Elizabeth would not allow her to travel through England, well, then, she must reach her kingdom by sea, 'and then the Queen your mistress shall have me in her hands to do her will; and if she be so hard hearted as to desire my end, she may then do her pleasure and make sacrifice of me'.[1] In the event, a few English galleys merely saluted the Scots queen's brave entourage of just sixty as they made their way to Leith. The timing of Mary's arrival was not deliberately provocative, but it could not have been more exasperating to Elizabeth. Since her coronation, she had not been allowed to forget the issue of the succession for a moment. Her romance with Leicester was effectively at an end, though its bittersweet shadow would stretch until the Earl's death and beyond. Now, not only was Mary Stuart claiming her rights north of the border, but the next designated heir in the English line, Katherine Grey, was discovered to be pregnant.

Katherine, the second daughter of Henry VII's granddaughter

Frances Brandon, had known the Queen since girlhood. She had
been married to Lord Herbert, the son of the Earl of Pembroke,
in the same ceremony which had united her elder sister Jane with
Guildford Dudley in 1553, though the marriage had subsequently
been dissolved under Mary Tudor. Katherine and her sister Mary had
been spared Jane's horrible end; six months after her execution they
had been invited to court with their mother Frances, who served
in Mary's Privy Chamber, and, like Elizabeth, they had waited out
her reign as compliant Catholics. Frances Brandon (who had never
pressed her own claim, which earned her Elizabeth's approval) died
in 1559, and Katherine assumed that she would be designated as Elizabeth's heir under the terms of Henry VIII's will. Instead, she found
herself demoted, within a court acutely sensitive to hierarchies of
physical space, from the Privy to the Presence Chamber. According
to the Spanish ambassador Feria, Katherine was unable to conceal
her sense of injustice, delivering 'arrogant and unseemly words' to
the Queen. The strength of her claim was, however, legally dubious.
Since her father, the Duke of Suffolk, had been executed alongside
his older daughter in 1554 in the aftermath of the Wyatt rebellion,
his family were technically under attainder for treason, but in the
absence of a royal husband, much less a royal baby, there were many,
evidently including Katherine herself, who considered it remained
valid. Elizabeth never betrayed any particular liking for Katherine,
but in 1560 she was reinstated to the Privy Chamber (where a closer
eye might be kept on her?) and accompanied the Queen on her first
summer progress, which included the palaces of Eltham and Nonsuch. Here she became close to Edward Seymour, Earl of Hertford,
another second-generation victim of the deadly power game of Tudor
politics. Seymour was the heir, through his second marriage, of the
former Lord Protector, the Duke of Somerset. By the late autumn,
the flirtation between the young couple had progressed so far that
they were emboldened to make a secret marriage, celebrated at Hertford's home at Cannon Row in the presence of just a single priest and
Hertford's sister Jane. Katherine continued in service to Elizabeth,
but by July 1561 she was in a desperate position. Somehow, in the
cramped and very public conditions of the court, she had managed

to conceal the fact that she was expecting a child, and she was now nearing its delivery. Her husband was away in Paris and in desperation she turned to the Earl of Leicester, once her fellow prisoner in the Tower, who agreed to inform the Queen. Elizabeth's reaction was swift and entirely unsympathetic. Katherine was tainted with her family's audacious treason, she had foolishly confided in the Spanish ambassador when she felt herself put aside, she had dared to marry – or claim to marry – without Elizabeth's consent, and she was heavily pregnant. Hertford himself was a minor descendant of Edward III – he had no claim of his own – but married to Katherine, the Protestant heiress and possibly the father of a son, he represented a threatening prospect. No one knew better than a Tudor that the slightest claim to a throne could sometimes be made strong enough to capture one. Elizabeth naturally suspected a plot. Katherine was sent to the Tower immediately, with Elizabeth declaring that she would 'have no manner of favour, except she will show the truth'. She was questioned on 22 August but could not or would not reveal anything of substance about her marriage. The only other wedding guest, Jane Seymour, had died aged nineteen the previous March and Katherine had no means of finding the priest who could corroborate her story. Summoned from Paris, Hertford, too, was in the Tower on 5 August.

In September 1561, William Maitland, the Queen of Scots' envoy, rode south to Hertford Castle on embassy to Elizabeth. His mistress had been in Scotland for just thirteen days, and her place in the English succession was among her priorities, so ingratiating herself with Elizabeth was, to Mary, natural. Had she not remarked to the Duke of Bedford that 'We are both in one isle, both of one language, both the nearest kinswoman that each other hath and both Queens'?[2] Only the last of these considerations ever carried any weight for Elizabeth; for the rest, it is a measure of Mary's stupendous political naivety that she even thought she had a hope. Charm was no substitute for submission, and beneath the niceties lurked the adamantine issue of the English succession. Maitland found Elizabeth in a state of obvious anxiety, 'To all appearance falling away . . . extremely thin and the colour of a corpse.'[3] Her irritation at his mission, that she should recognise Mary as her heir, was equally obvious. Elizabeth told Maitland she had expected quite another message from the new court in Scotland, that is, Mary's readiness to ratify the treaty of Edinburgh. She concluded their interviews with an explanation to Maitland as to why his own 'device for the succession' was impossible. Princes, she said, could never trust even their children in matters of succession. Moreover, 'I know the inconstancy of the people of England, how they ever mislike the present government and have their eyes fixed on that person that is next to succeed, and naturally men be so disposed: *plures adorant solem orientem quam occidentem* [more men worship the rising than the setting sun]'. Her final remark suggested that this maxim applied as much or more to the young woman in the Tower than the one in Edinburgh; there was 'more matter hid' in Katherine's marriage, she confided to Maitland, 'than was yet uttered to the world'. Two days after Elizabeth was greeted by adoring crowds as she returned to London, Katherine Grey gave birth to a son.

To have the weakness of the Elizabethan succession thus exposed was agonising for the government. For William Cecil it was also a personal embarrassment. His brother-in-law, William, was married to Katherine's cousin, the daughter of Lord John Grey of Pyrgo. Both Lord John and the Earl of Hertford's mother petitioned the Secretary to appease Elizabeth, but to no avail. Mary Stuart's response to Elizabeth's frank conversation with Maitland had been to have her Parliament question the validity of the clause in Henry VIII's will, which excluded the Stuarts, a month after the baptism of Katherine's son Edward, Lord Beauchamp, who was under the terms of that will the Protestant heir male which the nation so urgently required. The Queen would simply not countenance the baby's legitimacy, thus Cecil, despairing, to Throckmorton that Christmas:

> I do see so little proof of my travails by reason her Majesty alloweth not of them, that I have left all to the wide world. I do only keep on a course for show, but inwardly I meddle not, leaving things to run in a course as the clock is left when the barrel is wound up.

Elizabeth never forgave Katherine Grey. She and Hertford somehow contrived to get another son while both were imprisoned, but Elizabeth never even considered acknowledging the claim of Edward Seymour or his younger brother Thomas. Hertford was fined an astronomical £15,000, and remained in the Tower for nine years. Katherine was released after Thomas's birth and for the last four years of her unhappy life was moved from custodian to custodian, dying of tuberculosis at twenty-seven in 1568 at Cockfield Hall in Suffolk, exacerbated by several years of self-starvation.

Hertford managed to rehabilitate himself in 1591, when he gave a three-day entertainment at Elvetham for the Queen that may have cost as much as his fine. Featuring poetry by John Lyly, three artificial islands, a specially constructed withdrawing room in the garden and a water pageant where Nereus, prophet of the sea, delivered a speech to 'Fair Cynthia, the wide Ocean's Empress' as a warship with a cargo of jewels sailed towards the Queen, a banquet off a thousand pieces of plate, a fireworks display and a fairytale castle with the royal arms all built in sugar, Hertford's effort achieved the remark, as Elizabeth departed, that 'hereafter he should find the reward thereof in her especial favour'. Even after thirty years of disgrace, Hertford couldn't resist a subtle dig at Elizabeth's own lack of an heir. As the elderly Queen rode through the park towards the house, to the sound of verses proclaiming her 'a great Goddess whose beams do sprinkle heaven with unacquainted light', six virgins carried blocks away from her horse's path. The barriers had supposedly been laid by 'Envie'.

Elizabeth's refusal to settle the matter of the succession had consequences beyond the wretched fate of Katherine Grey. So long as England had no confirmed Protestant heir, the realm would remain vulnerable to Catholic incursion. This threat was brought into sharper relief by the events in France of March 1562. Much attention has been given to the St Bartholomew's Day Massacre which occurred in Paris a decade later, when the Huguenot magnates of France were murdered in a killing spree which engulfed the populace of the city, but the wars of religion which were to bloody Europe for thirty-six years might properly be said to have begun that spring, in a small town in what is now the province of Haute-Marne. It was as a result of Wassy that 'massacre', previously used to indicate the chopping block used by French butchers, took on a much more sinister connotation.

On 1 March, Mary's uncle, the Duc de Guise, was travelling through the town from his seat at Joinville when he stopped so that his men might hear Mass. Hearing bells in the streets, the Duc was informed that the town's Protestant community were proceeding to Sunday service. Wassy comprised part of Mary Stuart's royal dower, with Guise holding its lordship in protection of his niece's rights. He felt both challenged and outraged when it appeared that the Protestants, who in theory were permitted to conduct their own services beyond the town walls, were usurping his right to hear Mass by worshipping within Wassy's precincts, within sight and jurisdiction of the royal castle. Guise later claimed that he had invaded the Protestant gathering in order to reprove the congregation with their infraction, but his men lost control, or he lost control of them, with the result that fifty people were put to the sword.

Guise later dismissed the event, accounts of which were soon streaming off the printing presses in all European languages, as an 'accident', one not motivated by religious sectarianism, but by the 'arrogance' of 'vassals' who ought to have known better than to challenge his – and his niece's – authority. His assessment was just in that the religious conflict which came so powerfully to shape Elizabeth's reign had its birth in the interconnection between faith and authority, most particularly royal authority. The massacre at Wassy had two profound implications for Elizabeth's government. Firstly, Protestants were being openly slaughtered by a Catholic power. Secondly, the massacre was conducted, at least in terms of the feudal understanding of politics which the wars of religion would sweep away, in Mary Stuart's name. Mary's French allies, notably her Guise relatives, had proved the extent of their ruthlessness in quashing reformed religion, and it is important to consider this as a background to the relationship between Elizabeth and Mary in the 1560s. Woodcuts depicting the massacre were widely disseminated in London; their inked silhouettes were a reminder to Elizabeth of the extent to which her cousin in the north might be prepared to go in her pursuit of her claim to the throne.

In September 1564, Elizabeth received Sir James Melville as Mary Stuart's envoy to court. At a first reading, she does not come off well in Sir James's recollections of their encounter. Frankly, she showed off. 'Who was fairer?' she demanded. They were respectively the fairest of them all in their own countries, replied the diplomat, conceding that Elizabeth's complexion was whiter but that Mary was equally lovely. And which of them was taller? Melville was obliged to admit that Mary, at a model-like five feet eleven, had the advantage. 'Then,' crowed Elizabeth, 'she is too high, for I myself am neither too high nor too low.' Did Mary read, did she hunt, Elizabeth asked nosily, and what about music? Was Mary an accomplished performer? Melville replied that his mistress was reasonably skilled, for a queen. That evening, the Scots envoy was conducted to a gallery overlooking a chamber, and there Elizabeth was, beavering away on the virginals. Naturally, Melville was ravished at his 'accidental' intrusion and confessed the English Queen's musical superiority. The next evening Elizabeth exhibited herself on the dance floor, obliging Melville – who had extended his visit by two days in order to have the honour of watching the Queen dance – to remark that Mary's steps were not so 'high' nor well-disposed as her own.

Why would Elizabeth comport herself so foolishly? Certainly she was vain and certainly she was curious, but she was also quite aware that a great deal more was at stake than her skill at dancing. This retreat into femininity reads like a deliberate ploy, a presentation of herself as unthreatening, preoccupied with how well her 'Italian' dress set off her hair, for example, which was an effective distraction from, and a barrier to, Sir James's need for more penetrating inquiries. It is characteristic of Elizabeth's behaviour towards Mary that she consistently invoked models of the feminine when it suited her, to evade the more hard-headed realities in play. Indeed, in the entirety of her relations with Mary throughout the long Anglo-Scots crisis (and especially, as we shall see, at its conclusion), Elizabeth deployed the three main strategies of invoking contemporary clichés of femininity, arrogation of masculine qualities and references to the masculinity of her 'mystical body' which she had established, and employed according to circumstance, since her accession. Reconsidering her encounter with Maitland, it can be cast as a masterpiece of diplomatic choreography, not least because of its actual use of dance as a means of communication.

In 1589, one of Elizabeth's gentlemen of the chamber, John Stanhope, wrote to Lord Talbot on the state of the fifty-nine-year-old Queen's health, observing that 'six or seven galliards of a morning, besides music and singing is her ordinary exercise'. Elizabeth had been noted dancing with the Duke of Norfolk 'splendidly arrayed' at her coronation, and references to dancing at Elizabeth's court are abundant throughout her reign – from the Venetian ambassador Paolo Tiepolo in 1559, through Sir Thomas Smith on the Christmas balls in 1572, to approval of the 'magnificently robed women' of the 1585 Christmas court, to the curmudgeonly remark by a visiting Spaniard in 1599 that he had witnessed 'the head of the Church of England and Ireland dancing three or four galliards'. Yet dancing meant much more to Elizabeth than a pleasant and healthy pastime. As recent scholarship has shown,[4] dance in the sixteenth-century court was a signalling system, deeply integrated into any celebration or cultural event. Status could be indicated during a court masque or ball by who danced with whom and in what order, and the position of the monarch within that space. Authorities such as Castiglione, the Italian historian Francesco Guicciardini and Elyot concurred that dance was both a virtue and a means to virtue, Sir Thomas Elyot terming it 'a model of prudence in action'.[5] For the courtier, dance was a means of exhibiting the innate nobility which merited advancement and favour. A good dancer could achieve political and social success, witness Sir Christopher Hatton, who 'came to the court by the galliard', his prowess referred to in Ben Jonson's 1603 masque *The Satyr*:

> They came to see and to be seen/And though they dance before the Queen/There's none of these do hope to come by/Wealth to build another Holmby [Holmby being Hatton's grand country estate].

For a monarch, dance was a part of their political apparatus. Henry VIII was an accomplished dancer – the Milanese ambassador depicts him in 1514, in a sort of Renaissance *Saturday Night Fever*, barefoot and in his shirt, 'leaping like a stag' and spinning the girls into raptures. Dancing was one of the few means of physical display available to a female ruler (Catherine de Medici also employed it effectively), and as such it was also a virile, 'princely' activity, as the Duke of Alençon observed in 1581, declaring himself impressed with Elizabeth's conduct in 'matters of princely pleasure, as dancing, music, discoursing . . . and perfection of many languages'. The association of language and dance, the language of dance and the dance of language, is interesting here. Diplomatic conversations such as those between Elizabeth and Melville proceeded with the same stately measures as a dance, first the mutual reverence, then the courtesies offered and returned, then the movement through prearranged steps, with allowance for judicious improvisation on either side, then concluding as it began in a bow. Recast as a dance, linguistic and actual, Elizabeth's reception of Melville looks rather different.

The subtext of the interaction between Elizabeth and Melville glares, but never surfaces. Elizabeth's remarks may have been confined to competitive feminine trivialities, but the agenda both knew themselves to be discussing was whether or not Elizabeth was prepared to concede a serious conversation to the Scots ambassador on the urgent issue of the succession. She was not. After the interval of musical comedy when Melville had duly admired her performance, he attempted to use the 'occasion to press his dispatch'. Elizabeth was having none of it. Persuading him to remain at court for a further two days to watch her dance involved a loss of status for Melville, an admission that he was weak enough to have to attend on the Queen's pleasure. Thus Elizabeth used her dancing to invoke the practice of courtly love, forcing Melville into the role of attendant swain: 'Elizabeth's dancing is a key element in these conversations . . . she clearly incorporates her actual dancing or musical abilities as well as the discussion of her dancing in a manoeuvre that presents her as superior'.[6] When Melville grants that Elizabeth's 'Italian' manner of dancing is finer than that of his mistress, he admits a surrender. His 'dispatch' will not be pressed this time.

Elizabeth used dance on several similar occasions to make a diplomatic point. Roger Aston, a later messenger from the Scots court under James VI, was treated to a similar 'impromptu' performance, 'placed in the lobby, the hanging being turned him, where he might see the Queen dancing to a little fiddle'.[7] This was interpreted by Aston as meaning that he might 'tell his master by her youthful disposition how likely he was to come to the crown he so thirsted after'. In 1597, the ambassador of Henri of Navarre, de Maisse, came 'accidentally' upon Elizabeth playing the spinet in her chamber on Christmas Eve. When he had praised her execution of the piece, they watched her ladies dance, during which Elizabeth casually remarked that she had convened her council (which de Maisse had been unsuccessfully pressing for since his arrival), and suggested he attend. Only when the courtesies of diplomatic choreography had been observed was Elizabeth prepared to turn her attention to actual politics – assuming, of course, that her partner had performed with due 'honour, prudence and decorum'. In 1599, the Danish ambassador observed Elizabeth dancing with the Earl of Essex on Twelfth Night, 'very richly and freshly attired' – again, an important signal of favour towards an individual who was presently at the centre of much discord. In 1601, when Elizabeth entertained the Russian and Barbarian ambassadors along with the Duke of Brachiano, Virginio Orsini, she accorded him the great (if not quite truthful) honour of stepping out with him for the 'first time in fifteen years'. Orsini, a nephew of the grand Duke of Tuscany and a cousin of the Queen of France, was the most significant Italian figure yet to have visited Elizabeth's court. It was necessary to impress him, and Elizabeth did so, prompting him to write that he 'seemed to have become one of those knights travelling in enchanted palaces'.[8]

In 1563, Elizabeth made the distinctly peculiar proposal that Mary Stuart should marry her own favoured dancing partner, Robert Dudley. Melville's visit the following year was, in form at least, a pursuance of this bizarre alliance. To render the man whom Mary had once dismissed as her cousin's horse-keeper more attractive, Elizabeth took the opportunity to ennoble Dudley as the Earl of Leicester on 29 September, demonstrating their familiarity to a rather shocked Melville by stroking his neck above his collar as he knelt to be dubbed. It was a balletic gesture, at once girlishly unqueenly and also a reminder, given their physical postures at the time, of the threat incipient in regal favour. Since Elizabeth had no intention of marrying Leicester herself, the plan is not so strange as might first appear. Scotland would have a reformist consort and Elizabeth herself would have a loyal servant in Mary's very bed. Moreover, if Elizabeth settled the succession as Mary so ardently wished, Leicester's son might one day be king, the greatest reward Elizabeth could bestow for his service. When representatives of the two queens met at Berwick in November, Mary's envoys made it plain that she would not countenance marriage under any other condition. And Elizabeth stepped back.

Interpretations of Elizabeth's aim to push Mary into marriage with Leicester vary. Some argue that this was yet another diplomatic game, a means of encouraging Mary to think that Elizabeth had her interests at heart while buying time to keep more powerful suitors at bay. Others cast this as Elizabeth's first venture into controlling her own policy and judge it as 'a terrible miscalculation'.[9] On balance, the former view seems more probable, but in wasting time on the Leicester negotiations Elizabeth was making a misjudgement, in that she neglected the threat of a far more dangerous family than the Dudleys. Elizabeth's disgust with Katherine Grey's behaviour also plays into her misunderstanding of Mary's character. She simply never counted on Mary behaving in an unqueenly fashion. She could control herself, why could not Mary? Unlike Katherine, they were both born royal. And perhaps this is the key to Elizabeth's consistent bafflement, over the coming years, at Mary's behaviour. No matter how much Elizabeth strived to create herself as the serene, all-powerful monarch of the *Armada portrait*, a part of her always remained that contained, wary princess. The difference between their childhoods manifested itself in their endless frustrated communications – in a fashion Elizabeth never took her status for granted, while Mary, uncontested queen, darling of the French court before her seventh birthday, took it equally for granted that rules just didn't apply to her. Her hasty, passionately incautious marriage to Henry, Lord Darnley, was a disastrous case in point.

Elizabeth's cousin, Margaret Douglas, was the daughter of Henry VIII's elder sister, Margaret Tudor She was married to Matthew, Earl of Lennox, one of the most powerful Scots magnates. Margaret was given to vociferous meddling – her incautious remarks about uniting the Tudor blood of her eldest son, Henry Darnley, with that of Mary Queen of Scots, had already landed her under house arrest and her husband in the Tower – yet, despite this, in April 1564, Elizabeth apparently considered that the Earl of Lennox could be useful to her in Scotland. He travelled the same month as Robert Dudley was granted his earldom, but Elizabeth was 'hopelessly behind the game'.[10] Five months later, his son followed him. Darnley was vicious and rampantly ambitious, but all Mary saw when she set eyes on the 'properest and best proportioned long man' she had ever seen[11] was, to put it baldly, sex. She experienced a complete *coup de foudre*. By the following July, with flagrant disregard for Elizabeth's wishes, they were married, though not before Mary had recklessly, and without the support of her Parliament, had her darling proclaimed Prince Henry Duke of Albany, 'King of this Kingdom'. And on 24 June the next year, the news arrived in London that another couple with claims to the English crown had been blessed with a male child. As Elizabeth's second Parliament assembled in London that winter, Mary was contriving a spectacular display of dynastic magnificence for her son's baptism at Stirling. Her message could not have been more pointed: 'Our leader has transposed Mars ablaze with civil war into peace in our time . . . the crown of Mary awaits her grandsons.'[12] It seemed that the Scots queen had triumphed, 'the importance of kingship is eternal', and she, not Elizabeth, had produced it.

CHAPTER FIFTEEN

When Elizabeth was crowned in 1559, she received congratulations from reformed religious communities all over Europe, including that of the Consul and Senate of Bern, Switzerland, announcing their rejoicing at the news that the Queen 'has recalled those persons who have been exiled for the cause of Gospel truth . . . and has resumed the work of evangelical reformation commenced by her brother Edward'.[1] For the remainder of her reign, Protestant leaders were to encourage, exhort and frequently despair at Elizabeth's reluctance to commit herself, practically and ideologically, to the reformist cause at large. Elizabeth may have been determined to ensure the security of her own Church, but it was to be many years before she grudgingly conceded any help beyond words to the protection of anyone else's. Nowhere was this more apparent than in the English approach to the conflict between Holland and Spain which had begun early in the century, and which was to have profound effects on both the English economy and the nation's contumacious relationship with the great power of Spain.

The Seventeen Provinces of the Spanish Netherlands had been inherited by the Hapsburg Empire in 1482. Imperial–Dutch relations had proved fraught from the outset, with the Dutch objecting to heavy taxation, the neglect of clear governance on the part of the huge and unwieldy empire and an oppressive religious regime, which, in 1523, under Charles V, outlawed the 'heresy' of reform and saw over 1,000 people executed over the following forty years. When Charles V abdicated in 1555, his Spanish territories descended to Philip of Spain (soon to be technically King of England), whose commitment to the Counter-Reformation saw him revive these anti-heresy statutes which under his father's later reign had been less stringently applied. While the temporary exhaustion of the powers of France and Spain meant that Elizabeth began her rule within a diplomatic context which was generally desirous of peace, and which meant that initially English policy towards persecuted Dutch reformers was extremely circumspect, the importance of the economic relationship between England and the Netherlands soon exemplified the improbability of Elizabeth's government being able to distinguish between spiritual and secular issues.

In 1559, Philip appointed his illegitimate half-sister, Margaret of Parma, to the governorship of the Netherlands, a position previously filled, for a collective total of forty-eight years, by Margaret's great-aunt and aunt, Archduchess Margaret and Mary of Austria. Elizabeth sent warm congratulations to her fellow female ruler, which Margaret 'gratefully' received, and heard from her envoy, Sir Thomas Challoner, of the great 'wealth of prince and subject' of the Seventeen Provinces. Despite the fact that her own accession had prompted a wave of fearful Protestant emigration to England from the Netherlands (which Elizabeth personally saw no reason to rejoice in, as she disliked fanatical Protestants quite as much as she despised dogmatic Catholics), it was this wealth which immediately concerned English policy. Since her grandfather Henry VII had agreed a trade policy with the then Duke of Burgundy in 1496, the Netherlands, and Antwerp in particular, had been central to the English cloth trade, while loans raised on the Antwerp exchange were crucial to the English government in permitting a relative degree of independence from the need to raise funds through Parliament. Yet it was beyond the government's control to dictate a confessionally justified argument which was being fought out at sea. Challoner's correspondence is full of fearful detail of the persecutions enacted by the Spanish Inquisition, known as the Holy Office, which Philip refused to counter. Anglo-Spanish merchants were particularly vulnerable to charges of heresy and ever more convoluted justifications for their arrest and the confiscation of their goods, and English privateers now began a counter-attack on Iberian vessels. By 1563, some four hundred such ships, containing 25,000 sailors, were reported to be at large. In January 1564, Philip ordered that all English ships in Basque ports be seized and their crews imprisoned. Margaret's envoy to London, Christophe d'Assonleville, appeared before Elizabeth with a list of grievances against the privateers and an increase in English customs duties, and was given a soothing reception. Anxious to preserve accord with the Flanders trade, Cecil wrote to the Earl of Sussex:

> this matter of resort of pirates, or, if you will so call them, our adventurers, that daily rob the Spaniards and Flemings . . . is a matter of great long consequence. For God's sake I require you to employ some care therein, that some might be apprehended and executed.[2]

Unappeased, Margaret closed her ports to English vessels in November 1564. Elizabeth in turn demanded that unless the ban was lifted, and all English shipping and mariners released from Spain, she would suspend all trade with the Netherlands. What began as economic bravado on both sides – each wishing to prove their mercantile independence from the other – developed into something far more consequential in terms of the Spanish king's attitude towards Elizabeth. As the Flanders cloth trade collapsed for lack of English raw material, dispossessed and starving workers became more susceptible to the incendiary preaching of Calvinist divines. For Philip, the Flemish Protestants were not only heretics, they were a manifestation of a highly disturbing social revolution. The delicate and complex social fabric which had kept the Seventeen Provinces in such excellent fiscal order was being threatened by a reformed doctrine which encouraged ordinary men and women to disregard the rulings not only of priests, but of kings. Elizabeth's grand gesture provoked a degree of civil unrest which Philip viewed as an ungrateful return on his relatively tolerant attitude thus far to the heretic queen. Elizabeth had never intended to present herself as a Protestant champion, indeed she would maintain her resistance to that role for decades to come, but Philip was coming to see England as irremediably associated with his Flemish subjects' insurrection. It was the beginning of a cold war.

In the summer of 1566, Calvinist rebels succeeded in bringing Margaret of Parma's government to a standstill. The concessions the regent granted in the face of such widespread civil unrest, which included freedom of worship for Protestants, were impossible for Philip to admit. Margaret did succeed in restoring Hapsburg authority, but her brother's patience had snapped. A year later, the Duke of Alba arrived in the Netherlands with 10,000 Spanish troops. Where once Elizabeth had been worried about the possibility of French domination in the region, she was now confronted with a far more effective military power, and one far more concerned with expunging heresy. Moreover, the closure of the Antwerp exchange seriously affected her access to borrowing. Amidst shock news of Alba's persecutions and ever more urgent scrambling for credit, Elizabeth chose to make another inflammatory gesture.

In 1562 the English captain John Hawkins had undertaken a small expedition to Sierra Leone, where he had successfully traded several hundred slaves, returning with a profit so impressive that Elizabeth herself, along with her Lord Admiral and the Earls of Leicester and Pembroke, was prepared to invest in a further voyage. The fact that this amounted to a direct usurpation of Spanish prerogative did not deter her, and, by 1568, despite frequent assurances of Hawkins's loyalty to the Spanish king and a good deal of diplomatic fudging to disguise the Queen's involvement, three further voyages had been undertaken. Elizabeth was behaving in a wilfully provocative manner, choosing to remind Philip that she was his equal, but given the situation in the Netherlands she underestimated the diplomatic impact of profiting from illegal trade. As Alba's persecutions in the provinces mounted, fleets of 'Sea Beggars' – Protestant refugees, dispossessed members of the Netherlands aristocracy, plain criminals and numerous enterprising English sailors (encouraged by Elizabeth issuing commissions legitimising the harassment of French Catholic ships under cover of assisting the Huguenots) – were attacking Spanish traders and disrupting Alba's supply lines. Elizabeth clearly felt financially secure enough at this point to ignore Spanish displeasure – Hamburg had proved a viable alternative to Antwerp for the cloth trade and a recent alteration in customs duties had produced an excess – so when in November 1568 four Genoese ships carrying monies to pay Alba's troops limped into Plymouth harbour after escaping pursuit by the Sea Beggars, Elizabeth decided to help herself to the funds. Technically, this was not illegal, as the £85,000 the ships carried had not been made over to Alba, and its Italian owners were at liberty to lend the money to whomsoever they chose, but Philip's most recent, and deeply hostile, envoy, Don Guerau de Spes, did all he could to equate it with aggressive English policy and Elizabeth's active harbouring of heretics. Before Elizabeth had confirmed that she intended to retain the monies, de Spes's machinations prompted Alba in December to detain English ships and their cargoes in Netherlands ports and imprison their crews. For both sides, short of an outright declaration of war, escalation now seemed the only possibility – a staring contest in which both Elizabeth and Philip waited to see which of them would back down first.

As the Genoese ships nosed into port, a tribunal was sitting at Westminster Hall. Its task was to determine the fate of Mary Queen of Scots. Since the triumph of her son's christening the previous year, Mary's rule had been sliding into anarchy. The marriage with Darnley was a disaster, the Scots magnates increasingly resentful and ungovernable. On 9 February 1567 a conspiracy led by James Hepburn, Earl of Bothwell, had quite literally exploded at a house at Kirk o'Field in Edinburgh, where Mary's husband was convalescing from an illness. Darnley was murdered as he tried to escape from the burning ruin. By 15 May, Mary was married to Bothwell. By June, civil war had broken out in Scotland and Mary found herself an abandoned prisoner at Lochleven Castle. In July, utterly broken-spirited, she signed away the rights to her crown in favour of her son, who was proclaimed on the 29th with Mary's half-brother Moray as regent. Once the darling of European royalty, Mary had demeaned herself to the status of a homeless, stateless adulteress, one, moreover, who was accused of cooperating in the murder of her second husband. Elizabeth's personal sympathy for her kinswoman is perhaps best expressed by the fact that on the day Mary wrote to her, almost a year later, begging her to take pity on her 'good sister and cousin',

Elizabeth was inspecting a collection of pearls which had been sent south from Mary's collection by Regent Moray. Alongside six cordons strung 'paternoster' style (that is, looped like prayer beads) were twenty-five 'black Muscades', the size and colour of the grape, which Elizabeth, gloating covetously as she viewed them with Leicester, pronounced to be 'unparalleled'. She had them for 12,000 crowns, having the additional pleasure of besting Mary's former mother-in-law, Catherine de Medici, to the bargain. Sisterhood did not count for much when it came to stones.

Quite what was to be done with the once Queen of Scotland was initially uncertain, but Mary helped matters along in her own dashing way by escaping from Lochleven a few days after Elizabeth received the pearls and heading an army against Moray. Her troops were defeated, and on 16 May 1568 Mary arrived in Cumbria by fishing boat. As she never ceased to remind Elizabeth for the rest of her life, she had arrived not as a captive but as an anointed queen in search of succour. The best possible solution for Elizabeth's government, though, was to lock her up, which they did, for the next nineteen years. Challenging the legality of Mary Stuart's imprisonment is fairly easy. Primarily, she was a queen, and therefore subject only to God. She had come of her own free will to England after being herself illegally condemned by her subjects for Darnley's murder, to which she had been given no opportunity to answer personally or through Parliament. She had, if nothing else, the right to defend herself and claim restitution. To limit the rights and wrongs of the argument to the extremely hazy province of sixteenth-century laws concerning absconding monarchs, though, is rather to miss the point. As far as many of Elizabeth's ministers were concerned, Mary was the deadliest enemy their state possessed.

Mary Stuart embodied a new perception of Catholicism which was actively propagated in England in the 1560s and 1570s, in terms of both domestic and foreign policy. Elizabeth's Church was still new, vulnerable and unformed. The Catholic faith had to be repositioned as something foreign, something other, as opposed to what it had been until very recently, the accepted mode of worship for the majority. Confessional control was becoming part of statecraft: 'In all

sixteenth-century Christian states, non-conformity had profound political as well as spiritual implications: in England, it was a de facto
assault upon the ineluctable premise by which government defined
every aspect of its authority.'³ When Cecil analysed the situation in
1569, he identified the Pope and the monarchs of France and Spain as
the enemies of England and their instrument as Mary: 'the Catholic
powers of Europe were operating on Elizabeth like surgeons, using
Mary Stuart as their scalpel.'⁴ As far as Cecil was concerned, if the
government waited for a Catholic revolution, it would already be too
late to stop it.

The Moray regime had no interest in English support for Mary's
reclamation of her throne. Elizabeth, it seemed, was, however,
personally inclined to hear her cousin out. To counter this, Moray
conveniently produced a collection of letters, known as the Casket
Letters, which supposedly proved both Mary's adulterous relationship with Bothwell and her acquiescence to Darnley's murder,
described by Cecil as 'a full fardel of naughty matter tending to
convince the queen as devisor of the murder and the Earl of Bothwell her executor'. It was pathetically obvious that the letters had
been tampered with and in part downright forged, but it suited the
government to make use of them. After an initial tribunal at York,
the case was brought at Westminster, where Elizabeth agreed that,
should the evidence against Mary stand up, she would recognise
Moray's government and give her up. When the commissioners met
in the Painted Chamber at Westminster on 18 November, the letters
were produced, but only when Mary's envoys were out of the room.
Only 'copies' of the letters were seen by them, and at a second meeting at Hampton Court a month later it was stated before Elizabeth
that there was no discrepancy between the two versions. Mary, very
effectively, was framed. In part, the reduction of her standing was
a gesture to other powers, a performance of justice. It was also an
effective means of justifying an imprisonment that began at Tutbury
Castle and continued for nearly two decades. Cecil and his colleagues
sincerely believed that Mary could only ever be a threat to England,
and arguably in doing so, they brought about what they feared. The
politics of Elizabeth's reign were consistently those of opposition to

an overwhelmingly threatening foreign status quo. Whether she was indeed an enemy of Elizabeth's state at this point is moot. In 1569, she was the enemy it needed.

CHAPTER SIXTEEN

T he threat posed by Protestantism to the hierarchical social order of sixteenth-century Europe was not only an anxiety for the King of Spain. One of the many objections to Elizabeth from Rome was that she had dismissed such a number of noblemen from her council and replaced them with 'obscure' nobodies, an objection also felt by some of her most powerful subjects. To the Nevilles and the Percys, the great families of the Northern March, who had patrolled the Scots border for centuries, enjoying what was, in effect, princely privilege within their own fiefdoms, government policy in London had for some years appeared both confusing and insulting. The Earl of Northumberland, Thomas Percy, and the Earl of Westmorland, Charles Neville, felt marginalised by Cecil's regime and threatened by the religious settlement and the apparent lack of resolution over the status of Mary Stuart. Their disaffection, however, might not have taken radical form were it not for the incendiary provocations of a group of anti-Cecil activists, Richard Norton (who had been involved in the Pilgrimage of Grace, the uprising against Henry VIII three decades earlier), Thomas Hussey and Robert Tempest. Norton, Hussey and Tempest claimed that they had the support of the Duke of Alba, who would land troops at Hartlepool to aid them in rebellion. They played upon the wounded pride of the great northern families by vociferously deriding the 'new men' who were in power under Cecil in London, berating them as parvenus who were misadvising the Queen. Details of the latter's mood of insurrection were sufficiently alarming for Elizabeth's lieutenant in the north, the Earl of Sussex, to summon the two earls to court in late October 1569 to explain the persistent rumours of sedition. The earls refused, instead responding by calling out their troops in one of the moments of fission that characterised Elizabeth's reign; the summoning of what was to all intents and purposes a feudal host to confront the new order. Sussex had the earls declared traitors on 13 November, his reaction serving to coalesce what had been an incoherent reaction to general discontent into a specifically focused conflict.

Grumbling became rebellion. The earls had a cause – the release of Mary from Tutbury – though they did not announce an intention to push her to the throne. While they hoped to effect change, their cause was not specifically Mary's – they were conservatives who wanted to slow what they saw as the alarmingly radical absorption of Church by state while remaining theoretically loyal to the crown. Yet once the earls' affinities were mobilised, they were effectively in open rebellion and there could be no turning back. By the 24th, 10,000 men had reached Bramham Moor, about fifty miles from Tutbury, having celebrated Mass and burned English Bibles in Durham Cathedral en route. Emergency musters were held to provide an army of 15,000 men to protect Elizabeth, should the rebels succeed in attaining the capital, but even as the Queen's troops moved north, and Mary was removed to Coventry for greater security, the rising, which had never enjoyed much support beyond that of the immediate Neville and Percy affinities, began to peter out. After a last stand at Barnard's Castle, which they took but quickly realised they could not hold, the rebels scattered and by 15 December they were in flight to Scotland.

In January 1570, Leonard Dacre, a member of another significant northern family who was engaged in a wardship dispute over inheritance with the Duke of Norfolk, gathered about three thousand men at his seat at Naworth. He had been received by Elizabeth at Windsor as the rebellion was fomenting, and had returned to the north apparently as a loyal subject, but he had been in correspondence with Mary Stuart since 1566 and now attempted to attract her Scots supporters to his side. Elizabeth dispatched her first cousin, Henry Carey, from Berwick to confront Dacre, and in the Battle of Gelt Bridge on 20 February, Dacre was defeated and about three hundred of his men killed. Dacre himself escaped, fleeing first to Scotland and then to the Continent, where he died in Brussels, a pensioner of Philip of Spain, in 1573. Other rebels were less fortunate. Both Westmorland and

Northumberland were attainted for their treason; Westmorland and his wife eventually escaped to the Netherlands, but Northumberland was executed in 1572. Tudor propaganda was not only a celebration of dynastic magnificence; it could also serve in creating gruesome folk memories. The north could not be allowed to forget that royal justice held sway throughout the realm, so every bell tower which had sounded in favour of the rising was stripped of its carillon, leaving just one bell to remind the people of their disobedience. Many rebels were publicly hanged and their rotting bodies displayed 'for terror'.[1] In Cecil's view 'The Queen's Majesty hath had a notable trial of her whole realm and subjects in this time'[2] and Elizabeth was as keen as her Secretary that the country should be horrified into remembrance.

It is hardly surprising that the government in London believed that a storm was coming. In February 1570, the prediction Cecil had made in his 'Device' eventually came true. Pope Pius V promulgated the bull *Regnans in Excelsis*, the most literally damning Catholic challenge Elizabeth had yet faced. 'The number of the ungodly,' the Pope declared, 'has so much grown in power that there is no place left in the world which they have not tried to corrupt with their most wicked doctrines; and among others Elizabeth, the pretended Queen of England, and the servant of crime, has assisted in this.' The bull listed the offences of Elizabeth and her ministers, which included the oppression of followers of the Catholic faith, the institution of false preachers, the abolition of the sacrifice of the Mass, the promotion of heretical books, the ejection of bishops and priests, the forbidding of the acknowledgement of canonical sanction and the forced abjuration of the authority of Rome. Consequently, Pius declared Elizabeth a heretic, excommunicated her and deprived her of her 'pretended title to the aforesaid crown and of all lordship, privilege and dignity whatsoever'. Her subjects, the bull went on, were formally absolved of their oaths of loyalty to the Queen.

Since Elizabeth's accession, English Catholics had endured an uneasy truce with the religious settlement, but the bull rendered this untenable. 'The harsh reality was that the Pope had made it impossible to be a good Catholic and a good Englishman'.[3] As the Catholic priest John Hart, interrogated in 1580, was subsequently to express it 'if they obey her [Elizabeth] they be in the Pope's curse, and if they disobey her, they are in the Queen's danger'.[4]

Knowledge of the bull was well current at court by the end of the month, but attempts were made to suppress it as far as possible, until on 25 May, a young man named John Felton nailed a copy of it to the Bishop of London's garden gate. Writing later from the Catholic college at Rome, the English writer and spy Anthony Munday claimed the existence of a special book of martyrs from which inspiring stories were read to the students in the evenings. Felton, who had been executed for his action and had refused to give the traditional speech of submission to royal authority from the scaffold, was according to Munday celebrated in the book. *Regnans in Excelsis* had articulated what had previously been incoherent; it had given men such as Felton a clearly defined cause and the glorious prospect of dying for their faith to which they could aspire.

Elizabeth was now an official, legitimate target for prospective Catholic revolutionaries. Cecil had feared this since the beginning of her reign, and in the late 1560s he began to work closely with Francis Walsingham, who was to become his strongest ally in matters of security. Walsingham was familiar with Cecil's circle as a member of the Italian group of exiles under Mary Tudor, and on his return to England had been elected as a Member of Parliament in 1559. An active supporter of French reformists, known as Huguenots, in 1570, Walsingham became ambassador to Paris, and joined the Privy Council on his return three years later, eventually becoming Secretary in 1587. His involvement in what became known as the Ridolfi conspiracy is the first significant example of the close partnership he created with Cecil with the aim of protecting the Queen from what both men perceived as the principal threat to both her person and to the Protestant regime to which they were both passionately committed.

The Ridolfi conspiracy was finally exposed in 1571, but it forms the background of Anglo-Scots relations from 1569. There are two ways to read the plot as it was ultimately revealed. One is that Elizabeth and Cecil had made a potentially calamitous misjudgement and permitted a dangerous conspirator to go free. The other is that

Elizabeth herself was involved almost from its genesis in a scheme which would have efficiently compromised the Scots queen without Elizabeth apparently getting her own hands dirty.

Since the late 1560s Elizabeth's intelligence network had been keeping an eye on Roberto Ridolfi, a Florentine businessman, who was also a suspected papal agent. In December 1568, Francis Walsingham wrote to Cecil to report on a disturbing communication he had received from Paris, which claimed that the French and Spanish governments were considering an alliance for the overthrow of Cecil 'the great heretic' and the imposition of a total trade embargo on Elizabeth if she resisted a return to the Catholic fold. Within days of Walsingham's letter, the Spanish ambassador de Spes met with his French counterpart, la Mothe-Fénelon, to discuss the scheme. De Spes was in touch with Ridolfi, and in September 1569, as the first stirrings of the Northern Rising were heard in London, it was discovered that Ridolfi had made bills of exchange for the vast sum of £3,000 available to the Bishop of Ross, Mary Stuart's envoy. This was sufficiently alarming for Ridolfi to be detained on the advice of Cecil and the Earl of Leicester for questioning at Walsingham's London home in Seething Lane, near the Aldgate, a former medieval hospital known as the Papey. Ridolfi remained there from November until late January 1570 (that is, for the duration of the Rising), during which time he admitted his acquaintance with Ross and his knowledge of the plan to marry Mary to the Duke of Norfolk. His revelations were prompted by intervention from the Queen, who suggested that some of his responses were 'far otherwise than the truth is' and added threateningly that 'a harsher examination would reveal more'. So, was Ridolfi 'turned' during his residence at Walsingham's home, possibly under threat of torture? Elizabeth certainly seems to have displayed a curious degree of friendliness towards such a dangerous character.

After Ridolfi's release, on a promise to meddle no more in affairs which were beyond him, Elizabeth actually received him for an audience, in her garden at Greenwich Palace on 25 March. Ridolfi swore loyalty to her: 'he did in like sort make profession of great affection to serve Her Majesty and this crown'.[5] Shortly afterwards, he was on his

way to Rome, with a passport signed by Elizabeth herself. His journey also encompassed the Spanish Netherlands and Philip of Spain's
court, apparently with a view to promoting an invasion by the Duke
of Alba to set Mary on the throne, supported by an internal coup
led by English Catholics. Alba himself termed Ridolfi 'un gran parla-
quina' – a chatterbox – and dismissed his capacity to organise any
sort of insurrection, yet the view that:

> Ridolfi . . . was a man with an Italian love of intrigue, but . . . with
> little of the Italian Renaissance skill at diplomacy; he understood
> little of the workings of the English mind, or indeed the workings
> of England itself[6]

must be disputed. It is almost inconceivable that this supposed political lightweight should have successfully deceived Walsingham,
Cecil and Elizabeth at such a delicate moment, while it is a fact that
Ridolfi eventually died a respected senator in Florence, neatly avoiding the consequences of his revolutionary plotting. So

> there is another way to look at Ridolfi's career . . . that Ridolfi was
> a plant; that the whole conspiracy was a set-up from the start, a
> plot manufactured by [Cecil] to expose Mary Stuart and the danger
> he knew her to be and to reveal those in England and abroad with
> whom she had been plotting.[7]

Walsingham assured Cecil that Ridolfi 'would deal both discreetly
and uprightly, as one both wise and who standeth on terms of honesty and reputation', an assessment which hardly fits with the clumsy
blabbermouth of Alba's opinion. Unless, of course, Ridolfi's indiscretion and incompetence were part of his cover. That Elizabeth should
have chosen this moment to promote Walsingham to the French
embassy implies that she trusted his view. Moreover, Elizabeth's
resistance to French pressure to make a definitive statement about
Mary can be read in this light as a tactic to postpone action until the
plot had worked itself out. Ridolfi was a man whose 'manoeuvring
was so deft that we still cannot be sure whose side he was on'.[8] Was

he indeed working for Elizabeth, or fooling her into thinking he was a double agent while in fact remaining loyal to the Catholic cause? Recent historians have strongly inclined to the former view, but whatever Ridolfi believed himself to be doing, his activities indeed confirmed Cecil's worst fears for the security of Elizabeth and her state.

On 12 April 1571, a man named Charles Bailly, newly arrived from the Netherlands, was arrested at Dover and sent to Lord Cobham in London. Bailly's luggage had excited the suspicions of the port authorities when it was found to contain copies of *A Treatise Concerning the Defence of the Honour of . . . Mary Queen of Scotland*, as well as coded letters to the Bishop of Ross. Lord Cobham immediately sent Bailly to the Marshalsea prison, obviously having alerted Cecil, for Bailly's cellmate proved to be William Herle, a skilled informant who worked for the Secretary. Bailly discovered that his cell also possessed a convenient hole in the wall, through which he was able to communicate with an Irish priest, a secretary of the Spanish ambassador and two servants of the Bishop. Herle wrote daily letters to Cecil, who appeared to interrogate Bailly himself, and after several weeks of threats and a dose of the rack (the use of which Ross protested, though Cecil and Leicester denied it), Bailly confessed to knowledge of Ridolfi's discussions with Alba in the Netherlands and claimed that Ridolfi had requested Bailly to write two letters to be passed to Ross for delivery. Bailly knew only that the letters were intended for English noblemen, marked as '30' and '40'. On 13 May, Cecil, accompanied by Sir Ralph Sadler, the Earl of Sussex and Sir Walter Mildmay, visited Ross at his lodgings, and after lengthy questioning obtained the information that Ridolfi had in his possession letters from Mary to Alba, Philip of Spain and the Pope, and letters from Ross to Alba, all concerning plans for funds and troops to come to Mary's assistance.

After spending the summer on progress with the Queen, Cecil wrote an extraordinary letter on Elizabeth's behalf to the Earl of Shrewsbury, adding directions to the courier that it should go direct to Sheffield Castle, 'haste post haste, haste, haste, for life for life for life for life'. It is a rare and evocative little piece of poetry; one can hear the urgent gallop of the post horse's hooves in the repeated injunction.

Shrewsbury was instructed to press Mary to further revelations and to prevent her from sending or receiving any communication, for if Cecil had set a trap, he was very close to springing it. On 29 August, one Thomas Browne of Shrewsbury had been given a purse of silver by two of the Duke of Norfolk's clerks for delivery to another Norfolk servant, Laurence Bannister. Browne took the precaution of looking into the purse and discovered £600 in gold and two notes written in code. Within days, Norfolk's men were being interrogated in the Tower and Elizabeth claimed she was 'very inquisitive' to hear the news. The Duke of Norfolk was taken into custody at Howard House on 4 September, but not before he had had time to dispose of the key to the code. Norfolk refused to sign a statement put together by Sir Ralph Sadler, whom Cecil had employed to question him, and Elizabeth then instructed that Norfolk be sent to the Tower for further examination. Elizabeth sat next to Cecil at his desk as together they combed through the report. The Queen proposed that William Barker, one of the two Norfolk servants who had been given charge of the gold, should be questioned again, and she authorised the use of 'some extremity' against him. She was no longer prepared to listen to Norfolk's pleas for clemency, though he pleaded that 'when I considered with myself how far I have transgressed in my duty to your most excellent Majesty I dare not now presume to look up or hope for your grace's favour'. By mid-September, with the warrant for the torture of Norfolk's servants arrived at the Tower, Cecil was insisting on answers. A month later, he was sufficiently convinced of Norfolk's guilt to release a tract, *Salutem in Christo*, detailing the conspiracy to the public. In a method familiar to modern-day manipulators of the press, this was a 'private' letter from one 'RG' which 'accidentally' found its way into the public domain. Though the plot it detailed has become known by Ridolfi's name, his identity was concealed, referred to only as 'the messenger' (which again lends support to the notion that Ridolfi had been working for the English government all along).

The charges were as follows: that Mary was responsible for the Northern Rising, that she had conspired to marry Norfolk and with him orchestrate a plan to take London and receive troops from the

Netherlands, a scheme enabled by Ross, that 'instrument of all the duke's calamity'.[9] Mary was to be proclaimed Queen of England and Scotland and her son James kidnapped. It was an incendiary piece of propaganda, 'a sensational revelation from the heart of Elizabeth's government'.[10]

A week later, Ross was questioned again, in an investigation which stretched over days. Over and over again the bishop was asked about Ridolfi – and when he cracked it was clear that Norfolk was a dead man. Yes, Norfolk had 'discoursed' with Alba; yes, he had conspired with Philip and Mary, even proposing Harwich as the ideal port at which to land troops; yes, he had been in communication with the Pope; yes, the Duke was '40' and his ally Lord Lumley '30'. Further evidence of Ridolfi's agency came from the cipher he had prepared from Italian for Norfolk's use after his release from Walsingham's custody and kept in Norfolk's Bible. With only one code, it would be pathetically easy for Cecil to crack, and, as Cecil's biographer notes, 'Who but an English agent would have made such an obvious mistake?'[11] In November, Norfolk wrote a long letter to Cecil asking him to intercede with Elizabeth, but some days later the Queen herself charged her kinsman with six counts of treason drawn from his own confessions.

The Ridolfi plot reveals much about Elizabeth as a political strategist. From its inauguration, we see her working closely with Burghley, meeting with Ridolfi himself, her communications half protective, half threatening. We see her agreeing to the threat (and possibly the use) of torture on Bailly and Norfolk's servants. We see her going about her public business, meeting ambassadors, progressing through her realm, all the time patiently waiting for the threads of a conspiracy against her life to weave together. Yet in the days preceding Ross's interrogation, the strain was beginning to tell – Elizabeth suffered from painful bilious attacks which could only be relieved by emetics, the 'purging' cure the Queen usually despised. The effort required to maintain the mask of majesty under such circumstances demanded tremendous self-discipline, particularly as Elizabeth had been as duplicitous as her Secretary in engaging in a plot whose consequences could have been disastrous. Whether Ridolfi was indeed a stooge or just a chancer who loved intrigue can never fully be known, but Elizabeth was prepared to gamble with her own safety in order to bring down her enemies.

The churnings of the Ridolfi conspiracy illuminate Elizabeth's attitude to Scotland the previous year, when the assassination of the regent, Moray, on 23 January 1570, provoked a crisis. With the Protestant regime north of the border thrown into further disarray, Elizabeth was also under pressure from France to declare her intentions as to what she planned to do with Mary. At a meeting with the French ambassador on 6 February, Elizabeth asserted that she had 'used the Queen of Scots with more honour and favour than any prince having like cause would have done, and though she was not bound to make account to any prince of her doings, yet she would impart to the King, her good brother, some reasonable consideration of her doing'.[12] No such 'reasonable consideration', however, was forthcoming until April, when Sir Henry Norris was instructed to take a firm line in his statement to Catherine de Medici and her son. After detailing the incidents of the Norfolk marriage plot, the failure to ratify the Treaty of Edinburgh and the rebellion in the north, Elizabeth's envoy declared:

> If the requests that are made to us to aid her to our power to restore her forthwith to her realm shall be applied to the former things preceding, no indifferent person of any judgement will or can think it in conscience reasonable to move us to commit such a dangerous folly, as to be the author ourself to hazard our own person, our quietness of our realm and people.[13]

Personally, Elizabeth was still uncertain as to how she ought to proceed, and, despite the resolve of her Privy Councillors, who firmly opposed Mary's restoration, the Queen held a meeting at Hampton Court that same month to discuss the matter once again. Elizabeth's indecisiveness at this point has been read as typical of her character, as evidence of the 'feminine' nature of her governance, or, more realistically, as an inability to contemplate the enormity of striking at another of God's anointed. Yet given Elizabeth's personal engagement in the early stages of the notorious plot, it is possible to consider that her diplomatic stalling was based upon the assurance that Mary might soon be trapped by her own schemes.

The events of 1571 produced two further pieces of legislation, prompted in part by *Regnans in Excelsis* and in part by the Ridolfi conspiracy which further compromised the loyalty of Elizabeth's Catholic subjects and delineated the opposing sides in what was now an overt confessional conflict within the realm. The Treasons Act made it illegal to deny Elizabeth's right to the throne: to call her a heretic, a tyrant, an infidel or a usurper was treason. The Act Against Fugitives Over the Sea posed a more practical problem. Catholics who chose exile rather than conformity (expressed as leaving England without licence and failing to return within six months) were termed 'fugitives, rebels and traitors'. All English Catholics were now suspected of the treason which Catholic militants promoted, which is not to say that there were not many among them who attempted to find a way out of the theological labyrinth the Pope and the Queen had created between them. Many Catholic gentry were content to become 'Church papists', outwardly conforming to the requirements of the Act of Supremacy while holding to a certain freedom of conscience; others actively sought a place for loyal Catholics within the structure of the English state; still others maintained Catholicism as a system of social and cultural, rather than strictly religious practice: scholars working on the distinctions and interactions between these groups have ascertained considerable degrees of variation. Nor is it correct to assume that Elizabeth was staunchly opposing a monolith of Catholic conformity, however mighty the ultra-loyalist Hapsburg Empire at times appeared. For example, the French had never accepted the ruling of the 1563 Council of Trent which endorsed the Pope as the bishop of the universal Church, hence 'Gallicanism', as it became known, was increasingly influential in continental politics as the century drew on. Gallicanism argued for the ecclesiastical independence of Catholic kingdoms, especially, but not exclusively, in France, thus the English government was not unique in proposing that subjects should obey a monarch of a different confession than their own.[14] Many English Catholics saw 'ultramontanism', the assertion of the power of Rome over all other authorities, as a perversion of their faith, giving the temporal precedent over the spiritual. Anthony Copley, a Catholic polemicist writing at the end of the Elizabethan period, exhorted 'all English Catholics as well for that we are Catholics as English, explode and prosecute this doctrine . . . as impostural and disloyal'. As France descended into spiritual civil war, Gallican tracts became increasingly popular among English Protestants, with 130 such works having been translated and published by 1595. Dogmatic militancy no more universally obtained among European Catholics than insurrection among their English counterparts: the challenge Elizabeth faced was from an extremist minority.

Elizabeth's fine, supple intellect was in many ways brilliantly suited to the ever-shifting kaleidoscope of rainbow loyalties which formed Renaissance politics, but increasingly she was obliged to concede that her government could not afford to recognise subtleties, as the moral landscape was ineluctably reduced to black, or white. Post-*Regnans* legislation denied to English Catholics a position which both Elizabeth and Cecil had assumed during Mary's reign. Each in their own way had claimed that loyalty and conscience were not incompatible. Dying for one's beliefs had begun to look rather old-fashioned to these skilful proponents of a new political ideology, yet as the positions of both sides hardened there were increasing numbers of Catholic idealists prepared to rush in where pragmatists feared to tread.

For Norfolk, then, there could be no quarter. According to Cecil, Elizabeth was mindful of the Duke's nearness of blood and superiority of honour, and the death warrant was signed and rescinded four times before Elizabeth could bear to allow the execution to proceed. If Elizabeth had been engaged in the planting of Ridolfi, this would suggest that she was as eager as her ministers to learn the scope of the plots against her, but this did not mean she could easily reconcile herself with the consequences of that information. Yet she was even more reluctant to move against Mary Stuart than against Norfolk, and her Parliament would not permit her to spare them both. In late 1570, Dr Thomas Wilson, a Cambridge lawyer, had been commissioned by Cecil to 'translate' a work by George Buchanan, the tutor to James of Scotland. *A Detection of the Doings of Mary Queen of Scots*, a brutal summary of Mary's activities, had been sent to London by Elizabeth's ambassador in Scotland, Thomas Randolph, in 1568. Now Wilson doctored the text to make it appear that it had been written in 'handsome Scottish', after which it was sent to the French court with the aim of destroying what was left of Mary's reputation there. The text sums up the views of the Commons, who were determined on Mary's blood:

When rude Scotland has vomited up a poison, must fine England lick it up for a restorative? Oh vile indignity . . . Oh ambition fed with prosperity, strengthened with indulgence, irritated with adversity, not to be neglected, trusted, nor pardoned.[15]

Installed as ambassador in France, Walsingham added his opinion that:

So long as that devilish woman lives, neither Her Majesty must make account to continue in quiet possession of her crown, nor her faithful servants assure themselves of safety of their lives.

In the May parliament of 1572, member after member stood up to denounce this 'horrible adulteress' and 'subverter of the state'. It is notable that Mary's marital transgressions were conflated with her political treason, invoking the ancient association between sexual sin and perverted government, an association which anti-Elizabeth propaganda was also to adopt. Elizabeth pressed hard for a moderation of the House's wishes, pressing for a bill which would exclude Mary from the succession rather than the bill of attainder which would cost the Scots queen her life, a mercy which was very grudgingly accepted. In return, she finally agreed that Norfolk should go to the block. Mary heard the news in tears, and spent much time in private prayer for her lost suitor, but one does wonder whether she was truly grateful.

Norfolk was executed on Tower Hill on 2 June. The following evening, Cecil approached Elizabeth with a report from Walsingham containing research on the opinions of significant French Protestants on the Queen of Scots, but Elizabeth waved him away after a few moments, confessing that she was too distracted by her sadness over Norfolk's death to talk business. On 25 June, the moderated bill which Elizabeth had requested was read for the third time in the House of Commons. It stated that Mary Stuart had no right to the dignity, title or interest of Elizabeth's crown, and that if she should claim it, or seek to provoke any kind of war or invasion, then she would be a traitor and could be tried as such by the peers of England. If condemned, she would be executed. But Elizabeth did not give her assent, without which the bill was useless. She requested that it be deferred until the next parliamentary sitting in November. All that she permitted was a delegation to Sheffield Castle to read the brazenly unrepentant Mary yet another severe lecture on her treacherous ingratitude, a visit which had much the same effect as all its predecessors.

CHAPTER SEVENTEEN

The Elizabethan court has often been criticised for its artistic 'backwardness'. It is a 'commonplace that the adoption of an Italian Renaissance style came late to Britain, adopted tardily and only in part'.[1] Similarly, the second half of the sixteenth century is often viewed as a period of 'contraction', if not stultification. With regard to Elizabeth herself, such criticisms might at first appear to be justified. Her approach to artistic patronage was decidedly niggardly – 'it takes her very long, as she always gives with her words sure hopes to the petitioners that they will obtain what they desire but in fact without constant reminders and complacent friends and protectors one can hardly obtain anything which she doubts might cost her something from her purse,' sniffed Ubaldini. While it is true that Elizabeth's summer progresses around the south of England not only served a political purpose, a visual reinforcement of her authority to the people, but inspired the emergence of 'prodigy houses' such as Hardwick, Longleat and Holdenby, she herself built no palaces. And while the Queen may equally have inspired some of the greatest poetry in English during England's greatest poetic age, the books she actually owned represent a paltry legacy. Curiously, for such a self-styled and self-conscious intellectual, Elizabeth owned relatively few books. The Royal Library catalogue of 1760 assigns her 1,600, but of these only about three hundred were actually hers. 'The contents of the library of Queen Elizabeth I,' concludes a bibliographical historian crisply, 'are as enigmatic as the rest of her personality.'[2]

Elizabeth's Tudor predecessors to an extent confirmed their self-images through their books – Henry VIII saw himself as a 'Davidian' king, the spiritual leader of his subjects, as his earnestly learned marginal annotations on Luther's Latin Commentary on the Psalms support. Edward VI was styled as a Protestant David: he possessed, among other works referencing the comparison, a translation from the Hebrew of the Book of Job by Acasse d'Albric, which described him as 'Petite fleur d'esperance admirable/Petit David de Goliath vainceur'. Mary Tudor made a statement with her ownership of François de Billon's 1555 *Le fort inexpugnable de l'honneur du sexe féminine*, while her insistence on the (futile) republication of the work of Joannes Genesius, a scholar who had been one of the most significant defenders of Katherine of Aragon during the divorce, connects her with the queenly tradition of memorialisation through literature begun by Matilda of Scotland with the *Life of St Margaret*. Elizabeth's books are in the main distinctly unrevealing. She may well have owned her famous prayer book emblazoned with the Tudor rose between enamelled gold clasps, but, if so, she didn't use it much. The only poetry is some Latin verse by Thomas Drant, whose literary legacy is as familiar today as his name. Foreign literature is poorly represented, and of the two hundred or more books containing dedications to the Queen, she seems to have retained them more on the basis of their bindings than their contents. Many of the books attributed to Elizabeth in the catalogue belonged to her favoured courtiers, such as Christopher Hatton, or to her beloved tutor, Roger Ascham. Of these, the most pleasingly significant is perhaps a 1495 Venetian edition of Aristotle's collected works in Greek, which displays on the title page a handwritten inscription believed to be the entwined ciphers of Elizabeth and Robert Dudley, Earl of Leicester.

Equally, what painting Elizabeth commissioned was strongly medieval in tone, with its eye on replication rather than innovation; altogether the summation of the principal scholar on Elizabethan portraiture leads to the conclusion that 'the culture of Elizabeth I cannot bear comparison with . . . the aggressive splendour of Henry VIII'.[3] This image of Elizabeth as a reluctant and inadequate 'Renaissance' monarch, however, depends on several misconceptions: firstly an overemphasis on the importance of Italy, secondly on a particular inherited concept of what art meant to the Renaissance, and thirdly a neglect of the interiority, or 'psychological' revolution which has been identified as perhaps the primary characteristic of Renaissance thought. Elizabeth's England was not only very much part of the Renaissance currents which were transforming Europe; she and her court were as capable as any other major dynasty of displaying the *magnificenza* necessary to the sovereign dignity of a prince. The closeness with money which is one of Elizabeth's best-known characteristics concealed a different side to the Queen and her court:

'by many she is deemed generally reluctant and tight fisted, because only some of those closest to her and who can deal with her nature have earned not little by being patient, but with the foreign personalities sent by Princes she has always proved magnificent and munificent, as suits her dignity and royal condition'.[4]

While Italian culture was deeply influential, both politically and aesthetically, at Elizabeth's court, a deeper comprehension of its 'Renaissance' qualities also requires the consideration of Burgundy. Elizabeth's great-great-aunt, Margaret of York, had been Duchess and Regent of Burgundy, while her great-grandfather, Edward IV, had been exiled there during the Wars of the Roses, spending an influential period as the guest of the magnate Lord Gruuthuse. Burgundy was one of the capitals of luxury and learning of the fifteenth-century world, and Edward had returned to England intent on imitating its magnificence. The royal protocols which Elizabeth's paternal great-grandmother, Margaret Beaufort, had codified for the court, many of which were still in use in Elizabeth's day, were derived from the reorganisation of Edward's household in the 1470s. Edward's guide was Olivier de la Marche, commissioned by the king to produce *L'État de la Maison de Charles de Bourgogne*.

The relationship of the Burgundian dukes, who so dominated the cultural landscape of the fifteenth century, to French Renaissance art, has been compared to that of the Romans to the Greeks. The extraordinary refinements of Burgundian culture were adopted from the French court, but then adapted and melded with the urban culture of the Netherlands to produce a distinctive artistic expression of political ascendancy. What Edward IV absorbed during his sojourn in Burgundy was a whole system of princely living which incorporated hierarchies of status into every aspect of court life – not just ceremony or dress, but furnishing, food, the objects which were used and touched, tapestry, plate, music, even the layout of space. Edward's building projects, still extant in Elizabeth's time, showed explicit Burgundian influence, just as his court ceremony was derived from that of Charles the Bold. The staircase to the royal apartments at Nottingham was modelled on that of the Prinsenhof at Bruges, while at Eltham Edward used Burgundian models in the construction of the gallery and raised garden overlooking the river. Burgundian arts also influenced Elizabeth's grandfather Henry VII, who rebuilt Richmond Palace in 1501 with the 'donjon' design for the royal apartments, enclosed gardens and loggia-galleries. During the queenship of Elizabeth's grandmother Elizabeth of York, royal pageants directly imitated the displays of the Burgundian court, with elaborate floats featuring costumed dancers and musicians and, of course, the huge model beasts.

This is not to say that Edward IV was a unique innovator in bringing Burgundian arts to England.

Italian and French influences had been consistently important for centuries, but the Renaissance had effectively been arrested in its English progress by a century of civil war – the first generation of Tudor subjects had lived far closer to a more barbaric, violent age than to the refinements of Italian urbanity, but prior to the Wars of the Roses Richard II had presided over an aesthetically sophisticated court culture, of delicate fashions and elegant food, of scented bathwater and refined interiors. Like Elizabeth, Richard presided over a literary renaissance (though like her he functioned more as a dedicatee than a direct patron of writers such as Chaucer and Gower), and as Elizabeth was to do, he made his own magnificence and splendour the centre of all celebrations.

However, the visual language perfected by the Burgundian courts, or indeed Elizabeth's, was not one which was accessible to later critics. To the nineteenth century, which coined the term, 'Renaissance' when it did not mean ideas meant paintings. The great art which we now worship in museums was not understood by the sixteenth century in the same terms; paintings themselves were (relatively) low-status objects. Luxury arts, whether tapestries, clothes, furniture, plate, armour – what is now termed 'decorative' – were the key indicators of magnificence, and their deployment created the spectacle by which the ruler imposed it. The finest materials and the most skilful craftsmanship were used to achieve political, social and religious aims; they 'demarcated the transcendent from the mundane'[5] but also, in a form of visual apotheosis, translated the mundane to the transcendent. The appearance of a ruler was as the centre of a 'multisensory tapestry', created by writers, musicians, craftsmen of all kinds. Monarchs like Elizabeth did not just commission art, they *were* art. The desired effect was nothing short of sublimity.

It is short-sighted, then, to judge the English Renaissance on a single category of works, that is, pictures, privileged by different ages. The function of Elizabethan portraiture was, in the Queen's case, just one component of magnificence, but it was one in which she did do something unique. Her age's views on painting were quite different from our own. Originality was not prized, but the conception that the stilted, ornate sitters of Elizabethan 'corridor portraits' owe their stiffness to incompetence on the part of painters (the reasoning being that all the great artists were Catholic and therefore could not settle in England) is a canard. What was required was emblematic portraiture, a capturing of the inner self. The images of the Queen thus created, in dress, *maquillage*, jewellery, still leap towards us from the page or the portrait, even after nearly five hundred years. Yet though Elizabeth's motto, taken from her mother's *Semper Eadem* (always the same), is reflected in the consistency of her portraits, their apparently timeless immutability was part of an image that was constantly shifting. Elizabeth took great personal interest in the diffusion of her likeness, and that likeness, as the embodiment of her nation, was required to alter according to the nation's needs. Unlike her predecessors, Elizabeth was sensitive to the fact that 'the art of royal representation was transformed by the teeming marketplace of print'.[6] More people could now see the Queen than had ever been the case before. And just as the reformist faith had itself been disseminated through and exploited the revolution in printing, so the Protestant ideology of Elizabeth's court was changing the consciousness of identity into something more recognisably modern.

A changing concept of the self has been identified as particularly characteristic of the Renaissance period. The inner life, the distinction between the 'self' and the outer world, was being recognised as the core of human identity. Being and seeming, what one was as opposed to what one presented to the world, were identified as being recognisably discrete, which in political terms, as critics of Machiavelli identified, was morally disturbing. In sixteenth-century England, this new distinction was catalysed in confessional as well as psychological terms. A 'momentous ideological shift'[7] has been identified between on the one hand the universal consensus of the transnational Catholic Church and on the other the twin poles of a spirituality which depended on faith alone, and the monarch who was the declared leader of both that faith and the state itself. The spiritual and the temporal were being melded in an entirely novel way; therefore the self had to be redefined against the 'absolutist claims of the Book and the King'.[8] A new emphasis on individuality was created by the removal of the communicative bridges of priest and the Mass – within the reformed religion, people could in a new way speak directly to God. In a secular context, there was no 'Book', no Bible to establish this different individual consciousness within some communal framework; instead, there was the monarch. As God's lieutenant, Elizabeth's authority was personalised in a new model of power and subjectivity, which meant she was represented in a different way.

The apparent immutability of Elizabeth's image was less concerned with the need to appear constantly beautiful or desirable than with power. On one level it was a conquest over nature, on another the 'immortality' of the Queen's image correlated with that of her rule – so long as one lasted the other was not threatened. (The twentieth-century fashion for pickled dictators might be seen as having a similar motivation.) So successful was the Queen's imposition of a singular image that she remains instantly recognisable, even in the cartoons of Catholic propaganda, yet within the confines of that image symbolic transformations did occur throughout the reign, while the court ceremonial which framed her as its centre was also flexible and responsive to the needs and moods of the moment. In her manipulation of the courtly love tradition, Elizabeth can be seen as positioning herself intellectually as both stylised mistress and Protestant master; in the performance of her *magnificenza*, this is made visually, and variedly, manifest.

The 'internal' quality of the portraits of Elizabeth reflected the influence of an Italian theorist, Lomazzo, whose *Tratatto dell'arte della pittura* (1584) became very popular. Lomazzo was far more widely known in England at the time than Vasari, whose *Lives* of artists helped to create the legend of the innovative geniuses who constitute the Renaissance's greatest hits. Lomazzo stressed the importance of the idea contained within a painting, rather than its surface. Every aspect of Elizabethan culture was imbued with emblemology, allowing all forms of decoration, including paintings, to be 'read'. Increasingly popular tracts such as Geoffrey Whitney's *A Choice of Emblems* helped the public to keep up and offered a selection of suitable emblems for aspiring sitters. Elizabeth herself observed in a letter to her brother Edward that 'the inward good mind . . . might as well be declared as the outward face and countenance', and the symbolic readings of her portraits can, and do, fill volumes. Elizabeth's claim to originality in portraiture is limited, but equally it was so bold as to be revolutionary. Images of the Virgin Mary have been identified as the single most consistent source for Tudor propaganda painting, but it was Elizabeth, unlike any of her forebears, who dared to seat herself down square in the sanctuary of sacred art.

Two portraits by Nicholas Hilliard dating from 1572–6, known respectively as the *Phoenix* and the *Pelican*, are the first to include any personalised rather than generic iconography associated with the Queen. Their provenance covers the period of the papal excommunication and the Ridolfi plot, so it is considered likely that the emblems used are a reaction to these events. The pelican becomes associated with Elizabeth in the jewellery inventories as early as 1573, and the bird appears in bestiaries as a symbol of redemption and charity, noted by Lyly in 1580 as 'the good pelican that to feed her people spareth not to rend her own person', a reference to the fact that female pelicans will, if necessary, feed their young with their own blood. What has been overlooked is the connection of the pelican to earlier English queenship, in the gift of the bird by the citizens of Anne of Bohemia in the fourteenth century. The pelican was thus a highly appropriate emblem to represent Elizabeth's sacrificial, maternal relationship with her subjects, particularly given the atmosphere of insecurity and threat surrounding *Regnans* and Ridolfi. It is also – just – conceivable that, given Anne Boleyn's association with Anne of Bohemia through her interest in the vernacular Bible, the pelican may be a gesture on Elizabeth's part to her mother's 'sacrifice', though this connection can only be speculative. However, the pelican has a further association, with Christ Himself. In Catholic iconography, the pelican is Christ, who gave his blood for the spiritual nourishment of the faithful; thus 'Elizabeth has arrogated to herself a symbol which under the old religious order had been reserved for God himself'. What makes the symbol particularly daring is that since Henry VIII's edicts on idolatry, the use of such symbols was seen as blasphemous. The *Pelican* portrait thus represents an audacious irony in that sacred imagery is invoked in defence of a new political order which shifted its potency on to the figure of the monarch herself. No other ruler before Elizabeth had gone quite so far.

The court pageants staged by the Burgundian dukes of the fifteenth century were perhaps the most powerful visual indicators of their cultural pre-eminence, and such pageants were very much part of English royal display by the end of the period and continued into the seventeenth century in the form of the court masque. Yet their very nature, unlike pictures, makes them difficult to judge. They were temporary, ephemeral, designed as brief, dazzling displays of theatre which centred on the ruler, so that when the ruler departed, their magic left with them. The impact of such pageants was created through the 'layering of diverse arts, the simultaneous stimulation of all senses, the inventiveness with which political messages were delivered and the enormity of wealth expended on ephemera'.[9] Princely festivities were multimedia happenings, which even the beauty of isolated objects as viewed today in museums cannot possibly convey. In Elizabeth's reign, the Accession Day Tilts were among the most elaborate of such pageants, and they also provided a further instance, as in the *Pelican* portrait, of the absorption of the sacred by the secular.

Organised by Sir Henry Lee of Ditchley, the tilts had begun as an informal celebration of Elizabeth's accession day, 17 November, and by the 1580s had become the major court spectacle of the calendar, not only an opportunity for Elizabeth's knights and nobles to demonstrate their chivalric prowess, but a chance for thousands of members of the public to see (for a shilling) their Queen. They were thrillingly elaborate, packed with exotic costumes and decorations, as well as the violent excitement of the tilt itself, where the armoured combatants thundered head-to-head down the lists, to break their lances (and sometimes a good deal else) in a romantic display underpinned by both theological and political endorsement of the Elizabethan state. The inauguration of the tilt in 1581 as the principal state festival, as opposed to smaller tournaments such as that of *The Four Foster Children of Desire* organised for the French ambassadors that year, is notable in that it coincides with Elizabeth's 'official' entry into virginity. That year, Philip Sidney made an appearance as a shepherd, a likely connection with Spenser's Shepherd's Calendar, and his description of the Iberian jousts in the *Arcadia* recall the 1581 tilt, where Elizabeth was compared with Helen, virgin queen of Corinth, whose 'sports were such as carried riches of knowledge on streams of delight'. Sir Henry's public management of the tilts lasted until 1590, and he also gave two great pageants for Elizabeth, at Woodstock in 1575 and Ditchley in 1592. The relationship between these festivals, and the tilts which intervened, provide a picture across time of the emergent mythology of Elizabeth as 'Gloriana' and the manner in which the apparatus of chivalry was publicly exploited to translate religious tradition on to her person.

The Fairy Queen makes her first appearance in relation to Elizabeth at the first of Lee's pageants, which began with two knights, Contarenus and Loricus (one of Lee's pseudonyms in the tilt), and a Hermit recounted a story of a princess who fell in love with a lowly knight. Manuscript evidence suggests Lee as the author of this play, which was received so rapturously that Elizabeth was presented with three copies of it, in Latin, Italian and French the next Christmas. Part two of the drama, played the next day, had Princess Gaudina reject her humble lover for reasons of state, which brought Elizabeth and her women to tears. After the greeting, the Queen's party was led to an ivy-covered banqueting house, whose tables were covered with turf and flowers and set with gold plate, under an oak tree hung with posies and gilt emblems. The camouflaging effect made it appear that the 'fairy queen' and her ladies were dining in the tree, hovering above the ground.

Lee's pageant at Woodstock came some weeks after one of the most evolved celebrations of the 'cult' of Elizabeth, staged by the Earl of Leicester at Kenilworth. The sensational entertainment has been interpreted as a (failed) last attempt on Leicester's part to persuade Elizabeth to marry him, but also as a statement of the political agenda – military intervention in favour of European Protestants – which the Earl was hoping to press upon the Queen. As with all Renaissance conceits, it is difficult to disentangle one single element of meaning from the complex layerings of spectacle, and it may be that the Kenilworth fetes were also a tribute to the relationship between Queen and courtier staged at a moment when Leicester accepted, personally, that it was time to move on.

Elizabeth was nearing her forty-second birthday that summer. Her ability to bear children had been a constant source of speculation and gossip (Ben Jonson's later claim that she was prevented by a membranous growth from enjoying intercourse is topped only by recent speculation that she was, in fact, a man). There is no real evidence that her menstrual cycle was abnormal, and an examination by doctors when she was forty-six claimed that the Queen was still 'apt' to conceive, yet surely Leicester might now have accepted that while he still might – just – aspire to the power of the crown matrimonial, royal progeny were by now unlikely? Earlier in the reign, he had used performance to press both his own suit and the need for Elizabeth to produce an heir. One play at Whitehall in 1565 in which a dialogue on chastity between Juno and Diana resulted in Jupiter arguing for marriage had provoked the weary remark from Elizabeth that 'This is all against me'. Three years previously, in the wake of the Katherine Grey scandal, Leicester had brought a play originally performed at the Inner Temple to court for the New Year. *Gorboduc* is an extremely worthy and lengthy meditation on the reversion issue, derived from Geoffrey of Monmouth, in which a divided and heirless realm is left to the mercies of foreign powers. Elizabeth made no comment.

Leicester's ambitions at Kenilworth were considerably more subtle. The Queen arrived at about eight o'clock on the evening of 9 July, to be greeted by ten 'sibyls' dressed in white silk. A giant surrendered his keys to the Queen in the tiltyard as six eight-foot-high trumpeters played 'very delectably' as Elizabeth approached the Lake, where an artificial island bore a Lady and her nymphs. The Lady, who claimed she had been waiting since King Arthur's time, offered up her power, after which Elizabeth progressed to a new bridge, seventy feet long, past cornucopiae of songbirds, fruits, fish, wine, weapons, musical instruments, gifts from Pomona, from Neptune, from Mars, Phoebus, Sylvanus, Ceres. When the Queen dismounted in the courtyard, a cannonade announced the firework display, which echoed for twenty miles around.

The sibyls and their prophecies were an appropriate choice for Leicester to make his point about Elizabeth's role in the protection of the reformist cause. Sibylline prophecy had been a feature of early Christian writings and had been particularly adopted by Elizabeth's grandfather, Henry VII, as a means of connecting the sacred and the dynastic aspects of kingship through the work of his court poet Johannes Opicius, *Praises to the King*. As we have seen, sibylline prophecy had also featured at Anne Boleyn's coronation, where three women had held up tablets with the mottoes 'Come, my love, thou shall be crowned', 'Trust in God' and 'Lord God direct my ways'. The use of the sibyls, then, was a subtle affirmation of Elizabeth's own dynastic legitimacy. English reformists such as John Jewel and Foxe also made use of the sibylline motif, quoting such passages as: 'Sybilla sayeth . . . That the great terror and fury of the Antichrist's Empire and the greatest woe that he shall work, shall be by the banks of the Tiber and Antichrist shall be a bishop and placed at Rome.'

Several writers over the course of Elizabeth's reign identified her with the 'sibylline' figure in Revelation as the woman clothed with the sun, among them Jane Seager, who was in 1589 to translate ten of twelve sibylline prophecies concerning Christ from a fifteenth-century Latin text as a gift for the Queen. Her *Divine Prophesies of the Ten Sibyls* centre around a 'true Virgin' who will protect the Church. Jane was connected with Leicester through her brothers William and Francis, both of them militant reformers, and she was among the ten women who greeted Elizabeth at Kenilworth in the summer of 1575. Her speech presented the Queen as a 'prince of peace' who would preside over a safe realm until a final, apocalyptic battle in which the 'Last Emperor' (an image appropriated by both Henry VII and Henry VIII) would defeat the foes of Christianity. The sibyls provide a connection between Leicester's entertainment at Kenilworth and Lee's at Woodstock, where the 'Hermit' greeted Elizabeth with the announcement: 'And now best Lady and most beautiful, so termed of the Oracle and so thought in the world . . . what Sibilla showed, by your most happy coming is verified.' That is, both Leicester and Lee chose to emphasise the centrality of the Queen's role in the salvation of reform. In Lee's case, this met with Elizabeth's approval, but Leicester's magnificent entertainment, which over a week comprised the usual hunting, bear-baiting, dancing, masquerading and an extraordinary finale involving a twenty-four-foot-long singing dolphin, did not apparently amuse, or influence, her as much as the Earl hoped: 'one has the impression that it fell rather flat. Its classicism was slightly university-wittish and provincial, its romanticism slightly ridiculous'.

Perhaps Elizabeth was rather weary of endless nymphs and giants, or perhaps she was irritated by Leicester's ostentatious courtly tactics at a time when she knew perfectly well that he had recently conducted a clandestine affair (and possibly a secret marriage) with Lady Douglas Sheffield, who bore him a son. Either way, the Queen departed (as High Dudgeon?) while in a last-ditch effort to save his party, Leicester had his poet George Gascoigne improvise some eleventh-hour verses to be sung by 'Deep Desire' from a holly bush as Elizabeth rode by.

Or perhaps, while Elizabeth was content to position herself within the complex allegorical celebration of her queenship which presented her as the saviour of her people's faith, she simply objected to being pressured to act. Although Kenilworth has often been interpreted as a week-long proposal, featuring a 'rustic wedding' among the amusements, it may also be understood as a site of conflict between Leicester's agenda and that of the Queen. The armour Leicester wears in the portrait by Zuccaro he commissioned for the pageants is replete with Protestant imagery, and Elizabeth apparently disliked his self-presentation as a captain who would defend his faith in the Spanish Netherlands. The gauntlet of Lee's armour, featuring the motto 'Defensor Fidei', was less pointed and more acceptable.

Fifteen years later, at Henry Lee's retirement tilt of 1590, Sir Henry and his successor the Earl of Cumberland presented themselves to Elizabeth at her gallery window in front of a crowned pillar inscribed with Latin verses praising the Virgin and her empire. The pastoral allegories instituted at Woodstock and continued in the intervening tilts implied that Elizabeth had returned her nation to a golden age, indeed an Arcadia, conflating her through Protestant chivalry with Mary the Virgin. As Lee approached the Queen:

> Her Majesty beholding those armed knights coming towards her did suddenly hear a music so sweet and secret as everyone thereat greatly marveled. And hearkening to that excellent melody, the earth as it were opening, there appeared a pavilion made of white taffeta ... being in a proportion like unto the sacred temple of the Virgins Vestal ... arched like a Church, within it many lamps burning.

The enchanted pavilion of the fairy queen had been transformed into the sacred enclosure of the Virgin. Lee's verse address to Elizabeth combined the chivalrous pastoral with courtly love and religious worship:

> My helmet now shall make a hive for bees
> And lovers songs shall turn to holy psalms ...

And so from court to cottage I depart
My Saint is sure of mine unspotted heart.

Tournaments were one of the few forms of pageantry which survived from pre-Reformation times. That the tilts were consciously organised as a substitute for the old feasts of the Church is articulated in the manuscript for the last entertainment Lee gave for Elizabeth, at Ditchley, where the 'Curate' 'showed his parishioners of a holiday which passed all the Pope's holidays, and that should be on the 17th day of November'. The Ditchley fete was nostalgic in temper, recalling Woodstock fifteen years before. An 'old Knight' was awakened by music and explained that 'Not far from hence nor very long ago/The Fairy Queen the Fairest Queen saluted'. He then spoke of the tilts, which had been the annual tributes of 'Loricus's' love for his Queen – casting the tournaments as yearly instalments in a fifteen-year narrative of chivalrous romance. It is a beautiful image, one which encapsulates all the gleaming shimmer of Elizabethan *magnificenza*, yet by the time Lee delivered his last tribute Elizabeth had begun to learn the cost of such fanciful posturings as they played out in the real world. The poetry of Elizabeth's knights might come to represent a golden age, yet the reality of Elizabeth's rule as perceived in much of Europe was of a tyrannical, paranoid, repressive regime of torturers, a jarring contrast to the idealised dream worlds of the tilt.

CHAPTER EIGHTEEN

As a Renaissance ruler, Elizabeth was adept in the language of iconography. Courtiers who wished to flatter, persuade, celebrate (and, indeed, insult) the Queen had a huge range of iconographic analogies – classical, biblical, cosmographical – upon which to draw, producing a sometimes bewildering range of overlapping or contradictory imagery. Comparisons between Elizabeth and Diana are a case in point. Diana was the virgin goddess who asked Jupiter that she might retain her virginity; her iconography, with its symbols of bows and crescent moons, became something of a cult around the French royal mistress Diane de Poitiers. A tapestry commissioned by Diane for the Château d'Anet in 1550 shows Diana making her request to the gods, that she might be free not only from lust, but actively able to fight against it. Game was not the hunter-goddess's only quarry – according to the Anet inscription she also pursued 'unreasonable appetite', that is, anything which threatened the social order. Allusions to Elizabeth as Diana are relatively sparse early in her reign, when, in theory at least, the Queen was still contemplating marriage, though in the *Rainbow Portrait* and Hilliard's miniatures of the 1590s the crescent moon decorates her hair, and she received jewels which echoed Diana's imagery. While the virginal aspect of Diana, and her commitment to chastity in order to preserve social equilibrium, was appropriate to Elizabeth after the end of her last diplomatic courtship, there was also a darker side to the goddess. In some classical sources, Diana is the goddess of vengeance and death (the horrible fate of Actaeon, who spied on the bathing goddess and was transformed into a stag and ripped apart by her hounds, was alluded to in relation to Philip of Spain's early proposal to Elizabeth), since her virginity meant that her only currency was extinction. Elizabeth's resistance to becoming a figurehead for the Dutch Protestant cause is encapsulated in a particularly shocking reference to her as Diana, Pieter van der Heyden's 1584 *Elizabeth in Diana and Callisto*. Callisto's story is a tangle of macabre eroticism – the goddess's favourite nymph is raped by Jupiter in the form of his daughter Diana, and when her pregnancy is revealed Diana banishes her, then, when she gives birth to a son, Jupiter's wife Juno turns her into a bear. In the Heyden engraving, Elizabeth is shown, naked, as Diana, while at her feet the Pope, as Callisto, gives birth to a litter of monsters, his pregnant stomach exposed by the figures of Time and Truth, while the nymphs behind Elizabeth represent the Dutch provinces. Unsurprisingly, the composition failed to achieve its aim of persuading Elizabeth to become a more active champion of the Dutch. Elizabeth herself never appears to have identified personally with Diana, preferring, if at all, the more pacific lunar imagery of the moon goddess Selene, but for many English Catholics, relating her to Diana as the symbol of vengeance and death was becoming all too appropriate.

As the Titian parody makes clear, Elizabeth could not avoid being drawn into theological war games. Unlike her sister, Elizabeth never burned men for their faith. She tortured and hanged them for treason. A publication of 1583, *A declaration of the Favourable Dealing of her Majesty's Commissioners appointed for the Examination of Certain Traitors and of Tortures Unjustly reported to be done on them for matters of Religion*, authored by one Thomas 'Rackmaster' Norton, attempted to make this clear. Norton claimed that only guilty prisoners were tortured, that no man was racked for his conscience, only his treason, and that, besides, no such activity could be carried out without a warrant signed by at least six Privy Councillors. In the minds of many of the Queen's advisers, this was a necessary evil, but the perennial conditions of crisis and war which accompanied the European Reformation also created an atmosphere of conspiracy and fear which served to encourage the very threat it hoped to suppress – 'for all the uncertainty and unpredictability facing Elizabeth's England, it seems plain that the queen's ministers hypnotized themselves with fear'.[1] Hindsight is a poor rationale upon which to judge the actions

Elizabeth took against her Catholic subjects – we know that she survived, she believed she might not. The priest of the English College at Rome who denounced Elizabeth as 'That proud usurping Jezebel' and expressed his wish that 'I hope ere long the dogs shall tear her flesh, and those that be her props and upholders' was speaking for the majority of Europe. The Virgin Queen might have turned her face with relative serenity to the moon of chastity, but as her power as Protestant leader accrued around her, she had little choice in becoming not only an instrument of vengeance, but in modern terms, a tyrant.

The sixteenth-century term for the trade on which Elizabeth's security depended was 'spiery', the grimy underside of the magnificent cloak which overlaid Renaissance governance. Several writers have compared the Queen's mentality to that of a double agent, not only for her ability to preserve her privacy while living such an intensely public life, but for her dogged commitment to her own survival at all costs; an essential lack of interest in the merits of a cause so long as it advantaged her. Elizabeth just grasped, as Mary Stuart, for example, did not, that this was the new reality of the emergent modern state. Here Elizabeth is a true Machiavellian, not in the stereotypical sense of duplicitous, but more profoundly, as a ruler who fully apprehended that primary duty to self and state.

The passing of the Acts of Supremacy and Uniformity in 1559 had produced a confessional state in which political and religious loyalty were necessarily intertwined; they also produced a tension between these two elements which from the 1570s onwards gave disproportionate influence to a relatively small number of Catholic recusants (from the Latin, *recusans*, one who refuses) whose activities were the source of obsessively paranoid attention. Elizabeth had little choice but to give ear to the endless revelations of conspiracy, which involved her in a denial of those principles which were so much part of her self-presentation as a model of tolerance and peacefulness. Francis Walsingham encapsulated this necessity in his maxim 'there is less danger in fearing too much than too little'. Thomas Phelippes, Walsingham's codemaster, often used the modern-sounding phrase 'the security of the state', and security and suspicion were twins

– lose the latter, Elizabeth's ministers argued, and the former would vanish, too. The darker tempo which beat beneath the glittering rhythm of Elizabeth's magnificent public life was one of perpetual, thudding terror.

In 1579, it was estimated that the number of Catholic émigrés at large in Italy and France was some three hundred. This does not seem like many, but the majority were from gentry or upper-class backgrounds, with networks of connections and means which stretched back behind them to England. Their champion was William Allen, who in 1568 had founded the Catholic seminary at Douai, which later moved to Reims, while Allen himself travelled on to the English College at Rome. Propagandist accounts such as Anthony Munday's 1582 *Mirror of Mutabilitie* attempt to paint as sinister a picture as possible of the atmosphere of the College. Munday, a young spy posing as a Catholic sympathiser, details the incessant conversation about the need for a 'stout assaulting of England', while describing the macabre penances the Jesuit seminarians undertook in the refectory. Wearing hooded but backless cloaks, they lashed themselves with cords of wire until the blood ran on the floor. These faceless fanatics were plotting to destroy the Church of England, bring down the government and unseat the Queen from the throne. Allen argued that his priests were freedom fighters, their mission being merely to save endangered Catholic souls. The Pope did indeed support their mission, but it was a pastoral one, aimed at the succour of Catholic souls, not the overturning of governments. In 1580, a priest named John Hart was interrogated about papal recognition of the bull *Regnans in Excelsis*, promulgated a decade before. Hart confirmed that the bull as enacted under Pius was still legal, but that Pope Gregory, his successor, had made a dispensation permitting Elizabeth's subjects to respect her authority without threat to their souls. The government chose to ignore this. Hart, like so many of his fellows, was racked.

So far as the law was concerned, Norton's *Declaration* makes a distinction between faith itself, and the means by which that faith was to be conveyed to England. Torture was necessary not to persecute Catholics, but to 'understand of particular practices for setting up their religion by treason or force against the Queen'. And so, by the 1580s, torture was normalised. Alongside Rackmaster Norton, the government made use of the skills of Richard Topcliffe, who had been in Elizabeth's service since at least 1578. Described as a 'one man Stasi',[2] Topcliffe's relish for his work was such that his name became a verb: in the correspondence of Catholic exiles in Italy, 'topclifiz-are' was synonymous with the practice of torture. Yet so far as the eager schools of hopeful martyrs were concerned, even torture was no deterrent. In the text which became known as Campion's Brag, written in Southwark at the beginning of his English mission in 1580, Edmund Campion, a one-time Oxford favourite of the Earl of Leicester, affirmed that Jesuits were 'never to despair of your recovery, while we have a man left to enjoy your Tyburn, or to be racked with your torments or consumed with your prisons'. Campion's trial and execution are emblematic of the theological and legalistic elipses and evasions which coalesced into Elizabeth's policy of state security.

Campion's geographical progress inscribes the development of his commitment to the Catholic faith. From Oxford he had travelled to Douai, where he taught in Allen's seminary, and thence to Rome, where he was received as a Jesuit, after which he performed missionary work in the German states before arriving back in England, disguised as an Irish jeweller, in 1580. Accompanied by a fellow Jesuit, Robert Persons, Campion moved cautiously around the south of England, preaching in secret at Smithfield a fortnight before he composed his letter, intended for the Council in the event of his apprehension. Among the numbered list of intentions which summarised his mission, Campion made two key statements. He claimed that his charge was 'to . . . preach the Gospel, to minister the Sacraments, to instruct the simple, to reform sinners, to confute errors – in brief, to cry alarm spiritual against foul vice and proud ignorance'. Further, Campion claimed that 'I never had in mind, and am strictly forbidden by our Father that sent me, to deal in any respect with matter of state or policy of this realm, as things which appertain not to my vocation.' Officially, Campion maintained the same stance as Alan and Hart, that his presence in England was the fulfilment of his pastoral role as priest.

The 'Brag' was soon in wide circulation, and Elizabeth's printer,

Christopher Barker, was soon busy producing counter-propaganda. In January 1581, a proclamation was issued calling for the arrest of all Jesuits then in England, and for all members of seminaries on the Continent to return. Given Pope Gregory's dispensation, it was not strictly necessary that Catholics were automatically disloyal subjects, but the government was determined to make this so – loyalty to the Church of England and the crown were indissoluble. Once it was made high treason for a priest to reconcile a subject to Rome, converts were placed beyond the law, and hence vulnerable, without recourse, to its strictest punishments.

In this atmosphere, Campion became a trophy, a latter-day Most Wanted, and Walsingham's 'spiery' network was on his trail. George Eliot, a recent Catholic apostate who offered his services to Leicester, was among them. Eliot had recently confessed to knowledge of yet another conspiracy, in which a group of fifty men, selected by William Allen and another priest, John Payne, would assault Elizabeth on progress and kill her, Cecil, Leicester and Walsingham. Whether this was true, or a fabrication of Eliot's designed to demonstrate his willingness to betray Catholic families in which he had previously served, Eliot was authorised in mid-July 1581 to travel to Lyford Grange in Oxfordshire, where there was suspicion that Campion was hiding. Campion was discovered on the morning of the 17th, when a spike was driven through a hollow wall to reveal the 'priests' hole behind'. Campion was barely delivered to the Tower before rival presses were whizzing off triumphalist accounts of his impending martyrdom. There then began a curiously horrible process in which Campion was alternately tortured and vivaed, one day disputing scholarly points with the four commissioners appointed to try him at Westminster Hall, or even the Dean of St Paul's, the next strapped to the rack. This continued until the trial proper commenced in November. Now that Campion's case was an international *cause célèbre*, the government had to prove that he was a traitor, not a victim of confessional persecution. The 1581 act stated that:

> all persons [who] shall pretend to have power to absolve, persuade or withdraw any of the Queen's majesty's subjects from their natural

obedience to her Majesty, or to withdraw them to that intent from the religion now by her Highness's authority established within her Highnesses' dominions shall be to all intents judged to be traitors and being thereof lawfully convicted, shall have judgement, suffer and forfeit as in cases of high treason.

This was not the law that condemned Campion. The recent legislation was still not quite sufficient to prove that the Jesuit was on trial for treason, not faith, so the commissioners returned to an earlier statute of 1352 which made it treasonable to compass the king's death, excluding religion altogether. They claimed that Campion and his fellows had 'in divers other places . . . beyond the seas' conspired to 'deprive, cast down and disinherit' the Queen, to encourage her enemies to war and to produce insurrection and rebellion in the realm. To prove the case, Walsingham was obliged to bring in his spies from the cold, so that Londoners, eagerly awaiting every scrap of news, were treated to a vignette of the double agents, secret dossiers and coded communications on which their safety as Elizabeth's subjects depended. Or so the printers told them. From Rome, William Allen called the trial 'the most pitiful practice that ever was heard of to shed innocent blood by the face of justice'.

Campion was hanged, drawn and quartered at Tyburn on 1 December 1581. He prayed for Elizabeth from the scaffold. Elizabeth is absent, largely, from these proceedings carried out in her name. Supposedly, Lord Howard dared to confront her with the accusation that she had executed an innocent man, to which she replied that justice had been done according to the law. Her own feelings about the dirtiness of her government's hands cannot be known, while her behaviour in what amounted to her private life suggests that she had no particular personal hatred of Catholicism. And yet, she was the pious product of Katherine Parr's reformist court, happy to be associated, in pageantry at least, with the enemies of the Papal Antichrist. She signed the torture warrants, and the death warrants. She was anxious that the trials of Catholics should have the force of law, while being aware that in the eyes of Catholic states her authority to pass such law was in itself illegitimate. In 1559, she had acceded to the *Device for the Alteration of Religion* with awareness of its consequences. Campion's trial was a gift to Catholic propagandists, so much so that even Walsingham reportedly commented that it should have been better for the Queen to throw away 40,000 gold pieces rather than execute him publicly. The missionaries' cause was if anything enhanced by the threat of persecution; writing in 1597, one Jesuit observed that 'the rigour of the laws . . . has been the foundation of our credit'.[3] In Campion's case, both sides claimed victory in loss.

The contentiousness and subversion which surrounded the Campion case were very much products of Renaissance thought, and they demanded a peculiarly Renaissance solution. It was no longer the case, as an earlier Elizabethan scholar has suggested, that 'the dominant ruling idea of Renaissance England . . . was the belief in a cosmic order which governed both human institutions and natural phenomena'.[4]

Elizabeth may have held her power by divine right of that 'cosmic order', and she believed utterly in the concept, but she saw that different measures were required to secure that right's continued exercise. If Machiavelli is 'the single best source of that Renaissance view of politics which exalted cunning and cruelty over Christianity',[5] then Elizabeth's treatment of Campion is a perfect exemplar of that view. The rift created by reform was too deep to any longer accommodate scholastic debate. To use a modern term, the government saw the missionary priests as spiritual terrorists, and, like governments today, declared themselves unprepared to have dealings with them. Yet the extent to which Elizabeth's readiness to kill her enemies was fostered by genuine fear or by a ruthless determination to preserve her state is further confused by the debate as to the extremity England really faced. Was the Catholic threat as fearsome as it was perceived to be, or was that fear a product of the very vigilance upon which the government both insisted and depended? The corpses, though, are irrefutable.

CHAPTER NINETEEN

Elizabeth had never sought to become the champion of the Protestant cause in Europe. Confessional divisions in the 1570s were
causing her enough trouble at home; moreover, she was extremely
averse to the risk and expense that foreign intervention entailed. She
was, however, prepared to support her French counterpart, Charles
IX, in his aim of healing the religious breach that had already cost
France so many gruelling and destructive years of war. Charles's
plan was threefold – Elizabeth was to marry his brother the Duc
of Anjou, thus creating an Anglo-French alliance against Spain; his
sister Margot was to marry the Bourbon-Valois Henri of Navarre;
and, finally, the rift between two of his most powerful subjects, the
pro-Catholic Duc de Guise and the Huguenot Gaspard de Coligny,
Admiral of France, had to be repaired. Coligny and Guise had once
been friends, described as the 'two diamonds of France', but years
of vicious religious factionalism had set them at odds. Not only did
Charles's efforts at peace-making fail, but the enmity between the
two men would result in the 'greatest imponderable of sixteenth-
century history', the St Bartholomew's Day Massacre.[1]

In late 1571, Elizabeth's envoy Sir Thomas Smith arrived in Paris to
begin negotiations. Unfortunately the Duc of Anjou had no interest
whatsoever in marrying a thirty-eight-year-old woman he described
as a balding heretic, but his mother Catherine de Medici tactfully
proposed her eighteen-year-old youngest son, then Duc of Alençon,
as a replacement. Sir Thomas approved of the suggestion, writing to
Elizabeth that Alençon was not only less obstinate and bumptious
than his brother, but also less fervently Catholic and 'foolish and
restive like a mule'. To his disadvantage, Alençon was practically a
dwarf, with a complexion repulsively ruined by smallpox, though

his mother added protectively that he was growing a beard, which would conceal the worst of it. On 19 April 1572, England and France signed the Treaty of Blois, a defensive alliance agreement, but events in the Netherlands rendered the union frustratingly inadequate.[3]

Since the previous July, the rebel provinces of the north of Holland had recognised William, Prince of Orange, as their leader. Protestant leaders in France had been trying to persuade Catherine de Medici that France would benefit by assisting in the Netherlands' liberation from Spain, supported by the Dutch envoy Louis Count of Nassau, Orange's brother (an ally of Coligny). Charles IX and his mother had at least two secret meetings with Nassau, and though Charles was prepared to lend covert support to Nassau's campaign in the southern provinces, he would not take the definitive step of declaring war. England's perspective was key, but Blois held Elizabeth to no martial commitment in the circumstances, while the marriage with Alençon had made no progress. Without a firm commitment from Elizabeth, Catherine de Medici was not prepared to intervene. The royal council in Paris was in disarray – Catholics, supported by the Duc of Anjou, refused to countenance a war in favour of heretics, while the Coligny party argued that only intervention now would prevent a worse conflict in the future. If Spain was provoked, the Catholic party countered, Philip II might well invade from Italy and the Pyrenees. To Elizabeth, Walsingham wrote of the state of suspense in the city, and it was her refusal to engage – supported by the moderate party on the French Privy Council – which left Coligny defeated. Ironically, just as Elizabeth, fearful of potential French domination in the Netherlands, was considering a rapprochement with Alba (it was even proposed in council that England back him in the event of a French invasion), Philip was holding Elizabeth responsible for the whole mess:

> The king is informed [wrote a correspondent at Madrid to Cecil] that if it had not been for the Queen's Grace of England, Flanders had not rebelled against the Duke of Alba ... there be many Englishmen come into the Low Countries, of whose coming both the Queen and her Council do well know ... so that the King is very

angry with the Queen's grace, and . . . that he hath sworn that he will be revenged in such sort, as both the Queen and England shall repent that ever did they meddle in any of his Countries.[3]

Coligny, who had sworn a private oath to support the house of Orange, nonetheless felt himself bound in conscience to support the Dutch rebels, describing the Spanish, in a letter to Cecil, as the 'servants of Satan'. As Protestant magnates from the south gathered in Paris for the wedding of Henri of Navarre and Princess Margot, he announced that he intended to leave the city on 25 August with a company of 15,000 men. On 22 August, Coligny left the Louvre at about 11 a.m. to cross the river to his home. As he reached Saint-Germain, a shot was fired. Coligny survived, losing a finger and suffering a fractured arm, but who was it that wanted him dead?

In the days that followed the assassination attempt, Coligny was murdered in his bed by Guise's men. But Guise was not acting alone. St Bartholomew's Day was a massacre far beyond the scale of Wassy. Between two and six thousand Protestants were killed. More than six hundred homes in Paris were pillaged, women and children were horrifically slaughtered and for once the cliché that the streets ran with blood was all too appallingly accurate. Charles IX, attempting to save the French monarchy's face in the aftermath of the St Bartholomew's Day Massacre, gave out to his ambassadors that it 'happened through a private quarrel long fostered between . . . two houses', which has often given rise to the interpretation that the massacre was the consequence of a Guise/Coligny vendetta, but the massacre and the feud were two separate, though overlapping disasters. Guise was exonerated by Walsingham, himself an eyewitness to the terrible events of those few days: 'The duke of Guise is not so bloody, neither did he kill any man himself . . . He spake openly that for the admiral's death he was glad, for he knew him to be his enemy, but he thought for the rest that the King had put such to death as if it had pleased him might have done him very good service.' Evidence suggests that Guise was acting in collusion with Catherine de Medici and the Duke of Anjou, to prevent Coligny's departure and the civil war they believed would ensue. Once the assassination attempt failed, a series of late-night council meetings decided that the moment to move against the Protestant leadership had come and a list of seventy men was collated. What turned this horribly violent but specifically concentrated plan into a general massacre was the Paris Militia. Formed after the Wassy massacre to control religious tensions in the city, the Militia had been infiltrated by ultra-Catholics, and in the impossibly tense summer atmosphere of the capital it took one unfortunate phrase from Guise to produce a bloody explosion. As his men left Coligny's home in the early hours of 24 August, leaving the Admiral's corpse to be mutilated by the mob, Guise called out 'let us go on to the others, for the king commands it'. He meant the others on the original list of seventy, but the Militia understood differently. Their war cry was chillingly plain. 'Kill, kill!'

English responses to the massacre are epitomised by the reaction of Edmund Grindal, the generally moderate future Bishop of London, who demanded that all English Catholics be detained and that Mary Stuart's head be severed immediately. As descriptions of the horrors perpetrated on French Huguenots continued to reach England – for the original massacre soon spread to the French provinces – Grindal's demand for crisis measures spoke for many. Francis Walsingham, who had sheltered fleeing Huguenots in his home during the crisis, passed on a list of the names of the murdered to the Privy Council. Like many Protestants, Walsingham believed that Rome and Madrid were now colluding in what our century might understand as a 'final solution'. It was a view that would gain credence over the following years, in that St Bartholomew indicated that a negotiated solution was no longer tenable and that offence was the only possible strategy for the preservation of the Protestant faith.

In terms of international policy there could be no immediate question of proceeding with the French accords; conversely Charles IX, now completely cut off from his Protestant polity, needed England more than ever. If Elizabeth hoped to counter both the long-term imperial ambition of Spain and the apparently 'genocidal' policies of the ultra-Catholic parties in France and Rome, then she needed time, and for that the Spanish had to be conciliated. Both Elizabeth and Philip of Spain were now prepared to turn back from the impasse of the late 1560s. At the Treaty of Bristol in 1574, trade embargoes between England and the Netherlands were lifted. Elizabeth spent three days in the port city, arriving in a procession on a horse saddled in emerald green, trimmed with gold fringing. The saddle survives, having enjoyed considerably greater longevity than the treaty, which signalled the last brief period of peace between England and Spain for the remainder of the century.

Elizabeth's strategy towards Spain and the Netherlands during the next decade initially appears contradictory, if not self-defeating, a game of grandmother's footsteps with tentative appeasements to either side being proffered and then suddenly withdrawn. Whether the Queen liked them or not (and mostly she did not), cutting off the Dutch Protestants entirely was inconceivable. Spain could not be allowed to suppress them altogether, yet this had to be accomplished while simultaneously avoiding a direct confrontation with Philip, which would have escalated aggression to a position from which neither side could escape. Elizabeth continued grudgingly to channel funds to the Netherlands while claiming to the Spanish that her 'neutrality' was maintained in the hope of a settlement which would preserve both monarchical authority and a vague concept of 'ancient liberties'. Philip made some gestures towards the acknowledgement of the Orangist confederation, known as the States General, and the ultimate withdrawal of his armies, but by 1578, when the Protestants were defeated at Gembloux, their cause looked hopeless to English eyes unless Elizabeth was prepared to intervene, which both Leicester and Walsingham pressured her to do. Moreover, Don John of Austria was not discreet about his support of proposed papal measures to replace Elizabeth with Mary Stuart, which Gregory XIII was promoting with a view to marrying the Scots queen to a suitable Catholic candidate. Don John naturally saw himself as this candidate, and though his romance with Mary was never to be – he died of plague soon after Gembloux – the return of Spanish fortunes in the Provinces looked menacing.

Even more so was Philip II's accession to the throne of Portugal in autumn 1580. That he was the rightful claimant, through his mother Queen Isabella, was no comfort to the Portuguese, who initially claimed they had no intention of accepting Spanish sovereignty, but the arrival of the energetic Alba with 50,000 troops soon changed their minds. Philip now controlled not only the vast Spanish wealth of the New World, but Portuguese possessions there, too, as well as the Portuguese navy. Both the Atlantic and Pacific oceans were effectively under Spanish control, which meant that much of European trade was also. Philip was crowned in Lisbon in September, at the same time as Francis Drake sailed into Plymouth harbour, having successfully circumnavigated the globe.

Anglo-Spanish confrontations at sea had not ceased with the Treaty of Bristol. Elizabeth had forbidden attacks on Spanish vessels south of the equator for three years, while turning a blind eye to the lucrative (and to the Spanish more sensitive) operations of privateers to the north. John Hawkins funded several Caribbean expeditions, while Francis Drake made his personal fortune with a raid on a bullion fleet in Nombre de Dios during his third piratical voyage in 1572–3. Drake's propensity to bawl 'Victory to the Queen of England' during his raids looked bad for Elizabeth's professions of ignorance. In 1577 Elizabeth abandoned the pretence and, along with several members of her council, provided funds for Drake's attempt at circumnavigation. Drake's achievement was tremendous, as Elizabeth recognised when she welcomed him triumphantly on board his ship and knighted him, but the voyage had also exposed a weakness in Spain's Pacific possessions, one which Elizabeth declared herself openly to be ready to exploit. She announced to a seething Ambassador Mendoza that she had every intention of keeping her £140,000 share of Drake's booty, and that moreover Philip had no one but himself to blame, since 'the Spaniards had provoked unto themselves that evil through their injustice towards the English, in hindering against the right of nations, their negotiations'.[4] She continued grandly that she was perfectly entitled to state her right to 'bring in colonies' in regions where Philip had as yet no subjects living, since 'prescription without possession is of no validity'.[5] In case Mendoza failed to understand her, she wore the jewels Drake presented to her under the ambassador's nose at her New Year's gift-giving.

CHAPTER TWENTY

Even scholars who resist the notion of a 'cult of Elizabeth' often fall under her spell. Due to a noted 'aversion of English historians for all things Continental', theories about Elizabeth's governance frequently circle obsessively around the figure of the Queen, their orbit excluding the much wider trajectories described by the currents and counter-currents of sixteenth-century statecraft. The 'Throckmorton plot' is an instance of this. The conspiracy with which Elizabeth had to contend in 1583 represented more than another plan to usurp a heretic ruler; it evolved not from the English succession crisis, but from the French. 'They [English historians] refer to the invasion project as the "Throckmorton plot" as if Francis Throckmorton was something more than a parochial cog in a much bigger international mechanism' is an accurate dismissal.[1] The religious crisis which had begun in France with the massacre at Wassy had arrived at the doors of the royal palace – confessional divisions were now to determine the next ruler of France. It was the beloved project of the Guises, the Franco-British empire, which lay at the heart of a Europe-wide conspiracy.

Henri III, the third of Catherine de Medici's sons to ascend the French throne, had succeeded his brother Charles in 1575. A year later, he had signed the Edict of Beaulieu, which restored significant concessions to the Huguenots, but, under pressure from the Catholic League founded by Guise, had revoked the majority of them. Relations between the Guise family and Henri had thus been slowly deteriorating for some years. At his accession, the king had been anxious to conciliate his most powerful subjects, and had maintained them in apparent favour, but Henri had favourites of his own, a group of court dandies known as the *mignons* who succeeded in driving the Duc of Anjou from the French court in 1578 before turning their ire on the Guise. The Duc was prepared to watch his rivals, mostly members of the minor southern nobility, promoted, in the belief that the king would make him Constable of France, but as it became clear that Henri had no such intentions, his toleration evaporated. On the part of the childless king, there was suspicion that the Guises had ambitions to claim the throne of Navarre. Armed squabbles broke out between Guise retainers and those of the *mignons*, and by Easter 1582 the Duc had decided to retire from court. To his ultra-Catholic enemies, Henri III of France was a puppet in the hands of the English Queen. Elizabeth, meanwhile, saw Henri as harbouring her 'mortal enemy', the Duc de Guise, of whom she spoke words so 'foul' to the Spanish ambassador Mendoza that he felt unable to quote them to his master. With the Duc of Anjou now in the Netherlands, the Spanish feared that he would raise an army to come to the aid of the Dutch rebels, and they therefore sought allies at the French court. The Duc de Guise, under the exciting new code name 'Hercules', was prepared to offer his support, but he believed Scottish politics could determine the new direction of Europe's religious affinities.

Henri III spent the spring at Fontainebleau, while the Duc remained in Paris. On 14 May he attended a meeting at the house of the papal nuncio, Giovanni Battista Castelli. Also present were Claude Matthieu, the rector of the Professed Jesuits, the Archbishop of Glasgow, James Beaton, who represented Mary Stuart, and a Scots Jesuit, William Crichton. Crichton was connected with the Catholic League in Normandy, where he had first met Guise in late 1581, and was preparing to leave for Scotland to meet Esme Stuart, Duke of Lennox. That summer, Lennox had succeeded in usurping the trust of James VI in his Protestant regent, the Earl of Morton, leading the government himself when Morton was executed in June.

The close relationship between Lennox and James provoked accusations that their relationship was sexual, and while James had been raised a strict Protestant, under the precepts of his reformist tutor, the brilliant humanist George Buchanan, Guise believed that Lennox's influence might return James to the Catholic fold. At the meeting in May, Crichton delivered a report condemning those

English Protestants, including Leicester, who were denying the Stuarts their lawful right to succeed in England. According to Crichton, Lennox believed that he could muster 8,000 troops, to be equalled by a French force (led, Guise insisted, by himself, though some Jesuitical wrangling was required to absolve him of his oath to Henri III). With Scotland tamed, the Duc planned to invade England.

Crichton was dispatched to Spain, while his fellow priest, the erstwhile companion of the Catholic martyr Campion, Robert Persons, travelled to Rome to present the plan to the new Guise allies, the Spanish. It was estimated that the venture would require 400,000 crowns. Meanwhile, Guise was on the Normandy coast, procuring ships and supplies. But the plan began to unravel even at this early stage. Rome offered just 50,000 crowns of the required funds, while in Spain Philip proposed only 10,000. It did not suit Spanish interests to fund a Guise coup in England – they were more use to him in France as a counter to Henri, who had been sending funds to his brother Anjou in the Netherlands, supported by Elizabeth. Philip was, however, prepared to be generous to Guise personally, pensioning him to the sum of 40,000 crowns, 'not yet a formal alliance, but the first steps had been made in a commitment that would inevitably grow as the Anglo-French entente strengthened'.[2] While Guise profited personally from inaction, his manipulation of James's crush on Lennox achieved the opposite of his aims. The Protestant lords in Scotland were sufficiently alarmed by the king's flirtations with both Lennox and Catholicism to kidnap him (with Elizabeth's covert support) at Ruthven in 1582. The invasion of England was put off, while Scotland was once more in the hands of the reformers.

The web of espionage was growing impossibly tangled – Henri was receiving information from the English, while Walsingham was on the trail of Guise's agents on both sides of the Channel. As ever, it was almost impossible to know who was actually working for whom. The official English version of the 'Throckmorton plot' is explained in a pamphlet (possibly authored by Walsingham or Cecil himself), *A Discovery of the Treasons Practised and Attempted Against the Queen's Majesty*. Francis Throckmorton and his two brothers had been brought up as Catholics, and in 1581 Francis had joined the London household of the French ambassador, where he was soon selected to manage the secret correspondence between Mary Stuart and her French allies. In June 1583 he was contacted by Charles Paget, a member of the Guise household in Paris who had been spying for Walsingham for two years. Paget, known deliciously as 'Mope', a slippery creature, a most dangerous instrument in Walsingham's words, was in England in September to survey the most likely point on the Sussex coast for the landing of a Guisard force. To achieve this, he was courting the Earls of Arundel and Northumberland, the latter of whom was arrested in London on 15 December. Walsingham's investigations, which involved the questioning of hundreds of witnesses in Sussex, compromised Northumberland beyond his statement that his meeting with Charles Paget had merely been concerned with the affairs of the latter's elder brother. Throckmorton, though, had been in the Tower since early in the month and had already confessed under torture to meeting the Spanish ambassador and providing him with a list of potential harbours in Sussex.

If Philip of Spain had hoped that the Guises might undermine the more cordial relations obtaining between England and France, Spanish involvement in the plot had the opposite effect. In January 1584, Mendoza was unceremoniously ejected from England, shuffled on to the *Scout* and borne to Calais. In London, there was a mood of paranoid anxiety. The Earl of Northumberland committed suicide in the Tower in June; on 10 July Throckmorton faced the horrific traitor's death at Tyburn.

The charges against Throckmorton included the amassing of evidence to prove Mary Stuart's claim to the throne, listing potentially supportive magnates, and the intention of deposing Elizabeth with the aid of the Guise/Spanish army whose English coordinator he was. His death did not deter the Duc de Guise, who welcomed the expelled Mendoza in Paris and brazenly continued with his plotting. Guise dynastic pretensions in Britain were heightened by the French king's adherence to the succession of the reformist Navarrese branch of the house of Valois – pure anathema to the Guises. If Henri of Navarre did succeed, the Savoyard ambassador warned Guise, he should 'have no other doubt than that their House would be ruined and that as ancient enemies and Catholics, they would all be killed'.[3] The situation in France mirrored that of England – a childless monarch of one confession menaced by the ruler of a minor state of the opposing faith. So there was a curious parity between the situation of Elizabeth and that of Guise – both suspected and feared that while the next claimant lived, their own lives, and the authority of their dynasties, were in danger.

When Elizabeth conferred the Order of the Garter on Henri III the next spring, Guise mounted a propaganda campaign to publicise the danger of a Protestant succession, while expressing his hopes, in a conversation overheard by an English spy, that soon a 'pretty game' would be played out in England. But in June 1584, the news reached Paris that the Duke of Anjou had died. For the French, this initiated a war of succession which was to drag on for thirteen destructive years; for Elizabeth in England it was a poignant personal loss.

Elizabeth had had great fun with Anjou, not least because their play of courtship was a salve to her pride. In September 1578, Leicester had married Lettice Knollys, the widowed Countess of Essex, with whom he had been conducting an affair for some years. The couple had managed to keep their union a secret until 1579, when Elizabeth was informed of the marriage by Jean de Simier, who had arrived in England to conduct the diplomatic romance on his master's behalf. Elizabeth's shock and anger at the deception were exacerbated by Leicester's hypocrisy, since, as a married man himself, he had nonetheless been scheming to prevent the French marriage. Anjou made a brief visit to England in August 1579, returning in October 1581, and Elizabeth pronounced herself delighted and determined to proceed with the marriage. In November, she had created a sensation when she announced at Whitehall that the Duke would be her husband, kissing him on the mouth in public and giving him a ring. Elizabeth may have genuinely enjoyed Anjou's company, his charm and his flattery, yet she had never seriously intended to marry him. As ever, the real agenda of their courtship was the leverage England might purchase between France and Spain. Dangling a French alliance before Philip might conceivably keep him out of the Netherlands, and it was therefore in the Queen's interests to protract the negotiations as long as possible.

Elizabeth's greatest weapon in keeping her suitor at arm's length was the hostility of her subjects towards a foreign match. The process of annealing her own perpetual virginity to the nation's security, which was realised a decade later at Tilbury, begins in her manipulation of English fears of submission to an alien power as manifested in the reaction to the Anjou courtship. The rhetoric which in 1588 identified English interests indivisibly with the will of God in the aftermath of the Armada – 'we, in defence of ourselves, our native country, our anointed prince, our holy religion, our own Jesus Christ . . . against very antichrist . . . do withstand the injury done to us' – is present in the language of one of the many anti-Anjou tracts which appeared in the late 1570s, *The Discovery of a Gaping Gulf whereinto England is like to be Swallowed*. The author, a devout Norfolk reformist named John Stubbs, asserted in the most vulgar terms that the marriage 'must needs draw punishment from God' should Elizabeth take 'this odd fellow, by birth a Frenchman, by profession a papist . . . a fly worker in England for Rome and France in this present affair'. Stubbs had his hand cut off for his pains (managing to lift his hat and call 'God Save the Queen' before collapsing on the public scaffold), yet the very fury of his language indicated to Elizabeth how profoundly loathed the marriage was, providing her with the ideal excuse to call it off once she had achieved her diplomatic ends.

When the Dutch recruited Anjou as Prince of the Netherlands in the autumn of 1580, the courtship took on a more cynical angle on both sides. Elizabeth was still occupied with preventing Spanish dominion in the Provinces, and on Anjou's part, continuing the game appeared the best possible means of extracting English funds for his campaign. Given that Anjou's hopes were now more fiscal than flirtatious, Elizabeth's announcement of her commitment to the marriage in 1581 was a masterstroke. Since she desired the match, to which her subjects so objected, she herself could not be blamed if the French chose to be disobliging, which they could hardly help being, as the conditions she attached were frankly absurd. No funds would be supplied for the Netherlands, but France must agree to assist England in the event of a Spanish invasion. Anjou saw when he was beaten, and though both parties kept up their lovers' pose in public, the Duke was overheard cursing the lightness of women in general and the perfidy of islanders in particular.

Elizabeth played her regrets at the impossibility of the marriage perfectly. Since she no longer had to marry Anjou, she declared herself prepared to offer him £60,000 in two payments and kiss him goodbye. The Spanish ambassador Mendoza claimed that she danced with glee in her chamber at the success of her strategy, but Anjou persisted in lurking around, playing the heartbroken swain, until he had obtained an advance of £10,000.

The Queen may never seriously have intended to have Anjou, nor was she so foolish as to believe a blissful domestic life had truly been in prospect, but he had nonetheless represented the last chance at matrimony she could expect, and she grieved, if not for 'Monsieur' personally, then for the loss of a romantic dream. There is a certain melancholy pleasure to be had in mourning for things we never really wanted, and Elizabeth indulged it. The French ambassador described her as tearful and regretful, declaring herself 'a widow woman who has lost her husband'.

Anjou's loss was all the more cruel because Elizabeth was well aware that the Parisians had been sniggering over her last, failed courtship since the winter. In November, a 'foul picture' of Elizabeth had been pinned up about the city, depicting the Queen on horseback, exposing herself by raising her dress with her right hand, accompanied by a caricature of Anjou with a hawk on his wrist, 'which continually baited and could never make her still'. The engraver was Richard Verstegen, a Catholic exile and propagandist for the Guises, who had previously produced works such as *A Brief Description of the Diverse Cruelties which the Catholics Endure for their Faith in England*. When Elizabeth's ambassador complained, a set of Verstegen's plates were discovered at the Hôtel de Guise.

On 10 July 1584, William of Orange walked downstairs after dinner at his home, the Prinsenhof at Delft, to keep an appointment with a Frenchman, Balthasar Gerard. As the leader of the Netherlandish States General approached him, Gerard produced a pistol and shot William in the chest. For Gerard, this was the culmination of a three-year project. He had been pursuing William ever since 1581, when Philip of Spain had formally declared the prince an outlaw and placed a huge bounty on his head. Gerard was apprehended and died a particularly gruesome death, even by the standards of the time, so Philip kept his 25,000 crowns while achieving his objective. Spanish involvement in the Guise invasion plot marked a change in Philip's policy. He may not have been prepared to countenance a Guise-ruled puppet state in England, but, in a reversal of his position for the preceding twenty years, he was now contemplating war against Elizabeth.

The vehemence of the anti-Protestant campaign in France, coupled with the Spanish-inspired assassination of William of Orange, prompted William Cecil to believe that the law needed to take further measures to protect Elizabeth. As a preliminary step, he and Walsingham devised the 'Instrument of Association', signed at Hampton Court by the Privy Council in October. This lengthy document asserted that Elizabeth's murder had been 'most traitorously and devilishly sought' and swore those entering into the Association to solemnly defend her from any such future conspiracy: 'we shall never desist from all manner of forcible pursuit against such persons to the uttermost extermination of them, their counselors, aiders and abettors'.

Elizabeth, as usual, preferred to dismiss the necessity of protective legislation, at least in public. As the Instrument of Association began its travels across the nation, she appeared especially splendid at that year's Accession Day Tilt. An eyewitness account of the celebrations on 17 November describes the competitors entering the tiltyard at Whitehall to the sound of trumpets, accompanied by brightly dressed retinues who assembled behind the long barriers on either side of the course. Some wore horses' manes, others were disguised as 'wild Irishmen', others entered in a carriage drawn by horses themselves dressed up as elephants. Elizabeth stood in her canopied 'room' to greet the tilters, who approached to the bottom of the connecting staircase – their armour being too heavy to allow them to mount it – and heard an address from each, some in verse, at which she was noted to laugh appreciatively, studying with her ladies the devices of each knight's *impresa* (the emblem painted on a pasteboard shield). This image of the Queen, gay, courted, secure, could not have been in greater contrast to the privations being inflicted on Mary Stuart.

Mary had been removed from the custody of the Earl of Shrewsbury by an edict of September 1584 and, after a brief period with Sir Ralph Sadler as her custodian, was returned once more to Tutbury in early 1585. Her latest gaoler was Sir Amyas Paulet, Elizabeth's former ambassador to France. Paulet's instructions from Walsingham are interesting in light of the legislative developments progressing in London. Mary was to be kept in far stricter isolation than before, forbidden to walk out or ride, deprived of her custom of giving charity – lest she communicate with local people – and forbidden any letters except from the French ambassador. Even her servants were forbidden to take the air on the castle walls while her coachman could only leave the castle under guard. In a gesture reminiscent of the humiliations practised on Mary Tudor after Elizabeth's birth, Paulet removed Mary's precious cloth of state, one of the last visual symbols of her queenly status. Though Mary eventually succeeded in having it restored, its symbolic significance was poor comfort in the freezing conditions of Tutbury, which were ameliorated by the summer weather only to be replaced by the noisome stink of the castle's middens.

As Mary endured further privation, Parliament met in late November, to debate an act which was designed to protect Elizabeth from 'anything [that] shall be compassed or imagined tending to the hurt of Her Majesty's person'. Though her name was not explicitly mentioned, the object of the 'Act for the Queen's Surety', as it became known, was Mary Stuart. Offences against the Queen's surety were to be judged as such under the Great Seal of England by 'any person with or without the knowledge of anyone who pretended title to the English crown'. In affirming the Instrument of Association in conjunction with the Act, any English subject now had the right 'by all forcible and possible means to pursue to death every one of such wicked persons, by whom or by whose means assent or privity or any such invasion or rebellion shall be in form aforesaid denounced to have been made or such wicked act attempted, or other thing compassed or imagined against Her Majesty's person.'[5] That is, the Act provided for Mary's prosecution should anyone conspire against Elizabeth in her name, with or without her knowledge or consent. The anti-Catholic fear stoked by the Guisard invasion plot produced plenty of willing signatories to the Instrument when it was sent out through the provinces; even loyal subjects who were unable to write proudly set their mark to the document. At York, where the Northern Rising was still remembered, so many seals were appended that the commissioners were unable to post it. Elizabeth viewed the collated signatures at Hampton Court and declared herself pleased with this show of eager commitment on the part of her people. The signatories included Mary Stuart, who never lacked style, if not sense. Thus Mary slipped a noose around her own neck, and it was left to Cecil and Walsingham when to choose to draw it tight. They did not wait long.

CHAPTER TWENTY-ONE

T he deaths of Anjou and William of Orange presented Spain with complementary strategic advantages. Anjou's loss meant that the French royal house of Valois was effectively extinct, and the next heir apparent was the Protestant Henri of Navarre. This prompted Philip to formalise his alliance with the Guisard Catholic League, in order to prevent Navarre from inheriting, which in turn augmented his strength in the Netherlands. By declaring his intention to support the Leaguers against Navarre, Philip was able to assimilate their military power, which could now be deployed against the Dutch. With Orange gone and the Netherlandish rebels in disarray, Philip could proceed without fear that France would intervene against him. With the Spanish seizure of the majority of ports on the Flemish coast, the balance of power on the Continent seemed to be tilting inevitably towards the Hapsburgs. Philip's ambition appeared terrifying. The French ambassador in London reported Catherine de Medici's opinion that once Philip had definitively crushed the Netherlands he would turn his attentions to France, and thence to England.

After the expulsion of Mendoza in the wake of the Throckmorton conspiracy, the anti-Spanish position of Elizabeth's government was annealed. Psychologically, both sides were ready for conflict. On 10 October, Elizabeth summoned her councillors to discuss plans for resisting the King of Spain's 'malice and forces'. Philip concluded his alliance with the Guises in the Treaty of Joinville at the end of 1584, while at Nonsuch in August 1585 Elizabeth finally agreed to openly provide more than 7,000 men to come to the aid of the Netherlands. A month later Drake departed in another raiding mission, with a fleet of twenty-five ships, two of which belonged to Elizabeth. This time, he had his sovereign's express permission to attack both Spanish ships and the settlements of the Caribbean. After the long, fluid drift towards conflict, where both sides had been influenced as much by circumstance as specific policy, Drake's departure was an overt gesture of enmity.

The immediate concern was the Netherlands. Walsingham's question to Elizabeth in council 'if her Majesty shall not take them into her defence, then what shall she do or provide for her own surety against the King of Spain's malice and forces which he shall offer against this realm when he hath subdued Holland?'[1] summarised the Queen's choices. Either she ally with the rebels, or wait until Spain had crushed them, after which England would have to face Philip alone. The intelligence agents were filtering through news of the Joinville compact by the spring, and though the agreement contained no specific English aims, Elizabeth could no longer ignore the fact that the most effective military muster in France was now in league with the most powerful nation in the world, and that both were united in their loathing of Protestantism. Her hopes of Valois support were disappointed in March when Henri III conveyed that he was no longer prepared to engage in the Low Countries. Elizabeth had to support the Netherlanders, or stand in isolation against Spain. Nonsuch 'marked the final abandonment of Elizabeth's heartfelt aim of distancing herself from European entanglements'.[2] It is interesting to speculate on what could have happened had the Queen at this juncture accepted the offer of the grateful Dutch Protestants to assume the sovereignty of the States General. Cecil advised against this, observing that sovereignty would produce a 'perpetual quarrel', while protectorship would result in the lesser evil of a 'determinable war', which would hopefully be brought to an end by Philip of Spain's death. As a strategy, this proved hopelessly vague.

The subsequent campaign in the Netherlands showed neither the Queen nor its most ardent supporter, the Earl of Leicester, in their best light. They had argued a decade before during the Kenilworth festivities, when Leicester had dared to portray himself as the saviour-Captain of the Netherlands; when this became a reality, it precipitated the most furious quarrel of their relationship. Leicester's eagerness to serve was reportedly motivated by 'an itching desire of rule and glory', though he was also piously convinced that in serving he was doing God's work. As a commander, he had little to recommend him apart from his status and willingness to fund the mission from his own purse, as his active military experience had been confined to a single battle thirty years previously. But even Leicester was an improvement on Elizabeth herself, whose constant retractions of his orders and unwillingness to release sufficient finances left his starving soldiers deserting and his authority nugatory. Leicester's opponent, Farnese, the Duke of Parma, was the most brilliant commander of his generation, and though Leicester's troops (who soon looked like scarecrows, according to witnesses) were commendably brave, they were being deployed by a courtier, not a general. Given the English soldiers' ancient equipment, hopeless lack of organisation and ignorance of tactics, it 'is a miracle that some military action occurred'.[3] Parma drove a ruthless military machine, and all Leicester could really hope to do was delay its advance. Antwerp had surrendered even before his arrival, and for all that he was greeted with fireworks displays and ecstatic crowds, pageants featuring pleasingly grateful young ladies and banners extolling the Virgin Queen as the Provinces' saviour, he knew even before he set sail that the whole enterprise was hopeless, writing despairingly to Walsingham that 'I am sorry her Majesty doth deal in this sort, content to overthrow so willingly her own cause . . . There never was a gentleman or general so sent out as I am. My cause is the Lord's and the Queen's. If the Queen fail I trust in the Lord, and on him I see I am wholly to depend.'[4]

Having left Leicester to his own devices at the beginning of the campaign, Elizabeth furiously refused to grant him further discretion when the Earl accepted the title of Governor General of the United Provinces (the role she herself had refused) in The Hague in January 1586. Her letter to him was both hysterical and hypocritical:

How contemptuously we conceive ourselves to be used by you . . . that a man raised up by ourself and extraordinarily favoured by us, above any other subject of this land, would have in so contemptible a sort broken our commandment in a cause that so greatly toucheth us in honour.

It has been suggested that what particularly enraged Elizabeth in Leicester's careerings round the Netherlands was her jealousy that his wife Lettice was planning to join him 'with such a train of ladies and gentlewomen, and such rich coaches, litters and sidesaddles as her Majesty has none such, and that there should be a court of ladies that should far pass her Majesty's court here'. As ever with Elizabeth, there has been too much keenness to see the personal behind the political. Leicester was eventually permitted to keep his empty title, but in flaunting it he was drawing attention to the failure of the English venture as a whole. Elizabeth did pathetically mismanage the Netherlands campaign, but not because she was jealous of the Countess of Leicester's sidesaddle.

Parma had perceptively observed to Philip that Elizabeth was by no means fond of expense, yet even the inadequate monies she was prepared to grant absorbed half of the ordinary royal revenues in the three years before 1588. This expense was all the more intolerable in that the Netherlands enterprise was actually proving advantageous to Spanish interests. Any projected attack on England now had a justification, while the financial burden of the war could only diminish the likelihood of the English forces being prepared for it. Elizabeth had authorised the intervention in the reasonable fear of an imminent Spanish threat, and in doing so had made that threat ever more likely. The presence of Leicester's army was a provocation, but his force was too small and ill funded to present a serious challenge to Parma, while equally representing an unforgivable challenge to Spanish sovereignty. It was wasteful, horribly careless of life and ultimately fruitless. The 'hawkish' members of Elizabeth's council had seen the combination of Throckmorton and Joinville as the preparations for the long-feared Catholic crusade against reform, but in 1585 there was no pressing reason to seek confrontation. It was English policy which was influencing Spain, not the other way around. The rebels' cause looked more or less lost, particularly if England could be kept out of the equation, but after the first English forces landed at Middelburg, Philip finally acceded to the Pope's demands for the 'recovery of England'. When Leicester appeared in Holland, he might as well have been carrying an invitation to the Armada.

Sir Anthony Standen, a Walsingham agent at the court of the Grand Duke of Tuscany, provided a copy of a terrifying document to Elizabeth just weeks after Philip himself had seen it in April 1586. It detailed an invasion plan projected by the Marquess of Santa Cruz, numbering a fleet of 206 warships, 60,000 troops and 200 landing-barges, to sail from Spanish harbours to Ireland, where they would depose English authority. Elizabeth would then be offered a reprieve if she agreed to come to terms; if not, the vast fleet would sail on. The details were less threatening than the fact that the idea was being mooted so openly, as while Santa Cruz's suggestions were so absurdly expensive that neither Philip nor Elizabeth took them seriously, Parma was formulating an alternative strategy, of invading via Flanders. At the same moment, in London, Walsingham was examining another set of documents, the correspondence between Mary Queen of Scots and a young Catholic named Anthony Babington.

CHAPTER TWENTY-TWO

Video et taceo, 'I see and say nothing', was one of Elizabeth's mottoes; it applied very well, in the slow campaign against Mary Stuart of 1585–7, to William Cecil. Having enacted the legislation which would condemn Mary when the time came, he stayed quiet, waiting out the delicate scheme of entrapment which became known as the Babington plot. Key to this was one of the most intriguing characters of the Elizabethan secret world, the cryptographer Thomas Phelippes. Given the significance of Phelippes to the whole enterprise, it seems surprising that Elizabeth's later encounters with this quiet graduate of Trinity College should have been admonitory, but, then again, perhaps not. To favour the man who gave some of the most sensitive service of her reign would simply have been too compromising.

At some point in the mid-1580s, Phelippes returned from doing no-one-quite-knew-what for Walsingham in France and became the roommate of one Gilbert Gifford. A relative of Francis Throckmorton, Gifford was yet another double agent operating between the warp and weft of Catholic and reformist loyalties which tangled across the Continent – educated in the martyr-factories of Douai and the English College at Rome, he had worked with Mary Stuart's agent in Paris, Thomas Morgan, before being 'turned' by Walsingham. Mary trusted Morgan and Morgan trusted Gifford. So did Cordaillot, the French ambassador's secretary, when Gifford arrived at the embassy and offered to convey letters to Mary. At Christmas 1585, the Scots queen had been moved from Tutbury to Chartley in Staffordshire, a house belonging to the Earl of Essex, and after months of isolation under the stern eye of the pedantic Paulet, her joy can be imagined when she began to receive letters from Morgan, concealed in protective tubes slipped into the beer brewed for her household. What Mary did not know was that the 'honest brewer' of Burton-upon-Trent was in the pay of Paulet, who happened to be acquainted with Phelippes, who had served him in France. With Gifford acting as courier, Mary's letters were handed to Phelippes, who deciphered their coding and passed the documents on to Walsingham. The packets were then resealed (by a specialist named Arthur Gregory) so that Gifford could deliver them to the French embassy, whence they eventually made their way to Morgan in Paris. For incoming letters this process was reversed, and though it was time-consuming, laborious and dependent on the patchy communications which affected all sixteenth-century correspondence, it was remarkably efficient. When Elizabeth remarked tellingly to the French ambassador Guillaume de l'Aubespine in April 1586 that she was perfectly aware of his secretive communications with Mary, she added, 'believe me, I know everything that is done in my kingdom'. De l'Aubespine may have smiled confidently at her naivete, but she spoke the truth. Thanks to the beer-barrel system, the English government had obtained complete control over Mary's correspondence.

With the interceptions running smoothly, what Walsingham needed was an *agent provocateur*, and here he was spoiled for choice. Just as Elizabeth had absorbed the practices of courtly love and melded them with the dynamics of Protestantism in her self-presentation as a monarch, so there was an answering trope within the fervent atmosphere among Catholic sympathisers and exiles and the training colleges of the Continent. One of Edmund Campion's biographers discusses the scent of martyrdom which hovered in the very air of the English College at Douai. From a few years after its foundation, the seminary sent about twenty young priests a year to England, of whom 160 had been executed by the end of Elizabeth's reign: a whole generation of young men who 'gallantly squandered'[1] their lives for their faith. To the Elizabethan government they were effectively terrorists; to Catholic moderates the relays of martyrs seemed 'a gruesome and intolerable waste',[2] but there were many, including William Allen, the director at Douai, who saw martyrdom as 'the supreme privilege of which only divine grace could make them worthy'. It was a privilege which was talked of, and even prayed for. But many of the young men of Catholic gentry families educated on the Continent were more than products of what their enemies termed theological fanaticism. They were products of the education of their age, as saturated as Elizabeth's courtiers in the refinements of the classics and the tradition of courtly love. Elizabeth's 'suitors' played the game for places and preferment; those who chose Mary Stuart as their mistress offered their lives as love tokens. Mary's legendary beauty, her royal blood, her mistreatment and above all her faith lent her a dark glamour which blended with the sincere desire for 'gallant martyrdom' in some and adventurous meddling in others, produced an intoxicatingly heady concoction which provoked a 'confusion of conspiracies'.[3]

Anthony Babington, a Derbyshire native, had met Thomas Morgan in Paris in 1580. He also knew a priest named John Ballard, a member of the Guise/Mendoza set in the city. With the former Spanish ambassador's endorsement, Ballard was engaged in a plot to murder Elizabeth, and when he returned to England in 1586 he met Babington and encouraged him to believe that a plan to release Mary would be supported with aid from Spain and Rome. Babington had by now gathered around him a whole group of young men 'ready for any arduous enterprise whatsoever that might advance the common Catholic cause'.[4] With Ballard's promises in his ears, Babington decided not only to free Mary, but to crown her. In May, Mary received a letter from Morgan endorsing Babington as a contact, and in July Babington wrote her an extraordinarily indiscreet letter outlining the scheme for her deliverance. He described the foreign troops who would arrive to support Catholic musters, who would free Mary and depose Elizabeth, whom he called the 'usurping Competitor'. Babington's fanciful statistics make pathetic reading – Elizabeth was to be dealt with by six gentlemen, Mary to be released personally by Babington with the aid of a further ten, backed up by a hundred soldiers. At the time of writing, Babington had only about fourteen companions who were committed to the plot. In her reply of 17 July, Mary painstakingly dictated her own death warrant.

Mary's letter, like all her correspondence, was dictated in French to her secretaries, Claude Nau and Gilbert Curll, who made a simultaneous translation into Scots-English. If she was sensible enough at least to give nothing in her own hand, she could not have avoided knowing that, by merely responding to Babington, she was condemning herself under the Act for the Queen's Surety. Babington himself had been explicit about Elizabeth's death, which he termed 'that tragical execution,'[5] and while Mary made no direct reference to it, her acquiescence was signalled in the phrase 'time to set the six gentlemen to work' in regard to 'the queen that now is'.[6] Her eagerness was expressed in questions about Babington's arrangements for horses and troops, and suggestions for her own escape, such as the starting of a fire in the Chartley outbuildings, and the use of carts to block the gates. She even proposed persuading a powerful magnate – perhaps the Earl of Arundel or Northumberland – to act as a 'figurehead' for the revolt. Babington received her letter in London on 29 July, but by now something had been added to Mary's own ideas. Thomas Phelippes had received the original on 19 July, and had immediately sent a copy to Walsingham, adorned with a gleeful little cartoon of a gallows. He then doctored Mary's letter with the addition of a forged postscript, requesting that Babington explain 'as also from time to time particularly how you proceed, and as soon as you may, for the same purpose, who be already and how far everyone privy unto'. That is, Walsingham wanted Babington to name names.

The counterpoint to Babington's activities with Mary in July 1586 is a series of extraordinary encounters with Walsingham. One of his gang, Robert Poley, was Walsingham's man. His fellow plotters believed him to be a Catholic spy in Walsingham's household; in fact he was working for the government. Via Poley, Babington sought an audience with Walsingham at his country home early in the month, where he later claimed to have made an offer of 'general service' in return for a passport to leave the country. Was this a feint, designed to throw Walsingham off the scent? Or was Babington planning to betray his supposed future queen? Or was he simply terrified by the enormity of what he was about to engage with? The passport was not granted.

By 30 July Babington had deciphered Mary's letter of the 17th. On

31 July, Babington again sent word through Poley that he had evidence of a plan against the Queen. Walsingham was anxious. Had Babington seen through the forgery? It was time to draw the noose. On 4 August, the priest Ballard was arrested at Poley's home, along with Poley himself (presumably to retain the latter's cover). Later that day, Babington went to a tavern to eat with another Walsingham agent, Scuadamore. He had already sent word to Poley that 'The furnace is prepared wherein our faith must be tried. Farewell till we meet, which God knows when.' Babington clearly knew that the plot was hopeless, and that any last-minute attempt at a plea bargain with Walsingham was futile. There were no foreign ships, no fast horses, no loyal Catholics waiting at country crossroads, and there never had been. The whole plot had been romantic folly, a game of words in which, it transpired, Walsingham, not he, had been the player. Babington ran. When a note arrived for Scuadamore as they ate, he pretended to be going to pay the bill and escaped. He discovered two of his fellow plotters at Westminster and they made first for St John's Wood above the city, then for Harrow, where they were rounded up ten days later, bedraggled and starving. It was time for Cecil to take over.

In the first of nine interrogations, beginning on 18 August, Babington confessed to Cecil, Sir Christopher Hatton and Lord Chancellor Bromley. As search warrants for over thirty London houses were produced, and other members of Babington's group were hunted down, Cecil had to confront an essential problem. Babington had destroyed Mary's doctored letter of 17 July. The only document in the possession of the government was Phelippes's copy, which as a piece of evidence was almost worthless. His second difficulty was the Queen.

Elizabeth has been judged as having a greater taste for *realpolitik* than her minister. She was at ease with the demands of Machiavellian statecraft, at heart a political pragmatist. Yet she could not bring herself to indict Mary Stuart. She emphasised to Cecil that she had no wish to draw attention to the evidence against Mary, and while insisting that the punishment of the Babington conspirators should be left to her and her Council, maintained that 'no sharp speeches' should be 'used in condemnation or reproof of the Queen of Scots'.[7] She explained to a bemused Cecil that this was a measure of self-protection, lest Mary's supporters feared for the Scots queen's life. While Elizabeth wavered, Cecil and his legal team worked frantically to draw up the terms of a royal commission which would permit them within the framework of the law to put an anointed queen on trial. Finally, on 6 October, Elizabeth wrote to Mary from Windsor, informing her that she would be tried at Fotheringhay for her part in 'a most horrible and unnatural attempt on [Elizabeth's] life'.[8] She advised Mary to respect the officers of her commission and to respond to them, though Mary still stubbornly maintained that she had sent no letter to Babington, and that if her secretaries claimed she had it was under torture. By the time defence and prosecution were assembled at Fotheringhay on 12 October, Babington and his fellow plotter Chidiock Tichborne had already suffered the full horror of the traitor's death – first hanged, 'then they were . . . cut down, their privities were cut off, bowelled alive and seeing, and quartered', along with Ballard and four others.[9] Seven further members of the group were at least permitted to strangle before they were cut down and sliced up. The crowds at St Giles Fields roared 'God Save the Queen' as one by one the slippery heads were scooped up from the bloody swamp of the scaffold and impaled on stakes.

The involvement of Francis Walsingham in the Babington plot has led some writers to conclude that the whole thing was stage-managed from beginning to end as a means of entrapping Mary. Mary's own defence rested upon the fact that as an anointed queen she was answerable to no one: 'I am an absolute prince, and not within compass of your laws . . . for that I am equal to any prince in Europe'.[10] She stated truthfully that, since no word or writing of her own could be produced against her, she ought not to be charged. Yet her best defence would have required her to admit her own complicity in a plan which, while Walsingham had to a great extent controlled, he had neither incited nor, entirely, executed. Babington had destroyed the fatal 'gallows letter', but Cecil was able to produce a 'copy' of it at Mary's trial, re-encrypted by Thomas Phelippes but without the damning addition of the forged postscript. Mary knew that the letter was fake. But to have admitted her knowledge would have contradicted her assertion that she had not known anything of Babington. Destroying the crown's evidence against her would be effectively to admit her guilt. Mary was indeed a sovereign monarch, she had been detained illegally and entirely against her will, she had been harried, pressured, spied upon and conspired against for an intolerable length of time, yet under the terms of the law she was still guilty. She knew it, and the commissioners knew it, and the rest, like so much of Renaissance politics, was theatre.

Mary Stuart's trial commenced beneath Elizabeth's cloth of estate in the hall at Fotheringhay on 14 October. Cecil had arranged the stage carefully. Ten earls, one viscount, twelve barons, Lord Chancellor Bromley and Cecil himself faced one another, seated precisely according to rank, along the lengths of the room. A table in the centre was provided for clerks and notaries. Facing Elizabeth's throne sat Sir Christopher Hatton, Sir Walter Mildmay, Sir Amyas Paulet and Walsingham, with local notables packed in behind. Opposite was the door through which Mary made the entrance which had been thirty years in the making. All parties had rehearsed their roles long before that door opened. To the Duc de Guise, some weeks before the trial, Mary had written, 'I am resolute to die for my religion . . . With God's help I shall die in the Catholic faith.' Cecil had written to the Earl of Leicester on 1 October, 'I hope that God which hath given us the light to discover it [the conspiracy] will also give assistance to punish it. For it was intended not only Her Majesty's person, and yours, and mine, but utterly to have overthrown the glory of Christ's Church and to have erected the synagogue of Antichrist.'[11] So they faced one another, martyr and minister, for the opening of the last act.

The substance of the case against Mary was put by Lord Bromley and two serjeants, Puckering and Gawdy. Had Mary 'compassed and imagined' Elizabeth's death? After the terms of the royal commission and the Act for the Queen's Surety had been read, Mary protested that she could not submit herself to answer before this 'insufficient' law. Cecil countered that the law was adequate and that the trial would proceed whether or not Mary herself remained present. 'Then I will hear and answer,' she replied. As the Babington plot was delineated, Mary stated that she did not know him; even when confronted with his confession she persisted that 'I never wrote of any such letter . . . If Anthony Babington and all the world say of it, they lie of it.' When Mary was confronted with the forged copy of the gallows letter, she wept. Then she turned on Walsingham; 'Master Walsingham, I think you are an honest man. And I pray you in word of an honest man whether you have been so or no.'

Walsingham's response was an 'answer answerless' worthy of his mistress:

> I call God to record that as a private person I have done nothing un-
> beseeming an honest man; nor as I bear the place of a public person,
> have I done anything unworthy of my place. I confess, that being
> very careful for the safety of the queen and the realm, I have curi-
> ously searched out the practices against the same . . .

On the evening of the 14th, Elizabeth wrote that she wished any sentence to be delayed until she had been personally informed of the discoveries of the commission, which reconvened the following morning. Mary stated that she thought the charges against her were 'laid long and advisedly premeditated of'. Employing the biblical images so commonly associated with queenship, she claimed that she was no murderous Judith, but a peaceable Esther, who would pray for her people's deliverance, not kill for it. Elizabeth herself, she remarked, had suffered no such treatment during her time in the Tower during the Wyatt conspiracy of the 1550s, and therefore she refused to answer any further. In the absence of any meaning-ful defence, dignity was the last card she held. Mary in fact spoke aloud twice more, to assert that Serjeant Puckering's summation that her correspondence proved that she had claimed title to the English crown since the Act for the Queen's Surety was false, and then, as she left the hall, to ask Hatton to make her petition to Elizabeth. She added 'God bless me and my cause from your laws'. It was done.

But was it? Elizabeth ordered a ten days' stay on the commission, which met in Star Chamber at Westminster on 25 October. Nau and Curll were examined again and admitted 'without any threat or constraint' that the papers they had been shown earlier were accurate. Curll confirmed that Mary had personally instructed him to burn Babington's letter to her and the draft of her reply. The commissioners then pronounced a verdict of guilt. The only question which remained was whether Elizabeth would now be prepared to sentence Mary to death.

The actual killing of Mary was not such a moral complication to Elizabeth. Whatever residual sympathy or loyalty she felt towards her fellow queen had dissipated in her genuine fear of assassination, which Cecil and Walsingham had not been slow to encourage. In a private letter to Paulet, she described Mary's behaviour as 'wicked', 'vile', 'treacherous', 'dangerous and crafty'. She came precariously close to endorsing a private assassination, which would have solved the problem discreetly. There was even a precedent in the death of Henry VI, who had been simply (and to this day mysteriously) eliminated in 1471 when his continued existence proved an impossible political conundrum. A quiet murder was one thing, but what the council and Parliament demanded was the formality of a state-sanctioned execution. In her speeches to Parliament in response to its petition for such an execution, Elizabeth was careful to state how personally abhorrent she found the idea of Mary's death, and that, were it left to her, she would happily have been merciful, even to the extent of sacrificing her own life:

> And if even yet, now that the matter is made but too apparent, I thought she truly would repent (as perhaps she would easily appear in outward show to do) and that for her none other would take the matter upon them; or that we were but as two milkmaids with pails upon our arms, or that there were no more dependency on us than mine own life were only in danger and not the whole estate of your religion and well-doings, I protest . . . I would most willingly pardon and remit this offence.[12]

The dissonance Elizabeth had to resolve was that which Mary herself had identified. If a monarch could be tried and executed by Parliament, was that then not to reduce a sovereign to a subject? It was a dangerous precedent. Cecil believed that the only viable means of ridding the realm of the problem of Mary definitively had to be a public one – he knew as well as Elizabeth that princes were set on stages with the eyes of the world upon them. If Mary were disposed of privately the least damaging potential consequence would be to Elizabeth's reputation. The conflict between Elizabeth and her mentor, friend and servant was not, then, over whether Mary *ought* to die, but over the constitutional impact this would have. In effect, it was a debate about the limits of monarchical authority.

Inevitably, the dispute has been cast in terms of gender. It has been argued that Tudor ministers viewed the conciliar structure in terms of a marital relationship, with the king, the *imperium,* as the 'husband' and the counsellor, the *consilium,* as his subordinate 'wife'. According to this model, Elizabeth's relationship with her councillors represented a disturbing inversion of a 'natural' order. But divine right overrode such considerations, and neither Elizabeth nor her council ever recognised a diminution of her *imperium* –or at least not until now. So was the disagreement between Elizabeth and her ministers indicative of 'fundamentally different perceptions of the Elizabethan polity'?[13] Cecil, Walsingham, Hatton and Puckering believed that they were acting according to God's will – hence Walsingham had been able, in conscience, to reply to Mary at Fotheringhay. But how could Elizabeth claim that she was acting according to God's will in striking at another of His anointed? How to balance the princely imperative to protect the realm at all costs against a legislative gesture which ripped the heart from princely authority? It was a dispute Machiavelli might have enjoyed.

In the two answers Elizabeth made to delegations from the Lords and Commons, on 12 and 24 November, we can see her answer being worked out. First she emphasises that she is acting on sovereign authority and sovereign authority alone. In a draft of the Richmond speech on the 12th, Elizabeth altered the verbal reference to the Bond of Association from 'Which as I do acknowledge as a perfect argument of your hearts and a great zeal to my safety, *for which I think myself bound to consider carefully of it and respect you therein*' (italics mine) to, in the second part of the sentence, 'so shall my bond be tied to greater care for all good'. She repeatedly asserts her exclusive right to take counsel only from God. In her famous reference to princes being set upon stages, she acknowledges the Machiavellian principle that being seen to possess moral qualities is less important than their actual possession, and also alludes to the Machiavellian principle that virtue is no protection against evil. There is a curious echo here. Mary had referenced Elizabeth's own time in the Tower during her trial. During her incarceration in 1554, Elizabeth could not but have been aware of that earlier prisoner, her mother, and of the hopelessness of innocence in the face of political expedience. As Wyatt's witnessing poem has it:

> By proof, I say, there did I learn
> Wit helpeth not defence to yearn,
> Of innocency to plead or prate,
> Bear low, therefore, give God the stern,
> For sure, *circa Regni tonat.*

On her release, Elizabeth had written her own poem on the subject, from her captivity at Woodstock. Writing on Fate, she declares:

> Thou causeth the guilty to be loosed
> From bands wherein innocents enclosed,
> Causing the guiltless to be strait reserved,
> And freeing those that death had well deserved.

Henry VIII had executed an anointed queen for treason, according to the laws of the land. In her first declaration at Richmond, Elizabeth insisted that the statutes for her protection had not been made against Mary, as the Scots queen claimed; that is, she was not being legally manipulated into guilt. Like Anne, Mary was guilty under English law. But in balancing mercy against pragmatism, Elizabeth was confronting precisely the Machiavellian problem which had destroyed her own mother. Machiavelli's 'anti-Ciceronian' stance, which Elizabeth's tutor Ascham had rejected, argued that since virtue is in itself no defence, it can be ruinous. Mercy can create threat, while the preservation of the realm can be achieved only through action which can be perceived as vice. 'I have found treason in trust,' Elizabeth told the delegation, adding in her second reply that 'I am not so ignorant . . . as not to know it were a foolish course, to cherish a sword to cut my own throat.' If mercy was no option then vice required authority. *The Prince* endorses the idea that it is better to remove an individual, rather than allow discord to spread. Wyatt's advice is that only God can lead, and, as Elizabeth was later to write to Ralegh, the only power superior to Fortune is God's. In another of her poems, the Queen invoked a well-known description of Mary Stuart as:

> The daughter of debate,
> That eke discord doth sow,
> Shall reap no gain where former rule,
> Hath taught still peace to grow.

In her replies, Elizabeth stresses over and over again her divine appointment as a bringer of peace, one of the most ancient tropes of English queenship. Thus far, she fashions her justification in accord with the divine providence invoked by her ministers. But the authority for the destruction of the 'daughter of discord' must be Elizabeth's, lest her *imperium* be compromised. First, Elizabeth casts Mary as a Machiavelle. In her speech, with its cunningly disarming pastoral image of the queens as twin milkmaids, Elizabeth's urge to mercy is tempered by the Scots queen's duplicity, as she will only repent 'in outward show'. Recognising this, Elizabeth calls on her divine right, as she had so long ago in the conclusion of her poem written at Woodstock:

> But by her [Fortune's] envy can be nothing wrought,
> So God send to my foes all they have thought.

On 29 November the commissioners once more assembled in Star Chamber to 'subscribe the sentence' on Mary Stuart. A press campaign was under way, which included the publication of Elizabeth's speeches, alerting Europe to her dreadful moral predicament and showing her as regretfully adopting a necessary course which nonetheless was 'contrary to her own disposition and nature'.[15] The proclamation of Mary's guilt was made public all over London on 6 December. Meanwhile, Cecil had prepared the death warrant, which he gave into the keeping of Secretary Davison until the Queen should request it. On 1 February 1587, Elizabeth signed.

There are two ways to read what followed. Either Elizabeth countermanded her instructions and was ignored by her ministers, who proceeded to execute Mary without her permission, though with a signed and sealed warrant, or Elizabeth outmanipulated her beloved colleague and succeeded in placing both the initiative and the blame on Cecil. There can be no doubt that Elizabeth wanted Mary dead. On the same day that she signed the warrant, she ordered Davison and Walsingham to write to Paulet at Fotheringhay with a report of a conversation they had recently shared. Elizabeth gave out that she was somewhat surprised that under the terms of the sworn bond of Association, which made it a duty for citizens to kill anyone who threatened her life, Paulet had not already acted. The message was clear: assassinate Mary. Paulet was horrified. He returned a reply within an hour of the letter's receipt, declaring that such an act would make 'a foul shipwreck of his conscience' and that he could never compromise himself by such an illegal act.

Meanwhile, according to the ministerial version of events, progress towards Mary's execution was proceeding smoothly. Elizabeth had given the signed document to Davison, with instructions that it go to Lord Chancellor Bromley and Francis Walsingham. Davison claimed that he retained the warrant overnight and presented it once more to the Queen on the 2nd. Via Davison, Hatton and Cecil had now been informed. It was decided that Walsingham's brother-in-law, Robert Beale, should transport the warrant, which was shown to him by Davison at Walsingham's London home on 3 February. Paulet was informed that the executioner, Bull (who was to receive £10 for his performance), was on his way, accompanied by one of Walsingham's servants. The axe designated to sever the Queen of Scots' head was to be hidden in a trunk so as not to attract attention. Davison and Beale then rowed to Greenwich, where, in Cecil's lodgings, they met Leicester, Hatton, Lord Howard of Effingham and five other senior councillors, who presented Beale with letters to the Earls of Kent and Shrewsbury and Paulet. Beale reached Fotheringhay by Sunday the 5th, after alerting the Earl of Kent, then rode to fetch the Earl of Shrewsbury before returning to Fotheringhay. With Paulet's authority, a letter was written to the local deputy lieutenant, requiring his presence at Fotheringhay on the morning of 8 February. The company was fully assembled on the evening of the 7th, with the exception of Bull, who was lodged in a nearby inn.

Mary went to her death between eight and nine on the morning of the 8th. Her cloth of estate had once more been ceremoniously dismantled. In a particularly cruel gesture, she was informed that she would have to proceed to the block alone, without her women. Their weeping might create a scandal, she was told, and moreover they might seek to make blasphemous relics from linen dipped in her blood. Mary reminded Paulet of her cousinship to Elizabeth and argued that surely the Queen would not sanction something so improper; she was finally allowed to choose six ladies to accompany her. It was done with two blows of the axe, though, horribly, a saw was used to sever the final sinews of Mary's neck. At the end, Mary prayed in English, 'Even as Thy arms, O Jesus, were spread here upon the cross, so receive me into Thy arms of mercy and forgive me all my sins.' In her own mind, and in the eyes of Catholic Europe, the Queen of Scots died a martyr.

And Elizabeth was furious. She learned of Mary's death on the evening of 9 February. According to Davison, this was what she had wished. In their first interview after Elizabeth had signed the warrant, on 1 February, she had told her secretary that she did not wish for any further discussion of the case until Mary should be dead, 'she for her part [as she said] performed all that in law or reason could be required of her'. The next day, Davison affirmed that when re-presented with the warrant, the Queen appeared uncertain but 'still resolved to proceed therein according to her former directions'. Elizabeth, though, denied that such a conversation had taken place. In her version, she had indeed requested Davison to take the signed warrant to Bromley, but then sent one of the gentlemen of her chamber, William Killigrew, to find Davison, and, had he not already found Bromley, to return with the warrant to await further instruction. Davison was apparently nowhere to be found, and when he eventually informed Elizabeth that the warrant had been ratified by the Lord Chancellor, she berated him for his precipitancy. And yet, six days went by when Elizabeth knew the warrant was at large, and she did nothing. Had she actually wished to stay Mary's execution, she could have done so. In a letter dated 26 January 1587, that is just days before she signed the warrant, James of Scotland had warned Elizabeth that the projected events at Fotheringhay would prejudice her 'general reputation, and (almost) universal misliking of you, may dangerously peril both in honour and utility your person and estate'. Elizabeth knew this perfectly well. So she perpetrated an act actless, a gross hypocrisy which left her own hands technically clean. She stormed and raged at the councillors who had gone behind her back, refused to see Cecil, condemned poor Davison to the Tower (where he remained until 1598, though he was not restored to her service even after his release) and thus, quite neatly, followed the Machiavellian principle that crime, where necessary, is best delegated to others. Moreover, in giving out that her ministers had acted without her full consent, she conceded just the necessary amount of authority to conscience. The assessment of Cecil's principal biographer that 'For all the evasions, contradictions, omissions and fabrications in the accounts . . . of the events leading to Mary's execution, there is really no doubt that [Cecil] and his colleagues acted in effect on their own authority'[15] is quite correct. They did, which was just what Elizabeth, with magnificent cynicism, wished them to do.

CHAPTER TWENTY-THREE

At the New Year gift-giving of 1585, Elizabeth's present from Leicester was 'a sable skin, the head and four feet of gold, fully furnished with diamonds and rubies'. As was the way with formal Renaissance presents, this magnificent piece was loaded with meaning. It was in a sense a parting gift, a forget-me-not. Leicester had been pressing for years to lead an expedition to the beleaguered Protestants of the Netherlands, and, after Elizabeth had reluctantly signed the Treaty of Nonsuch the previous August, he had finally taken up his commission in late December. It was also a timely reminder not only of the contribution made by the Dudley family to the important Russian trade, but, in this time of crisis, of the significance of the alliance with the Russian imperial family, which had been imperilled since the sudden death of Tsar Ivan (the Terrible) the previous year.

Until 1553, there had been no diplomatic contact between England and Russia. The mysterious empire to the north had been a place of legend, the 'Russland' of the masquerade performed for Henry VIII in 1509. This changed with the arrival of the *Edward*, captained by Richard Chancellor, at Novgorod on the shores of the White Sea. Leicester's father, Northumberland, had been instrumental in correcting 'our former gross ignorance in maritime causes',[1] and it was his involvement in the voyage which promoted the growth of 'a genuine maritime culture, founded on the scientific understanding of maps and astronomy [which] had laid the basis for the flowering of English enterprise under Queen Elizabeth'.[2] It was this culture, in turn, which was to prove so crucial in England's engagement with the Armada in 1588. It was Northumberland who recognised the lack of indigenous expertise in shipbuilding and navigation during his time at the Admiralty under Edward VI, and he who imported craftsmen from Normandy and Brittany, many of them Huguenot refugees, to instruct their English counterparts in, for example, the art of making the sail canvases known as 'poldavies'. It was also Dudley who recognised the potential of the 'joint stock' company in financing merchant exploration of a possible trade route to the north. The company which financed the 1553 voyage was the first of its kind, shrewdly exploiting the venturesome mood of the economy in the 1550s. The dissolution of the monasteries had created a new class of wealthy men, and a concurrent demand for luxury goods. Dudley was aware of Italian joint stock practices through his protégé, the navigator Sebastian Cabot, and the Muscovy Company, as it became, allowed for a novel form of investment – raising capital to finance expeditions with relatively small individual outlay (the share price for the first voyage was fixed at £25), and potentially huge returns. One of the last joyful sounds the dying boy-king Edward heard was the cannon fire from the *Edward*, the *Bona Speranza* and the *Bona Confidenzia* as they set sail from Greenwich on 10 May, just a few months before Northumberland's fall.

Chancellor's crew eventually made contact with the imperial court at Moscow, and left many extraordinary recollections of the customs and sights of the Kremlin, not least Ivan himself. After impressing the tsar with samples of English cloth, they returned from their first voyage with an agreement that English merchants might trade freely, and with the tsar's protection, within his vast domains. Thus began a diplomatic and economic relationship which endured throughout Mary's reign, and then Elizabeth's. More than ninety letters survive from the English government to the Russian between 1554 and 1603, and Elizabeth herself corresponded with three tsars, Ivan himself, his son Feodor Ivanovitch, and the regent and then usurper Boris Godunov. The Muscovy Company proved hugely successful, but Elizabeth's interest in Russia was more than merely commercial. The empire, and, curiously, its Orthodox religion, took on new significance as the Queen began to engage in both mercantile enterprise with the Ottomans and pro-Reformation diplomacy with eastern European states. There was also a cultural element.

Ivan was keen to modernise his court through contact with the west (in opposition to the Poles and Danes, who wished precisely to prevent it), requesting Elizabeth early in their correspondence to send 'an architect to build castles, towns and palaces, a doctor, an apothecary and other artificers such as can seek for gold and silver'.³ And Ivan was interested in something else, as well as artisans – arms. In his strategy of expanding his lands and defeating the Muslim khans on his eastern borders, Ivan recognised that English raw materials could provide him with a much-needed advantage, so in a profitable relationship which prefigured her dealings with the Sultan at Istanbul, Elizabeth set about providing them.

From the first, Elizabeth had to balance the essential protection of her merchants' privileges (and persons) with the insistent and often mercurial demands of Ivan for a closer political alliance. In 1569, she promised the tsar her 'eternal friendship', and in 1570, in a letter co-signed by ten members of the Privy Council, including Leicester, she agreed to receive Ivan and his family in England if insurrection obliged them to go into exile. She resisted, however, his demands for a formal alliance, citing the reluctance of Parliament as her reason, but here the two rulers reached an impasse. Ivan was unable to comprehend the function of Parliament, or of any form of consensual politics, and wrote frustratedly to the Queen: 'We had thought that you had been a ruler over your land and had sought honour to yourself and profit to your country . . . now we perceive that there be other men that do rule . . . and you flow in your maidenly estate like a maid.'⁴ (Only Ivan the Terrible had the nerve to refer to Elizabeth I as an actual woman!) In a fit of pique, the tsar suspended English privileges, which Dutch and French merchants were by now eagerly pursuing, and confiscated the Muscovy Company's goods, but Elizabeth's response was cool: 'Our ambassador will tell you in all truth that no merchants are governing the estate and our affairs, but that we rule ourselves with the honour befitting a virgin queen appointed by God.'

By 1572 Elizabeth had succeeded in smoothing over the misunderstanding; the impounded goods were returned, the imperial protection reobtained, and she declared herself satisfied with Ivan's respect for her wishes. Two years later, the alliance was again proposed, and discussed in a memorandum 'certain notes touching the benefit that may grow to England by the traffic of English merchants into Russia', but by 1576 Ivan had lost patience and announced that he intended instead to conclude a treaty with the Holy Roman Empire. Since the Emperor Maximilian (and subsequently Rudolf, who succeeded him the same year) controlled territories from Romania to the Adriatic, this could potentially open Russian trade routes to Italy and the East, greatly to England's disadvantage. Elizabeth was anxious, and dispatched an embassy to Russia, but unfortunately the ambassador, Sylvester, was killed suddenly by a stroke of lightning at Kolonogori just as he was trying on the yellow satin suit he had ordered for his audience with the tsar, an incident which the deeply superstitious Ivan interpreted as an unfavourable sign from God. Discussions were once more suspended. But in 1580, Ivan sent an Englishman living in Russia, Jerome Horsey, to Elizabeth with a request for military supplies concealed in a flask hidden in his horse's mane. Elizabeth obliged the next year, sending Horsey back with thirteen ships loaded with arms.

The munitions trade with Russia had proved almost as lucrative as the Muscovy Company's declared interest in furs. During Mary's reign, a Company employee named Thomas Alcock had been arrested in Poland, and charged with supplying 'Thousands of ordnance, as also of harnesses, swords, with other munitions of war, artificers, copper and many other things'. Alcock denied it, but subsequent correspondence with Ivan confirmed that Elizabeth had provided him with materials 'which Her Majesty does not suffer to be transported forth of her realm to no other prince of the world'. This was not quite true. By 1580, Elizabeth had become a serious arms dealer, supplying not just Russia but the Ottoman Empire, and it is here that her secretive dealings with Ivan connect with the broader politics of the Counter-Reformation.

After Horsey's delivery, Ivan gave out that he was considering an English marriage, with Lady Mary Hastings selected as the lucky bride. Mary was a kinswoman of Elizabeth's, of Plantagenet descent, and Ivan declared himself enthusiastic at an English royal marriage. Mary may have been less so, since the tsar was by now on his seventh wife, whom he proposed to discard to make her the eighth. In 1582, Ivan sent two ambassadors, Pissemski and Neovdatcha, to inspect Lady Mary, who remained unmarried in her late twenties (Cecil having snatched her intended husband, his ward the Earl of Oxford, for his own daughter Ann). Elizabeth was positive, as she hoped that the marriage might secure exclusive English rights to the port of St Nicholas. Mary was duly inspected, walking in a garden accompanied by Leicester's sister Katherine, and found satisfactory, but Elizabeth then instructed her new ambassador, Sir Jerome Bowes, to dissuade the tsar from the match, as Mary was scarred from smallpox and professed herself reluctant to convert to Orthodoxy and abandon her English relatives. Confusingly, having first apparently desired the marriage, Elizabeth had made the ambassadors wait eight months to see Mary, and then again scotched the alliance. Poor Mary, who had to endure being referred to as the 'Empress of Muscovia' by court wags, never married at all, but her putative betrothal had concealed quite another level of diplomatic intrigue.

Since the early 1580s, Elizabeth's intelligence network had been active in Poland, which was believed to be a supporter of the claim of Mary Stuart to her throne and, more generally, a Counter-Reformation ally of Rome and Spain. Until 1582, Poland had been at war with Moscow, in part over the disputed territory of Protestant Livonia. In 1577, Ivan had invaded Livonia, which was seen by Catholics as a 'bulwark for European states',[5] his success there not only being seen as a 'calamity' by the emperor, but directly attributed, according to the English ambassador at Antwerp who had canvassed the rulers of the German principalities, to 'the furniture of ammunition which the English sent to the Russians'.[6] In a counter-gesture, Magnus of Livonia recognised the rule of Poland and its king, the Catholic Stefan Batory. With the help of a truce with the Ottoman Empire, Batory succeeded in claiming much of Livonia's territory back from Ivan at the end of the war, which both Moscow and Protestant Sweden viewed with alarm. The German Protestant rulers, according to a report to Walsingham, 'are suspicious of the king of

Poland and dread his prosperity and greatness'. The marriage negotiations with Lady Mary were therefore a smokescreen for a different
project, an alliance against Poland.

Ivan's ambassadors arrived in England in September 1582. On 23
January 1583, Elizabeth conducted a 'secret meeting'[7] with Pissemski,
and in April held a series of banquets for the envoys, in the presence
of Francis Walsingham, Leicester, Sir Christopher Hatton and Sir
Philip Sidney. Mary was finally viewed at her garden walk in May,
and the ambassadors departed, but in June Prince Albertus Laski
appeared at court. Laski was an odd character, one of the flotsam
thrown up by the religious storms engulfing Europe. He was a descendant of a prominent Polish Protestant, John Laski (whom Cecil
had covertly assisted in escaping the Marian persecutions in 1555), for
a time a member of the Polish Calvinists and the author of several
Latin treatises on religion. Laski has been described as an impoverished magnate who was 'honourably received' at Elizabeth's court
before being obliged to flee in the face of his debts, but his time in
England was divided between Winchester House and Oxford, where
he toured the colleges and enjoyed, or endured, the usual entertainment of verses and disputations. On 23 June, accompanied by Philip
Sidney, he was rowed by the Queen's men in a barge draped in her
colours and to the music of her trumpeteers down the river to Mort-
lake, the home of John Dee.

Dee was another Cambridge man, an alumnus of St John's and a
friend of John Cheke, with whom he shared an ambition to promote
the study of mathematics, a much-neglected subject at the time of
his residency at the college in the 1540s. By his own account, Dee
devoted eighteen hours a day to his studies, in science as well as the
ancient languages, which former interest he subsequently pursued
during wide travels in Europe. Returning to England in 1551, Dee was
introduced by Cheke to Cecil, through whom he gained an entrée
at both Edward VI's court and later Elizabeth's. Often described as
a 'magus', Dee was an extraordinary polymath, proficient in mathematics, astronomy, geography, history and theology, as well as the
more occult studies which in later life aroused dangerous suspicions
of witchcraft. To Elizabeth, he was 'her philosopher'. Although Dee's

reputation was dogged by accusations of sorcery, Elizabeth was alert to the suspicions provoked by ignorance of Dee's studies, and in his own words 'promised unto me great security against any of her kingdom that by reason of any my rare studies and philosophical exercises unduly seek my overthrow'.[8]

Elizabeth was a frequent visitor to Dee's house, where he had built up the largest library in England, and she was eager to meet Laski on his arrival. Although Laski had impeccable Protestant credentials, he had recently converted to Catholicism, which makes the warmth of his reception, and Elizabeth's gift to him of a Protestant Bible with a pair of her gloves inside, rather curious. Laski was a spy, a very effective one, and Catholicism was part of his cover. His connections included the secretaries to the Polish Cardinal, the papal nuncio and the King of Poland, and perhaps most importantly Antonio Possevino, a Jesuit priest with vehemently anti-English views who was close to Batory's nephew, who was serving with the Duke of Parma in the Netherlands. Poland was advocating military and naval action against England to prevent further intervention against Spain in the Netherlands. Laski was therefore able to provide Elizabeth with details of an east–west Catholic front, for which she rewarded him on several occasions before his departure for Poland in September 1583. He travelled with John Dee, whom he intended to present to Batory as a 'conjuror', with a view to placing a spy at the centre of the Polish court. Laski was not entirely reliable – Dee described him as 'a wanton and very prone to sin' – and somehow the men lost one another, with Dee eventually ending up alone in Prague. He made several visits to Poland, but never succeeded in getting close to Batory, who died in late 1586.

The continuance of English trade with Russia now depended on a more malleable candidate for the Polish throne, and here Laski was more useful. Since 1582, Elizabeth had supported the candidacy of Sigismund Vasa of Sweden, the nephew of her old suitor King Erik, despite the fact that he had been raised as a devout Catholic. A friendly Catholic in Poland was better, in her view, than a hostile one in Sweden, a view shared by her Swedish Protestant allies and also by Ivan. (Sigismund did eventually become King of

Sweden in 1592.) Laski was active in promoting Vasa, who became King of Poland in 1587. Just when it appeared that the Poles had been outmanoeuvred and the Russian trade secured, though, Ivan died.

Elizabeth continued her correspondence with the new tsar, Feodor, and with the regent, his brother-in-law Boris Godunov, but now it was Feodor who was interested in a political alliance. In a reversal of a contemporary situation, the English merchant community in Moscow were criticised for living in high style, parading in silks and velvets, racing horses, buying pedigree hunting dogs and provoking such hostility that the ambassador, Sir Jerome Bowes, was imprisoned by rioters in his home and barely made it back to England alive. New trading privileges were denied, and by 1589 Elizabeth's letters complained of the damage done to her monopoly by the encroaching Dutch. By April 1590, she was claiming that the enormous sum of 60,000 roubles was owed to her, having been lost to the English through Ivan's fault during his reign. When Feodor was usurped by Godunov, Elizabeth wrote to congratulate him and the privileges were renewed, though she continued to grumble that the Muscovy Company was being denied its due. Godunov grumbled in turn that England was now too engaged with Polish politics and Ottoman trade, for during the previous decade Elizabeth had made another exotic, and lucrative, alliance.

Elizabeth's long-standing engagement with Russia not only throws light on the extent and complexity of the diplomatic and covert intelligence network which the English deployed in Eastern as well as Western Europe; it was, arguably, one of the foundation stones of English, and then British imperial dominance in the centuries to come. Leicester's gift of a sable cloak is a sensuous reminder of the skill, courage, and – why not? – greed, which galvanised not only the crafts of shipbuilding, map-making and navigation for which the English became renowned, but of the beginning of an economic system which has left the City of London as one of the financial powerhouses of the world even today. The Muscovy Company, the Eastland Company and the East India Company were all founded during Elizabeth's reign, and 'in the trade of these chartered companies . . . lay the practical and intellectual origins of the . . . British Empire'.[9] One more highly significant charter was also granted, to the Levant Company. And in that instance, Elizabeth would be doing business with the enemy.

CHAPTER TWENTY-FOUR

E lizabeth I's speech at Tilbury hardly needs an introduction. Her presence among the troops at Tilbury camp on 8 August 1588 and the words she spoke to inspire them are legendary:

> Although I have the body of a weak and feeble woman, I have the heart and stomach of a King, and a King of England too – and take foul scorn that [the Duke of Parma] or any other Prince of Europe dare to invade the borders of my realm.

The speech has taken its place in the English national consciousness as much as John of Gaunt's 'sceptered isle' eulogy in Shakespeare's *Richard II*; it echoes through the dauntless valiance of Churchill's great wartime broadcasts, it tugs the patriotic heartstrings as it establishes for the first time an image of England, that plucky little island facing down a military superpower, which still resonates, both sentimentally and politically, in the twenty-first century. But did Elizabeth ever actually speak these now immortal words? Crucially, there is no eyewitness account of the speech at Tilbury. Certainly, the accessories which successive historians have bestowed upon the Queen that day have no origins in fact. One writer speaks confidently of Elizabeth's 'silver breastplate worn over her white velvet dress', another adds a 'helmet with white plumes' to a steel corselet, another adds a white horse, another a silver truncheon. Yet there is no contemporary evidence that Elizabeth wore armour that day, no engraving or painting which reveals her to have been carrying a truncheon, nor any contemporary record of what she said.

Elizabeth and her councillors had been anticipating full-blown war with Spain for some years. Intelligence gathered by Cecil's network indicated that Philip had determined upon invasion as early as 1585. The execution of Mary Stuart was not a catalyst for the unleashing of the Armada, though it provoked Philip to expedite his plans. A memo written up by Cecil in February 1588 assesses the likely tactics of the Spanish, the relative provision of English ships and their capacity to hold off a naval attack, the possibility of Philip persuading – that is, bribing – James of Scotland to assist him, and the overall costs of defence, which Cecil estimates as well into the tens of thousands of pounds. About 140 ships were available, a fleet consisting of Elizabeth's navy of forty ships, a further thirty funded by the City of London and the remainder provided through other port towns, by collectives of merchants as well as private citizens. Cecil was uncertain enough of the strength of this force to consider in his memo the possibility of obtaining further ships from Denmark and Scotland. On 25 April, Pope Pius blessed the Armada banner, and by May, after receiving several direct communications from Drake stressing the importance of acquiring more vessels and suggesting the possibility of a counter-attack, Elizabeth had determined her policy.

The fleet was to muster at Plymouth under the command of Lord Howard of Effingham with Drake as vice-admiral, while Lord Henry Seymour was to deploy forty ships in the Channel. The Armada set sail from Lisbon under the command of the Duke of Medina Sidonia on 28 May. Between 30 May and 24 June, the English sailed out three times in attempts to engage the enemy, but each time the English ships were driven back to port by bad weather. The Armada was aiming to proceed to the coast of the Spanish Netherlands, where it would meet 30,000 soldiers under the Duke of Parma, to augment the 18,000 already embarked with Medina. The weather conditions also hampered the Spanish, who diverted their course towards England. The beacons which had waited along the coast since the spring were fired on 19 July, as the Armada was sighted off the narrow Lizard peninsula at the tip of Cornwall, and as the alarm burned its way back to London Drake and Howard manoeuvred their ships into position. Two skirmishes between the fleets on 21 and 23 July proved inconclusive, but the English were able to prevent Medina's ships from entering the shelter of the Solent Strait. The Armada returned

The *Pelican* portrait. Elizabeth's arrogation of religious imagery was subtly revolutionary.

A coloured woodcut of Tsar Ivan, known as Ivan the Terrible. Elizabeth's dealings with Russia signalled her engagement with the Protestant cause in Eastern Europe.

Dealing with the enemy: Sultans Murad III and Mehmet III. Elizabeth profited from arms trading with the 'infidel'.

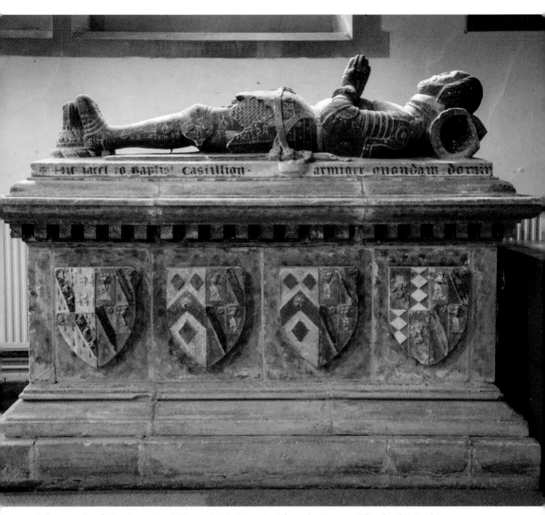

The tomb of Battista Castiglione in St Mary's Church, Speen. Elizabeth's Italian tutor was a key connection in her dealings with the anti-Catholic underground.

Henry Lee organised the complex propaganda festival of the Accession Day Tilts.

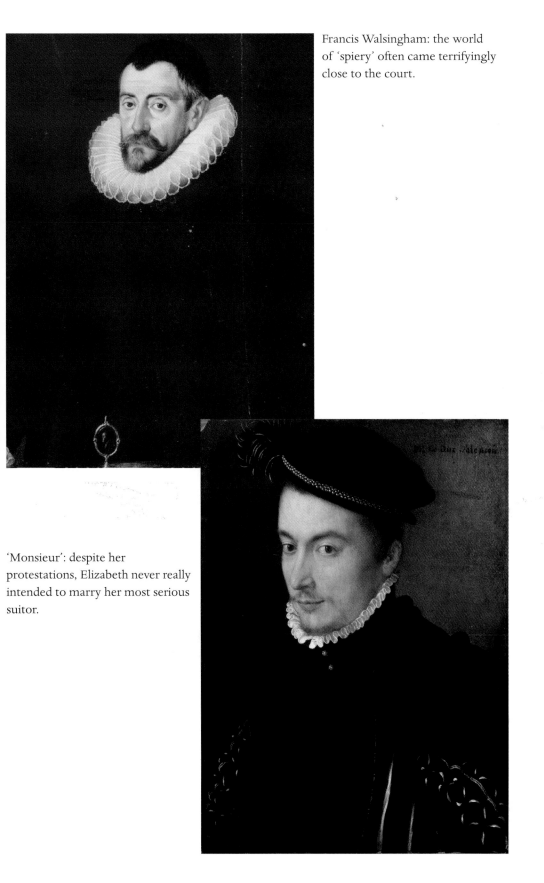

Francis Walsingham: the world of 'spiery' often came terrifyingly close to the court.

'Monsieur': despite her protestations, Elizabeth never really intended to marry her most serious suitor.

MARIE
REINE
D'ESCOS
S

Mary Stuart's execution was perhaps the greatest personal and
political challenge of Elizabeth's rule.

The apotheosis of the Armada: Elizabeth as victorious goddess.

Weary but triumphant, Elizabeth the statesman at her most human.

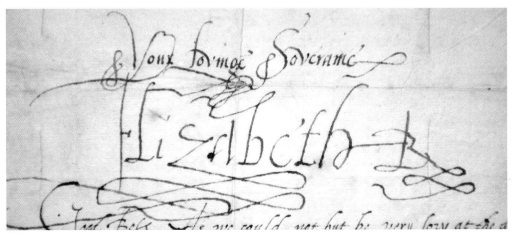

'My skirting hand' – when Elizabeth signed her name, she did so as a Prince.

to deep water and made for Calais, Parma's troops being now expected at Dunkirk. However, the Spanish were unable to establish
contact with Parma as the Dutch had blockaded the port. Moreover,
they were now vulnerable, as there was no harbour deep enough to
accommodate the great Spanish warships. At midnight on 28 July,
the English sent eight fireships into the Spanish line, and though no
enemy ships were burned, many of the panicked crews slashed the
anchor cables and fled. Medina's formation was now severely disor-
dered, and at Gravelines the next day the English had them cornered.

Medina planned to use a technique which had proved successful
at the Battle of Lepanto, of bringing his ships in close and having the
soldiers board those of the enemy, but Howard and Drake had anticipated this. Their craft were lighter and faster, and they were able
to dance around the Spanish, firing on their ships from a safe range.
The Armada used relatively little of their ammunition, while the
English maintained the bombardment for eight hours. By the time
they pulled away, at about 8 p.m., the Spanish had lost five ships,
with many more damaged. Their boats scattered and made north
for Scotland, with Howard continuing the pursuit until 2 August.
While invasion by Parma's army was still considered a serious possibility, by the time Elizabeth supposedly made her immortal speech
at Tilbury the danger was certainly significantly diminished, if not,
indeed, banished.

We know that Elizabeth left St James's Palace on the royal barge on
the morning of 8 August, catching the tide downriver. We know that
she was accompanied by further boats carrying her Gentlemen Pen-
sioners and the Yeomen of the Guard. At Tilbury she was received by
Leicester and Lord Grey, with her footmen, guards and a group of
her ladies behind her. We know that she reviewed the troops twice,
on the 8th and 9th, before returning to London on 10 August. And
then, we know nothing, for twenty-four years.

A painting on the north wall of the chancel at St Faith's church,
Gaywood, Norfolk, dated 1588 and commissioned by the then rector,

Thomas Hare, shows Elizabeth at Tilbury. A version of the famous speech is painted beneath it. The quotation claims to be from a sermon preached on the Armada by a clergyman named William Leigh, yet the text in question was not printed until 1612. The speaker invokes similar themes to the better-known version, though the words are by no means identical:

> I have been your Prince in peace, so will I be in war, neither will I bid you go and fight, but come and let us fight the battle of the Lord. The enemy may challenge my sex for that I am a woman, so may I likewise charge their mould, for they are but men.

The casting of Elizabeth in the masculine, the playing on the contrast between physical sex and martial gender, is the same rhetorical technique, but the Gaywood version differs sufficiently from the 1612 publication to the extent that it is extremely unlikely that the painted version derived from the subsequently published sermon. It is not until 1623 that the most familiar version of the Tilbury speech appears, this time in a letter from Leonel Sharps to the Duke of Buckingham, as part of an argument against the proposed marriage of Prince Charles (later Charles I) to the Infanta of Spain. In 1654, part of the letter was reproduced in *Cabala: Mysteries of State*, with the explanation that it was written after the fruitless eight-month marriage embassy to Spain thirty-one years earlier. The letter invokes the perfidy of the Spanish in 1588 as a reason to mistrust the alliance:

> While they were treating of peace in '88 they even then did invade us. I pray God they have not used this treatise of marriage to as bad a purpose.

Of the two possible versions, it seems more likely that the Gaywood/Leigh text is closer to what Elizabeth actually said at Tilbury, concentrating as it does on confrontation with the enemy, rather than Elizabeth's own feelings and actions. Sharp has further been dismissed as a 'generally unreliable' witness.[1] Yet one argument in favour of Sharp's rendition is Elizabeth's own education as a modern,

Renaissance ruler. There was nothing aberrant about her appearance on a battlefield. Women may have been excluded from what was conventionally 'a privileged site of patriarchal history',[2] but queens, in this respect, were not women. A century earlier, Marguerite of Anjou, Henry VI's queen, had led the Lancastrian troops in battle, as had Isabelle of France and Matilda of Boulogne. The fact in itself of a queen rallying an army was not new in English history. But while Elizabeth's actual presence at Tilbury is well documented and, arguably, customary, her words remain contentious.

In 1549, Elizabeth's tutor Ascham observed that 'She admires, above all, modest metaphors and comparisons of contraries well put together and contrasting felicitously with one another.' The Queen was known to dislike wordy orations: in her own utterances she was notably brief – though admittedly not always to the point. Her own rhetorical style was much influenced by Latin, the 'male' language of power and privilege, deriving its manner from Cicero and its directness from Seneca. A contemporary audience would have registered (as we do) Elizabeth's use of synechdoche, the expression of a whole by a part, as well as her employment of 'contraries', *comparatio*. In almost all of the Queen's speeches where she alludes to her femininity, she makes use of *comparatio* – acknowledging 'yes, I am a woman' then contrasting 'but I do (therefore am not) such'. The Tilbury oration in the Sharp version, then, is consistent with Elizabeth's classically formed style. This does not entirely compensate, however, for the lack of eyewitness accounts of the speech on that August day. Why, then, should Tilbury become the site for the coalescence of so much nationalistic sentiment? Whatever Elizabeth indeed said, and whatever she indeed wore while saying it, the fictions constructed around the Queen were essential to her government at the time and to a developing conception of English identity over the following centuries.

Nations are more than territories, peoples or systems of governance. They are also ideas, collective beliefs about a place's history or values which create a sense of commonality. The sculpting of the 'English' nation was taking place during the Renaissance, and Elizabeth's self-presentation as Queen was very much part of that process. To see this more clearly, it is perhaps worth considering the imaginative projections which surrounded her not only at Tilbury, but at a very different stage of her reign, ten years previously.

In 1578, the Anjou marriage discussions had reached their climax. In August that year, the Queen was at Norwich, where she witnessed a pageant, *Cupid's Fall from Heaven*, the first public occasion on which she was celebrated as the Virgin Queen. Between then and 1583, as the anti-French party moved against the marriage in council, a curious visual and literary propaganda conflict took form. The poet Edmund Spenser was a Leicester man, and therefore opposed to the Anjou match. In his *Shephearde's Calendar* (1579), the *April Eclogue* features Elizabeth as a 'mayden queene', albeit one surrounded by blooming spring flowers, evoking a paradoxical fertility. Spenser hints that Elizabeth may be possessed of a holy virginity which can be compared with that of the Virgin Mary, the patron saint of maternity as well as chastity, though since such a comparison could be read as potentially idolatrous, Elizabeth is compared to Venus Virgo, locating the analogy safely within Renaissance classicism. A further reference to Venus Virgo illustrates the frontispiece to the manuscript of *Regina Fortunata*, by Henry Howard, Earl of Northampton, and here the Marian connection is made plain by means of the book in Elizabeth's lap, featuring the quotation 'Pax tibi analla mia' ('Peace be with you, my handmaiden'). This typically Renaissance combination of Marian and pagan motifs allows for Elizabeth's ambiguous status while the marriage was, theoretically at least, going forward, but a more assertive claim as to the centrality of virginity to Elizabeth's successful rule is made by John Lyly in *Euphues and His England* (1580). Notably, Lyly uses 'prince' as Elizabeth herself did, as a gender-neutral category: 'As this noble Prince is endued with mercy, patience and moderation, so is she adorned with singular beauty and chastity . . . But such is the grace bestowed on this earthly Goddess, that having the beauty that might allure all to Princes, she hath the chastity to refuse all, accounting it no less praise to be called a Virgin, than to be esteemed a Venus.' Lyly goes on to cite the case of Tuccia, the Roman Vestal who proved her virtue by carrying a sieve full of water from the River Tiber to the temple without spilling a drop. The sieve, in turn, is central to a series of portraits of the Queen produced amidst the uncertainty of her last venture in the marriage market. The first of these, attributed to George Gower, and dated 1579, features Elizabeth holding a sieve in her left hand, with a quotation from Petrarch's *Triumph of Love*, describing the 'error and dreams' which attend the throne of Cupid. Those who follow him, the poet suggests, will be subject to 'false opinion' and bound by force in an 'eternal darkness'.

Elizabeth herself had acknowledged the fact that she would now never marry in her sonnet *On Monsieur's Departure*:

Some gentler passion slide into my mind,
For I am soft and made of melting snow,
Or be more cruel, Love, and so be kind,
Let me float or sink, be high or low;
Or let me live with some more sweet content,
Or die, and so forget what e'er love meant.

The poem played into the official strategy of the Queen's grief – she even managed to weep in front of Leicester and Walsingham, claiming that her life was worthless but for the hope of seeing her beloved 'Frog' once more. It shows Elizabeth deploying all the skills of a Renaissance ruler – her dexterous talent for courtly idiom is put in play to 'humanise' her, to present her as a suffering lover, while glossing over the functional realities of Anjou's dismissal.

Spenser's *Eclogue* of 1579 provides the final aspect of the symbolic virginity which reached a form of apotheosis in the *Armada Portrait*, even as the Anjou negotiations continued. His allusion to the Song of Songs:

For she is Syrinx daughter without spot,
Which Pan the shepherd's God of her begot,
So sprung her Grace
Of heavenly race,
No mortal blemish may her blot

figures Elizabeth's parents, Henry VIII and Anne Boleyn, as Pan and

Syrinx, dismissing those rumours to which Elizabeth had proved so sensitive, that she was 'the bastard child of a licentious coupling'.[4] Implicitly, she is immaculately conceived, fathered by Christ himself. The defeat of the Armada, in propaganda terms, vindicates this position – looking backward, Elizabeth's refusal of her last chance at matrimony foregrounds her triumph as the virgin protectress of her state. Thus the Tilbury speech (whatever Elizabeth actually said) represents the culmination of the role Elizabeth had been creating since she had come to the throne. The army at Tilbury did not go storming into battle after hearing their Queen's rousing words in 1588. Most of them just went home. Effectively, the threat of the Armada was dissipated by the time Elizabeth, with or without her breastplate, addressed her troops. The Tilbury speech was crucial in that it encapsulated the politics of the Queen's image as they had developed since 1578. Elizabeth's person was connected with the defeat of the Spanish through her virginity; her body politic was England itself, repelling the violent rape of the Armada and confirming the quasi-divine myth of chaste invulnerability that Elizabeth and her ministers had perpetuated since the collapse of her final marriage negotiations. It would not be an exaggeration to suggest that, in terms of imagery, Elizabeth's hymen protected her nation.

CHAPTER TWENTY-FIVE

While the Armada could not truly be claimed as an extraordinary military victory, symbolically it represented the zenith of Elizabeth's achievements. She barely had time to rejoice. Leicester had left London at the end of August, planning a visit to the spa at Buxton in the hope of relieving a persistent stomach complaint before moving on to Kenilworth. Amidst the outburst of jubilation which overtook the capital in the aftermath of the Armada, he and Elizabeth had seemed replete with a quieter satisfaction, content to watch the victory celebrations together from a window and dining quietly in the evenings. Neither was in the best of health, and perhaps they had a comfortable time together comparing their ailments. Leicester wrote a chatty note to Elizabeth on his journey, from Rycote, 'to know how my gracious lady doth, and what ease of her late pain she finds, being the chiefest thing in the world I do pray for, for her to have good health and long life'.[1] He added that he hoped to find his own cure at the springs, but his sickness was worsening, forcing him to pause at Cornbury, near Oxford, to recover. He died there on 4 September.

Elizabeth grieved acutely and privately. For some days she remained shut in her bedroom at St James's. Walsingham and Cecil noted that she refused to conduct any business; her women hovered anxiously outside the chamber. Eventually, the story goes, Cecil had the doors broken down. When she emerged, she had suffered a *coup de vieux*, she was visibly 'much aged and spent'. All she said was that she didn't want to talk about it. In response to a delicately phrased letter of condolence and congratulation from the Earl of Shrewsbury, she responded:

We desire rather to forebear the remembrance thereof as a thing whereof we can admit no comfort, otherwise by submitting our will to God's inevitable appointment. Who notwithstanding His goodness by the former prosperous news hath nevertheless been pleased to keep us in exercise by the loss of a personage so dear unto us.

Elizabeth did submit her will, as she had often counselled others to do. She continued her round of official duties, yet beneath her rigid 'mask of youth' there was inconsolable grief. The letter was as near as Elizabeth ever came to admitting that she was angry with her God.

The hint of a personal religious crisis in Elizabeth's reaction to Leicester's death suggests that the Queen's piety was not always quite so serenely confident as she would have the world believe. Yet in her relations with the Ottoman Empire she evinced a degree of certainty of her divine right to mingle piety with pragmatism that shocked even those critics who already dismissed her as a heretic tyrant. Within western diplomatic relations, the papal bull *Regnans in Excelsis* of 1570 had obviously been a political as well as a theological disaster for Elizabeth. Yet in economic terms, her reaction was both shrewd and robust.

For centuries, and more particularly since the Ottoman conquest of Constantinople in 1453, generations of popes had confirmed the illegality of Christian trade with the eastern empire, banning the sale of any materials which could be used by the 'infidel' to prosecute anti-Christian aggression. Based on the Codex Justinianus, successive legislation had threatened excommunication to anyone who exported munitions or foodstuffs to the enemies of the Church. Since the Pope had chosen to declare Elizabeth an illegitimate heretic, there seemed no longer any good reason to recognise Rome's authority in this matter, and English merchants were now effectively freed to profit from the vast Ottoman market. The conquest of Cyprus and the naval defeat at Lepanto had created a need for armaments beyond what the indigenous Ottoman market could supply, so in a wonderfully defiant gesture Elizabeth's merchants set about turning the scrapheap left by the Reformation – metal from bells and broken statuary, even the lead from dismantled ecclesiastical buildings – back into gold.

During the fourteenth and fifteenth centuries, Venice had been the hub of trade with the eastern Mediterranean, with spices, silks and carpets arriving in England on a merchant fleet of 'Flanders Galleys'. Woollen cloth, lead, tin and rabbit and calfskin were re-exported via Venice from England, so that the notoriously fearsome Janissaries (the armed units recruited by kidnapping non-Muslim boys from within the empire) wore uniforms of English cloth. While the first Turkish trade document issued on behalf of an Englishman was granted by Suleiman I to Anthony Jenkinson in 1553, permitting him to trade throughout the empire, until 1580, the English had traded in the Levant through a customary arrangement with France. Even with nominal legal agreements in place, trade with the East was an extremely risky business, as if ships were captured their crews could be, and were, enslaved. Or worse, in the case of Samson Rowlie, the son of a Bristol merchant, who was castrated by his new owners (though the 'English eunuch' made the best of it by converting to Islam and under the name of Hasan Aga rising to become Treasurer to the Beglerbeg of Algiers). Between 1562 and 1582, £4,000 had been spent for the relief of English captives from the Ottomans, making the costs of legally dubious expeditions even higher.

But with *Regnans in Excelsis*, this was about to change. By 1577, when John Hawkins proposed a venture to the Ottoman ports, effective trade had been under way for several years, as confirmed in a report by the Spanish ambassador Mendoza to Philip of Spain. Hawkins's cargo list included fernambuck (a hardwood), tin, lead and cloth, about one fifth of the cargo comprising those prohibited goods which could be used for arms manufacture. The Turkish market was hungry for such products, as in 1578 the empire began a protracted conflict with Persia, but in her first letter to the Sultan Murad III Elizabeth, whose political hypocrisy was nothing if not audacious, described herself as:

the most invincible and most mighty defender of the Christian faith against all kinds of idolatries, of all that live among the Christians and falsely profess the name of Christ.

Elizabeth was responding to a letter whose 'importance and unique-ness . . . cannot be overemphasised',[2] that is, the first communication of an Ottoman Sultan with England. Admittedly, the English trav-eller Fynes Morrison recorded that when the Sultan was shown England on a map, he wondered aloud why the King of Spain did not take a spade, dig it up and throw it into the sea; nevertheless he admitted himself impressed by English achievements, particularly in the light of its governance by a woman. Yet Murad had person-al reasons for admitting women's capacity to rule. His own mother, the beautifully named Nur Banu (which means 'lady of light'), was a blonde Venetian originally named Cecilia. Some archival conflation has occurred between Nur Banu and another woman of Venetian origin, Murad's favourite and the mother of his son, Mehmed III, whose name was Safiyye ('the pure'), and with whom Elizabeth was subsequently to correspond, but as queen mother, Nur Banu was very much a force in her own right. The Sultan Murad, described as 'minute, pale, huge-eyed and full of melancholy', was not much in-terested in government affairs, being 'weak and pleasure loving', and he allowed considerable power to devolve on his mother, whose rule, contemporaries claimed, was 'absolute'. Nur was the first woman to achieve political influence at the Ottoman court, and indeed had one Grand Vizier deposed for daring to remark that 'emperors do not govern with the counsel of women'. Nur died in 1583, which meant that when Elizabeth's correspondence with her son was initiated, she was still a considerable authority in the Seraglio. While it is perhaps too far-fetched to suggest that Nur influenced her son in favour of another ruling woman, it is certainly the case that Murad himself did not see Elizabeth's sex as a reason not to do business.

Elizabeth's letter, written at Greenwich in October 1579, went on to request that the Sultan extend his protection to all English subjects, hinting heavily as the advantages of a supply of 'prohibited goods':

the bestowing of which so singular a benefit your Highness shall so much the less repent of by how much the more fit and necessary for the use of man those commodities are, wherewith our kingdoms do abound, and the kingdoms of other princes do want.

Among the customary exchange of gifts, alongside several mastiffs in red coats was a clock, decorated with a forest of intarsia silver trees 'among which were deers chased by dogs and men on horseback following, men drawing water, others carrying mine ore on barrows', an equally unsubtle hint as to the wealth of raw materials available in England.

By 1580, Murad had consented to a pledge of safe conduct, *ahidname*, for English merchants in Ottoman ports, an extremely significant development in trade with the Levant and North Africa. In the case of the latter, a clandestine trade in munitions had occurred in Morocco from the 1550s, but this had proved too dangerous and lapsed. Revivified by Murad's grant, the Turkey Company was formed in 1581, amalgamated with the Venice Company eleven years later to form the Levant Company, while a similar joint-stock venture, the Barbary Company, was given a royal grant in 1585 to trade along the Atlantic coast of North Africa. These developments were of enormous importance to English trade, not only for the new availability of silks, spices, goatskin, cotton yarn, carpets, dates, aniseed and indigo dye, but for the general augmentation of Mediterranean commerce now that the threat of piracy and slavery was diminished. The ships required to make the journey to the East stimulated the boatbuilding trade and added to England's stock of potential naval power, while an entirely new commercial field was opened by the possibility of exporting goods to northern Europe via England – and English customs houses. And, of course, there was the central profit derived from dealing with the enemy.

Elizabeth was entirely aware that in the view of her Catholic fellow monarchs, and moreover critics within her own realm, she was guilty 'of active collusion with England's greatest enemy'.

She was therefore reluctant to commit to a formal alliance with the infidel through the customary sending of an embassy. Her letter to Murad of 8 January 1580 strikes a very different tone from the initial rather bombastic confidence of their first exchange. Elizabeth excuses her prevarication on the grounds that:

> We would have sent some embassy long ago to testify to which advantage and to how much we ascribe to your Imperial Majesty's goodwill towards us had not princes hostile to us, who are making a disturbance within our Kingdom with their own external soldiery and the influenced minds of certain people who are conspiring for civil destruction, diverted us from that plan and purpose.

She goes on to concede rather plaintively that she has been obliged to 'yield a little to these stormy times', adding with a surprising degree of frank bitterness that 'Meanwhile he shall keep his affirmed goodwill towards us and account us, merely by the luck of the moment and in no way as just deserts, the least among his allies, or rather the last.' In other words, Elizabeth is conceding her own weakness, as a product of momentary fortune.

In 1588, William Harborne was succeeded as ambassador to Constantinople by Edward Barton. From the first, Barton's concern was to promote discord between Turkey and Spain, the policy which had been successfully practised, on the instructions of Walsingham, by his predecessor. But as with the Cold War in the twentieth century, the conflict between the two superpowers evolved as a series of skirmishes between satellite client states, and Elizabeth's government was intricately involved. Elizabeth recognised that Eastern Europe was of particular importance in the struggle between Reformation and Counter-Reformation and used the influence England had acquired in Turkey to promote both trade and theological war. Intervention in Transylvania, controlled by the Ottomans, had begun as early as 1581, when Peter Cercel, a pretender to the Wallachian throne, had made contact with the English party in Constantinople. Cercel was sent to John Woolley, Elizabeth's Latin Secretary, to beseech the Queen's protection, and did succeed as voivode between 1583 and 1585.

Yet this was only the beginning of a consistent and influential English policy in the region. In 1568, King Stefan Batory of Poland (who had not yet taken the troublesome step of invading Livonia) had granted mercantile privileges to the Eastland Company, giving a strong impetus to trade between England and the Baltic. This trade passed through the state of Moldavia, which between 1588 and 1591 was subject to a campaign of intense Jesuit propaganda. In an attempt to counter this, Barton allied himself with the Greek Orthodox see at Constantinople, denouncing the Spanish Roman Catholics as 'idolaters'. He furthered the Protestant cause by sending for preachers from Geneva to officiate in both Constantinople and Chios. When the Catholic leader of Moldavia was deposed, Barton had achieved sufficient leverage via this alliance to prefer his own candidate, Aaron Ferhad, to the throne, on the condition that Aaron carry out a pro-Protestant policy which would smooth the Anglo-Polish trade route. Simultaneously, Barton was active in preventing a truce between Turkey and Spain in January 1590, going on to mediate between Turkey and Poland, who faced a potential war over an alliance between the latter and the Hapsburg Empire. Barton's deputy, Thomas Wilcox, was sent via Moldavia to the court of the Polish King Sigismund III to work against the treaty, effectively enacting a pro-Turkish policy which furthered advantageous relations between Turkey and Poland while isolating the Spanish. The papal nuncio to Poland attempted to counter-attack, warning Sigismund against the danger of entering into any concords with 'such a pernicious woman', that is, Elizabeth, and Sigismund assured the legate with a smoothness worthy of his ally that he was entirely unaware of any English intervention proceeding from 'that pretended queen'.

Aaron's reign in Moldavia might have been a coup for England, but the Moldavians took a different view, deposing him in 1592 after a reign described as the most 'oppressive and miserable' in the country's history. Barton's prestige in Constantinople was severely diminished, but he remained influential enough to persuade the Janissaries (who were key to any enactment of imperial power) to reinstate Aaron, again on the condition that Protestants would be permitted freedom of conscience and their churches restored. Thus Moldavian Protestants found themselves praying 'dailie' for the 'long life and good prosperitie' of Queen Elizabeth I. The Archbishop of Lemberg was so alarmed by Barton's success that he warned the papal nuncio Malaspina that the English were plotting to effect a union between the Greek and Calvinist Churches and that Elizabeth herself was planning to become a Turk (i.e. convert to Islam) in order to 'trouble the state of Christendom'.

Moldavian affairs might have seemed far removed from the more urgent challenges Elizabeth was facing, but they intersect curiously both with the perceived perennial foreign threats to Elizabeth's life and the factionalism which in the 1590s the Earl of Essex was beginning to create at her court.

Even, or perhaps especially, after Leicester's death, Elizabeth could not bring herself to stomach Lettice Knollys's company, but for her son, Robert Devereux, the Earl, she showed an immediate and to both her contemporaries and subsequent writers, embarrassing, weakness. She never, though, took him as seriously as he did himself, and it was this mismatch between the perceptions of their relationship which was to bring about Essex's downfall thirteen years after the Earl arrived at court in 1584. Leicester, who knew the Queen's tastes perhaps better than anyone, had been quick to promote his stepson, who accompanied him to the Netherlands without having to bear any of the responsibility and consequent disapprobation which fell upon Elizabeth's first favourite. When Essex returned in 1587, it swiftly became obvious that Elizabeth was utterly smitten. Maybe, just for once, Elizabeth judged that she could afford to behave like a woman, and though (as had also been the case with Leicester) she never loosed the reins of their political relationship, her infatuation has attracted far more squirming contempt than it might have done had the genders of the couple been reversed. Essex was pretty, and naively grand, but he was also intelligent and witty, perfect company for Elizabeth in the aftermath of Mary Stuart's execution and then when she had to deal with the complex grief of Leicester's death.

Essex was not a dancing man, but in every other respect he was the model of the Renaissance swain. Despite the fact that they were a generation apart, he participated apparently unselfconsciously in the courtship rituals which were the accepted paradigm for intimacy with the Queen. Elizabeth was not averse to advancing his career, giving him his stepfather's office of Master of the Horse when she promoted Leicester to Lord Steward in late 1587 and giving him Leicester's former apartments at Whitehall after the latter's death, but she was impatient with his hasty, untried ambition which constantly set her against the old guard of her trusted ministers.

Dr Roderigo Lopez was a victim of precisely this ambition. Lopez had long-standing connections with the swarm of Catholic plots and counter-plots that massed around the Queen. The son of a Portuguese *marrano* (one of the many Jews who had been forced to convert to Christianity in Spanish dominions), Lopez was a skilled medical practitioner by the standards of the time. In 1571 he had cured Sir Francis Walsingham of kidney stones while he was living in Paris, and also assisted in helping Walsingham to develop 'invisible' inks to pass secret messages. Walsingham clearly recognised his utility, since Lopez not only went on to become physician to Elizabeth in 1586, but took his place in the intelligence network operated by Walsingham and Lord Burghley. Like many of the spies they used, Lopez was a double agent. He had been commissioned as an intelligencer by the ambassador to France, Mendoza, and passed on his reports, destined for the king of Spain, through a third party, a fellow Portuguese named Manuel de Mandrada. In 1591, Mandrada was arrested, and Burghley sent Lopez to push forward his interrogation. Mandrada confessed, and with Lopez's encouragement was 'turned' on threat of his life, into counter-spying for the English. Lopez remained in his post, as Burghley could make use of his reports on Spanish intelligence and the information he provided through the *marrano* community. It may seem extraordinary that Burghley should have permitted a known agent to enjoy such privileged and physically intimate access to the Queen, but clearly it suited him to do so. Yet when the Earl of Essex accused Lopez of treason in 1594, Burghley was ruthlessly prepared to sacrifice his protégé to politics.

The atmosphere around the Queen in the 1590s was paranoid and febrile. The Catholic threat was nothing new, but with the country again at war and the succession of the ageing Queen still unsettled, it provoked an aggressive hysteria. In London, Christopher Marlowe had just premiered *The Massacre at Paris*, a gory reminder of the slaughter on St Bartholomew's Day two decades earlier, while at court the Earl of Essex was determined to assert his supremacy over the Cecils. While the dangers were real enough, this visceral political contest might be cast as a gruesome form of chivalric quest, with the rival heroes battling to save their lady from mortal danger, a tiltyard masquerade where the combatants played for horribly real stakes. Essex worked for three months to bring down Lopez, eventually claiming that his own care and diligence had unmasked a plot whereby the doctor would poison the Queen for 50,000 Spanish crowns. 'I have uncovered a most dangerous and desperate treason,' the Earl crowed in a letter.[3] 'The point of conspiracy was Her Majesty's death. The executioner should have been Dr Lopez, the manner poison.' Elizabeth herself was alarmed but unconvinced. She chastised Essex, calling him 'a rash and temerarious youth' and claiming that she was personally convinced of Lopez's innocence. Characteristically, Essex sulked until Elizabeth conceded that he might pursue the inquiry.

Essex had chosen to make his denunciation while Burghley was ill and incapacitated, but Burghley moved swiftly to prevent his rival claiming credit for Elizabeth's rescue. Disregarding both the extreme unlikeliness of the plot and his own knowledge of Lopez's intelligence activities, Burghley enlisted Thomas Phelippes to turn government reporting of the case to his own ends. The helpless Lopez was publicly accused of confessing his intention to poison Elizabeth with 'physic', encouraged by Mandrada, and of receiving a gold jewel set with diamonds and rubies as a token. Under questioning in the Tower, Lopez admitted that he had 'spoken of this matter and promised it', but added that it had all been to fool the King of Spain – precisely as Burghley had wished him to do. Yet Burghley could not afford to seem any less zealous than Essex for the royal security, and Lopez, a Jew and a foreigner, was too pathetically easy a target. Robert Cecil was a witness at Lopez's trial for treason in February 1494, and declared himself satisfied that the 'vile Jew' was guilty 'in the highest degree'. Burghley's secretary, Henry Maynard, wrote up the official account of the proceedings, which conspicuously failed to mention Essex. The plot had been discovered by 'the great diligence and carefulness of one of the Lords of Her Majesty's Privy Council'.

Even with Burghley's endorsement and the verdict of the jury (who calmly ignored Lopez's protests that his confession had been made under torture), Elizabeth was unable to bring herself to send Lopez to the gallows. In the three months before she signed the warrant, Alvaro Mendas, an agent of Don Solomon, the Duke of Mytelene, arrived in London. He claimed to wish to report on the involvement of Edward Barton in the affair of the Moldavian throne, and, further, to offer intelligence on the advantages which England might gain from the war between Turkey and the Hapsburgs in Hungary. In fact, he had been sent to free Lopez. Does this mean that Lopez was indeed guilty, or that the double-agent cover which Burghley had so mercilessly ignored was so successful that the Spanish were still convinced he was their man? How much Elizabeth knew is uncertain, yet she permitted Lopez's widow to retain a property which in law ought to have been attaindered to the crown after the doctor was finally executed on 7 June. The presence of Mendas demonstrates the extent and complexity of clandestine Elizabethan diplomacy, of which Lopez so cruelly found himself the victim.

Back in Constantinople, Edward Barton found himself in an awkward position. In 1593, a second English present had been offered with tremendous ceremony to the Sublime Porte. The Sultana Safiyye wrote to Elizabeth, in just the kind of terms the Queen adored, as:

> the most gracious and glorious, the wisest among women and chosen among those which triumph under the standard of Jesus

Christ, the most mighty and rich governor and most rare among womankind in the world . . . I send Your Majesty so honourable and sweet a salutation of peace that all the flocks of Nightingales with their melody cannot attain to the like.

Elizabeth replied on paper scented with camphor and ambergris, in ink perfumed with musk, her letter accompanying a gift of eight chests of cloth, including scarlet, violet and 'sad green' colours, bottles, silver and gilt flagons and rabbit skin, as well as a jewelled picture of herself for the Sultana, set with rubies and diamonds, three 'great pieces' of gilt plate, two pieces of fine Holland cloth, ten garments of cloth of gold and a case of glass bottles 'richly ornamented' in silver. In turn she received a Turkish-style costume consisting of an upper gown of cloth of gold, an under gown of cloth of silver and a girdle in the Turkish manner.

This gracious exchange had gone very well, but three years later, on the accession of the new Sultan, Mehmet, Barton desperately needed to provide similar gifts in order to ensure English privileges under the new regime. Technically, though, Barton was not employed directly by Elizabeth's government, but by the Turkey Company, which meant that with characteristic stinginess Elizabeth was able to regulate her ambassador's diplomatic ventures without troubling herself over paying for his maintenance. It was therefore to the Turkey Company that Barton was obliged to apply for his gift, but the merchants baulked. He resorted to creating a 'dodgy dossier' designed to persuade Elizabeth to assist the Company with a suitable present.

Elizabeth received a detailed document, transcribed in Italian by one Salamone 'the Jewish man', describing the former Sultan, Murad, and the circumstances of the accession of the new. Compared with an account of the same events delivered by the Venetian ambassador Marco Venier, it is apparent that Salamone's rendition has been doctored. The altered version presents the situation in Constantinople as considerably more precarious, with the aim of persuading Elizabeth to pay up for the required gift. A promise was evidently forthcoming, as Barton was permitted to accompany Mehmet on campaign in

Hungary the same year. Eventually, in 1599, one Hector arrived with Thomas Dallam, who had constructed a mechanical organ for the Sultan's pleasure, along with a gilded carriage for Sultana Safiyye.

CHAPTER TWENTY-SIX

I n the years following the scattering of the Armada, Elizabeth appeared to have achieved the serene sovereignty promised by the monarch of the eponymous portrait. The Spanish threat was vastly diminished, Mary Stuart was gone, the reform of religion was firmly established. As Elizabeth approached her sixties, her status as Virgin Queen might have appeared as both unique and unassailable. But the mask was corroding even as it fixed: 'the very years which provide the strongest evidence of a cult at its zenith also produced reactions of negativity and even iconoclasm towards the Queen'.[1] Elizabeth had faced down many challenges to her authority over the years, but in the 1590s she confronted a different kind of threat – the sexual misdemeanours of her own court. The strain between duty and desire was one that Elizabeth had known personally all too well, and in the Queen's view succumbing to emotion over obligation was not only a shameful weakness, but also a threatening one. Renaissance culture has been characterised as 'obsessively taken up with the kaleidoscopic aspects of transgressive sexuality, most particularly the insistent pull off family relationships and the counterweight of desire',[2] and Elizabeth's response to those who elevated feeling over duty had always been strict. In 1574, she had so far forgotten herself as to break the finger of her lady Mary Shelton with a candlestick when it was discovered that she had secretly married John Scudamore. One witness to her fury observed 'she hath dealt liberal both with blows and evil words . . . I think in my conscience never woman bought her husband more dear than she [Mary] hath done.'[3] Mary was ultimately restored to favour, and Elizabeth in fact did promote what she considered to be suitable marriages among her maids, but she has nevertheless been left with a reputation for violent sexual jealousy; in the phrase of one critic, an 'anger with love'. Yet seeing Elizabeth as a sexually thwarted creature who manifested her frustrations on those who enjoyed what she had never had is to neglect the importance of monarchs' roles in regulating both marriage and sexual conduct at their courts. What Elizabeth's actual feelings about sex were we cannot know, as she never expressed them on record. Her poem on Anjou's departure contains erotic imagery – gentle passions sliding into soft snow – but to read sexual jealousy into her reaction to the exceptional number of scandals which beset the court in the 1590s is as rational as suggesting that the Queen's enthusiasm for riding was a form of sublimated sexual gratification.

Forbidden liaisons were a test to Elizabeth's princely and personal authority, and their increase was a disturbing signal of its decline. Women rulers, as has been noted, were particularly susceptible to charges of licentious misconduct at their courts (hence, for example, those excessively positive accounts of the propriety of Anne Boleyn's). The decency, or not, of a court was seen as deriving from its ruler, so women needed to distance themselves from this negative stereotype as a means of reinforcing sovereignty. Promiscuity could produce political discord, as in the case of Henri III's notorious *mignons*, if not actual violence. When the Earl of Oxford, the husband of Cecil's daughter Anne, seduced the fifteen-year-old Anne Vavasour in 1580, Elizabeth imprisoned the pair of them, but his offence provoked a series of duels and aggressive encounters between retainers which continued for years. Elizabeth saw herself as a substitute 'mother' to her maids, for whom she was responsible *in loco parentis*, and conceivably where this dynamic was threatened, her role as 'mother' to the nation was also undermined. Court life had always been sexually charged – the combination of young men and women closeted in physical proximity without a great deal to do, combined with the prestige of 'courtly love' exchanges, could not but lead to intrigues – yet in the 1590s there was practically a sexual revolution.

Not all the women at court met such a disgraceful end as Lucy Morgan, who had served Elizabeth in the 1570s and 1580s. Lucy was abruptly expelled from court, after which she found a new career as a bawd in Clerkenwell, reappearing in the records beating hemp in

Bridewell, the prostitutes' prison, in 1600. But sex was very much in the air. In 1590 the Earl of Essex secretly married and impregnated Sir Philip Sidney's widow. Two years later, Walter Ralegh was exposed in a secret marriage with Elizabeth Throckmorton. In 1594, Lady Bridget Manners secretly married Robert Tyrwhit, whom Elizabeth imprisoned, placing his wife in the custody of the Countess of Bedford. In 1595, Essex's relationship with Elizabeth Southwell was revealed when she gave birth to his son, while three years later Elizabeth Vernon was pregnant by the Earl of Southampton. Essex, meanwhile, began an affair with Elizabeth Stanley in 1596. Elizabeth was Cecil's granddaughter, the child whose paternity Oxford had denied in the Vavasour scandal. Mary Fitton became pregnant by the Earl of Pembroke in 1601. He refused to marry her and ended up in the Fleet prison. By this time, Lady Rich, who had started an affair with Lord Mountjoy in 1590, had given birth to several of his children (she had fourteen in total, six of whom were Mountjoy's).

The case of Elizabeth Stanley was particularly compromising. Lady Anne Bacon wrote disapprovingly of Essex 'infaming another man's wife and so near about Her Majesty'. Elizabeth was the Queen's goddaughter, married by royal invitation to William Stanley, Earl of Derby, at Greenwich in 1595 (one suggestion as to the first performance of *A Midsummer Night's Dream* connects it, appropriately enough, with this wedding). Elizabeth Stanley was ordered to retire to her husband's estate, but her affair caused such outrage that three correspondents, Lord Cobham, the Countess of Warwick and Lady Ralegh, wrote to her husband about it, and only Cecil's personal and highly embarrassing intervention prevented a divorce. Essex continued in his shameless career as a seducer. Two of the Queen's maids were discovered to have crept secretly through the palace galleries to watch a group of male courtiers, including Essex, playing sport in their shirts – 'the Queen of late hath used the fair Mrs Bridges with words and blows of anger and she with Mrs Russell were put out of the Chamber' (the girls were taken in for three nights by Lady Stafford). Ten months later Essex was still in love with his 'fairest B' – either Elizabeth Bridges, Lord Chandos's daughter, or Elizabeth Russell, Lady Russell's.

Essex's conduct was all the more scandalous as by 1590 he was a married man. His bride was Frances Walsingham, the daughter of Elizabeth's closest councillor after Cecil, and the widow of Sir Philip Sidney. Their first child, named Robert (who grew up to command a parliamentary army against Charles I), was born in 1591. Given that Frances was mentioned in her father's will in December 1589 by her first married name, Sidney, and that the boy was born just a year later, the union may have been hastened by Frances's pregnancy. Elizabeth expressed weary outrage when she learned of the marriage, though this did not prevent her continuing favouritism towards Essex.

On and on it went. Mr Vavasour, who had challenged Oxford to a duel over his sister Anne (making him the uncle of Elizabeth Stanley), was imprisoned for impregnating Mrs Southwell. Robert Dudley Junior, Leicester's illegitimate son by *his* lover, Lady Douglas Sheffield, was engaged to Frances Vavasour, who jilted him to make a secret marriage with Sir Thomas Stanley, who had been having an affair with Frances Lady Stourton, Robert Cecil's sister-in-law. Dudley consoled himself with Margaret Cavendish, and he, too, was imprisoned when they were caught. He went on to marry Margaret, then Alice Leigh, in 1596, before eloping with Elizabeth Southwell. Mrs Jones, the 'mother of the maids', found herself in the Tower with Francis Darcy, who had secretly married Katherine Leigh. Altogether, Elizabeth despaired of girls such as her carver, Lady Howard (née Carey), who was more interested in flirtations than her duties, once being otherwise engaged when it was time for her to bring the Queen's mantle when she wished to walk out, being late to serve at table in the Privy Chamber and then being absent entirely when she was due to accompany Elizabeth to chapel. In 1591 alone, half of Elizabeth's maids of honour were dismissed for scandal, 'All of which doth so disquiet Her Highness that she swore she would no more show . . . any countenance, but out with such ungracious flouting wenches.'[4]

It is easy to have sympathy with the maids. Their mistress was highly demanding and often querulous. Even she had behaved indiscreetly with Leicester in those impossibly long-ago days when she had, it was rumoured, been young. And, after all, the whole purpose of their presence at court was to find suitable husbands, while the Queen herself was mistress bar none of the art of flirtation. Outside the supposedly chaste atmosphere of Whitehall, London in the 1590s was full of prostitutes, directed to eager clients by 'guidebooks' such as Robert Greene's *Notable Discovery of Cozenage*. Even gently bred Protestant misses could hardly avoid the sight of these women and their customers in the streets, not to mention the rotted faces and collapsed eyes which their exchanges often produced – for the city was at the time in the grip of a syphilis epidemic. Sex was dangerous, not only because of the risks of childbirth, but because even virtuous wives risked contracting the pox from straying husbands. And danger is always alluring to adolescents – many of Elizabeth's maids were still in their teens. Sometimes the girls took revenge on the double standard which kept them so strictly enclosed while their male contemporaries were granted so much licence. Sir William Knollys, the comptroller of the royal household, was a well-known old goat, given to complaining at the 'disturbances' caused by the maids, whom he enjoyed peeping at by night. On one occasion he appeared in their chamber, naked but for a pair of spectacles, attempting to shock them by reading pornographic passages from Aretino. The girls nicknamed him 'Party Beard', for the stripes of white, yellow and black in his whiskers, and responded to his invasion by making up rude ditties about him.

Elizabeth needed her maids. It was they, after all, who were practically responsible for the construction of Gloriana – the wigs, the make-up, the lacing of the gowns, the placing of the jewels – and perhaps her reaction to their rebellious indiscretions was less erotic envy than a sense of outraged vulnerability. These young, attractive women knew her in her diminished physical self, an ageing, wrinkled woman with bad teeth and sagging breasts. Their fecundity underlined her own childlessness, but that in itself was a source of power, what made her exceptional. Their flouting of her authority rendered her *politically* sterile, as it represented a refusal to collude with an image of whose falseness only they knew the intimate extent.

Elizabeth was not always hard on girls who strayed. When Abigail Heveringham became pregnant she was found a husband in Sir

George Digby, while Emilia Bassano, who had been Lord Hunsdon's mistress, was respectably married off to one of the royal musicians. Elizabeth despised sexual incontinence where it threatened order, but in the highly charged atmosphere of the court of the 1590s she made one notorious exception – the Earl of Essex.

The defeat of the Armada had not put an end to the war with Spain, and while the iconography associated with Elizabeth continued to present her as a victorious bringer of peace, the 1590s saw a period of conflict on various fronts. The Netherlands remained one theatre, which was expanded by war in France, where Henri IV was attempting to overthrow the Catholic League and retain the succession, while in Ireland, which increasingly attracted the interest of Spain as the decade progressed, English resources were as overstretched as English rule was threatened. Not only did this require a delicate juggling of limited military powers, it created serious divisions within Elizabeth's council. Two main strategies were pursued, on land and at sea. At sea, the aim between 1588 and 1594 consisted mainly of privateering, with the objective of raiding Spanish funds to finance English expeditions and to protect the Channel ports, while on land the Spanish were repelled both in the Netherlands and in France, where Elizabeth committed 20,000 troops between 1589 and 1595. However, in neither case did Elizabeth have any effective long-term ambition on the Continent – her aim was simply the preservation of England. Essex thought differently. He wished to pursue a more aggressive strategy in the Netherlands which would give more active help to the Dutch Protestants. This was countered by the supporters of Cecil, and increasingly of his son Robert, his right-hand man, who believed that action at sea was both more flexible and less costly.

From 1589, England had had little choice but to support the cause of the Protestant pretender to the French crown, Henri of Navarre. News of Mary Stuart's execution had reached Paris on 1 May 1587. So violent was the reaction to her death that the preacher of Saint-Eustache (possibly the Queen's former confessor René Benoiste) was obliged to leave the pulpit before concluding his sermon, as it had practically caused a riot. On 13 November a Mass was said for Mary at Notre-Dame, but the Duc de Guise did not attend. Mary had been practically useless to the Guise attempt to gain control of French politics for some time, but now she could become a serviceable martyr. It was rumoured that Henri III had acquiesced in the execution, and anti-royalist Catholic preachers were encouraged to speak out against the king.

From England, Elizabeth encouraged Henri to go to war against Guise, yet without being prepared to do much to aid him, and by the end of the year Henri had almost lost control. Protestant supporters of Henri of Navarre arrived on 18 September, adding a further insurrectionary element to the stand-off between king and subject. By May 1588, Paris was in the control of the Guises, whose ally, Philip of Spain, was pushing for a complete rupture with the crown. Guise was delighted to work with him to bring down Elizabeth, but baulked at the possibility of setting up a Spanish client monarchy in France. Guise and Henri III were therefore forced into uneasy collaboration, convening in October at Blois. Guise now found himself, embarrassingly, at the head of what amounted to a proto-democratic party. In November, deputies of the Third Estate threatened to leave if the king refused to lower taxation, arguing that 'the Queen of England, wicked though she is, is not maintained by these means'.[5] The English Parliament, they argued, was able to pass resolutions without interference from the royal council. Thus the ultra-Catholic Guise found himself the spokesman of what was in effect an attempt at a constitutional revolution based on the model of his great enemy.

Henri was equally disgusted, and his solution was the murder of Guise. He was assassinated (after a sensible breakfast of Provençal prunes) in the king's antechamber early on a December morning by the king's bodyguard. The murder of Guise did not preserve the ailing house of Valois. A month later, the Sorbonne lodged a decree in the French Parliament which deposed Henri III and replaced him with a council. Desperately, the king turned to Henri of Navarre, and the two mounted a campaign against the Leaguers over the summer, but in 1 August Henri was murdered by a zealous Dominican monk.

At this point, Henri of Navarre sought assistance from England. His correspondence with Elizabeth proceeded in the conventional language of courtly love, with one of Europe's most famous philanderers professing to be ravished by the portrait of the fifty-six-year-old Queen. Elizabeth was not impressed by Henri's subsequent gift of an elephant, neither an aesthetically pleasing nor economical choice, but she permitted him to go through the motions of a 'courtship', while remaining aware that she had little choice but to assist him. With the Leaguers proclaiming their own candidate, Charles, Cardinal of Bourbon, she faced the possibility of a Spanish-ruled puppet state across the Channel, or at best the emergence of two confessionally divided states, Catholic north and Bourbon south. Twenty thousand pounds and 4,000 troops were promised to Henri in September, prompting Cecil to remark on the vagaries of political fortune: 'The state of the world is marvellously changed when we true Englishmen have cause for our own quietness to wish good success to a French King and a King of Scots.'[6]

France was the first site of Essex's ambitions. Like Leicester before him, Essex's ideas of his own military prowess were based more on his lineage and his ability to make an impressive appearance in the tiltyard than on actual soldiering experience. The evidence of the field showed him up as little more than a flouncing amateur. In 1591, Elizabeth sent a small expedition under Sir John Norreys to Brittany, where it met with some success. Essex was given the generalship of the French forces the same year, but his campaigning consisted of little more than dubbing an inordinate number of knights (twenty-four, more than Elizabeth herself had made in a decade), and hanging around waiting for Henri IV, who, despite having given Essex a private interview, without the outraged Elizabeth's permission, never actually showed up in the field. Trudging round in the mud of northern France was not Essex's idea of military glory, however much it may have been a realistic experience of actual warfare. Having obtained a seat on the Privy Council in February 1593, the Earl set about sowing discord among Elizabeth's advisers, with the aim of displacing Robert Cecil from what appeared to many as his natural inheritance now that his father was evidently in declining health.

The exposure of poor Rodrigo Lopez was claimed as a victory, but Essex had little understanding of, or interest in, the daily grind of political business at which the Cecils, father and son, so thoroughly excelled. He wanted power, and action, and flash, without having to bore himself too much with the somewhat middle-class business of detail.

The struggle for dominance in France continued for four years, which proved an intolerable strain on Elizabeth's resources. So when Henri made his peace with Rome on 22 July 1593 at an elaborate ceremony at the royal abbey of St Denis, her feelings were ambivalent. She described Henri as 'the most ungrateful King that liveth',[7] but was encouraged by his promise to continue religious toleration for Protestants. In a move which gave the lie to the idea that conservative opinion still rejected the concept of female rule, Philip of Spain was pushing for his daughter, the Infanta Isabella, to succeed instead of Henri. It was Isabella's foreignness, rather than her sex, to which the French Estates objected in their rejection of the scheme. For her part, Elizabeth did consent in 1594 to support an expedition to oust the Spanish from Brest, though for the next two years she refused any further support for Henri, despite considerable pressure from the more militant among her council.

Elizabeth's choice to make her translation of Boethius's *The Consolation of Philosophy* is notable at this juncture. She began the work, her first major translation since her gifts to her father and Katherine Parr as a princess, at Windsor, shortly after hearing the news of Henri's conversion. Despite the French king's compliments on her portrait, Elizabeth knew that, visually, the game was up. She has been criticised for her failure, during the 1590s, to reposition her symbolic image, 'the aged actress looked foolish as she continued to play the part which had once made her famous',[8] yet the translation may be seen as precisely such a gesture, a reclaiming of intellectual authority. Elizabeth's looks may have been waning, not so her mind. Boethius was a sharp choice, and one which, as we have seen above in her exchange with Ralegh, played to her own self-conception as divinely appointed monarch. It was also a subtle response to a literary challenge. In 1593, another lady had been at work on a translation. Mary Herbert (née Sidney), Robert Dudley's niece, had attended on Elizabeth before her marriage to the Earl of Pembroke in 1577. As sister to the courtier-poet Philip Sidney, Mary created an intellectual circle around her home at Wilton which has been described in the most glowing terms of Renaissance comparison as 'the English Urbino'. After her brother's death in the Netherlands, Mary, whose own excellent education had included Hebrew, continued his translation of the Psalms, eventually publishing them in 1599. The Sidneys were allied with the militant party at court, and the Psalms were particularly important to radical Protestants – the Huguenots sang Psalm 68 as a battle hymn. Mary was keen to present her late brother as a Protestant martyr, and her dedication of the work, to both the Queen and Philip himself, can be read as a challenge. The expenses of the French campaigns amounted to over £300,000 by the time of Henri's 'apostasy', and though Parliament wished to reduce subsidies by two-thirds, and Elizabeth had been forced to sell off crown lands to raise funds, many considered that she had not gone far enough in her support for the Huguenots. In counter-translating Boethius, Elizabeth is asserting the authority of her judgement.

Above all, Boethius counselled patience. By implication, Protestant zealotry is to be mistrusted: 'Each thing seeks out his own proper course/And do rejoice at return their own/No order given to any remains/Unless he joins to end his first/And so steadies his holy round.' It is by acceptance of God's (and therefore Elizabeth's) will that things will return to their true nature; it is presumptuous to seek to illuminate the Holy mind. Thus, Elizabeth subtly reminds her reader of the spiritual pride of the Protestants who advocate further armed conflict, and of her own unique status as a channel of communication with God. Contending with the changes in her council, the pressure from militant Protestants and the frustration of Henri's conversion, Elizabeth looks for succour in Boethius's injunction to seek the truth by rising above the pettiness of worldly matters: 'Man alone his head upward bends/On high thy mind should raise, lest overweighed/Thy body made aloft, thy mind should/Lower sit.' This rendering reads as a recollection of Sidney's observation in the *Defense of Poesie*, then in circulation, that 'our erected wit maketh us to know what perfection is, and yet our infected will keepeth us from reaching unto it'. In other words, Mary and her fellow advocates of intervention would do well to remember the thoughts of their pet martyr, that it is the mind which raises us to the quality of divine grace, and excessive dependence on action reduces us to mere bodies.

Just as Henri had employed the vocabulary of courtly love in seeking Elizabeth's favour, so, more broadly, did Protestant intellectuals in seeking to associate her with the cause of transnational Protestantism. Literature, often in Latin, formed an important connection between Elizabeth's court and the Protestant centres of northern Europe, another strand of connection between Elizabethan England and the continental Renaissance. Paulus Melissus was another member of the Sidney circle, a German writer and refugee who had known Philip Sidney in Heidelberg in 1573. He arrived at court in 1585, soon after which he dedicated his first poetry collection, *Schediasmata Poetica*, to the Queen. His ambition of an official appointment remained unfulfilled, but his work expresses all the hope of European Protestants that they would find a champion in her, casting himself as the supplicant lover in the mingling of the erotic with the divine which Elizabeth had so successfully arrogated to herself. Elizabeth functions as both lord and lady, sexually idealised as 'Rosina' (one can see why the well-read Queen baulked at giving poor, earnest Melissus a job) and as an armed *princeps ignotus*, his weapons burnished by heavenly light. True piety, he argues, will only be achieved by a prince worthy of God's love, couched in the most yearning of courtly terms: 'For twenty Mays I have been able to creep through acanthus and often been subjected to pricking thorns and brambles/There the Queen was permitted to gather a gleaming flower which Venus is always accustomed to love above all others/But spring has never had any regard for me and summer glances back towards my face . . . No rose is to be seen . . . When will that cup of the rose reach out to me?' Melissus articulates the despair of Protestants who saw Elizabeth as the object of long-standing and fruitless devotion, but Elizabeth had as much regard for the German as spring did, and by the early 1590s Melissus's 'ideal prince' had mutated into Henri of Navarre.

Henri's conversion was thus in a sense a bitter vindication of Elizabeth's policies, which she expressed in her own translation, that interfering in the workings of the sacred mind was a vanity, a spiritual puffery which would be thwarted by fortune. Patience was also considerably cheaper.

CHAPTER TWENTY-SEVEN

I n September 1598, Elizabeth lost the last of the three men of
her life, her brother–suitor–enemy Philip of Spain. For all the
vagaries of their relationship, his portrait was still kept in the
royal bedroom, which was also the site of Elizabeth's final stand-off
with Essex, who had left for Ireland several months previously. English authority there, never particularly strong, had received a serious
blow in the defection in 1595 of Hugh O'Neill, Earl of Tyrone.
Although plagued by almost incessant rebellion, English subjugation of Ireland had proceeded throughout the previous five years
until some form of consistent English government had been established all over the country, with the exception of Ulster. Tyrone had
been an effective instrument in this, but now he demanded that he
should be given Ulster to govern in Elizabeth's name. When he was
refused, he rebelled. In the summer of 1598, O'Neill was besieging
the English castle of Blackwater in the north, overpowering the
English army sent to relieve it at a cost of 2,000 lives. With Cecil
gone and Ireland in need of a commander, Essex saw an opportunity and returned to court. When Elizabeth refused to see him, he
feigned illness, at which the Queen relented, sending her own doctors to tend him and allowing herself to be persuaded, against her
better judgement, that the Earl should have the command in the next
Irish campaign. Essex realised too late that he was a victim of his
own arrogance, admitting that the role was 'the hardest task that
ever gentleman was sent about', but unable to back down. Elizabeth,
whose own view of Ireland as an albatross on England's neck was
summed up in her remark 'The like burden and charge is not found
in any place in Christendom', hoped that for once Essex's bragging
might turn to the good, and was prepared to equip him far more

thoroughly than she had been Leicester in the Netherlands fourteen years earlier.

Elizabeth later remarked angrily that she had paid Essex £1,000 per day to strut about the countryside. The purpose of the 1,400 horse, 16,000 foot (with quarterly reinforcements of 2,000) and the £23,000 worth of *matériel* was the immediate subjugation of Tyrone. Essex had vaunted his view that anything 'that was done in other kind in Ireland was but waste and consumption'.[1] Yet after a summer of what Elizabeth scornfully referred to as a 'progress' he had not only failed to engage Tyrone but complained loudly that he received nothing from England except discomfort and wounds to his soul. Essex was disobedient, promoting his crony the Earl of Southampton to General of the Horse, a position Elizabeth had forbidden as Southampton was in disgrace over his entanglement with Elizabeth Vernon, whom he had married after a spell in the Fleet prison. He also continued his scatter-gun dubbings, not having learned from Elizabeth's disapproval of the number of knights he had made in France. The Queen was altogether disgusted, particularly as, rather than admit his faults, Essex whined and wheedled and blamed others. Essex returned to Dublin for three weeks in the middle of the summer, then set off again on campaign, but still he failed to do anything definitive about Tyrone. In August, Elizabeth wrote sardonically that 'if sickness in the army be the reason, why was not the action undertaken when the army was in better state. If winter's approach, why were the summer months of July and August lost? . . . surely we must conclude that none of the four quarters of the year will be in season for you . . . for you had your asking, you had your choice of times, you had power and authority more ample than any ever had.'[2] Finally, on 5 September, Tyrone himself took the initiative and organised a private conference with the Earl on the banks of the River Lagan, where a truce was settled upon. Essex did not see fit to inform Elizabeth of the terms he had negotiated, throwing the council into a panic. He had been specifically instructed not to return without formal permission, yet now he considered that his only course was to explain his conduct in person.

The eglantine, the delicate rose so often associated with Elizabeth, and which she had taken as her badge from her grandmother Elizabeth of York, flowers in late spring and early summer. To Elizabeth, who was well accustomed to discovering the messages of *imprese*, the verbal/visual conceits displayed at the tilt and in miniature paintings, one of Essex's gifts might now have attained a sorry irony. One of the best-known paintings of the period, Hilliard's *Young Man Amongst Roses*, is widely considered to be a portrait of Essex. The earliest dating for the picture is 1585, so if it is indeed Essex he would have been about nineteen, which fits well with the beardless face, the moustache barely discernible, of the elegantly posed youth depicted. Dressed in Elizabeth's colours, the black and white she had worn so long ago to indicate her commitment to virginity, the boy stands with his hand to his heart, the first time such a gesture is deployed in English painting, and reminiscent, in its exaggerated suppleness of line, of the Mannerist stucco works at Fontainebleau which influenced Hilliard's style at this point in his career. The portrait may be read as an *impresa* expressing love for a woman (the Queen), but possibly also of friendship with a man, a suggestion reinforced by the powerfully upsurging trees in the background. This would fit appropriately with the mingling of genders often applied to Elizabeth as master/mistress, and the composition also recalls Elizabeth's figuring in this fashion as the source of erotic authority in Paulus Melissus's rendering of his entrapment in the tangled rose fronds in his contemporaneous poem. The motto, 'Dat poenas laudata fides' (my praised faith is my pain), is from Lucan's *De Bello Civili*, which Elizabeth would have recognised as associating the young man with Pompey, the great Roman general who by the age of twenty-five had already been granted two triumphs. The size of the picture, slightly too large to be worn as a miniature, reinforces the hand-on-heart gesture, its 'status as a precious object to be held and admired in the palm of the hand deepens its iconographic focus upon physically touching the heart'.[3] If the picture was made as a gift to the Queen, its resonance had altered considerably between its production and the autumn of 1599. That Elizabeth held Essex's faith in her hand, that his heart was hers, twined perennially in her motto, was an elegant conceit, but now the roses were browned and faded, and the career of the ambitious young general proved to be as deceptive as the carefully laid-on colours of his lover's complexion.

Essex left Dublin on 24 September and made straight for the court at Nonsuch, which he reached at about ten o'clock in the morning on the 28th. Of a previous absence from court he had written to her 'the delights of this place cannot make me unmindful of one in whose sweet company I have joyed as much as the happiest man doth in his highest contentment; and if my horse could run as fast as my thoughts do fly, I would as often make mine eyes rich in the beholding the treasure of my love as my desires do triumph when I seem to myself in a strong imagination to conquer your resisting will'.[4] Now Essex's image would be put to the test. For both players in the charming game of love which had sustained the relationship between the young aristocrat and his Queen, it was a cruel encounter with reality. The swooning lover crashed into Elizabeth's chamber in his filthy travelling clothes 'so full of dirt and mire that his very face was full of it' to confront his fair mistress, barely out of bed, her wrinkles brutally exposed in the morning light and her wig off. Elizabeth kept her countenance and played for time, uncertain as yet whether his precipitate arrival was yet more recklessness, or if it heralded the beginning of a *coup d'état*. Once she was assured that Essex had arrived with only a small party of servants she dismissed him to bathe and dress and received him again to dine. By the afternoon, now dressed and made up, Elizabeth was ready to attack. She demanded that he account for his disgraceful conduct and after two sessions of interrogation by Council, Essex was instructed to keep to his rooms. Effectively, he was under arrest, confirmed three days later when Elizabeth commanded that he should be confined at the residence of Lord Keeper Egerton, York House, where he remained until the following March, when he was permitted to return to Essex House, though still under arrest. On 6 June, the Earl was called before a committee of judge and councillors, and knelt bare-headed as he was censured for contempt and insubordination. He was deprived of all his offices excepting Master of the Horse and warned that he had narrowly escaped perpetual imprisonment in the Tower and extensive fines. In August, Essex was once again a free man, only to be rendered ever more desperate by Elizabeth's decision that the tax monopoly he had been granted on the import of sweet wine should revert to the crown now that the ten-year lease was up. Furious, humiliated and in terrifying debt, Essex took himself off to stew in the country.

By the winter of 1600, Essex's anger and paranoia had reached boiling point. Sir John Harrington recorded that he seemed 'devoid of good reason or right mind', so suddenly did he shift between 'sorrow and repentance, rage and rebellion'.[5] During his last disgrace Essex might have written to Elizabeth begging to be permitted to kiss her hand, and claiming that until he was able to see her 'time itself is a perpetual night and the whole world but a sepulchre to your humblest vassal',[6] but amongst the rowdy cabal of chancers he was assembling around him at Essex House he sneered at the 'treasure of my love' as 'an old woman . . . no less distorted and crooked in mind than she is in body'.[7] Until now, Essex's own plans had been wild and formless. Convinced that Elizabeth was no more than a puppet of the Cecil faction which he had convinced himself was barring him from his proper place in government, Essex had as early as his service in Ireland talked of collecting two hundred resolute gentlemen to take control of the Queen's person, he had also attempted to enlist the services of Lord Mountjoy in bringing over a force from Ireland, and had long been engaged in a correspondence with James VI in an attempt to persuade him that, as he confided in a letter of Christmas Day 1600, James must intervene 'to stop the malice, the wickedness and madness of these men, and to relieve my poor country which groans under her burden'.[8] It has been suggested that James fell for Essex's arguments as to Cecil's 'unquenchable malice', and that his agreement to send an ambassador to demand a change of ministers from Elizabeth once Essex had effected his plan was an endorsement of the Earl's aims, but given that Cecil was in covert negotiations with James over his accession from 1601 onwards, his acquiescence is more likely to have been a means of giving Essex a little more rope to hang himself with. Nonetheless, Essex was sufficiently encouraged to lay out his scheme at a meeting at the Earl of Southampton's house in early February 1601. Along with Essex and Southampton, the key conspirators were Sir Charles Danvers, Sir Ferdinando Gorges, Sir

John Davies, Sir Christopher Blount and John Littleton. The object was to isolate Elizabeth, after which Essex would beg her contritely to bring his enemies to trial 'and having called a Parliament, to alter the form of commonwealth'.[9] Blount would man the gate, Davies the Hall, Danvers the great Chamber and the Presence Chamber, upon which Essex would emerge from the stable called the 'Muse' with his escort and throw himself upon the Queen's mercy. Once the court was controlled, the plotters would take the Tower and subdue the City.

That Essex was able to convince his supporters that this was a plausible scheme was a testament to his personal charisma, as the project was patently fantastic, if not merely stupid. Firstly, Essex had severely underestimated the scope of Cecil's intelligence network and therefore overestimated the support of James VI. Secondly, in believing that he was standing up for the 'countless host of the discontented'[10] he had not considered how paltry his backing was among powerful magnates and wealthy burghers. Thirdly, he was utterly unable to keep his mouth shut. Under Essex's steward Meyrick, who dished out provisions to anyone with a sword, Essex House had become a general canteen for 'bold confident fellows, men of broken fortunes, discontented persons and such as saucily used their tongues in railing against all men'. Obviously, the authorities knew something was going on. Essex gave out that the increase in guests at his home was for the purpose of hearing sermons, but this pretext only made matters worse when it was suggested that 'some words . . . had dropped from the preachers' mouths as of the superior magistrates had power to restrain kings themselves'.[11] Unlike the network Elizabeth herself had constructed around her in the last year of Mary's reign, this was no efficient court-in-waiting, but an inchoate mass of discontents with no real programme and no real power.

On 7 February, Essex was summoned to appear before the Privy Council, but he rejected this, and a further summons, claiming that he was ill. He learned that a barricade of coaches had been erected between Whitehall and Charing Cross, preventing access to the palace, and that the guard in the Great Chamber had been augmented. That evening, a specially commissioned performance of Shakespeare's

Richard II was given at the Globe Theatre in Southwark. Supporters of Essex, including Charles and Joscelyn Percy, younger brothers of the Earl of Northumberland, paid forty shillings to persuade the Chamberlain's Men to stage the piece, which the actors felt was too out of date to appeal to many spectators. Eleven of Essex's men (though not the Earl himself) were in the house. At ten the next morning, four councillors, headed by Lord Egerton, arrived at Essex House to persuade Essex to petition the Queen in correct form if he felt that there was a wrong to be redressed. Essex had already spread a rumour that he had refused to attend Council because a fatal ambush was planned for him, and now set off into the city with about two hundred armed followers, having locked the delegation in the library at Essex House. Just as Essex entered the City, en route for the Tower, Thomas Lord Burghley (Burghley's older son) and Garter king of Arms arrived, proclaiming Essex and all his followers to be traitors. Elizabeth was at dinner at Whitehall while Essex's rabble confronted her guards at Ludgate Hill. The only allusion she made to the menace in the streets was that 'He that had placed her on that seat would preserve her in it', and whatever she was feeling, she concealed it 'marvellously'.

The skirmish at Ludgate cost the life of Essex's page, Henry Tracey, but the Earl escaped with a couple of bullet holes in his hat. There was never any possibility of attaining the Tower – the rebels scattered at the first sign of a serious engagement and Essex's small remaining party commandeered a few boats to row themselves desperately back downriver from Queenhithe, hoping to use the hostages to negotiate a settlement. Back at Essex House, now surrounded on the land side by royal troops, Ferdinando Gorges had had the sense to see that holding the councillors could only make matters worse, and freed them before Essex returned. At about nine that evening, Essex surrendered his sword to the Earl of Nottingham. He spent the night at Lambeth Palace before being rowed to the Tower, already a condemned man. To the last, Essex would maintain that he had never intended any harm to Elizabeth's person, refusing to sue for pardon and insisting that he had only wished to state his grievance. Might Elizabeth have forgiven him one last time?

Robert Cecil was determined to preclude this possibility. Immediately following the failed coup, the details of the Earl's treason were proclaimed in London, and thanks given to the people for refusing to join the rebels. With the citizens' resistance praised so publicly, Elizabeth could not fail to execute Essex without appearing impossibly weak. Yet this time the Queen gave no sign of wavering. From the moment Essex had exposed her ageing frailty in her bedchamber to the staging of Shakespeare's drama, his actions had struck not only at Elizabeth's government but at the mystical core of her personal power.

Elizabeth Tudor was the granddaughter of a usurper and the product, according to many, of an illegal marriage, if not of an ignominious adultery. From the moment of her coronation, she had identified herself with Richard II, the last undisputed possessor of the divine right, and linked herself further to him through mystical virginity. These latter had been the compasses of her queenship. But Elizabeth was also a modern ruler, a monarch who had absorbed the principles of Renaissance political theory, combining in her person that uneasy blend of might and right which had fractured the consistency of her father's theory of kingship, as exposed in *Henry VIII*. In the drama which was played out with Essex, Elizabeth's self-identification with Richard inevitably casts Essex as Bolingbroke, the rationalist who sees through the 'deeply Machiavellian'[13] construct that royal magnificence is merely a device for control: as the play has it 'Art thou aught else but place, degree and form/Creating awe and fear in other men?' The tragedy of *Richard II* is that of the dismantling of the king's 'two bodies',[14] the gradual and brutal demystification of Richard's person until he is rendered a man as other men. From the moment the king acknowledges that he is human, that he 'live[s] with bread like you, feel want/Taste grief, need friends—subjected thus/How can you say to me, I am a king?' to the point when he reverses the sacraments of his consecration as monarch (a scene performed but never printed or published in Elizabeth's reign), the audience witnesses the undoing of a sacred fiction. Time and time again, Elizabeth herself had played on the distinction between her 'body natural' and her 'body politic', but no exposure of the dislocation between those entities could have been more brutal than the scene played out with Essex in her bedroom. But might Elizabeth not be seen as a Bolingbroke? Might that not, ultimately, have been Essex's error? For, as Marlowe's Machiavel has it, did not 'Might first make kings?'

Essex was a jouster, not a soldier, a sonneteer, not a politician. Elizabeth was serenely assured of her own divine right (or at least, she played it that way), and no one knew better than she the importance of image to the making of monarchy, yet throughout her reign she had undertaken, albeit sometimes reluctantly, to preserve her state at any cost, the first principle of the Renaissance prince. Essex, not Elizabeth, was the throwback, the believer in chivalric kingship. His glamour and his aristocratic birth may have made him popular, but the future belonged to the 'goose-quilled gentlemen', the pen-pushers, who so offended his sensibilities. Elizabeth suffered from no such delusions. As she wrote to James of Scotland, she was not so unskilled in kingship that she would wink at any fault. To the French ambassador, when he congratulated her on her delivery from the rebellion, she declared that if Essex had made it to Whitehall, she should have gone out to meet him, 'in order to know which of them ruled'. Perhaps Elizabeth's particular qualities as a Renaissance prince can be cast as the inheritance of her mixed Yorkist and Lancastrian blood – York the house of romance and chivalry, Lancaster as pragmatism and statecraft. If Elizabeth, rather than Essex, was Bolingbroke, then she showed that when it came to an emergency she was Lancastrian through and through.

Perhaps Essex can be seen, like Anne Boleyn before him, as yet another victim of the game of love. He never quite appreciated that Elizabeth only saw it as a game, that he would never be master of his mistress. Essex maintained a jaunty insouciance throughout his trial, which began at Westminster Hall on 19 February, persisting in his refusal to plead for mercy. Only when the Dean of Norwich visited him in the Tower to warn him of the danger to his soul did Essex apprehend that he was actually going to die. His nature had always been depressive and mercurial – Elizabeth dismissed him as a 'mad ingrate' – now he suffered some form of hysterical nervous breakdown. Elizabeth signed his death warrant the next day. Five days later, his head was struck off as he recited the fifty-first Psalm. Though she subsequently confided to the French ambassador that she would have spared Essex if she could, this was merely a formulaic echo of Elizabeth's professed grief at the execution of Mary Stuart. To the public, responsibility for Essex's death fell firmly upon Cecil, but the promptness of Elizabeth's action suggests that the decision was hers.

CHAPTER TWENTY-EIGHT

⟨✧⟩

The Essex rebellion has been seen as the point of tergiversation in Elizabeth's rule, the moment when the long and so carefully cultivated image of majesty began to decay. The tinsel was looking tawdry; behind the glittering edifice of the monarch's person an old, exhausted woman could be all too clearly seen. Elizabeth's godson John Harington noted in 1598 that among university scholars, discussion 'did light on one question that bewailed a kind of weariness of this time, *mundus senescit*, that the world waxed old'.

Elizabeth had always been quite aware, as she had remarked early in her reign, that her people would incline more to the rising than the setting sun, and now, finally, she had to acknowledge that the long love affair between queen and subject, in which she had always believed, was coming to an end. On 30 November 1601, the Queen addressed 140 members of the Commons in the council chamber at Whitehall. The members had officially come to formally express their gratitude for the resolution of the monopolies question; what they and she knew was that many of them had come to say goodbye. Elizabeth accepted the thanks 'with no less joy than your loves can have desire to offer such a present', which she claimed to 'esteem more than any treasure or riches; for those we know how to prize, but loyalty, love and thanks I account them invaluable'. Her greatest happiness as a Queen, she went on, had been to reign over 'so thankful a people'. As the members stood, she continued 'it is not my desire to live or reign longer than my life and reign shall be for your good. And though you have had, and may have, many mightier and wiser princes sitting in this seat, yet you never had, nor shall have, any that will love you better.' As they bent over the Queen's hand in farewell, many of the men were seen to be weeping. Her words became known instantly as 'the Golden Speech', but 'its themes, like the Queen, were exhausted'.[1]

Was Elizabeth herself convinced? 'Affection is false' she had remarked tartly to Mistress Fitton at the wedding masque a year before, and yet, still, she had risen and danced. To the end of her life, she performed the role she had been born for, and perhaps the criticisms of her conservatism, her inability to change, her lack of concern for the succession, need to be balanced against the enormous psychological cost of so doing. Elizabeth ruled as a prince, and princes just could not be as other men. Possessed of 'two bodies', Elizabeth could never entirely inhabit either. She has been described, perfectly, as a 'political hermaphrodite',[2] but, as this book has attempted to argue, it was not the division between her 'masculine' political body and her 'feminine' mortal body which entirely made her unique, but the fusing in that female person of the material and the divine. As Shakespeare's *Henry V* puts it:

> What infinite heart's ease
> Must kings neglect that private men enjoy?
> What kind of god art thou, that suffers't more
> Of mortal griefs than do thy worshippers?[3]

In her Golden Speech, Elizabeth declared that she had no wish to outlive her usefulness to the realm, yet, as Bacon put it in his treatise *Of Great Place*, 'retire men cannot when they would, neither will they when it were reason, but are impatient of privateness, even in age and sickness, which require the shadow'.[4] In her last years, perhaps more than ever before, Elizabeth performed the dance of monarchy, yet the shadows were stealing close.

From 1592 onwards, the Queen's portrait was no longer taken from life. That year she had sat to Isaac Oliver, Hilliard's pupil, who produced a pattern model for a portrait intended for mass repetition. Described as 'the most revealing portrait ever painted of Elizabeth',[5] in the Queen's eyes it was a disaster. For once, we see Elizabeth's face, the slightly hooked nose, high forehead with just a suggestion of lines, the lips withered with age. Elizabeth's large eyes, sunk deep in their sockets, possess the hooded alertness of a resting hawk. If anything, since the picture was painted when Elizabeth was almost sixty, it shows what an attractive woman she must have been, yet Elizabeth expressed herself greatly offended and the Privy Council gave out that 'all likenesses of the Queen that depicted her as being in any way old and hence subject to mortality'[6] ought to be impounded. The matter was not entirely one of vanity. To suggest that the Queen was ageing was to allude to the still uncertain matter of the succession. 'In the later time,' wrote John Clapham, 'when she showed herself in public she was always magnificent in apparel, supposing happily thereby that the eyes of her people, being dazzled with the glittering aspect of those accidental ornaments would not so easily discern the marks of age and the decay of natural beauty.'[7] There was a very real fear that, beyond the gleaming aura of the Queen's person, anarchy was waiting.

In a sense, Elizabeth was becoming the victim of her own legend. As the decade progressed, still with no confirmation of the next heir, the demeanour of splendid majesty was too difficult to maintain. A 1591 poem by that most patriotic of writers, Edmund Spenser, entitled *The Tears of the Muses*, announces a slippage in the process of civilisation, a descent into dark savagery. In turn, the Muses lament that their verses have lost their power and that the only hope they have of stalling the slide into degeneracy is a queen called 'Pandora'. Their complaint echoes Elizabeth's apparent despair as she began to lose control of the court in the sexual free-for-all of the 1590s. The Muses claim that Pandora is the only means by which culture can be preserved, but it was Pandora who unleashed 'black Chaos' upon the world. Two years later Shakespeare's bestseller *Venus and Adonis* goes further. As the poem opens, the goddess of love is captivated by the beauty of a young man who is more interested in boar hunting than making love. Venus sneers at Adonis for being no man, but 'a lifeless picture, cold and senseless stone/Well-painted idol, image dull and dead'. Venus's failure to consummate her passion descends into an undignified (and very funny) brawl, concluding with Venus departing as a 'disappointed and bitter goddess, no longer the goddess of justice, nor even ... the goddess of love, retiring in disgust from a wilderness in which she no longer has a place'. Renaissance readers of the racy sensation of the 1590s would have caught the allusion to Juvenal's *Sixth Satire*, which begins with Chastity departing the earth in the company of her sister Astraea, who was placed among the constellations at the end of the Golden Age as Virgo. Within the satire is a description of the transience of women's physical appeal: 'Why does Sartorius burn with love for Bibula? If you shake out the truth, it is the face he loves, not the woman. Let three wrinkles make their appearance, let her skin become dry and flabby; let her teeth turn black, and her eyes lose their lustre: then ... "Pack up your traps and be off! You've become a nuisance."' Spenser's and Shakespeare's works represent a tide of viciously satirical literature which emerged in the 1590s, which suggests that the rich brocade of royal allegory was wearing rather thin. Or, bluntly, the Virgin Queen was past her sell-by date. The currency of Diana was death; unlike the Holy Virgin, Elizabeth had produced no offspring. Her legacy, so the murmurings of dissent which emerged at the end of the reign suggested, was a risible barrenness. Elizabeth, her Church and her government had survived against extraordinary odds, and to do so they had employed a politics of 'raw survival'.[8] Yet was all the struggling, all the vigilance, all the compromise to now be rendered futile by Elizabeth's ultimate and stubborn refusal to preserve the future of her state?

Elizabeth's opponents had their own solutions to the reversion crisis. Robert Persons, safely ensconced at the English College at Rome, produced *A Conference about the next Succession to the Crown of England* in 1594. Interestingly, of the fourteen claimants discussed in the tract, which was banned in England, Persons favoured the Infanta Isabella, once proposed as the Queen of France, 'a princess of rare parts, both for beauty, wisdom and piety'. The only feasible Protestant candidate remained James VI of Scotland, with whom Elizabeth had been conducting a personal correspondence since the mid-1580s. In her relationship with James, Elizabeth invoked the split between her 'two bodies' as she had done at the time of Mary Stuart's execution, capitalising on contemporary expectations of her 'body natural' to create a fiction of political sympathy.

Intercession had always been an important trope of English queen-ship, the means by which a king could exercise clemency without diminishing his authority. Since in Elizabeth's case she was both king and queen, she was obliged, rhetorically, to absorb both aspects, of supplicant and gracious bestower of mercy. She had entirely ignored Mary's message after her trial, but in her two speeches to Parliament she exercised both her 'natural' 'feminine' inclinations, stressing her sorrow, her kinship with Mary and their shared gender, while simul-taneously acceding to the demands of her mystical body in respecting the Act of Association by signing the death warrant. A widely circu-lated propaganda text, *The Copie of a letter to the Right Honourable Earl of Leicester . . . And Her Majesty's answers thereunto by Herself delivered*, which appeared in French in 1587, gestured towards the interces-sion trope with its mention of Elizabeth's 'abundant gracious *natural* clemency and *Princely* magnanimity' (italics mine). Writing to James, Elizabeth elides the fact that she had sliced off his own mother's head by casting herself as a surrogate maternal figure, stating after the ex-ecution that 'since you first breathed, I regarded always to construe it as my womb it had born you'. James took part enthusiastically, sign-ing himself 'brother and son' to his 'dearest mother' and claiming that he trusted Elizabeth as 'a good mother'.

Still, James had no guarantee of his claim. At this point, Robert Cecil took charge, using that remarkable Catholic survivor, Lord Henry Howard, as a go-between. Between March and June 1601, he began a secret, coded correspondence with James, insisting that Elizabeth should know nothing of it, since 'her age and orbity, joined to the jealousy of her sex, might have moved her to think ill of that which helped to preserve her'.[9] During the following two years, Robert slowly slotted the provisions for the succession into place. In-structions were prepared, to be sent to the county lieutenants, the London watches were to be augmented, the Privy Council were alerted to summon the nobility. Robert even had the draft for James's proclamation at the ready, with a plan drawn up as to where it should be read.

Only Robert's father could have claimed to have been a more sea-soned politician than his Queen, yet his decision to treat her like a woman, protected from political realities which would distress her, reflects the mood of sterility and decay which was expressed, in the 1590s, by a renewed focus on Elizabeth's decaying natural body. As the image of immortality inevitably cracked, Elizabeth found herself the object of even cruder sexual rumours than the satire of *Venus and Adonis*. In 1592 a Lincolnshire priest, Thomas Pormort, complained to the Privy Council about allegations he had claimed to have heard from Elizabeth's 'rackmaster', Topcliffe. Topcliffe, he claimed, had stated that he had seen and felt Elizabeth's legs, that she had 'the softest belly of any of womankind' and that he had also fondled her breasts and neck. The Queen had supposedly asked him whether 'be not these the arms, legs and body of King Henry?', and when he assented he received a gift of white silk stockings. Imprecations on the Queen's chastity were by now surely beyond belief, but it is a measure of Elizabeth's declining power that people felt free to make them. In Essex, a couple were arrested for claiming that Elizabeth had had several children by Leicester, who had been stuffed into a chimney to kill them, while in Dorset one Edward Francis claimed that Elizabeth had given birth to three illegitimate offspring.

The absurdity of such present accusations only rendered them more cruel. Elizabeth was neglecting her appearance, barely eating, and England's Amazon now walked with a cane. Sometimes the Queen appeared disoriented, her 'lonely, diminished state', as John Harington described it, painfully emphasised by her new habit of pacing her chamber with a rusty old sword, 'stamping her feet at bad news and thrusting her . . . sword into the arras in great rage'. On better days, though, the Queen still rode out, and she showed a flash of spirit at an inept sermon preached by Dr Rudd before her seventieth birthday. 'I said ye are Gods but ye shall all die like men,' quoted the doctor, to which Elizabeth snapped, 'Mr Rudd, you have made me a good funeral sermon, I may die when I will.' By 1603, it was clear that this was indeed what the Queen wished.

That spring, the court moved from Whitehall to Richmond. By March, it was apparent that Elizabeth was ailing. She was not yet ill, but suffering from dreadful insomnia and was almost unable to eat. On 15 March, she was diagnosed with an inflammation of the breast and throat, but persisted in refusing any medicine. The throat abscess burst, and she found some relief in having her temples bathed with rosewater. Anxiously, the ambassadors exchanged what news they could glean – she had been given up, she was sleeping again, she had lost her mind, she was suffering from confusion, she was exhausted and refused to stir from her floor cushions, where she spent hours staring into space and sucking her finger. Perhaps the best indication of Elizabeth's real state was that Robert Cecil began the operation for the succession. Even as the Earl of Shrewsbury was being instructed to 'suppress all uncertain and evil rumours' concerning the state of the Queen's health, the government was rounding up vagrants and potential troublemakers, claiming that they were being sent to serve in the Netherlands. Five hundred 'foreigners' were escorted to Holland and numerous Catholics imprisoned. Theatres and ports were closed, Elizabeth's jewels and plate were sent to the Tower and the royal guard around Richmond was doubled.

By 19 March, Elizabeth was so weak that she could not attend chapel, instead hearing the service from cushions laid on the floor of the Privy Chamber. The rhythm of life in the capital slowed to mimic the Queen's struggling breaths. One priest locked up in the Tower described the atmosphere: 'a strange silence descended on the whole city, as if it were under interdict . . . Not a bell rang out, not a bugle sounded.' Elizabeth had by now given up changing her clothes or washing, lying in a torpor on the floor of her chamber, surrounded by her ladies. Ben Jonson claimed that for years, Elizabeth had not viewed her own reflection, that the women of her chamber had smashed their looking-glasses rather than allow the Queen to catch a glimpse of her raddled features, but now, she called for a glass and contemplated her face 'then lean and full of wrinkles . . . which she a good while very earnest beheld, perceiving thereby how often she had been abused by flatterers'. It was not her countenance which distressed her. Years before, Elizabeth had written a poem in her French psalter:

No crooked leg, no bleared eye
No part deformed out of kind,
Nor yet so ugly half can be,
As is the inward suspicious mind.

Elizabeth refused to go to bed because, as she explained to her Lord Admiral, the Earl of Nottingham, as he coaxed her to take some rest, 'if you were in the habit of seeing such things in your bed as I see in mine, you would not persuade me to go there'.[10]

By 23 March, Elizabeth was beyond speech, locked in with her ghosts. When the Privy Council attended her she was able, by a movement of her hand, to signal her acceptance of the succession of James of Scotland. She died quietly among her women the next morning.

The image we have of Elizabeth as she looked in the years before her death is not one which would have flattered her notorious vanity. The posthumous *Allegorical Portrait* of 1620 does not show the fresh young Queen of the *Three Goddesses* portrait, nor the triumphant empress of the *Armada* depiction, but someone else entirely. The Elizabeth who slumps dejectedly at the centre of the allegory looks like what she is – a tired old woman. The lines of the composition echo those of the *Coronation Portrait*, with the old Queen's arm following the curve of the ermine of the young Queen's robe; the hand that proudly held the sceptre taut in the first is now curved, in the second, to support her weary head. Behind her leers Death, come to claim her; on her right, Time sleeps, his hourglass tumbled and forgotten. Above her pearled false curls, two *putti* descend, preparing to set a crown upon her head. For this picture, in its way, shows a triumph. The Queen will transcend death, it tells us, she will be immortal in eternity. This may be the end for the 'body natural' – Elizabeth's eyes are hollow, her elegant fingers seem barely to have the strength to hold the book in her left hand, yet the strongly modelled contours of the worn face are possessed of a beauty quite absent in the other, more stringently controlled visions of the Queen. Here, Elizabeth, at last, is human.

EPILOGUE

Three years after Elizabeth's death, King James held a series of entertainments for King Christian of Denmark at her old home at Hatfield. The hollow, spectral atmosphere of the last years of the Elizabethan court was filled with a rambunctious vivacity, the pinched, cobwebby ghost of the old woman who had stalked and muttered through her last years was laid. Convention had returned: in the pageant the Queen of Sheba was to pay tribute to King Solomon; things were as they had always been. As the Queen approached the royal dais, carrying gifts for His Majesty, she missed her step, collapsed at his feet and tipped her caskets into the Danish king's lap. He attempted to rise, but was so inebriated that he too fell down and had to be carried to his bed of state, much besmeared with jelly, cream and custard. 'The entertainment and show went forward, and most of the presenters went backwards, or fell down, as wine so occupied their upper chambers.' Three maids of honour, as Faith, Hope and Charity, made their entrance, but Hope was beyond speech, only able to murmur an apology for the brevity of her performance. Faith staggered from the royal presence, leaving Charity to remark that her gifts were futile as heaven had already given its all to King James. She joined Hope and Charity in the lower hall, where all three were sick. Victory made no appearance at all, having dozed off in the antechamber, leaving Peace to beat the remaining courtiers about the heads with her olive branch.

NOTES

CHAPTER ONE

1. Garin, Eugenio, *L'Uomo del Rinascimento* (Rome, 1988), p. 10.
2. Ibid., p. 8.
3. Rickert, Edith (ed.), *The Babees' Book* (London, 1908), p. xxiii.
4. Kristeller, Paul Oskar, *Renaissance Thought and the Arts* (Princeton, 1990), p. 71.
5. Bobbitt, Philip, *The Garments of Court and Palace: Machiavelli and the World that He Made* (London, 2013), p. 3.
6. Ibid., p. 7.
7. Bate, Jonathan, *Soul of the Age: A Biography of the Mind of William Shakespeare* (London, 2010), p. 320.
8. Berlin, Isaiah, 'The Question of Machiavelli', *New York Review of Books*, 17 November 1971, p. 22.
9. Ryan, Alan, *On Machiavelli: The Search for Glory* (New York, 2014), p. 41.
10. Smith, G. Gregory (ed.), *Elizabethan Critical Essays* (Oxford, 1904), p. xxxviii.
11. McBride, Tom, '"Henry VIII" as Machiavellian Romance', *Journal of English and Germanic Philology*, Vol. 76, No. 1 (1977), p. 189.
12. Eisaman Maus, Katherine, *Inwardness and Theatre in the English Renaissance* (Chicago, 1995), p. 18.
13. Cited in Lake, Paul, *Moderate Puritans and the Elizabethan Church* (Cambridge, 2004), p. 11.
14. Ibid., p. 11.
15. Allinson, Rayne, '"The Prince" and Queen Elizabeth I: A New Perspective on the Development of English Machiavellianism', *Melbourne Historical Journal*, Vol. 34 (2006).
16. See particularly Praz, Mario, *Machiavelli and the Elizabethans* (London, 1972).
17. Gibson Jonathan, 'The Queen's Two Hands', in Petrina, Alessandra and Tosi, Laura (eds), *Representations of Elizabeth I in Early Modern Culture* (London, 2011).
18. *Hamlet* 5: 2, 33–5.
19. Strong, Roy, *Gloriana: The Portraits of Queen Elizabeth I* (London, 1987), p. 131.

CHAPTER TWO

1. Taylor-Smither, Larrisa J., 'Elizabeth I: A Psychological Profile', *Sixteenth Century Journal*, Vol. 15, No. 1 (Spring 1984), p. 51.
2. Scarisbrick, J. J., *Henry VIII* (New Haven, 1968), p. 323.
3. Laynesmith, Joanna, The Last Medieval Queens: English Queenship, 1445–1503 (Oxford, 2004), p. 112.
4. Ibid., p. 24.
5. Ibid., p. 27.
6. Borman, Tracy, *Elizabeth's Women: The Hidden Story of the Virgin Queen* (London, 2010), p. 22.
7. Luke, Carmen, *Pedagogy, Printing and Protestantism: The Discourse on Childhood* (New York, 1989), p. 64.
8. Borman, op. cit., p. 3.
9. Ibid. p. 81.
10. Luke, op. cit., p. 34.
11. Ibid., p. 135.
12. *Calendar of State Papers, Spain*, Vol. VII, No. XLIII(a), pp. 91–4.
13. Shulman, Nicola, *Graven with Diamonds. The Many Lives of Thomas Wyatt: Courtier, Poet, Assassin, Spy* (London, 2011), p. 123.
14. Ibid., p. 127.
15. Ibid., p. 146.
16. Castiglione, *The Book of the Courtier*, Book 1, Section IX.
17. Shulman, op. cit., p. 199.
18. For the suggestion that Wyatt's evidence was crucial to the case against Anne Boleyn, I am indebted to Nicola Shulman's analysis in the work cited above.
19. Shulman, op. cit., p. 194.

CHAPTER THREE

1. Allen, William, *An admonition to the nobility and people of England and Ireland concerninge the present vvarres made for the execution of his Holines sentence, by the highe and mightie Kinge Catholike of Spaine* http://quod.lib.umich.edu/e/eebo/A16774.0001.001?view=toc
2. Brewer, J. S., Gairdner, J. and Brodie, R. H. (eds), *Letter and Papers, Foreign and Domestic, of the Reign of Henry VIII, 1509–47* (London, 1862–1932), Vol. XVIII, 364, p. 214.

3. Cited in Wilson, Katharina M. (ed.), *Women Writers of the Renaissance and Reformation* (Athens, Georgia, 1987), p. 452.

4. Heywood, Thomas, *England's Elizabeth*, Rider, Philip R. (ed.) (New York, 1982), pp. 25–6.

5. Cited in Gristwood, Sarah, *Elizabeth & Leicester* (London, 2007), p. 117.

6. Bendor Grosvenor in an interview with the author.

7. Starkey, David, *Elizabeth* (London, 2000), p. 31.

8. Belozerskaya, Marina, *Rethinking the Renaissance: Burgundian Arts Across Europe* (New York, 2012), p. 105.

9. Ibid.

CHAPTER FOUR

1. Whitelock, Anna, *Elizabeth's Bedfellows: An Intimate History of the Queen's Court* (London, 2013), p. 9.

2. Middlebrook, Leah, 'Tout Mon Office: Body Politics and Family Dynamics in the Verse Epitres of Marguerite de Navarre', *Renaissance Quarterly*, Vol. 54 (Winter 2001).

3. Ibid.

4. 'My poor soul, ecstatically imprisoned / Heavy footed with concupiscence / Without hope of end', translation author's own.

5. Ives, Eric, 'The Fall of Anne Boleyn Reconsidered', *EHS*, 107 (1992).

6. Weir, Alison, stated in interview with NPR October 2011.

7. Cited in Carroll, Stuart, *Martyrs and Murderers: The Guise Family and the Making of Europe* (Oxford, 2009), p. 105.

8. Bernard, G. W., *Anne Boleyn: Fatal Attractions* (London, 2010), p. 96.

9. Ibid. p. 97.

10. Wycliffe, John, *De triplici vinvi amors,* in Deanesley, M. (ed.), *The Lollard Bible and Other Medieval Biblical Versions* (Cambridge, 1920), p. 248.

11. Bernard, op. cit., p. 114.

12. Brewer, Gairdner and Brody (eds), op. cit., Vol. X, p. 797.

13. Dowling M. (ed.), *William Latymer's Chronickille of Anne Bulleyne, Camden Miscellany* (London, 1990), p. 50.

14. Strype, J., *Ecclesiastical Memorials* (London, 1816), Vol. VI, p. 312.

15. See Watkins, Susan *Elizabeth I and her World* (London, 1988), pp. 188–9.

CHAPTER FIVE

1. Starkey, op. cit. p. 61.
2. Lemon, Robert and Everett Green, Mary Anne (eds), *Calendar of State Papers Domestic Series of the Reigns of Edward VI, Mary, Elizabeth, 1547–1625* (London, 1871), Vol. X, *Edward VI*, p. 92.
3. Strickland, Agnes, *Lives of the Queens of England*, Vol. IV, p. 35.
4. Lemon and Everett Green (eds), op. cit., p. 210.
5. MacCulloch, Diarmaid, *The Later Reformation in England, 1547–1603* (London, 2011), p. 25.
6. Ibid., p. 28.

CHAPTER SIX

1. Halls, Julie, *Aristotle and Dudley: Books as Evidence* (London, 2011) http://www. history.org.uk/resources/student_resource_4356_106.html
2. Hume, Martin A. S. (ed.), *CSP Spain* (London, 1896–9), Vol. I, p. 263.
3. Cited in Gristwood, op. cit., p. 70.
4. Nichols, J. G. (ed.), *Chronicle of Queen Jane and two years of Queen Mary* (London, 1850), p. 101.
5. Alberi, E. (ed.), *Relazioni degli ambasciatori veneti al Senato* (Florence, 1839–63), Vol. II, pp. 329–30.
6. Brown, Rawdon and Cavendish, Bentinck G. (eds), *Calendar of State Papers and Manuscripts Relating to English Affairs, Existing in the Archives of Venice and Other Libraries of Northern Italy* (London 1864–1947), Vol. V, p. 539.
7. Hume (ed.), op. cit., Vol. XI, p. 418.
8. Nichols (ed.), op. cit., p. 5.
9. Foxe, John, *Acts and Monuments*, Vol. XI, pp. 414–15, cited in Starkey, op. cit., p. 133.
10. Foxe, ibid., p. 53.

CHAPTER SEVEN

1. Manning, C. R. (ed.), *State Papers Relating to the Custody of Princess Elizabeth at Woodstock in 1554* (Norwich, 1855), p. 146.
2. Ibid.

3. Ibid., p. 182.
4. Weisner, Louis, *La Jeunesse d'Elizabeth d'Angleterre* (Paris, 1878), p. 339.
5. Manning (ed.), op. cit., p. 177.
6. Alford, Stephen, *Burghley: William Cecil at the Court of Elizabeth I* (Padstow, 2011), p. 71.
7. Overell, Anne, *Italian Reform and English Reformations* (Farnham, 2008), p. 141.
8. Ibid.
9. For this observation I am indebted to Dr Alessandra Petrina for her permission to read her then unpublished article '"Perfit readiness": Elizabeth Learning and Using Italian'.
10. The revelation of this meeting is credited to Stephen Alford in his cited biography of Lord Burghley.

CHAPTER EIGHT

1. Cited in Kantorowicz, Ernst H., *The King's Two Bodies: A Study in Mediaeval Political Theory* (Princeton, 1997), p. 7.
2. Castiglione, op, cit., Book 1, Section IX.
3. Hilton, Lisa, *Queen's Consort: England's Medieval Queens* (London, 2008), p. 94.
4. Ibid.
5. Davis, R. C. H. (ed.), *Gesta Stephani* (London, 1976).
6. Laqueur, Thomas, *Making Sex: Body and Gender from the Greeks to Freud* (Harvard, 1990), p. 6.
7. Ibid.

CHAPTER NINE

1. Hayward, John, *Annals of the First Four Years of the Reign of Queen Elizabeth* Bruce, John (ed.) (Cambridge, 1840), p. 15.
2. Brown and Cavendish (eds), op. cit., Vol. VII, No. 10.
3. De Lisle, Leanda, *The Sisters Who Would Be Queen: The Tragedy of Mary, Katherine & Lady Jane Grey* (London, 2009), p. 183.
4. Rowse, A. L, *The Coronation of Queen Elizabeth* (1953) *http://www.historytoday.com/al-rowse/coronation-queen-elizabeth*
5. Knighton, C. S. and Mortimer, Richard (eds), *Westminster Abbey Reformed* (Aldershot, 2006), p. 147, italics mine.
6. Ibid.
7. Starkey, op. cit., p. 277.

CHAPTER TEN

1. Ribeiro, Aileen, *Dress and Morality* (Oxford, 2003), p. 63.
2. Ibid., p. 67.
3. Ibid., p. 70.
4. Sharpe, Kevin, *Selling the Tudor Monarchy: Authority and Image in Sixteenth-Century England* (New Haven, 2009), p. 414.
5. Dolan, Frances E., 'Taking the Pencil out of God's Hand: Art, Nature and the Face-Painting Debate in Early Modern England', *PMLA*, Vol. 108, No. 2 (March 1993).
6. Sharpe, op. cit., p. 414.
7. Belozerskaya, op. cit., p. 83.

CHAPTER ELEVEN

1. Hartley, T. E. (ed.), *Proceedings in the Parliaments of Elizabeth I*, Vol. I (Leicester, 1981–95), p. 34.
2. Alford, op. cit., p. 91.
3. Hartley, op. cit., Vol. I, p. 7.
4. Cited in Haigh, Christopher, *Profiles in Power: Elizabeth I* (Harlow, 1998), p. 32.
5. McDermott, James, *England & the Spanish Armada: The Necessary Quarrel* (New Haven, 2005), p. xii.
6. Malham, J. (ed.), *The Harleian Miscellany*, Vol. II, p. 261.
7. Ibid., p. 317.
8. Cited in McDermott, op. cit., p. 325.

CHAPTER TWELVE

1. Von Klariwill, Victor *Queen Elizabeth and Some Foreigners: being a Series of Hitherto Unpublished Letters from the Archives of the Hapsburg Family*, trans. Nash, T. H. (London, 1928), p. 112.
2. Cited in Skidmore, Chris, *Death and the Virgin: Elizabeth, Dudley and the Mysterious Fate of Amy Robsart* (London, 2010), p. 167.
3. Ibid., p. 366.
4. Clifford, A. (ed.), *The State Papers and Letters of Sir Ralph Sadler* (Edinburgh, 1809), 70/19, f.39r.

5. Stevenson, Joseph et al. (eds), *Calendar of State Papers, Foreign Series, of the Reign of Elizabeth* (London, 1863–1950), p. 243.

6. Ibid.

7. Skidmore, ibid., p. 371.

8. St Jerome cited in Caferro, William, *Contesting the Renaissance* (Chichester, 2011), p. 6.

9. Strong, op. cit. p. 38.

10. Orgel, Stephen, *I Am Richard II*, in Petrina and Tosi, op. cit., p. 16.

11. Jones, Dan, *The Plantagenets: The Kings Who Made England* (London, 2012), p. 559.

12. Cited in Jones, op. cit., p. 558.

CHAPTER THIRTEEN

1. Baumgartmer, F., *Henry II King of France 1547–1559* (Durham, NC, 1988), p. 25.

2. Ritchie, P., *Mary of Guise in Scotland 1548–1560: A Political Career* (East Linton, 2002), p. 67.

3. Carroll, op. cit., p. 91.

4. Fraser, Antonia, *Mary Queen of Scots* (London, 1969), p. 56.5.

5. Durot, Eric, 'Le Crepuscule de l'*Auld* Alliance: la legitime du pouvoir en question entre Ecosse, France et Angleterre 1588–1561', *Histoire, Economie, Société*, Vol. 26 (2007), p. 105.

6. Alford, op. cit., p. 111.

CHAPTER FOURTEEN

1. Keith, Robert, *History of the affairs of Church & State in Scotland from the beginning of the Reformation to 1568* (Edinburgh, 1844), p. 45.

2. Stevenson et al. (eds), Vol. III, p. 573.

3. Nichols (ed.), op. cit.), p. 63.

4. See Mirabella, Bella, 'In the Sight of All: Queen Elizabeth and the Dance of Diplomacy', *Early Theatre*, Vol. 15, Issue 1 (January 2012).

5. Ibid.

6. Ibid.

7. Osborne, Francis et al. (eds), 'Antony Weldon's Court and Character of King James' and 'Osborne's Traditional Memoirs' in *Secret History of King James the First* (Edinburgh, 1811), p. 26.

8. Wyatt, Michael, *The Italian Encounter with Tudor England: A Cultural Politics of Translation* (Cambridge, 2005), p. 181.

9. Alford, op. cit., p. 129.

10. Ibid.

11. Melville, James, *Memoirs of Sir James Melville of Halhill*, Donaldson Gordon (ed.) (London, 1969), p. 107.

12. Robertson, J. (ed.), *Inventaires de la Royne d'Ecosse. Douairiere de France* (Edinburgh, 1883), p. 36.

CHAPTER FIFTEEN

1. Lemon and Everett Green (eds), op. cit., 11 January 1559.

2. BL Cotton MS Titus B XIII, f.99.

3. McDermott, op. cit., p. 93.

4. Alford, op. cit., p. 155.

CHAPTER SIXTEEN

1. Alford, op. cit., p. 161.

2. Ibid.

3. Somerset, Anne, *Elizabeth I* (London, 1991), p. 313.

4. Cited in Alford, Stephen, *The Watchers: A Secret History of the Reign of Elizabeth I* (London, 2012).

5. Lemon and Everett Green (eds), op. cit., 12/66, f.92r–v.

6. Fraser, op. cit.

7. Alford, *Burghley*, p.168.

8. Cooper, *The Queen's Agent: Francis Walsingham at the Court of Elizabeth I* (London, 2011), p. 56.

9. Lemon and Everett Green (eds), op. cit., 12/88, ff.47r–50r

10. Alford, *Burghley*, p. 178.

11. Ibid., p. 180.

12. *Scriana Ceciliana: Mysteries of State & Government in Letters of the Late Famous Lord Burghley* (London, 1663), p. 181

13. Digges, Dudley (ed.), *The Compleat Ambassador* (London, 1655), p. 9.

14. Reid, Clare, 'Anthony Copley and the Politics of Catholic Loyalty 1590–1604', *Sixteenth Century Journal*, Vol. 43, No. 2 (Summer 2012).

15. Cited in Alford, *Burghley*, p. 181.

CHAPTER SEVENTEEN

1. Howarth, David, *Images of Rule: Art and Politics in the English Renaissance, 1485–1649* (Oakland, 1997), p. 1.
2. Birrell, T. A., *English Monarchs and Their Books* (London, 1987), gives a full and surprising inventory of the books whose ownership can definitively be credited to Elizabeth I.
3. Iamartina, Giovanni, *Under Italian Eyes: Petruccio Ubaldini's Verbal Portrayals of Queen Elizabeth I*, in Petrina and Tosi, op. cit.
4. Belozerskaya, op. cit., p. 115.
5. Sharpe, op. cit., p. 388.
6. Greenblatt, Stephen, *The Swerve: How the Renaissance Began* (London, 2011), p. 157.
7. Ibid.
8. Belozerskaya, op. cit., p. 135.

CHAPTER EIGHTEEN

1. Alford, *The Watchers*, p. 14.
2. Lyons, Mathew (2012) *http://mathewlyons.wordpress.com/2012/06/25/richard-topcliffe-and-the-capture-and-torture-of-robert-southwell/*
3. Cited in Aveling, J. C. H., *The Handle and the Axe* (London, 1976), p. 67.
4. See Tillyard, E. M. W., *The Elizabethan World Picture* (London, 1990).
5. McBride, op. cit.

CHAPTER NINETEEN

1. Carroll, op. cit., p. 193.
2. François, Duke of Alençon, heir to the French throne from 1574, became Duke of Anjou in 1576. For clarity he will be referred to from now on as Duke of Anjou.
3. Cited in McDermott, op. cit., p. 89.
4. Camden, William, *Annales* (Leiden, 1639), p. 426.
5. Ibid.

CHAPTER TWENTY

1. Carroll, op. cit., p. 243.
2. Ibid., p. 247.
3. Boucher, Jacqueline et al. (eds), *Histoire et dictionnaire des guerres de Religion* (Paris, 1998), p. 311.
4. *Act for Surety of the Queens Person 1585*, in Luders, A., Tomlins T. E., Raithby, J. et al. (eds), *Statues of the Realm*, Vol. 4, p. 704.
5. Ibid.

CHAPTER TWENTY-ONE

1. Cited in McDermott, op. cit., p. 150.
2. Ibid., p. 157.
3. Ibid., p. 159.
4. Cited in Gristwood, op. cit., p. 398.

CHAPTER TWENTY-TWO

1. Waugh, Evelyn, *Edmund Campion: Jesuit and Martyr* (London, 2012), p. 41.
2. Ibid.
3. Alford, *Burghley*, p. 261.
4. Caraman, Philip, *William Weston: The Autobiography of an Elizabethan* (London, 1955), p. 99.
5. Cited in Cooper, op. cit., p. 218.
6. Ibid.
7. Read, Conyers (ed.), *The Bardon Papers: Documents relating to the Imprisonment & Trial of Mary Queen of Scots* (London, 1909), pp. 46–7.
8. Cited in Steuart, A. Francis (ed.), *Trial of Mary Queen of Scots* (London, 1951), p. 135.
9. Camden, op. cit., p. 618.
10. Cited in Cooper, op. cit., p. 191.
11. Cotton MS, *Galba*, c.10f.49r
12. Elizabeth I, cited in Wilson (ed.), op. cit., p. 540.
13. Allison, op. cit.
14. Hartley, op. cit., p. 111.
15. Alford, *Burghley*, p. 292.

CHAPTER TWENTY-THREE

1. Cited in Evans, James, *Merchant Adventurers: The Voyage of Discovery that Transformed Tudor England* (London, 2013), p. 7.
2. Ibid.
3. Lubimenko, Irina, 'The Correspondence of Queen Elizabeth with the Russian Czars', *American Historical Review*, Vol. 19, No. 13 (April, 1914), p. 529.
4. Ibid., p. 531.
5. Cited in Evans, op. cit., p. 295.
6. Ibid.
7. Kasprzak, Jan, 'A Riddle of History: Queen Elizabeth and the Albertus Laski Affair', *Polish Review*, Vol. 14 (Winter 1969).
8. French, Peter, *John Dee: The World of an Elizabethan Magus* (London, 1972), p. 7.
9. Evans, op. cit., p. 321.

CHAPTER TWENTY-FOUR

1. Frye, Susan, 'The Myth of Elizabeth at Tilbury', *Sixteenth Century Journal*, Vol. 23, No. 1 (Spring 1992).
2. Radkin, Phyllis, *Genealogical Anxiety and Female Authority*, in Logan, Marie Rose and Rudnytsky, Peter (eds), *Contending Kingdoms: Historical, Psychological and Feminist Approaches to the Literature of C16th England and France* (Detroit, 1991), p. 339.
3. Hackett, Helen, *Virgin Mother, Maiden Queen: Elizabeth I and the Cult of the Virgin Mary* (London, 1995), p. 109.

CHAPTER TWENTY-FIVE

1. Cited in Gristwood, op. cit., p. 49.
2. Skilliter, S. A., *William Harborne and the Trade with Turkey 1578–1582: A Documentary Study of the First Anglo-Ottoman Relations* (Oxford, 1977), p. 50.
3. Hume, M. A. S., 'The So Called Conspiracy of Doctor Lopez', *Transactions of the Jewish Historical Society of England*, VI (1908–10).

CHAPTER TWENTY-SIX

1. Hacket, op. cit., p. 35.

2. Haynes, Alan, *Sex in Elizabethan England* (Stroud, 1997), p. 17.

3. HMS, *The Manuscripts of His Grace the Duke of Rutland KG, Preserved at Belvoir Castle,* (London, HMSO 1888–1905), Vol. 4, p. 81.

4. Hammer, Paul E. J., 'Sex and the Virgin Queen: Aristocratic Concupiscence and the Court of Elizabeth I', *Sixteenth Century Journal*, Vol. 31, No. 1 (2000).

5. Constant, Jean-Marie, *Les Guise* (Paris, 1984), p. 191.

6. Cited in Somerset, op. cit., p. 613.

7. Somerset, op. cit., p. 620.

8. Elizabeth I, *Letters of Queen Elizabeth*, Harrison, G. B. (ed.) (New York, 1968), p. 225.

9. Haigh, op. cit., p. 172.

CHAPTER TWENTY-SEVEN

1. Hamilton, H.C. et al. (eds), *Calendar of State Papers Relating to Ireland* (London 1860–1905), VIII, p. 42.

2. Devereux, Walter Bouchier, *Lives and Letters of the Devereux Earls of Essex*, 1853, Vol. II, p. 63.

3. Leonard, Amy E. (ed.), *Masculinities, Violence, Childhood: Attending to Early Modern Women – and Men* (Newark, DE, 2003).

4. Devereux, op. cit., Vol. I, p. 292.

5. Cited in Somerset, op. cit., p. 689.

6. Ibid.

7. Harrison, G. B., *A Last Elizabethan Journal: Being a Record of Those Things Most Talked of During the Years 1599–1603* (London, 1933), p. 132.

8. Devereux, op. cit.

9. Cited in Loades, David, *Elizabeth I* (London, 2010).

10. Strachey, Lytton, *Elizabeth and Essex* (London, 1985), p. 277.

11. Loades, op. cit., p. 278.

12. Camden, op. cit., p. 606.

13. Bate, op. cit., p. 313.

14. Kantorowicz, op. cit., p. 26.

CHAPTER TWENTY-EIGHT

1. Haigh, op. cit., p. 172.
2. Ibid.
3. *Henry V*, IV.i.25.
4. Alford, *Burghley*, p. 344.
5. Strong, op. cit., p. 143.
6. Cited in Devlin, C., *The Life of Robert Southwell* (London, 1956), p. 243.
7. Ibid.
8. Alford, *Burghley*, p. 321.
9. Elizabeth I, *Letters of Queen Elizabeth and James VI of Scotland*, Bruce John (ed.) (London, 1849), pp. 35–7.
10. Carey, Robert, *The Memoirs of Robert Carey*, Mares, F. H. (ed.) (Oxford, 1972), p. 59.

EPILOGUE

1. Harrington John, cited in Pullar, Philippa, *Consuming Passions* (London, 1977), p. 129.

BIBLIOGRAPHY

PRIMARY SOURCES

CALENDARS OF STATE PAPERS

CSP Domestic Series, Addenda, 1566–1579 Green, M. A. (ed.) (London, 1871)

CSP Spain, Hume, Martin A. S. (ed.) (4 vols) (London, 1896–9)

Calendar of State Papers Domestic Series of the Reigns of Edward VI, Mary, Elizabeth, 1547–1625, Lemon, Robert and Everett Green, Mary Anne (eds) (12 vols) (London, 1871)

Calendar of State Papers and Manuscripts Relating to English Affairs, Existing in the Archives of Venice and Other Libraries of Northern Italy Brown, Rawdon and Cavendish, Bentinck G. (eds) (38 vols) (London, 1864–1947)

Calendar of State Papers, Foreign Series, of the Reign of Elizabeth, Stevenson, Joseph et al. (eds) London, 1863–1950)

Calendar of State Papers Relating to English Affairs Preserved Principally at Rome at the Vatican Archives and Library, Rigg J. M. (ed.) (London, 1916–26)

Calendar of State Papers Relating to England and Mary Queen of Scots, Bain, Joseph (ed.) (5 vols) (Edinburgh, 1898–52)

Relazioni degli ambasciatori veneti al Senato, Alberi, E. (ed.) (3 vols) (Florence, 1839–63)

Relations des ambassadeurs venitiens sur les affaires de France au XVe siècle, Tommaseo, M. N. (ed.) (2 vols) (Paris, 1838)

State Papers Relating to the Custody of Princess Elizabeth at Woodstock in 1554, Manning, C. R. (ed.) (Norwich, 1855)

Hughes, Paul L. and Larkin, James F. (eds)*Tudor Royal Proclamations*, Volume 2, *The Later Tudors 1553–1587* (New Haven, 1969)

Brewer, J. S., Gairdner, J. and Brody, R. H. (eds), *Letter and Papers, Foreign and Domestic, of the Reign of Henry VIII, 1509–47* (21 vols) (London, 1862–1932)

ELIZABETH I

Elizabeth I, *Letters of Queen Elizabeth and James VI of Scotland*, Bruce, John (ed.) (London, 1849)

Elizabeth I, *Letters of Queen Elizabeth*, Harrison, G. B. (ed.) (New York, 1968)

Elizabeth I, *Elizabeth I: Devotions* (trans. Fox, A.) (Gerrards Cross, 1970)

Elizabeth I, *Elizabeth I, Collected Works*, Marcus, L. S., Mueller, J. and Rose, M. B. (eds) (Chicago, 2000)

Elizabeth I, *Autograph Compositions and Foreign Language Originals*, Mueller, Janel and Marcus, Leah S. (eds) (Chicago, 2003)

Elizabeth I, *Elizabeth I: Translations*, Mueller, Janel and Scodel, Joshua (eds) (2 vols) (Chicago, 2009)

★★★★★★★★★★★★★★★★★★★★★★★★

Ainsworth, Mitchell C. (ed.), *The Evidence of the Casket Letters* (London, 1927)

Allen, William, *A True, Sincere and Modest Defence of English Catholicques that suffer for their Faith at home and abroad* (Rouen, 1584), in A Short-Title Catalogue of Books 1475–1640, Jackson, W. A., Ferguson, F. S. and Pantzer, Katherine F. (eds) 3 vols (London, 1986–91)

Anon., *The Passage of Our Most Drad Soveraigne Ladye Queen Elizabeth through the Citie of London to Westminster the Daye before Her Coronacion* (London, 1559)

Aylmer, John, *An Harborowe for Faithful and Trewe Subiectes, Against the Late Blowne Blaste, Concerninge the Gouernmet of Wemen* (London, 1559)

Bacon, Francis, *The Works of Francis Bacon*, Spedding, James, Ellis, Robert Leslie and Heath, Douglas Denon (eds), 7 vols (London, 1857–61)

Berry, Lloyd E., *John Stubbs's "Gaping Gulf" with letter and other Relevant Documents* (Charlottesville, 1968)

Bonadella, Peter (trans.), *The Prince* (Oxford, 2008)

Bonadella, Peter and Conway Bonadella, Julia (trans.), *Discourses on Livy* (Oxford, 2009)

Brice, Thomas, *Register of Martyrs* (London, 1559)

Buchanan, George, *The Tyrannous Reign of Mary Stewart* (ed. and trans. Gatherer, W. A.) (Edinburgh, 1958)

Calendar of the Manuscripts of the Marquess of Salisbury at Hatfield House, 24 vols (London 1883–1976)

Camden, William *Annales* (Leiden, 1639)

The Great Bragge and challenge of M. Campion a Jesuite, commonlye called Edmunde

Campion, lately arrived in Englande, containynge nyne articles here severallye laide downe, directed to him by the Lords of the Counsail (London, 1581)

Castelnau, Michel de, *Memoires*, de Castelnau, Jacques (ed.) (Paris, 1621)

Clapham, J., *Elizabeth of England: Certain Observations Concerning the Life and Reign of Queen Elizabeth*, Read, E. P. and Read, C. (eds) (Oxford, 1951)

Clifford, A. (ed.), *The State Papers and Letters of Sir Ralph Sadler*, 2 vols (Edinburgh 1809)

Coke, John, *Le débat des hérauts d'armes de France et d'Angleterre*, Pannier, L. and Meyer, P. (eds) (Paris, 1877)

Collins A. F. (ed.), *Jewels and Plate of Queen Elizabeth I: The Inventory of 1574* (London, 1955)

Constantine, Peter (trans.), *The Essential Writings of Machiavelli* (New York, 2009)

D'Ewes, Simonds, *The Journals of All the Parliaments in the Reign of Queen Elizabeth* (London, 1682)

Doleman, R., *A Conference about the Next Succession to the Throne of England* (Amsterdam, 1595)

Hakluyt, Richard, *The Principal Navigations, Voyages and Discoveries of the English Nation*, 2nd edition (London, 1598)

Hartley, T. E., *Proceedings in the Parliaments of Elizabeth I* (Leicester, 1981)

Hayward, John, *Annals of the First Four Years of the Reign of Queen Elizabeth*, Bruce, John (ed.) (Cambridge, 1840)

Heywood, Thomas, *England's Elizabeth*, Rider, Philip R. (ed.) (New York, 1982)

Holinshed, Raphael, *Chronicles of England, Scotland and Ireland*, Ellis, Henry (ed.), 6 vols (London, 1807)

HMS, *The Manuscripts of His Grace the Duke of Rutland KG, Preserved at Belvoir Castle*, 4 vols (London, HMSO, 1888–1905)

Labanoff, A. (ed.), *Lettres, instructions et memoires de Marie Stuart* (Paris, 1844)

Laneham, Robert, *A Letter Wherein part of the Entertainment unto the Queenz Maiesty at Killingworth Castle in Warwicksher in this soomerz progress 1575 is Signified* (London, 1575)

Lemaire de Belge, Jean, *Traite des Schismes* (trans. Gough, John) (London, 1539)

Lomazzo, Giovan Paolo, *Trattato dell'Arte della Pittura* (trans. Haydocke, Richard) (Pittsburg, 2013)

L'Himne de la Paix au tres-auguste et serenissime Roy d'Angleterre d'Escosse et d'Irlande (Paris, 1604)

Mahon, R. H., *Indictment of Mary Queen of Scots* (London, 1923)

Melville, James, *Memoirs of Sir James Melville of Halhill*, Donaldson, Gordon (ed.) (London, 1969)

Nau, Claude, *Memorials of Mary Stewart*, Stevenson, J. (ed.) (Edinburgh, 1883)

Nichols, J. G. (ed.), *Chronicle of Queen Jane and two years of Queen Mary* (London, 1850)

Rodriquez, Salgado J. and Adams S. (eds), *The Count of Feria's Dispatch of 1558* (London, 1984)

Sander, Nicholas, *De origine et progressu schismatis Anglicani* (Cologne, 1585)

Seager, Jane, *The Divine Prophesies of the Ten Sibyls* (London, 1589)

Smith, Sir Thomas, *De Republica Anglorum* (London, 1583), Dewar, Mary (ed.) (Cambridge, 1982)

Stubbes, Philip, *The Anatomy of Abuses* (London, 1583)

Thomas, Marcel, *Le process de Marie Stuart: Documents originaux presentes par Marcel Thomas* (Paris, 1956)

Von Klariwill, Victor, *Queen Elizabeth and Some Foreigners: being a Series of Hitherto Unpublished Letters from the Archives of the Hapsburg Family* (trans. Nash, T. H.) (London, 1928)

SECONDARY SOURCES

Alford, Stephen, *Burghley: William Cecil at the Court of Elizabeth I* (Padstow, 2011)

— *The Watchers: A Secret History of the Reign of Elizabeth I* (London, 2012)

Arnold, Janet, *Queen Elizabeth's Wardrobe Unlock'd* (London, 1988)

Aveling, J. C. H., *The Handle and the Axe* (London, 1976)

Bate, Jonathan, *Soul of the Age: A Biography of the Mind of William Shakespeare* (New York, 2009)

Bates, Catherine, *The Rhetoric of Courtship in Elizabethan Language and Literature* (Cambridge, 1992)

Baumgartmer, F., *Henry II King of France 1547–1559* (Durham, NC, 1988)

Bicheno, Hugh, *How the English Became the Scourge of the Sea: Elizabeth's Sea Dogs* (London, 2012)

Belozerskaya, Marina, *Rethinking the Renaissance: Burgundian Arts Across Europe* (New York, 2012)

Bernard, G. W., *Anne Boleyn: Fatal Attractions* (London, 2010)

Birrell, T. A., *English Monarchs and Their Books* (London, 1987)

Bobbitt, Philip, *The Garments of Court & Palace: Machiavelli and the World that He Made* (London, 2013)

Borman, Tracy, *Elizabeth's Women: The Hidden Story of the Virgin Queen* (London, 2010)

Boucher, Jacqueline et al. (eds) *Histoire et dictionnaire des guerres de Religion* (Paris, 1998)

Bredbeck, Gregory W., *Sodomy and Interpretation: Marlowe to Milton* (Cornell, 1991)

Broaddus, James W., *Spenser's Allegory of Love: Social Vision in Books III, IV and V of "The Faerie Queene"* (London, 1995)

Bull, Malcolm, *The Mirror of the Gods: Classical Mythology in Renaissance Art* (London, 2006)

Burke, Peter, *The Fortunes of the Courtier: The European Reception of Castiglione's "Cortegiano"* (Pittsburgh, 1996)

— *The European Renaissance: Centres and Peripheries* (Oxford, 1998)

Caferro, William, *Contesting the Renaissance* (Chichester, 2011)

Caraman, Philip, *William Weston: The Autobiography of an Elizabethan* (London, 1955)

Carlton, Charles, *State, Sovereigns and Societies in Early Modern England* (Stroud, 1988)

Carroll, Stuart, *Martyrs and Murderers: The Guise Family and the Making of Europe* (Oxford, 2009)

Castor, Helen, *The Women who Ruled England before Elizabeth* (London, 2010)

Chauvire, R., *Le Secret de Marie Stuart* (Paris, 1937)

Cross, Claire, *The Royal Supremacy in the Elizabethan Church* (London, 1969)

Cole, Alison, *Virtue and Magnificence: Art of the Italian Renaissance Courts* (London, 1995)

Collins, William Edward, *Queen Elizabeth's Defence of her Proceedings in Church and State* (London, 1958)

Constant, Jean-Marie, *Les Guise* (Paris, 1984)

Cooper, John, *The Queen's Agent: Francis Walsingham at the Court of Elizabeth I* (London, 2011)

Cooper, Tarnya, *A Guide to Tudor & Jacobean Portraits* (London, 2008)

— *Elizabeth I & Her People* (London, 2013)

David, Elizabeth, *English Bread and Yeast Cookery* (London, 1977)

De Grazia, Margreta, Quilligan, Maureen and Stallybrass, Peter, *Subject and Object in Renaissance Culture* (Cambridge, 1996)

De Lisle, Leanda, *The Sisters who would be Queen: The Tragedy of Mary, Katherine & Lady Jane Grey* (London, 2009)

De Maio, Romeo, *Donna e Rinascimento* (Milan, 1987)

Devlin, C., *The Life of Robert Southwell* (London, 1956)

Dillon, Anne, *The Construction of Martyrdom in the English Catholic Community* (Aldershot, 2002)

Dollimore, Jonathan, *Radical Tragedy: Religion, Ideology and Power in the Drama of Shakespeare and his Contemporaries* (London, 1989)

Donaldson, Gordon, *The Scottish Reformation* (London, 1960)

343

Doran, Susan, *England and Europe 1485-1603* (Abingdon, 1996)

— and Jones, Norman (eds) *The Elizabethan World* (London, 2011)

Dunlop, Ian, *Palaces and Progresses of Elizabeth I* (London, 1962)

Eisaman, Maus, *Inwardness and Theatre in the English Renaissance* (Chicago, 1995)

Evans, James, *Merchant Adventurers: The Voyage of Discovery that Transformed Tudor England* (London, 2013)

Ford, Boris (ed.), *The New Pelican Guide to English Literature: 2. The Age of Shakespeare* (London, 1982)

Fraser, Antonia, *Mary Queen of Scots* (London, 1969)

— *The Six Wives of Henry VIII* (London, 1995)

French, Peter, *John Dee: The World of an Elizabethan Magus* (London, 1972)

George, Margaret, *Elizabeth I: A Novel* (London, 2012)

Greenblatt, Stephen, *Renaissance Self-Fashioning From More to Shakespeare* (Chicago, 2005)

— *The Swerve: How the Renaissance Began* (London, 2011)

Gristwood, Sarah, *Elizabeth & Leicester* (London, 2007)

Gruber, Alain, *The Renaissance and Mannerism in Europe* (London, 1994)

Guy, John, *Tudor England* (Oxford, 1990)

Hackett, Helen, *Virgin Mother, Maiden Queen: Elizabeth I and the Cult of the Virgin Mary* (London, 1995)

Haigh, Christopher, *Profiles in Power: Elizabeth I* (Harlow, 1998)

Hale, John, *The Civilization of Europe in the Renaissance* (London, 1993)

Hanning, R. W. and Rosan, David (eds), *Castiglione: The Ideal and the Real in Renaissance Culture* (London, 1983)

Harbison, Craig, *The Art of the Northern Renaissance* (London, 1995)

Haynes, Alan, *Robert Cecil, Earl of Salisbury* (London, 1989)

— *Sex in Elizabethan England* (Stroud, 1997)

Hearn, Karen, *Nicholas Hilliard* (London, 2005)

Heller, Agnes, *A Renaissance Ember* (Budapest, 1967)

Hibbert, Christopher, *The Virgin Queen: A Portrait of Elizabeth I* (London, 1990)

Horrox, Rosemary and Ormrod, W. Mark (eds), *A Social History of England, 1200–1500* (Cambridge, 2006)

Howarth, David, *Images of Rule: Art and Politics in the English Renaissance, 1485–1649* (Oakland, 1997)

Hurstfield, Joel, *Elizabeth I and the Unity of England* (London, 1971)

Jardine, Lisa, *Worldly Goods: A New History of the Renaissance* (London, 1996)

Jouanna, Arlette, *La Saint-Barthélemy: les mystères d'un crime d'état* (Paris, 2007)

Kantorowicz, Ernst H., *The King's Two Bodies: A Study in Mediaeval Political Theory* (Princeton, 1997)

Kekewich, Lucille (ed.), *The Renaissance in Europe: The Impact of Humanism* (New Haven, 2000)

Knighton, C. S. and Mortimer, Richard (eds) *Westminster Abbey Reformed* (Aldershot, 2006)

Kristeller, Paul Oskar, *Renaissance Thought and the Arts* (Oxford, 1980)

Lake, Paul, *Moderate Puritans and the Elizabethan Church* (Cambridge, 2004)

Laqueur, Thomas, *Making Sex: Body and Gender from the Greeks to Freud* (Harvard, 1990)

Le Person, Xavier, *Praticques et Praticquers: La vie politique à la fin du regne de Henri III* (Geneva, 2002)

Loades, David, *Elizabeth I* (London, 2010)

— *The Boleyns: The Rise & Fall of a Tudor Family* (Amberley, 2011)

Leonard, Amy E., *Masculinities, Violence, Childhood: Attending to Early Modern Women – and Men* (Newark, DE, 2003)

Levin, C., *The Heart and Stomach of a King: Elizabeth the First and the Politics of Sex and Power* (Philadelphia, 1994)

Lovell, Mary S., *Bess of Hardwick: First Lady of Chatsworth* (London, 2005)

Luke, Carmen, *Pedagogy, Printing and Protestantism: The Discourse on Childhood* (New York, 1989)

Lyons, Matthew, *The Favourite: Raleigh and His Queen* (London, 2012)

MacCulloch, Diarmaid, *The Later Reformation in England, 1547–1603* (London, 2011)

McDermott, James, *England & the Spanish Armada: The Necessary Quarrel* (New Haven, 2005)

Marcus, Leah S., 'Queen Elizabeth I as Public and Private Poet' in *Reading Monarchs Writing: The Poetry of Henry VIII*, Herman, Peter C. (ed.) (Tempe, 2002)

Merriman, Marcus, *The Rough Wooings: Mary Queen of Scots 1542–1551* (Edinburgh, 2000)

Montrose, Louis, *The Subject of Elizabeth: Authority, Gender and Representation* (Chicago, 2006)

Nash, Susie, *Northern Renaissance Art* (Oxford, 2008)

Nolan, John S., *Sir John Norreys and the Elizabethan Military World* (Exeter, 1997)

Overell, Anne, *Italian Reform and English Reformations* (Farnham, 2008)

Penn, Thomas, *Winter King: The Dawn of Tudor England* (London, 2012)

Petrina, Alessandra and Tosi, Laura (eds), *Representations of Elizabeth I in Early Modern Culture* (London, 2011)

Plumb, J. H., *The Penguin Book of Renaissance* (London, 1991)

Praz, Mario, *Machiavelli and the Elizabethans* (London, 1972)

Pullar, Philippa, *Consuming Passions: A History of English Food and Appetite* (London, 1970)

Raab, Felix, *The English Face of Machiavelli: A Changing Interpretation 1500–1700* (London, 1964)

Ribeiro, Aileen, *Dress and Morality* (Oxford, 2003)

Rickert, Edith (ed.), *The Babees' Book* (London, 1908)

Ritchie, P., *Mary of Guise in Scotland 1548–1560: A Political Career* (East Linton, 2002)

Rivers, Isabel, *Classical and Christian Ideas in English Renaissance Poetry* (London, 1994)

Rosedale, H. G., *Queen Elizabeth and the Levant Company* (London, 1904)

Ryan, Alan, *On Machiavelli: The Search for Glory* (London, 2012)

Sharpe, Kevin, *Selling the Tudor Monarchy: Authority and Image in Sixteenth-Century England* (New Haven, 2009)

Shephard, Amanda, *Gender and Authority in Sixteenth-Century England: The Knox Debate* (Keele, 1994)

Shulman, Nicola, *Graven with Diamonds. The Many Lives of Thomas Wyatt: Courtier, Poet, Assassin, Spy* (London, 2011)

Skidmore, Chris, *Death and the Virgin: Elizabeth, Dudley and the Mysterious Fate of Amy Robsart* (London, 2010)

Skilliter, S. A., *William Harborne and the Trade With Turkey 1578–1582: A Documentary Study of the First Anglo-Ottoman Relations* (Oxford, 1977)

Smith, Gregory, *Elizabethan Critical Essays* (Oxford, 1937)

Solnon, François, *La Cour de France* (Paris, 1987)

Somerset, Anne, *Elizabeth I* (London, 1991)

Starkey, David, *Elizabeth* (London, 2000)

Strachey, Lytton, *Elizabeth and Essex* (London, 1985)

Strickland, Agnes, *Lives of the Queens of England*, Vol. IV (London 1841)

Strong, Roy, *Gloriana: The Portraits of Queen Elizabeth I* (London, 1987)

Tillyard, E. M. W., *The Elizabethan World Picture* (London, 1990)

Trill, Suzanne and Zunder, William (eds), *Writing and the English Renaissance* (New York, 1996)

Varotti, Carlo, *Gloria e ambizione politica nel Rinascimento. Da Petrarca a Machiavelli* (Milan, 1998)

Viroli, Maurizio, *From Politics to Reason of State: The Acquisition and Transformation of the Language of Politics 1250–1600* (Cambridge, 1992)

— *Niccolo's Smile: A Biography of Machiavelli* (New York, 2002)

Waller, Gary, *English Poetry of the Sixteenth Century* (Harlow, 1993)

Waller, Maureen, *Sovereign Ladies: The Six Reigning Queens of England* (London, 2006)

Waterhouse, Ellis, *Painting in Britain 1530–1790* (New Haven, 1994)

Watkins, Susan, *Elizabeth I and Her World* (London, 2007)

Waugh, Evelyn, *Edmund Campion: Jesuit and Martyr* (London, 2012)

Weir, Alison, *Elizabeth the Queen* (London, 2008)

Weisner, Louis, *La Jeunesse d'Elizabeth d'Angleterre* (Paris, 1878)

Whitelock, Anna, *Elizabeth's Bedfellows: An Intimate History of the Queen's Court* (London, 2013)

Wilkinson, Alexander, *Mary Queen of Scots and French Public Opinion* (Basingstoke, 2004)

Wilson, A. N., *The Elizabethans* (London, 2011)

Wilson, Katharina M. (ed.), *Women Writers of the Renaissance and Reformation* (Athens, GA, 1987)

Wolf, Norbert, *Holbein* (London, 2004)

Woolgar, C. M., *The Senses in Late Medieval England* (London, 2006)

Wyatt, Michael, *The Italian Encounter with Tudor England: A Cultural Politics of Translation* (Cambridge, 2005)

Wyatt, Sir Thomas, *Selected Poems* (Manchester, 2003)

JOURNALS

Allinson, Rayne, '"The Prince" and Queen Elizabeth I: A New Perspective on the Development of English Machiavellianism', *Melbourne Historical Journal*, Vol. 34 (2006)

Anglo, S., 'Ill of the Dead: The Posthumous Reputation of Henry VII', *Renaissance Studies*, Vol. 1 (1967)

Axton, Marie, 'The Queen's Two Bodies: Drama and the Elizabethan Succession', *Royal Historical Society* (1978)

Barberis, W., 'Uomini di corte nel "500"', *Storia d'Italia, Annali*, No. 4 (Turin, 1981)

Barton, Edwarde and Pears, Edwin, 'The Spanish Armada and the Ottoman Porte', *English Historical Review*, Vol. 8, No. 31 (July, 1893)

Benkert, Lisbeth, 'Translation as Image-Making: Elizabeth I's Translation of Boethius's "Consolation of Philosophy"', *English Modern Language Association*, Vol. 6, No. 3 (2001)

Bowers, R. D., 'The Chapel Royal, the First Edwardian prayer Book and Elizabeth's Settlement of Religion', *Historical Journal*, Vol. xliii, No. 2 (2000)

Boswell, Chris, 'The Subjective Petrarchan Heroine in the Verse Answers of Elizabeth Tudor and Frances Parnell Seymour, Countess of Hertford', *The Culture and Rhetoric of the Answer Poem 1485–1626*, University of Exeter (2003)

Burian, Orhan, 'Interest of the English in Turkey as Reflected in English Literature of the Renaissance', *Oriens*, Vol. 5, No. 2 (December, 1952)

Carroll, Stuart, 'The Revolt of Paris, 1588: Aristocratic insurgency and the mobilization of popular support', *French Historical Studies*, Vol. 23 (2000)

Clover, Carol J., 'Regardless of Sex: Men, Women and Power in Early Northern Europe', *Representations*, No. 44, University of California Press (Autumn 1993)

Crane, Mary Thomas, '*Video et Taceo:* Elizabeth I and the Rhetoric of Counsel', *Studies in English Literature 1500–1900*, Vol. 28, No. 1 (1988)

Dolan, Frances E., 'Taking the Pencil out of God's Hand: Art, Nature and the Face-Painting Debate in Early Modern England', *PMLA*, Vol. 108, No. 2 (March, 1993)

Durot, Eric, 'Le Crepuscule de l'*Auld* Alliance: la legitime du pouvoir en question entre Ecosse, France et Angleterre 1588–1561', *Histoire, Economie, Société*, Vol. 26 (2007)

Fabri, Frank, 'Sidney's Verse Adaptations to Two Sixteenth Century Italian Songs', *Renaissance Quarterly*, XXIII (1970)

Felperin, Howard, 'Shakespeare's "Henry VIII", History as Myth', *Studies in English Literature 1500–1900*, Vol. 6 (1966)

Forney, Kristine, 'A Gift of Madrigals and Chansons: The Winchester Part Books and the Courtship of Elizabeth I by Erik XIV of Sweden', *Journal of Musicology*, Vol. 17, No. 1 (Winter 1999)

Frye, Susan, 'The Myth of Elizabeth at Tilbury', *Sixteenth Century Journal*, Vol. 23, No. 1 (Spring 1992)

Gajda, Alexandre, 'The State of Christendom: History, Political Thought and the Essex Circle', *Historical Research*, No. 81 (2008)

Green, Janet M., 'I My Self: Queen Elizabeth's Oration at Tilbury Camp', *Studies: The Sixteenth Century Journal*, Vol. 28, No. 2 (Summer 1997)

Hammer, Paul E. J., 'Sex and the Virgin Queen: Aristocratic Concupiscence and the Court of Elizabeth I', *Sixteenth Century Journal*, Vol. 31, No. 1 (2000)

Heisch, Alison, 'Arguments for and Execution: Queen Elizabeth's "White Paper" and Lord Burghley's "Blue Pencil"', *Albion*, Vol. 24 (1992)

Horniker, Arthur Leon, 'Anglo-French Rivalry in the Levant from 1583 to 1612', *Journal of Modern History*, Vol. 18, No. 4 (December 1946)

Hume, M. A. S., 'The So Called Conspiracy of Doctor Lopez', *Transactions of the Jewish Historical Society of England*, VI (1908–10)

Ives, Eric, 'The Fall of Anne Boleyn Reconsidered', *EHS*, 107 (1992)

Jardine, Lisa, 'Gloriana Rules the Waves: Or, the Advantage of Being Excommunicated (And a Woman)', *Transactions of the Royal Historical Society*, Sixth Series, Vol. 14 (2004)

Kasprzak, Jan, 'A Riddle of History: Queen Elizabeth and the Albertus Laski Affair', *Polish Review*, Vol. 14 (Winter 1969)

Kendrick, Laura, 'The Game of Love: Troubadour Wordplay', *Speculum*, Vol. 65, No. 4 (October 1990)

Kewes, Paulina, 'Henry Savile's Tacitus and the Politics of Roman History in Late Elizabethan England', *Huntingdon Library Quarterly*, Vol. 74, No. 4 (December 2001)

Labriola, A. C., 'Painting and Poetry on the Cult of Elizabeth I: The Ditchley Portrait and Donne's "Elegie"', *Studies in Philology*, Vol. XCIII (Winter 1996)

Lubimenko, Irina, 'The Correspondence of Queen Elizabeth with the Russian Czars', *American Historical Review*, Vol. 19, No. 13 (April, 1914)

Marshall, Peter, 'Religious Exiles and the Tudor State', *Studies in Church History*, No. 43 (2007)

Mateer, David (ed.), *The Renaissance in Europe: Courts, Patrons and Poets* (New Haven, 2000)

McBride, Tom, '"Henry VIII" as Machiavellian Romance', *Journal of English and Germanic Philology*, Vol. 76, No. 1 (January, 1977)

Menage, V. L., 'The English Capitulation of 1580', *International Journal of Middle East Studies*, Vol. 12, No. 3 (November, 1980)

Middlebrook, Leah, 'Tout Mon Office: Body Politics and Family Dynamics in the Verse Epitres of Marguerite de Navarre', *Renaissance Quarterly*, Vol. 54 (Winter 2001)

Mirabella, Bella, 'In the Sight of All: Queen Elizabeth and the Dance of Diplomacy', *Early Theatre*, Vol. 15, Issue 1 (January, 2012)

Piepho, Lee, 'Paulus Melissus and Jacobus Falchenburgius: Two German Protestant Humanists at the Court of Queen Elizabeth', *Sixteenth Century Journal* Vol. 38, No. 1 (Spring 2007)

Podea, I. I., 'A Contribution to the Study of Queen Elizabeth's Eastern Policy 1590–1593', *Mélanges d'Histoire Générale*, II, *CLUJ* (1938)

Redworth, Glyn, '"Matters Impertinent to Women": Male and Female Monarchy under Philip and Mary', *English Historical Review*, Vol. 112, No. 447 (June, 1997)

Reid, Clare, 'Anthony Copley and the Politics of Catholic Loyalty 1590–1604', *Sixteenth Century Journal*, Vol. 43, No. 2 (Summer 2012)

Richards, Judith M., 'To Promote a Woman to Bear Rule: Talking of Queens in Mid-Tudor England', *Sixteenth Century Journal*, Vol. 28, No. 1 (1997)

Rossi, Ettore, 'La Sultana Nur-Banu (Cecilia Venier-Baffo) Moglie di Selim II (1566–1574) e Madre di Murad III (1574–1595)', *Pubblicazione dell'Istituto per l'Oriente, Roma* (1953)

Rossi, Ettore Studio, 'Turcologica: Memoriae Alexii Bombaci Dicata', *Istituto Universitario Orientale di Studi Asiatici, Napoli*, No. XIX (1982)

Schleiner, Winifried, 'Divina Virago: Queen Elizabeth as an Amazon', *Studies in Philology*, Vol. 75, No. 2 (Spring 1978)

Skilliter, S. A., 'An Ambassador's Ta'Yin : Edward Barton's Ration on the Egri Campaign, 1596', *Revue d'Etudes Turques*, No. XXV (1993)

Taylor-Smither, Larrisa J., 'Elizabeth I: A Psychological Profile', *Sixteenth Century Journal*, Vol. 15, No. 1 (Spring 1984)

Warnicke, Retha M., 'Henry VIII's Greeting of Anne of Cleves and Early Modern Court Protocol', *Albion*, Vol. 28, No. 4 (Winter 1996)

Wright, Celeste T., 'The Amazonian in Elizabethan Literature' *Studies in Philology*, Vol. 37 (1940)

Zaharia, Oana-Alis, 'Fashioning the Queen: Elizabeth I as Patron and Dedicatee of Translations', *Gender Studies*, Vol. 1, No. 11 (2012)

ONLINE RESOURCES

Allen, William, *An admonition to the nobility and people of England and Ireland concerninge the present vvarres made for the execution of his Holines sentence, by the highe and mightie Kinge Catholike of Spaine* http://quod.lib.umich.edu/e/eebo/A16774.0001.001?view=toc

Castiglione, Baldassare, *The Book of the Courtier* https://archive.org/stream/bookofcourtieroocastuoft/bookofcourtieroocastuoft_djvu.txt

Copley, Anthony, *Another Letter of Mr AC to his Dis-jesuited Kinsman* (London, 1602) http://quod.lib.umich.edu/e/eebo/A19321.0001.001?view=toc

Doran, Susan, *Elizabeth I* (June, 1977) http://history.org.uk/resources/student_resource_487.html

Green, Karen, *Phronesis Feminized: Prudence from Christine de Pisan to Elizabeth I* (2007)
http://link.springer.com/chapter/10.1007%2F978-1-4020-5895-0_2#page-1

Halls, Julie, *Aristotle and Dudley: Books as Evidence* (London, 2011) http://www.history.org.uk/resources/student_resource_4356_106.html

Knox, John, *The First Blast of the Trumpet Against the Monstrous Regiment of Women* (Geneva, 1558)
http://www.swrb.com/newslett/actualNLs/firblast.htm

Lyons, Mathew (2012) http://mathewlyons.wordpress.com/2012/06/25/richard-topcliffe-and-the-capture-and-torture-of-robert-southwell/

Machiavelli, *Il Principe* *http://www.classicitaliani.it/machiav/critica/pricipe_traduzione_bonghi.htm*

Malham, J. (ed.), *The Harleian Miscellany* (12 vols) *https://archive.org/details/harleianmiscell20malhgoog*

Meikle, Maureen M., *John Knox and Womankind: A Reappraisal* (London, 2003) *http://www.history.org.uk/resources/general_resource_625_70.html*

Regnans In Excelsis *http://www.papalencyclicals.net/Pius05/p5regnans.htm*

Rowse, A. L., *The Coronation of Queen Elizabeth* (1953) *http://www.historytoday.com/al-rowse/coronation-queen-elizabeth*

Woodhead, Christine, *England, the Ottomans and the Barbary Coast in the Late Sixteenth Century* (Reading, 2009) *http://www.google.co.uk/url?sa=t&rct=j&q=&esrc=s&source=web&cd=1&ved=0CCM-QFjAA&url=http%3A%2F%2Fg*

ACKNOWLEDGEMENTS

I should like to thank Dr Carlo Bajetta at the University of Val d'Aosta and Dr Laura Tosi at the Ca'Foscari University for so generously giving time to my inquiries. Dr Alessandra Petrina at the University of Padova was also extremely helpful, and kind enough to allow me access to a then- unpublished paper, *"Perfit Readiness" Elizabeth Learning and Using Italian.* The staff of the History Faculty at the Mohammed V University at Rabat were also extremely kind.

Dr Kate Fleet, director of the Skilliter Centre at Newnham College, Cambridge was invaluable, especially in selflessly hauling material out of the archive. Many thanks to Owen and Xenia Matthews for hosting me during my time researching in Istanbul.

Thanks also to Kate Williams, Ian Kelly, Dominique de la Basterrechea and above all Rosie Apponyi and Edgware Tone for eleventh-hour assistance. To my brilliant agent, Georgina Capel, and my editor, Alan Samson: the latter's patience was Cecil-esque. Simon Wright at Orion was fantastically quick and thorough on the picture research.

I am also grateful to Bendor Grosvenor for the benefit of his time and expert opinion in the matter of Elizabeth's pendant. It was a privilege to work alongside Professor Philip Bobbitt on Machiavelli.

Most loving thanks to my parents, Linda and Paul, my sister Anna and my stepmother, Judy, without whose support in so many ways this book could never have been finished. And to the editor of *The Posky Times,* researcher extraordinaire.

As ever, the staffs of the London Library, the British Library and the Bodleian were wonderfully efficient and patient.

Most of all, thanks to Lady Antonia Fraser, without whom this book could not have been conceived of or written at all. I hope it is, in some way, worthy of the debt.

I should like to point out that the works of four scholars, Stephen Alford, Stuart Carroll, James McDermott and Nicola Shulman have been particularly influential in the shaping of this book.

NOTE ON SPELLING AND NAME (somewhere at the front)

ACKNOWLEDGEMENTS

Elizabethan spelling is notoriously whimsical – I have generally modernized it where it seemed necessary for clarity. And William Cecil, Baron Burghley ought properly to be referred to as Lord Burghley from 1571, but somehow has remained Cecil, since that was how I thought of him for four years.

INDEX